Castaways in Question

British naval interrogation
in two world wars

First published 2020 by Derek Nudd
Second printing 2021, First eBook edition 2021
Third printing 2024
Copyright © 2020, 2021, 2024 Derek Nudd.

A catalogue record for this book is available from the
British Library.

ISBN 978-1-8380943-1-7

Cover design by Art of Communication

Cottage Grove Editions

Dedication

To Sue

All the best interrogators have a certain way with them, some personal characteristic they have learned to turn into a weapon of persuasion. Some present themselves as the soul of sweet reason, others strive to scare or unsettle; others to overwhelm you with their frankness and charm.

John le Carré, *The Pigeon Tunnel*.

★★★★★

IF FURTHER CIRCULATION OF THIS REPORT IS NECESSARY **IT MUST BE PARAPHRASED**, SO THAT NEITHER THE SOURCE OF THE INFORMATION NOR THE MEANS BY WHICH IT HAS BEEN OBTAINED IS APPARENT

[*Standard header of WW2 SR (eavesdropping) report*]

Contents

List of Illustrations

List of Tables

FOREWORD

My last book, *Castaways of the Kriegsmarine*, examined the contribution of prisoner of war interrogation to British Naval Intelligence at the system's peak in early 1944. I illustrated it from the experience of five crews who were guests of the Combined Services Detailed Interrogation Centre (CSDIC) at the time.

My intention in starting this project was to work back from there and see how the system achieved such a high state of tune, focussing on the role played by Trent Park between 1940 and 1942. It quickly dawned on me that the naval team which came together in 1939 was almost entirely drawn from people who had learnt their trade in the First World War, and moreover that these veterans were probably the first in the world to exploit prisoners systematically as a source of intelligence.

Certain characters who provide continuity across the story will pop up at intervals. This is not their biography, but they do propel the narrative at critical points.

Anyone interested in the topic will have come across Helen Fry's excellent work in *The Walls Have Ears*, *The London Cage: The Secret History of Britain's World War II Interrogation Centre* and *Spymaster: The Secret Life of Kendrick*. This work complements Helen's by looking specifically at the naval domain, digging a little deeper into the technology war, and expanding the field of view both geographically and temporally.

In the Second World War we have the priceless gift of thousands of transcribed conversations between captives who were unaware that their cells were bugged. 'Listening' to these unguarded conversations brings home the variety of people sucked into the service of one of the most vicious regimes the world has ever seen. Some bought the whole, sick story and their words send shivers down the spine even at this distance. Others were disgusted by the depths to which their country had sunk and may have seen capture as a blessed release from an intolerable dilemma. The majority mapped the whole spectrum of confused and contradictory views in between.

Marine Frank Shippey helped guard the thirty-six survivors of the battlecruiser *Scharnhorst* during their voyage to Scapa Flow aboard HMS *Duke of York* and subsequent 24-hour train journey to London on the 'Jellicoe Express.' This highly cohesive and well indoctrinated group was a tough project for the naval interrogators but when Shippey's son asked him much later for his impressions of the men he got the reply, *'They are just like us, son.'*

The questions I am most often asked when admitting to an interest in this topic are, 'Did it work?' and 'Did we use torture?'

The answer to the first is an emphatic yes. Considering just the naval dimension, the Battle of the Atlantic was the only clash which ran from the first day of World War 2 to the last. Arguably it could have changed the outcome in the west. At several points prisoners yielded information which allowed the Allies to forestall or counter German technology which might have tipped the balance.

My reply to the second question is a qualified no. The first qualification is that I focus mainly on service centres (CSDIC in World War 2) in the UK. Questions have been asked (and remain open) about the London District Cage[1] and there were suggestions of mistreatment at CSDIC Middle East. Internees were certainly ill-treated at No 74 CSDIC Bad Nenndorf in Germany after the war. The second qualification is that, while CSDIC UK was careful to avoid physical abuse, the psychological pressures applied sometimes sailed close to the wind. Verbal intimidation, implied threats that the Russians or the mythical British 'Secret Service' might be interested in them, or that they could be tried for piracy or spying were all in the armoury. Solitary confinement may also have been used.

I therefore attach the relevant passages from the 1907 Hague Convention and the 1929 Geneva Convention in appendices so that the reader can make up their own mind.

This account will trace the development of the interrogation system over time, painting in the steps which led to its spectacular successes in the Second World War. I focus on the naval element, at least in part because that's where it all started.

At first, battle survivors were interviewed shortly after rescue by fellow seamen who happened to speak German. Both were interested in discussing their mutual experience and any information of intelligence value was almost a by-product. The onset of professional interrogators introduced a standard process for handling prisoners and a central facility (later shared with the army) to carry out interviews. The team was finding its way, learning its craft as it went along, but quickly devised a critical aid to direct interrogation: a card index summarising everything known about enemy vessels, individuals, and locations. This allowed the questioner to present himself as omniscient, throwing his victim instantly off balance.

The team still lacked two tools of critical value in the next conflict: microphones in prisoners' cells and stool pigeons ('gun dogs' in the US). They allowed a change of emphasis, in which the relatively small naval group could focus on using direct interrogation to unsettle a prisoner, plant ideas in his head, and rely on subsequent chat in what he thought was privacy to harvest intelligence. Both techniques had been used in army cages during the Great War and were integrated with the naval experience to create the spectacularly successful Combined Services Detailed Interrogation Centres (CSDIC) in the later conflict.

The Second World War saw a pace of technological development undreamt of in the first. Most of the equipment used in September 1939 directly descended from that which the 1918 veterans knew. Six years later homing torpedoes, electronic warfare, jet aircraft, air-independent propulsion, mini-submarines, acoustic countermeasures, and atomic bombs were all a reality. Younger, more eclectic and above all more scientifically literate personnel were needed.

Finally, the Armistice on 11th November 1918 abruptly ended the need for prisoner interrogation. VE Day on 8th May 1945 did not. There was an urgent need to dismember the monster called Nazism and render accounts for the suffering of its victims.

World War II was a truly global cataclysm. I have focussed mainly on the European theatre here, the equally interesting work of centres operating in the Indian and Pacific Oceans and eastern US must wait for later attention.

When quoting prisoners' conversations and statements I use the contemporary English translations. I keep the transcribers' practice of capitalising significant names, although it can be distracting to a modern reader. They were careful to avoid interpolation and guesswork, so inserted a line of dots where the speaker's words were unclear or a question mark if they were unsure of the word used. Speakers are identified in the transcripts by a CSDIC index number; up to 1944 a simple sequence beginning 'A' for air force, 'M' for military or 'N' for navy. The suffix '(Am)' indicates a prisoner taken by US forces. A more complex structure was adopted after D-Day.

Please look up my web site, https://www.dnudd.co.uk/ for up-to-date news.

---

[1]   See Fry, *The London Cage* and Lomas, *The Drugs Don't Work*.

ACKNOWLEDGEMENTS

It was a review of Helen Fry's *The M Room* (now revised and updated as *The Walls Have Ears*) that first sent me walking down this road. I bought the book, found my grandfather's name in it, contacted Helen with a little extra information from family records, and the story rapidly acquired a momentum of its own. Helen's support, advice, and professionalism throughout have made these books possible.

While researching the book I have been privileged to meet some remarkable people, including two of the last 'secret listeners' who eavesdropped on German captives: Erich Mark and Fritz Lustig. Sadly, neither of them is still with us.

For the historian, the written record is almost invariably the main rope by which we descend into the past, and the UK National Archive remains a priceless resource for serious research. At the time of writing its priorities seemed to be under review. I hope that review will not dilute its value.

The library of the National Museum of the Royal Navy is a greatly underrated resource. It was there I discovered the diaries of Bernard Trench with his delightfully indiscreet account of the early years of World War 2. I am indebted to archivists Heather Johnson at Portsmouth and George Malcolmson at the Submarine Museum for their encyclopaedic knowledge of this treasure trove. Developments under way at the museum will greatly improve public access to the library.

I am grateful to Lance Shippey for information about his father's role in the Battle of North Cape and subsequent events, and to Peter Hore for additional information about Gwendoline Neel-Wall.

Then there is the troop of reprobates whose variously smiling and scowling faces over breakfast at Kew help to make my visits to the National Archives much more fun than they might be. You know who you are. Thanks.

The second printing brought two new characters to the cast: Christine Hammacott who produced the superb cover design and Hannah Hargrave who had the thankless task of trying to bring my work to the notice of the wider world. You have my thanks, anyway.

It goes without saying that all mistakes are mine alone. There would be many more of them without the help of people who have generously given their time and attention to read through the manuscript before it was let loose on the unsuspecting world. Here I must particularly thank my colleague at the Society for Nautical Research (South) Richard Blake MA, M Phil, FSNR and Dr Marcus Faulker of King's College London.

Saving the best for last, I do not have the words to express my feelings for the woman who has, unbelievably, stayed with me for over forty years and put up with my crouching over a hot keyboard during the gestation of this book.

Tongue-tied as always.

Derek

GLOSSARY AND ABBREVIATIONS

All full stops are removed for consistency.

Term	Expansion
AB	Able Seaman
ACOS	Assistant Chief of Staff
AIF	Australian Imperial Force
AMC	Armed Merchant Cruiser
ANCXF	Allied Naval Commander, Expeditionary Force
Asmiralstab	German naval staff up to and during the First World War
Abwehr	German military intelligence from 1920-1945
ADNI	Assistant Director of Naval Intelligence
ASV	Anti-Submarine Visualiser (or possibly Air to Surface Vessel). Airborne radar
ATIS	Allied Translator and Interpreter Section
ATS	Auxiliary Territorial Service
AWM	Australian War Memorial
B-Dienst	*Beobachtungs-Dienst* (observation service), the German naval decryption unit.
BdU	*Befehlshaber Der U-Boote* (U-boat Commander-in-Chief)
BEF	British Expeditionary Force
CAFO	Confidential Admiralty Fleet Order
CIOS	Combined Intelligence Objectives Sub-Committee
Coy	Company (army)
CPO	Chief Petty Officer
CSA	Consular Shipping Adviser
DA/SW	Director of Anti-Submarine Warfare[1]
DKM, KM[S]	Deutsche Kriegsmarine: prefix of WW2 German warships (usually omitted)

Term	Expansion
D/F	Direction Finding
DID	Director of Intelligence Division
DNI	Director of Naval Intelligence
DPW	Directorate of Prisoners of War
DPW&I	(Australian) Directorate of Prisoners of War and Internees
DSC	Distinguished Service Cross
DTM	Director of Torpedoes and Mining
DTMI	Department of Torpedoes and Mines Investigation Section
E-Boat	German fast torpedo-boat (short for Enemy boat, also known as S-boat or *Schnellboot*)
ERA	Engine Room Artificer
EPES	Enemy Personnel Exploitation Section (UK Foreign Office)
FAT	*Federapparat Torpedo*, a pattern-running attachment used in WW2, which allowed German torpedoes to steer a wandering course with regular 180° turns until they hit something or ran out of fuel or battery power. Useful against convoys. See also LUT.
FIAT	Field Information Agency Technical
FIC	Foreign Intelligence Committee (predecessor of NID)
FIU	Forward Interrogation Unit
GAF	German Air Force (*Luftwaffe*)
GCCS	Government Code and Cypher School (the cryptographic centre)
GHz	Gigahertz (billions of cycles per second)
GM/SA	German Minesweeping Admin¬istration
GPO	General Post Office
GSR	German Search Receiver – British name for a variety of radar warning receivers used by the German Navy

Term	Expansion
HTP	High Test Peroxide: a solution of hydrogen peroxide in water. It has been used at high concentration as fuel for rockets, torpedoes, and submarines. It can be dangerously unstable. Also known as *Ingolin*.
HMT	Hired Military Transport
ID	Intelligence Division ('NID' before 1912 and after WW1)
Ingolin	See HTP.
JIC	Joint Intelligence Committee
JSIW	Joint Services Interrogation Wing
Kaiserliche Marine	Imperial German Navy
LUT	A more sophisticated version of FAT with more pattern options, but only used toward the end of the war
'M' Room	Microphone Room (or Map Room): where the secret listeners eavesdropped remotely on prisoner conversations – 'Map' was a deliberate distraction
MG	Machine gun
MHz	Megahertz (millions of cycles per second)
MI9, MI19	MI9 was a branch of Military Intelligence formed at the beginning of WW2 to look after both enemy prisoners in British hands (MI9a) and vice versa (MI9b). In December 1941 MI9a was split out to a separate organisation, MI19
MiD	Mention in Dispatches
Nxxxx	Sequential index numbers given to naval prisoners of war during their stay with CSDIC UK. Different numbers were used by centres abroad, and the convention changed in 1944.
N(Am)xxx	Sequential index number, as above, given to naval prisoners of war captured by US forces

Term	Expansion
NCSO	Naval Control Service Officer
NID	Naval Intelligence Division
NMRN	National Museum of the Royal Navy (+P – Portsmouth)
OKM	*Oberkommando der Marine* (German naval high command)
Outpost Patrol	Small craft used as a picket to warn of enemy forces' approach
Pistol	Torpedo fusing mechanism
PO	Petty Officer
Pte	Private (army)
PW, P/W	Prisoner of War (plural PsW, Ps/W)
PWIB	Prisoner of War Information Bureau
PWIS(H)	Prisoner of War Interrogation Section (Home)
Q Ships	Merchant ships taken into naval service and fitted with concealed guns in the hope of decoying U-boats into a surface attack, where they could be overwhelmed
QF	Quick-Firing
RAAF	Royal Australian Air Force
RAF	Royal Air Force
RAN	Royal Australian Navy (+VR = Volunteer Reserve)
RCA	Radio Corporation of America
RCN	Royal Canadian Navy (+VR = Volunteer Reserve)
RFC	Royal Flying Corps
RM	Royal Marines
RMA	Royal Marines Artillery
RMLI	Royal Marines Light Infantry
RNAS	Royal Naval Air Service
S-boat	See E-Boat

xvi

Term	Expansion
SBT	Submarine Bubble Target, a.k.a. *'Bold Verfahren'*, *'Pillenwerfer'*, 'Tube 6' (or 7). Effervescent 'pills' which a submarine could eject, creating a bubble cloud to confuse a pursuing vessel's sonar
SEAC	Southeast Asia Command
SEATIC	Southeast Asia Translation and Interrogation Centre (New Delhi, India)
Seehund	('Seal'): German code name used both for an infra-red optical device and a midget submarine
Sicherheitsdienst	Intelligence agency of the SS and the Nazi Party
SIR	Subject Interrogation Report
SMS	*Seiner Majestät Schiff* ("His Majesty's Ship"). Designation of German Navy (*Kaiserliche Marine*) ships before and during the First World War
Zentner	Unit of weight (50kg)

German Naval Ranks and British Equivalents

German nomenclature for the same role/rank may differ between the First and Second World War.

Rank	Equivalent
Bootsmannsmaat	Leading Seaman or Bo'sun's Mate 2nd Class
Fähnrich zur See	Junior Midshipman.
Feldwebel	PO (Mechanical)
Fregattenkapitän	Commander.
Funkegefreiter	Telegraphist.
Funkmaat	Leading Telegraphist.
Funkmeister	PO Telegraphist
Funkobergefreiter	Telegraphist.
Heizer	Stoker

Rank	Equivalent
Kapitän zur See	Captain.
Kapitänleutnant	Lieutenant.
Koch	Cook
Konteradmiral	Rear Admiral
Korvettenkapitän	Lieutenant-Commander.
Leutnant zur See	Junior Sub-Lieutenant.
Marinestabarzt	Surgeon Lieutenant.
Maschinengefreiter	Stoker, 1st Class.
Maschinenmaat	Leading Stoker and ERA, 5th Class.
Maschinenobergefreiter	Stoker, 1st Class.
Maschinistenmaat	Engine Room PO
Matrose	Ordinary Seaman.
Matrosengefreiter	Able Seaman.
Matrosenobergefreiter	Able Seaman.
Mechanikersmaat	Leading Seaman (S.T.)
Mechanikerobergefreiter	Able Seaman (S.T.), Artificer 1st Class
Oberassistenzart	Surgeon Lieutenant.
Oberbootsmannsmaat	PO (Seaman's Branch) or Bo'sun's Mate 1st Class.
Oberfähnrich zur See	Senior Midshipman.
Oberfunkmeister	CPO Telegraphist
Obergefreiter	Able Seaman
Oberheizer	Leading Stoker
Oberleutnant zur See	Sub-Lieutenant.
Obermaschinenmaat	Acting Stoker PO and ERA, 4th Class
Obermaschinist	Chief Stoker and Chief ERA, 1st or 2nd Class.
Obermaschinistenmaat	Engine Room CPO
Obermatrose	Leading Seaman
Obermechanikersmaat	Acting Petty Officer
Obersteuermann	CPO (Navigation)
Signalgäst	Signalman
Signalmaat	2nd Yeoman of Signals
Steuermann	Helmsman, Warrant Officer
Steursmannsgefreiter	Able Seaman (Navigator's Yeoman)

Rank	Equivalent
Steursmannsmaat	Navigating Petty Officer
Steward	Steward
Zimmermannobergefreiter	Shipwright AB Rating

(*ing*) denotes engineering branch.

German Army Ranks and British Equivalents

Rank	Equivalent
Feldwebel	Deputy Platoon Sergeant
Oberfeldwebel	Platoon Sergeant

Italian Naval Ranks and British Equivalents

These ranks apply to *La Regia Marina* in the Second World War.

Rank	Equivalent
Grande Ammiraglio	Admiral of the Fleet
Ammiraglio di Armata	Admiral
Ammiraglio di Squadra designato di Armata	Vice Admiral (Upper Half)
Ammiraglio di Squadra	Vice Admiral (Lower Half)
Ammiraglio di Divisione	Rear Admiral
Contrammiraglio	Commodore
Capitano di Vascello	Captain
Capitano di Fregata	Commander
Capitano di Corvetta	Lieutenant-Commander
Tenente di Vascello	Lieutenant
Tenente Genio Navale	Engineer-Lieutenant
Sottotenente di Vascello	Sub-Lieutenant
Guadiamarina	Midshipman, Acting Sub-Lieutenant
Capo Silurista	Chief Petty Officer
Capo Elettricista	Chief Petty Officer (Electical)
Capo di 1a classe	1st Class Chief

Rank	Equivalent
Capo di 2a classe	2nd Class Chief
Capo di 3a classe	3rd Class Chief
Secondo Capo	2nd Chief

---

[1] This and the following 'Director' entries refer to Admiralty divisions.

ORIGINS

Naval Intelligence Division

The Board of Admiralty set up a Foreign Intelligence Committee (FIC), later Naval Intelligence Division (NID), in December 1882. Its first director was Captain William Henry Hall. The navy thus had a thirty-year start on the domestic and foreign intelligence agencies (later MI5 and MI6), plus a ready-made global contact network in every British naval attaché, shipping consul, naval captain, merchant master and Lloyd's agent.

The Curious Cruise of HMS Cornwall, 1909

William Hall's son Reginald, nicknamed 'Blinker' for a facial tic, followed his father into the navy and rose to command the armoured cruiser HMS *Cornwall*. In May 1909 she set out on a five-month cruise of the Baltic. Shortly before departure two junior officers joined her crew: Marine Lieutenant Bernard Trench and RN Lieutenant Vivian Brandon.

Bernard Trench was born in 1880, the son of a railway engineer who had been apprenticed to George Stephenson. Bernard joined the Royal Marines Light Infantry (RMLI) as a Second Lieutenant in 1899, was promoted to Lieutenant the following year and qualified as a German interpreter in 1907.

He gained an early reputation for clandestine work. While serving aboard HMS *Venus* in 1905 he earned Admiral Charles Beresford's appreciation for *'the interesting and valuable report on a suitable landing place near Palma and the defences in the vicinity.'*[1] He was urgently recalled from France for the Baltic assignment and personally briefed by the Deputy Adjutant General (the professional head of the Royal Marines staff).

Brandon, born in 1882, was a qualified marine surveyor whose stellar examination results and glowing fitness reports seemed to set him on course for a high-flying naval career. In May 1909 he had just recovered from sickness contracted while working in the Far East, and which was to plague him for the rest of his life.

The overt purpose of the *Cornwall*'s voyage is remarkable enough. It was ostensibly – and genuinely – a cadets' training cruise taking in the North German, East Danish, and South Norwegian coasts, and going as far as Libau (now Liepāja, Latvia) and Reval (now Talinn, Estonia). The cadets were intensively drilled in navigation, gunnery, and engineering. On one occasion the ship lost both anchors in foul weather and had to steam slowly out to sea until the conditions abated and they could return to retrieve them. The officers entertained numerous dignitaries including the Kaiser, the Queen of Sweden and the King and Queen of Norway – harvesting information which Hall assiduously reported to the Admiralty.[2]

During the voyage Brandon and Trench industriously surveyed navigable passages, coastal defences and potential landing beaches in east Denmark north Germany west Russia (now the Baltic States), southern Sweden and Norway.[3] On 31st July for example, they borrowed a boat to examine a small island near Drøbak in Oslo Fjord. Trench notes,

> *'Immediately below the 30.5 cm gun and about 25 feet above the sea level we found a small battery containing one – 57 mm QF gun on a pedestal mounting, all being on a travelling platform, enabling the gun to be absolutely concealed when not in use. … We measured the calibre & took off the breech cover & examined the breech, it is the same action as our 3 & 6 pdrs.'[4]*

They also submitted a report on '*Coast Defences at Kiel*', as well as one on '*Brunsbüttel, Tönning and the Kaiser Wilhelm Canal*'[5]. All this was exactly the kind of information a planner would need to bring a fleet into the Baltic through lesser-used channels – Brandon's survey for navigation and Trench's for coastal defences that had to be neutralised or bypassed. First Sea Lord 'Jacky' Fisher's staff would have dusted off their work while planning his unrealised 1915 Baltic Project, to land an army on Germany's northern coast. Their records may well have been the most recent and detailed information available to the Royal Navy's 1919 Baltic expedition. How differently might today's history books read if the Dardanelles expedition had started with the detailed information about its target that these two gathered in the north?

Just two years earlier Fisher caused a diplomatic storm by admitting that in the event of war with Germany Britain would not hesitate to seize a foothold in newly independent Norway as a 'northern Gibraltar' to control the Baltic exits.[6]

There is an oft-quoted incident during a courtesy visit to Kiel. With a full-scale naval arms race under way the Admiralty was anxious to learn as much as possible about German warship construction, a matter which their hosts were equally keen to keep private. Hall borrowed a fast motor launch from the Duke of Westminster, who was visiting, and went for a cruise around the harbour apparently with Brandon and Trench disguised as artificers. A 'convenient' breakdown opposite the dockyard gave them plenty of time to take covert photographs, bearings and notes while dismantling and rebuilding the perfectly good engine. This wonderful story deserves to be true but must be told with caution. The only source is Admiral Sir William James' biography of Hall, *The Eyes of the Navy*. Careful reading suggests Brandon and Trench were not the officers involved. Trench's diary for 4th September 1906 to 24th August 1909 does not mention the incident, while it is delightfully indiscreet in other matters.[78]

Brandon's service record includes the statement '*Aug 09 Apprecn. expressed for useful report on German naval matters & writing addl. Sailing Directions for the Belts, Kattegat & Baltic.*'

The Riddle of the Frisian Islands

The two lieutenants were reunited the following year, posing as tourists in a survey of the Frisian Islands. Their luck ran out when they were caught investigating the fortification of Borkum island, off the mouth of the river Ems. After a highly publicised trial (in which *Cornwall's* exploits were brought up as evidence) they were sentenced to four years' fortress imprisonment. Luckily they were released in 1913, in an amnesty to mark King George V's visit to Germany for the Kaiser's daughter's wedding. During their trial Brandon was questioned about the intended recipient of the information he was gathering and replied, '*I will call him "Reggie," though that is not the person's name.*'[9]

This was Captain Cyrus Regnart RMLI, who had briefed them for the mission. On their return both suffered a humiliating official refusal either to admit that their trip had been authorised or to cover their expenses, despite Trench having been given leave for language study in Denmark as a cover story and at least some updates on their brief during the trip.

The Band Comes Together

As the light faded on a century of '*Pax Britannica*' in the early twentieth century the political, economic, and military landscape looked startlingly different than it had at the start of the era. Industrialisation and empire had left Britain uniquely dependant on a global network of maritime trade routes for her prosperity and very survival. The Royal Navy was still the unquestioned owner of the oceans, but no major sea battle had occurred since 1815. In that time wooden, sailing two- and three-deckers had given way to armoured, steam-powered behemoths that could throw an explosive shell over ten miles. Nobody knew, really knew, what effect this revolution would have on a future conflict. Different interest groups took directly opposing lessons from the Russo-Japanese War of 1904-5.[10]

Worse, there were new, radically different kinds of weapon which threatened to level the playing field and allow weaker nations to engage stronger on equal terms. The mine, the torpedo and the submarine were all at an early stage of development but had shown the potential to sink even a capital ship.

Then there was the diplomatic landscape. The Admiralty was used to thinking about France, Japan, Russia, Italy, perhaps the USA as potential competitors. Now there was a new, insistently aggressive kid on the block – the German Empire.

In a different place, a different time and a different world John Thomas Cope, a talented artist in glass, divorced his wife Eliza Annie in November 1883. Repeated allegations of adultery (denied by his wife) enabled him to keep custody of their three children. The following month he married Eliza Julia Rivers.

The resulting tension may have made a change of scenery convenient, for he quickly decamped with his family to Munich as a stained-glass painter at the *Mayer'sche Hofkunstanstalt*. Mayer's studio had opened a London branch in 1865 so he might simply have changed sites while staying with the same employer.

This business, founded in 1848, was riding the boom in demand for stained-glass both at home and for export,

5

specialising in ecclesiastical work. The art had however declined on the continent until the early 19th Century so British craftsmen trained in the Arts and Crafts movement were in great demand. Cope's abilities secured promotion to head of the stained-glass department and allowed him to buy two houses in the city.

Burton Scott Rivers Cope, John Thomas' fourth child and his first with Eliza Julia, was born in in June 1885 – not long after John's arrival in his new home. He was followed by three more between 1890 and 1896.

1: *Laisser-Passer* issued to Burton in 1906

2: Burton and Berta at about the time of their marriage

There is almost no documentation of Burton's schooling and early life, but he may have been apprenticed to his father's trade. In later life he certainly took a detailed interest in the stained-glass window over the main staircase of Latimer House.

By 1906 Burton clearly felt the need to travel. There is a *Laisser-Passer* issued to him by the British consulate in Munich.

He also appears on an undated Antwerp police immigration record in the early 20th Century; this may be where he first learnt Flemish, demonstrating a natural aptitude for languages which would stand him in good stead throughout his life.

About 1908 Burton married Berta Burghard in Munich. She was a strikingly good-looking woman, but nothing else is known about her.

As the clouds of war broke most of the family returned to Britain. Burton's younger sister Florrie married a local man on 7th August 1914 and stayed with her husband through both wars. His elder half-brother Charles left it too late to make a run for it and was interned at Ruhleben Camp on the outskirts of Berlin.

The approaching cataclysm would weave together the fates of Hall, Brandon, Trench, Cope, and others in an intelligence revolution.

---

[1]   *Private Papers of Bernard Trench* in the National Museum of the Royal Navy, NMRN(P) 2107/24/7/9.

[2]   Publications of the Navy Records Society, Vol 152 *Naval Intelligence from Germany*. xxiii.

[3]   Brandon's meticulous documentation of coastal landmarks is now available in the ADM 344 series of the UK National Archives.

[4]   *Private Papers of Bernard Trench* in the National Museum of the Royal Navy, NMRN(P) 2107/24/7/9. Diary from 4/9/1906 to 24/8/1909.

[5]   Navy Records Society, *Op Cit.*

[6]   *Private Papers of Bernard Trench*, Trench diary 1908-9. TNA ADM 53/18956. ADM 344/436,437, 443-445, 450-455, 463, 478, 480, 498. Kristiansen, *The Norwegian Armed Forces and the Coming of the Second World War* P.298.

[7]   James, Admiral Sir W. *The Eyes of the Navy*. P.7-8. Ramsay, D. *'Blinker' Hall: Spymaster*. P.19. TNA ADM 53/18956.

[8]   Admiral James incorrectly gives 1908 as the date of *Cornwall's* cruise.

[9]   *The Sunday Post*, 16/02/19 has a full account of the trial on P.6.

[10] See Towle, *The evaluation of the experience of the Russo-Japanese War* in Ranft (ed).

WORLD WAR 1

"The lamps are going out all over Europe…"
"… we shall not see them lit again in our life-time."

Sir Edward Grey, British Foreign Secretary, reflected the dismay of many people at the unexpected and unlooked-for upheaval in their lives even before the shooting started. Most of the Cope family made their way back to Britain in a desperately uneasy atmosphere for the many people whose background, family and culture straddled both nations. Berta, in particular, must have felt very strange. Michael Foley brings out how tightly interlinked the two societies were, and how difficult it was to tie down the concept of 'enemy alien'. He relates anecdotes of Germans marching into internment singing *Tipperary* to show where their loyalties lay, and a Royal Navy crewman pulling a survivor of SMS *Blücher* from the sea to discover he was a former next-door neighbour.[1] Equally poignantly, the ship's senior surviving officer was a certain *Korventtenkapitän* John Ross.[2]

On his release from prison Bernard Trench was posted to the Plymouth Division and then to the cruiser HMS *Highflyer*, an obsolescent training ship which was immediately deployed on operations when war broke out. In the first month of hostilities she intercepted a Dutch merchantman carrying German troops and bullion and sank the armed merchant raider *Kaiser Wilhelm der Grosse*. Trench's contribution earned a later commendation from his captain:

> *"…Capt Trench was of the utmost assistance to me during 18 months on the trade routes owing to his intimate knowledge of the Germans – their language, habits & machinations."*[3]

Reginald 'Blinker' Hall's career had prospered meanwhile; he was by then captain of the new battlecruiser *Queen Mary*, but in October 1914 his deteriorating health forced him reluctantly to accept a posting ashore. Coincidentally the post of Director of Intelligence Department (DID, later DNI) was vacant at the time. Hall was to prove one of the most successful and influential spymasters in history.[4]

He set about reforming and invigorating his new command, bringing in new blood to tackle the ever-expanding scope and scale of the Division's tasks in wartime.

It can be no coincidence that Vivian Brandon, who had distinguished himself in 1909, was recalled from command of the gunboat *Bramble* on China Station to Intelligence Department at the end of 1914. He was promoted to Commander and took charge of the German section (ID14), where he set up a naval prisoner of war interrogation facility.

He had qualified in seamanship, gunnery, torpedoes, and as an interpreter in French and German. The Department placed a note on his record that *"This officer is retained at the Admiralty on account of his special qualifications for work in the Intelligence Department and his retention in a shore appointment … is not to militate against his chances of promotion when he becomes eligible under the regulations."* By the end of the war he had risen to Acting Captain and Assistant DNI.

Perhaps at Brandon's instigation Trench was assigned on 16th July 1915 to the new interrogation section. Owing to the exigencies of ship movements and onward travel he did not physically join it until 20th August. It was a role he was to reprise twenty-four years later.

Attempts to extract information from enemy captives, with varying degrees of coercion, are as old as conflict. What was new was a systematic, structured intelligence-gathering process. The team had to be built from scratch and their methods worked out as they went along. Ironically, they were helped by the 1907 Hague Convention which, by codifying prisoners' rights, assured a minimum standard of treatment, care and accounting, and explicitly approved the confiscation of military documents in their possession.

The flip side of the coin, unnoticed at the time, was that the duty of warring nations to record, feed, house and keep track of captives also created an opportunity for systematic information gathering from them. British Naval Intelligence was probably the first in the world to grasp this.

The Battle of Dogger Bank on 24th January 1915 produced an object lesson in how *not* to do it. Survivors of the armoured cruiser *Blücher* were interviewed aboard the battleship *King Edward VII* and a report produced within two days. It contained a great deal of colour about conditions during the battle and the sinking, but little of intelligence value.[5]

By July 1915 Intelligence Division had learnt enough to prepare a Confidential Admiralty Interim Order (CAFO) for the Fleet on how to handle survivors:

'Whenever German Naval Prisoners of War are taken the Senior Officer at the port where they are landed should immediately report to the Admiralty by telegraph the number of prisoners and their ranks and ratings, together with particulars of the arrangements proposed to be made for their disposal.

It is pointed out that information of the greatest importance may occasionally be obtained from prisoners of war, but as a rule this can only be done by a duly qualified officer, and the above reports will enable arrangements to be made by the Director of the Intelligence Division for a qualified officer to be detailed at the earliest possible moment to undertake such an investigation.

Until this officer can interrogate the prisoners it is desirable that they should be kept separated, so far as circumstances permit, both before and after arrival at the port of landing. If individual separation is not possible it is important at least to isolate the officers from the men. The prisoners should not be allowed to communicate with their friends without permission from the Admiralty, and unless the manner in which their submarine has been captured or destroyed is officially published no reference to this should be allowed to pass in their letters.[6]

Some key principles which would endure through both wars were already emerging: leave interrogation to the professionals, segregate officers to prevent them synchronising stories or giving their men a security briefing, and delay news of a sinking until it is clear the vessel is not going to return. A separate note covered censorship of prisoners' mail.

The point was reinforced the same month by two officers from HMS *Taranaki* who attempted to interrogate the three survivors of *U-40* while escorting them to London. To ID's frustration much of the information they reported was either inaccurate or well-known, and they gave away as much as they got. The event also highlighted a need for more specialist knowledge within Intelligence Division.

'This is a very interesting and useful report although it cannot be implicitly relied on.

Two points arise which are of special departmental interest

(1). The great advantage of first hand technical knowledge, when dealing with questions of this nature. A corollary is that the first possible opportunity should be taken to get a suitable submarine officer permanently attached to I.D.

(2). The great disadvantage of allowing these cross-examinations to be conducted by an Officer completly [sic] out of touch with intelligence, matters and requirements. This is shown

(a) By the fact that Lieut. Commdr Edwards openly discussed with the Germans the methods employed against them, and apparently took no subsequent steps to ensure that they should not have the

possible opportunity of transmitting to Germany what they had learnt.

(b)   By the fact that in the report several assertions, which are in conflict with positive statements in the German War Vessel Book, are made without comment; and other facts are mentioned as though they were new, when actually full information on these points is given in the War Vessel Book.'[7]

Growing experience led Intelligence Division to publish an updated and expanded instruction in 1916 and quickly taught the need to record and remove prisoners' effects, especially any documents, before they could dispose of them. A key tool in the interrogator's kit was to overwhelm with the impression of omniscience, as demonstrated by a typed extract from the *Western Morning News* forwarded to Bernard Trench in 1940 but referring to the previous war:

'WHAT THE BRITISH KNEW.

To illustrate the extraordinary cleverness of the British Intelligence service, the German Paper "Norddeutsche" tells a couple of excellent stories which it attributes to ex-prisoners. One German airship commander, taken prisoner by this country but exchanged and now in Switzerland, sent the following report of experiences to Germany:-

"On the fourth day three officers from the War office arrived for the purpose of interrogating me, one of them being Maj. Trench, who at one time was arrested for spying at Borkum. When I told these officers that I could not answer any questions, Maj. Trench remarked sarcastically, 'Then we will tell you something.' He then read me from a notebook my whole career, giving every detail concerning my taking over the airship, the exact period of leave on every occasion, every journey made, and its precise objective, with the dates even when the airships returned without having accomplished their object, and where they landed. He showed me a drawing of our new type of airship, and asked me if I recognised my own ship. He told me the

secret names of our airships, and stated that they were able to follow
the various ships on their journeys with the greatest exactitude from
their direction stations. He also knew where the individual ships
were stationed, and when, how long, and for what reason an airship
was laid up."
Very similar testimony was given by the German N.C.O. of another
airship. Not only did the British officers given them all details about
their own record of service, but also the changes in the personnel of
their ships. Photographs of the new sheds in ------ and groups of
officers at the new casino were also shown them. This N.C.O. was
asked by one of the English examining officers whether he
remembered where he had been at Friedrichshafen on a particular
day. When he answered "no," the officer told him that he had been in
Lindau, and that he (the officer) had been there himself and seen
him. The public here will be glad to get this unsolicited testimonial to
the thoroughness and alertness of the British naval and military
authorities in a department in which it is (erroneously) supposed we
are sometimes wanting."[8]

In 1917 the section (ID16b) moved from Wandsworth
Detention Barracks into Cromwell Gardens Barracks, a block of
large houses known as Admiralty Annex II near the Victoria and
Albert Museum, with their army colleagues in MI1(a). By this
point at least we can see the genesis of the joint service working
that was such a multiplier of their effectiveness in the Second
World War.

Intelligence Division needed time to grow into the integrated
information harvesting, sharing, planning and operational body
that made it so effective and influential. William Clarke of Room
40, the breathtakingly successful cryptographic team, recalled,

'One other matter may be mentioned, which was the complete
watertight division of our party and other intelligence sections of the
I.D.; we could have helped them and they could have helped us, but

it was not till late we heard of the work, valuable as it was of Brandon and Trench in their section.[9]

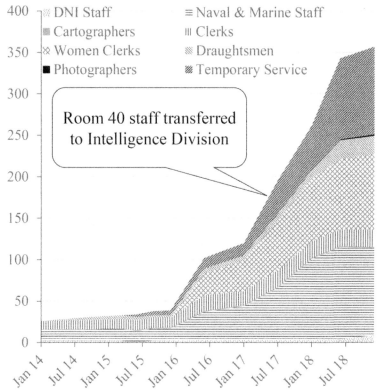

3: Growth of Intelligence Division staff during WW1
Source: Navy Lists Intelligence Division pages, which may understate the total. 'Temporary Service' includes both male and female staff, service and civilians, often unpaid and from a wide variety of backgrounds. Note the rapid recruitment of women clerks from 1916.

It is unclear what Burton Cope was doing for the first two years of the war. His father bought a house in Bexleyheath, Kent, and it is possible that they continued creating stained-glass designs for anyone who had the will and the wherewithal to buy. After all, they would not have been the only ones expecting a short war and a quick return to normality.

By April 1916 this was clearly a futile hope. Cope, approaching his 31ˢᵗ birthday, signed up as an officer in the Royal Naval Volunteer Reserve (RNVR). The fact that the army extended conscription to married men under the age of forty-one soon afterward may not be unrelated.

His first posting in early 1917 was as Assistant Paymaster to HMS *Pekin*, a minesweeper base at Grimsby. Although Paymaster was nominally an administrative function the (*I*) for interpreter against his name in the Navy List suggests that he already had an intelligence role. His responsibilities would have included collating sighting reports from Grimsby's extensive fishing fleet and forwarding them to the Admiralty. For example, Anthony Roland Wells' PhD thesis on Naval Intelligence cites the Grimsby trawler *Elmira*, which was stopped and questioned by a German destroyer in 1914 and duly gave full details to the base intelligence officer.[10] Similarly the trawlers *Thistle*, *Mayfly* and *Petrel* were stopped by a submarine on 29ᵗʰ January 1917. The U-boat sank *Thistle* with gunfire, intending to do the same with *Mayfly* and bring *Petrel* and her cargo back to Germany, but was chased off by a patrol boat leaving her boarding party behind.[11]

Cope's facility with languages was too useful to languish in Yorkshire. In September 1917 he was posted to Commander Brandon's and Major Trench's rapidly growing team as 'Interpreter in German and Acting Interpreter in French,' and promoted to Lieutenant. His nodding acquaintance with Flemish was no doubt useful for translating Dutch press articles. As an interpreter he was paid an extra shilling a day, but only when he used his language skills.

World War 1

The Maturing System

Interrogation reports in 1915 and 1916 show evidence of a team feeling its way into the job. They are typewritten and of variable structure, apparently following the whim of the officer concerned or the course of the interview. For example, Lieutenant-Commander Walter Bagot's account of the survivors of the trawler *Otto Rudolf*, brought ashore at Grimsby in March 1916, is in narrative form. It describes the vessel, her crew and last voyage, the organisation of the patrol flotilla, new construction under way, smoke boxes, aircraft, anti-submarine devices, High Seas Fleet organisation and the emergency disposal of confidential books. Hall's covering memo drew the reader's attention to important information about portable smoke generators, which otherwise would have been easy to miss. He surprisingly dismissed the warning that the battleship *Bayern* was nearing completion.

By 1917 reports were increasingly typeset, presumably reflecting wider distribution, and settling into a standard structure. This took the form of introductory remarks and general narrative about the vessel, survivors, and the circumstances of their capture, followed by the vessel's history, home port and place in the enemy's organisation. Then came specific technical intelligence about (for instance) wireless telegraphy or torpedoes, information about the commanders, activities and losses of other vessels, and finally political and social intelligence such as the state of rationing and morale in Germany. Translations of prisoners' letters, diaries and other captured documents were included as appendices. This format was clearly successful as it survived with little change throughout the Second World War. Unlike their Army and later RAF colleagues the naval branch almost invariably reported on a vessel as a unit rather than an individual interviewee.

UB-81 hit a mine which flooded her two aft compartments on 2nd December 1917, about ten miles south of Selsey Bill. Luckily, the sea was shallow enough for the crew to bring her bow above water by blowing tanks until the boat was almost vertical. It took six hours to make a torpedo safe and unload the tube, allowing seven men to exit through it before the open tube was accidentally flooded by the wash from a rescuing vessel. More might have survived but some of those who did escape returned to the boat, choosing to die warm rather than face the freezing waters of the winter Channel.

The interrogation report gives an interesting insight to kind of pressures available to the intelligence team.

'Heinrich Bäthke, Navigating Warrant Officer, belongs to the Reserve. He proved to be a very stubborn subject and at first refused to make any statements at all. He was much annoyed that his diary had fallen into our hands, and it was only when it was suggested to him that the publication of this diary might be the cause of a great deal of unpleasantness to him, that he became more tractable.'[12]

They tried a different ruse on Hans Bruhn, the tight-lipped second-in-command of *UC-29*.

'In order to ascertain the dates on which "U.C.29" was cruising, Bruhn, the officer, was accused of having been concerned in the sinking of certain vessels on certain dates. He admitted having stopped the Norwegian S.S. "HAAKON VII" on 24 January 1917, and having captured six Russians from her. He said he didn't know what had become of these prisoners.

He denied having stopped any ships on 11 February 1917, as he said that "U.C.29" had not been at sea on that date.

He then refused to give any further information.'[13]

If Bruhn was a tricky customer, Werner Fürbringer of *UB-110* sounds infuriating. The report on his boat comments,

'Fürbringer was most reticent during his interrogation, being apparently under the impression that if he answered the most simple

and harmless questions he might betray valuable naval secrets. He
admitted, however, that he had sunk about 110,000 tons of shipping
during his career in command of submarines.'[14]

In this case we are fortunate to have Fürbringer's own account of his interrogation by a *'tall British naval officer, clean-shaven, with red hair and small fanatical eyes.'* We cannot be certain who his interviewer was but Burton Cope, five foot eleven inches and shown in a contemporary portrait[15] with ginger hair and piercing blue eyes, is a strong possibility.

Fürbringer describes being met at Kings Cross and transferred to a detention barracks *'in Hyde Park near the Kensington Museum.'* The interviews began the next day. Both accounts agree that Fürbringer was open about his pre-war career and said nothing about subsequent events. When asked about the sinking of the *Lusitania* Fürbringer's reply (unspecified) apparently prompted the interrogator to say that he deserved to be hanged as a pirate.

At this point the interviewer threw Fürbringer off balance by tossing the nicknames of four of his fellow U-boat commanders, one of whom sailed after he did, into the conversation. Like others before and after him he instantly jumped to the conclusion that the British must have an efficient espionage system in his home port. It is much more likely that the information came from carefully indexed snippets picked up in previous interrogations.

We should mention one more matter before we leave Fürbringer's story. There is a major discrepancy between his account of *UB-110*'s sinking and that in the interrogation report. The Admiralty's version reads,

'The clips of the conning-tower hatch, which had jammed on account
of excessive air-pressure in the boat, were finally prised open, and the
crew tried to escape through this and the forward hatch. The
combined effect of the gunfire and the heavy list of the boat seem to

have led to a panic. The crew tried to force their way through the hatches in a body, and it was probably owing to this that a large number failed to escape.

Shortly after U.B.110 came to the surface a destroyer again rammed her with such force that she capsized and sank.'[16]

According to Fürbringer the entire crew got away from the boat but were shot at and pelted with lumps of coal from convoy escorts while in the water. Only the arrival of neutral merchantmen as independent witnesses put an end to the carnage.[17]

UB-110 was rammed (twice) and sunk by HMS *Garry* under the command of Lt Cdr Charles Lightoller (former second officer of RMS *Titanic*) after the boat had been depth charged and machine-gunned by motor launches *ML49* and *ML263*. *Garry* was seriously damaged by the collisions. Lightoller's memoir shows little sympathy for U-boat crewmen in general, stating in an oft-quoted passage '*when one did surrender to us, I refused to accept the hands-up business. In fact it was simply amazing that they should have had the infernal audacity to offer to surrender, in view of their ferocious and pitiless attacks on our merchant ships*'. Writing specifically of the *UB-110* incident he is more circumspect, saying '*I left the rescue work to the others, who picked up fifteen out of the water.*'[18]

When reading Fürbringer's account it is worth recalling that he learnt his trade under the notoriously trigger-happy Walther Schwieger in *U-20*, wondering why a well-run warship would have lumps of coal lying around ready for use as projectiles, and why he waited until 1933 to level his allegations.

We may never know the truth of the matter. Either way the upshot was nineteen dead and thirteen survivors who, between them, provided Intelligence Division with useful information.

Some captives like *Oberleutnant zur See* Kurt Utke of *UC-11*, considered it their duty to mislead. The limits of their truthfulness were explored with test questions to which the interviewers already knew the answers, painstaking cross-examination, and the interrogator's reliable fall-back of omniscience. Surely matters which your enemy is chatting knowledgeably about can no longer be a military secret? Even so, Utke managed to pull the wool over their eyes to some degree. Their report repeated in good faith his understated account of the damage sustained by the battlecruiser *Von der Tann*, in which he had served at the Battle of Jutland. He also denied, probably inaccurately, that the High Seas Fleet used 'ladder' salvoes (in which each of a ship's turrets fired at slightly different elevation) for rapid ranging. Better coordination between the silos of Naval Intelligence might have allowed the interviewer to call his bluff.[19]

There is an occasional hint of more robust measures.

'One informant had served for over three years in the Derfflinger, where his action station was in 'B' turret. This prisoner was at first unwilling to answer questions, but after a certain amount of persuasion, furnished the following information: ...'[20]

Brandon, Trench, and their colleagues evolved a well-tuned process of direct interrogation. The inactivity of the High Seas Fleet and poor survival rates of U-boat crews meant that they had relatively few customers and the luxury of taking their time with each one – a typical stay at Cromwell Gardens was several weeks. The key was to use what they did have from previous interrogations, captured documents, letters to and from prisoners, and agent reports to undermine the unfortunate subject's confidence.

Prisoners' correspondence could be a surprisingly valuable source of intelligence on its own. Once clear of formal interrogation many relaxed and became garrulous in their communications home, while gossip in family letters about who was posted to which ship could be equally revealing. *Kapitän-leutnant* Kurt Tebbenjohanns, in command of *UC-44*, sunk on 4th August 1917, chatted with *Oberleutnant zur See* Schiwig who passed his news on to his friend Gerhard von Wenkstern at Colsterdale internment camp.

> *'Losses – 3 boats per month. The total tonnage agrees with what we publish monthly. The returns published by the British are difficult to check, as each of our submarines reports separately on her return.*
>
> *Helfferich and the Admiralty Staff made a miscalculation with their 6 months, but the enormous losses must have their effect.'*[21]

His mention of six months may have been the Admiralty's first indication of the strategy behind the 1917 unrestricted U-boat campaign: to force Britain out of the war before the expected result of drawing in the USA could take effect.

There is no record of the Second World War's more sophisticated measures in the First. The Navy did not at this stage exploit hidden microphones or stool pigeons.

There is however evidence of inexpert interrogation before prisoners reached the professionals, a practice that NID tried hard to stamp out in WW2. Then-Lieutenant Stephen King-Hall of HMS *Maidstone* escorted Lieutenant Vicco von der Lühe, CO and sole survivor of *UB-16*, from Harwich to London in May 1918. In the words of the covering letter to the report he '*made good use of the opportunity for conversation. Lieut. Von der Lühe, however, fully realised that he had been 'pumped', and it was rather difficult to extract any further information from him.'*[22]

Curiously enough the two had come within sight of each other at the Battle of Jutland when King-Hall, serving aboard HMS *Southampton*, helped drive off a destroyer attack led by von der Lühe's ship *G-86*.[23] Sadly, the latter died of influenza while still a prisoner of war in 1919.

The exigencies of housing prisoners on a small ship meant that officer and rating captives were too often left together between capture and interview. In at least one case a prisoner managed to throw documents overboard after rescue, provoking the fury of Intelligence Division.[24] Interviews were carried out by senior staff up to and including 'Blinker' Hall himself as well as dedicated interrogators. The team was learning fast – but still learning.

There was a rather inept attempt to infiltrate an informer at an internment camp. Cope had to revisit an earlier interrogation when an Air Force intelligence report seemed to produce information he had missed. He concluded that this was down to the inexpert use of an unreliable stool pigeon and observed,

> 'The use of 'decoys' is a very risky procedure, as in many cases such a decoy is liable to invent information in order to make a good impression and to obtain material benefit.
>
> Kröllich and Elser state that Wolf [the stool pigeon] made a very strange and shifty impression on them, that he was most voluble, a braggart, and on the whole an undesirable person. He had told them he was captured in March, and they were wondering why he was still in London [this was September 1918].'[25]

Intelligence officers were also increasingly uneasy about the risk of information leakage back to the enemy. The October 1917 record of an unsatisfactory interview with *Oberleutnant zur See* Alfred Arnold, former commander of *UC-33*, noted the following concern:

> 'In view of the fact that many German naval officers distributed amongst the various P/W camps in this country may be expected to be interned in a neutral country in the near future, it becomes a matter for consideration whether it is at all desirable to attempt to extract more than general information from German submarine officers. In only very rare cases do officers give away information of any real value. Also, when a number of these officers, who have been under examination, meet at the same prisoner of war camp, they are in a position to compile a useful report on the amount of information known by the British Admiralty, and to transmit it to Germany whenever an officer is repatriated.'[26]

The danger of mishandling prisoners' intelligence potential was illustrated by the case of *UB-68*, sunk in the Mediterranean on 4th October 1918. Her skipper was *Oberleutnant zur See* Karl Dönitz, of whom much more would be heard in the next war. Following a chain of errors, the boat was forced to surface in the middle of the convoy she was trying to attack and was fired on by the escorts. Unable to dive, Dönitz gave the order to abandon ship. The engineer, who was below opening vents, went down with the boat and two or three seamen (accounts vary) drowned before they could be rescued. The remaining survivors were brought to Malta for interrogation.

The authors were evidently conscious that the ensuing report was unsatisfactory, commenting in the preamble,

> *'There is unfortunately little to be got from this interrogation as the submarine had almost entirely recommissioned just before coming out from Pola and while the officers were exceedingly reticent, the men were so inexperienced that they could give little evidence of value.'*

In view of his later career their comment on the commanding officer is worth repeating.

> *'Oberleutnant zur See Donitz … was very moody, and almost insolent at times, and it was very hard to make him talk at all. …. As he had previously said he was done with the sea and ships, it seems probable that the loss of UB 68 was due to the direct fault of the Commander.'*

The most interesting aspect of the report is the response it provoked from Brandon, by then promoted to Assistant DNI while retaining his responsibility for prisoner intelligence. In a thinly veiled reprimand over the failure to bring captives quickly to the attention of professional interrogators and, worse, their ruination by poor handling and inept prior questioning he wrote on 22nd October,

> *'Dear Temple [Brigadier-General Frank V Temple RMLI],*

Can you do anything to help us in the matter of German prisoners captured in the Mediterranean? On each occasion on which prisoners have been captured during the past year or so, either it has proved impossible to get the prisoners sent to England at all, or the process of getting them home has occupied so long, and so many amateur interrogations and so much contact with other prisoners have intervened, that very little information of value was derived when we finally did get hold of the prisoners.

We are now having the usual struggle in regard to the prisoners from "U.B.68", and the only reply I can get to my remonstrances in regard to the matter is that the C.-in-C. has more important things to bother about at the present moment. I cannot for the life of me conceive why the C.-in-C. should be bothered about this; surely it is a matter which can be settled by some comparatively subordinate member of his Staff. However, perhaps you can explain the riddle and suggest some remedy for our cases. I leave the matter in your hands in the assurance that you understand our difficulties here and will do all you can to assist us.

There seems to be no clear realisation in the Navy at large of the possibilities latent in the capture of prisoners, though I had hoped that some of our O.X.O. books[27], mere beginnings as they are, might have awakened a little interest in the matter. On the West Front it is considered worth while to expend thousands of pounds' worth of ammunition and lose the lives of a hundred men or so, to capture a handful of prisoners from the particular positions about which information is required. I have no hopes of our reaching this stage of enlightenment during the present war, but we might at least try to make good use of such material as the gods send.

In conclusion I may mention, in case you have not heard it already, that during the stay of the survivors of "U.B.53" at Malta, a most serious leakage of information to the enemy took place. It is the greatest pity that naval prisoners there should have to be turned over to the Military, and I wish you could use your influence in the

direction of their being retained in naval custody whenever it is
humanly possible.

Our best remedy of course is to have them sent straight home, making
an opportunity if one does not exist. They are surely of as much
importance as a British Minister General or Ambassador, for whose
benefit ships are freely detached from their proper work and sent
hither and thither.'

Temple wrote back explaining the difficulty of segregating
prisoners before interrogation and suggesting that a direct order
from Admiralty to keep submarine survivors in naval custody
until they reached the UK would make them such a nuisance
that their departure would be expedited by any means possible.
By the time his letter reached Brandon the Armistice had been
signed and the issue was irrelevant.[28]

Trench was posted in April 1918 to Base Intelligence Officer
at HMS *Colleen*, a 'stone frigate' or shore base at Queenstown
(now Cobh).

In the closing months of the war the scope of MI1(a)
expanded to provide the newly formed RAF with bombing target
intelligence, for which prisoners were a useful source. Cromwell
Gardens was too small for the extra workload, so a large house
in Wimbledon was requisitioned and fitted with 'special
technical apparatus' – presumably microphones. With exquisite
timing it was ready for occupation on 11th November 1918,
Armistice Day, so was never used.[29]

When the interned ships of the High Seas Fleet were scuttled
by their crews at Scapa Flow in June 1919 there was a desperate
scramble to find out whether they had done so was on their own
initiative or on orders from Germany, in breach of the Armistice.
There is no mention of the Fleet senior officers meeting
professional interrogators, implying the section had been
disbanded by then.

Lessons from Jutland

Burton Cope's initiation to Intelligence Division in 1917 came at a busy time. The previous year's Battle of Jutland, or the Skagerrak, had given both sides much to think about. Jellicoe and Beatty had not delivered the crushing victory the British public expected and instead brought home a soberingly high butcher's bill. Compounding the shock, the German version of events was promulgated first and loudest whereas the official Admiralty communique was muted and sounded almost apologetic by comparison.

4: Cope's First War Naval Intelligence Pass

One factor contributing to the disappointing outcome was the hermetic isolation of Room 40's cryptanalysts, forced to report through a tiny cadre of officers in Operations Division who were both sceptical of what these uppity civilians could contribute and paranoid that secrets might escape. A delayed consequence of intelligence miscommunication during the battle was that Room

40 became part of Intelligence Division in a May 1917 reorganisation, propelling its civilians into uniform and bolstering ID's already growing strength.

Part of Hall's genius was his talent for exploiting secret knowledge without giving away its source which, combined with a switch to issuing appreciations rather than raw decrypts, finally allowed the codebreakers to realise their potential.

The Admiralty was not long deceived about the extent of damage to the High Seas Fleet. Two agents ('R.16' and 'D15') infiltrated Wilhelmshaven and other dockyards on Hall's behalf and reported back by the end of June 1916.[30] 'R.16' (also referred to as TR16 and H16) was a resentful former *Kaiserliche Marine* engineering officer, Karl Krüger, who offered his services to the MI6 Rotterdam resident in November 1914. With unrestricted access to German naval dockyards and contractors he provided a priceless stream of intelligence throughout the war and inter-war period.

Over time, a procession of first-hand witnesses helped Brandon and Trench put flesh on these skeletal reports.

Scheer and Hipper, on the other hand, had failed to break through Jellicoe's wall of steel or significantly reduce the Royal Navy's numerical superiority. The resulting constraints placed on capital ship operations led to the resumption of unrestricted submarine warfare in February 1917.

The German High Seas Fleet made few sorties in strength after Jutland. The only prospect of action for veterans of the battle was transfer to the dangerous life of U-boats or destroyers. For those left behind the combination of idleness, harsh discipline and short, vile rations led to mounting disillusion. A steady drip of deserters found their way to the Netherlands or Denmark and presented themselves, sometimes with gifts of drawings or components, to the British Consulate.

Desertion and capture brought customers into Cromwell Gardens. One of the first was Louis Jütte, an ordinary seaman from Hamburg who had gone to America in 1912 to avoid military service – only to be conscripted by the German Consul when his ship put into Naples. He eventually found himself helping feed the shell-hoist for the aft turret of the battleship *König* at Jutland. Before drydocking the ship for repairs the turret crew had to remove fuses from the unused ammunition. Jütte, with an eye to the future, kept one back – it was a new delayed-action design for armour piercing shells. When finally granted leave at the end of November 1916, he and two others tried to cross the Danish frontier by boat but were frustrated by a destroyer[31] patrol. He finally made it, alone, a couple of days later and presented himself at the British consulate in Copenhagen on 6th December, whence he was sent to London via Bergen. His sole ambition was to get back to America and, after willingly draining his knowledge to Brandon's interviewers, he got his wish. Jütte was a passenger on SS *New York* departing Liverpool for New York on 3rd February 1917.[32]

Kapitänleutnant Claus Lafrenz, captain of the minelaying submarine *UC-65*, described his capture in a letter to his friend Lieutenant Ulrich Meier at Kiel, dated 4th November 1917.

'*DEAR MÜMMELMANN ['HARE'],*

This evening I intended to go home on leave and to contribute to the food supply by shooting numerous hares and duck. Instead of this I am here in London as a prisoner in the Prisoners of War Detention Barracks in Cromwell Gardens and feel very down on my luck. I fell a victim to the very worst of bad luck. If I had not personally seen the periscope and the torpedoes fired, they would have missed us. As it was, owing to my turning, one of them struck us aft, I believe at the rudder. The boat sank quickly, and 20 men with her. With me Lieutenant Braue, Leading Seamen Ostergaard and Fügner, and Telegraphist Bremer, were picked up by the British submarine and were treated very well, as also later on on board a trawler. Yesterday evening we were brought here from Portsmouth. It is also quite bearable here, if it were not for the boredom and the consequent gloomy thoughts. The many fine fellows who have been lost – I wish I had gone with them!

The rescued are all uninjured, with the exception of myself: I received a severe blow to the chest.[33]

Matrose Fritz Leiss, a survivor of *UC-75*, wrote home describing his situation in glowing terms.[34]

Dear Mother,

Fancy, I am now in London. I can only tell you that we were rammed and then rescued by a destroyer. Half of the crew were saved, including myself.

It was simply touching, we were received so well. We were given everything we needed, clothes, food, and smokes. We arrived in London at about noon and went off at once to the barracks in a motor. We live in the centre of the town and our rooms even face the street. From this you can see what nonsense people talk in Germany; things are just the opposite of what was said. We are better cared for in every respect than when in His Majesty's (the Kaiser's) service. You might send me some money, then we can buy a lot here.

I must close now, trusting that you will receive this letter soon. The next letter will contain more about the cruise. Fondest love.

Your Son,

(Signed) FRITZ.[35]

Some former participants in the battle transferred to naval airships, or 'Zeppelins.'[36] They had begun raiding the British mainland with impunity in 1915 but were now finding it a much tougher proposition as anti-aircraft gunners and fighters found the range. Their crews worked in the brutal cold and thin air at operating altitudes up to 20,000 feet, under gas bags full of highly flammable hydrogen and (until late in the war) without parachutes. They were tough and brave and, as naval personnel, many of the captured survivors met Brandon's team. Even hard-boiled interrogators were sometimes taken aback by their apparent callousness: joking about the screams of crewmates trapped in a burning section, or ground crew killed as they ditched ballast while manoeuvring to land.[37]

At the same time Trench's energetic pursuit of crashed Zeppelins and generous bounty for divers to enter sunken U-boats helped feed Room 40's cryptanalysts with up-to-date code books.

The steady flow of Jutland veterans allowed interrogators to build a picture of the battle from the German viewpoint: tactics, damage suffered, casualties beyond the official lists and the enemy's view of British performance.

The most serious German loss was the battlecruiser *Lützow*, abandoned and sunk by her own escort during the night when it became clear she stood no chance of getting home. Six men trapped in the auxiliary dynamo room were claimed to have gone to their deaths with patriotic resolution. Armand Denny was a disaffected stoker from Alsace who had been sent to front line *Stosstruppen* (shock troops) as punishment and deserted from there. He had a different view.

> '*They asked permission to come out, as the water was beginning to rise, but the compartments on either side were full of water, and it proved impossible to get them out. They were consoled with the story that they were just outside Wilhelmshaven, and would soon be in safety. The rest of the crew then abandoned the ship, which was finished off by a German torpedo.'*[38]

Lieutenant Loebell of *UB-110*, had been first lieutenant of the destroyer *V.153* at Jutland. On gunnery, he '*considered that, had our salvoes had a greater spread, a larger number of hits would have been registered on German ships. Salvoes appeared to fall over, short, right or left, but seldom to hit.*'[39] This may have been a reflection on the Battle Cruiser Squadron's lack of live-fire practice and obsession with rate-of-fire. He also observed that German destroyers, which at first sheltered some 1,500-2,000 metres behind the battleships, were ordered to move further away because British fire was falling so far beyond its targets.

Importantly, interrogation yielded technical details of topics such as turret and ammunition design where the Germans were ahead. It was very noticeable that despite horrific pounding they had *not* lost any ships to the catastrophic magazine explosions that made the day so painful for the Royal Navy.

Other prisoners revealed that both main and secondary turrets in German ships had been modified after the battle to increase their guns' maximum elevation and thus range. The equivalent modernisation of British battleships' armament was not complete by the start of World War 2.[40]

A revealing insight into German ships' survivability appears in the interrogation report on a prize crew captured from the Norwegian SS *Older* on 18th November 1916. An engine-room PO who had previously served with *Grosser Kurfürst* supplied the information that,

> *'All considerations of convenience or handiness appear to have been subordinated to making the subdivision as complete as possible. Each boiler room is reached by a separate entrance from the armoured deck. All important bulkheads are stiffened in a very thorough manner and tested at 30 ft. head of water.'*[41]

The difference of approach persisted into the next generation. In 1943 *Scharnhorst* survivors expressed shock at, in their view, *Duke of York's* excessively large compartments.

Fear of German torpedoes had limited Jellicoe's options in the battle, and the apparent disparity in the effectiveness of British and German gunnery had come as an expensive wake-up call. Both had to be investigated. Admiral Beatty, by then Commander-in-Chief (C-in-C) Grand Fleet wrote to Hall on 27th December 1916 with the request,

'… I shall be glad if you will make every effort to ascertain by interrogation details as to torpedo armament, ranges and speeds of torpedoes, in the latest vessels of the German Navy.[42]

Hall replied that, since none of the recent captives were torpedo ratings or had any special knowledge of the subject, the previously disseminated information was the best available.

Jellicoe, by then First Sea Lord, asked Hall on 21st January 1917 to,

'…give the Officers of the Grand Fleet more information about the damage inflicted by our shells on the German High Sea Fleet than they now possess. Otherwise their confidence in their ammunition will eventually be destroyed.[43]

Hall submitted a draft response on 29th and a formal paper the following month, both of which relied heavily on Jütte's evidence.[44]

Intelligence Division investigated German ammunition handling, damage control, sensors, fire control, signalling, tactics, and the relative merits of British and German rangefinder design, which are still debated today.

A Seaman Petty Officer survivor from *U-58* had been a range-taker in the gun control tower of *Prinzregent Luitpold*. He supplied details of the number and type of rangefinders carried, their method of operation, and the training regime. A minute on the C-in-C (Admiral Beatty's) advance copy of the report comments,

'There appears to be no doubt that the Germans have stuck to and developed the Stereo Range Finder.

It appears probable that this Range Finder is advantageous for taking Ranges of Indistinct Objects & that it may be desirable to carry one or even two in each ship. From Private Information, a 15ft Stereo Range Finder is on order for Grand Fleet. Meanwhile we can try the one at present supplied, to see if it can take ranges when the Barr & Stroud cannot.'

The Admiral wrote underneath, '*Let this be done.*'[45]

Information continued drifting in. Some prisoners who had snatched an unofficial look through a rangefinder without understanding what they saw were at least able to describe it. More usefully a survivor of *UB-124*, sunk on 20th July 1918, had qualified in rangetaking earlier that year and was persuaded to give a detailed description of the course, equipment, and procedures.[46]

Some lessons were learnt, others not quickly enough. In the febrile atmosphere of 1917/18, the interrogators' priority was naturally to counter the U-boat menace. Nonetheless the two battle fleets, glaring at each other across a North Sea infested with mines and submarines, still chafed for another encounter. The High Seas Fleet had taken delivery of the super-dreadnoughts *Bayern* and *Baden* (roughly equivalent to the British *Queen Elizabeth* class) with another two launched in November 1916 and June 1917. The new battlecruiser *Hindenburg* was almost ready for sea until stripped to repair other ships after Jutland. In the words of the report,

> '*After the Jutland Battle several of her armour-plates were removed and fitted in the "DERFFLINGER" and "SEYDLITZ". Two of her turrets were taken out and installed in other ships. All the guns were also removed from the remaining turrets and distributed among the ships of the fleet.*'[47]

This delayed her availability for trials until May 1917. A successor, *Mackensen* (formerly *Ersatz Freya*), then on the stocks was launched in April 1917, with another in September. Two more battlecruisers had been laid down when the war ended but none of the *Mackensen* class was completed.

Nor was the threat merely theoretical. On 17th October and 12th December 1917 German cruisers and destroyers surprised and successfully attacked convoys between Norway and Shetland. The unavoidable British reaction was to give the frequent sailings a capital ship guard, handing Scheer the chance to chip away at Britain's numerical dominance. On 23rd April 1918, the entire High Seas Fleet set out in radio silence to find and annihilate a Norwegian convoy and its escort. As it happened there was no sailing that day.

At the end of October 1918, with U-boats withdrawn from commerce warfare in preparation for the Armistice, Admirals Scheer and Hipper prepared one last, desperate throw of the dice: an attack in force on the Thames Estuary to draw the Grand Fleet out over lines of the newly released submarines. It was frustrated only by their crews' refusal to join an unauthorised suicide mission which risked prolonging the war.

Informants provided surprisingly detailed information about the new super-dreadnoughts *Baden* and *Bayern*, and the light cruiser *Königsberg*, none of which were ready in time for Jutland. They confirmed and expanded on material gleaned from survivors of the trawler *Otto Rudolf*, sunk off Sylt on 25th March 1916. Captain Hall was sceptical at the time.

'This information, which was elicited by Lieutenant-Commander Bagot, appears to be generally reliable, but it is considered out of the question that the "BAYERN" (late "T") or any other new battleship can be nearly completed at Kiel.'[48]

In fact, *Bayern* was already working up in the Baltic.

Prisoners' correspondence and new captives provided a running commentary on the progress of these and other new ships. The interrogation report on *UC-61*, for example, updated news on the battlecruiser *Hindenburg*, light cruiser *Emden* ('*Ersatz Nymphe*'), minelaying cruisers *Brummer* and *Bremse* as well as *Bayern*, *Baden* and their proposed sister *Sachsen* which was never completed.[49] These fast, modern vessels were an incremental improvement on their predecessors and represented a serious threat.

Castaways in Question

Unrestricted Submarine Warfare

As in the Second World War it was the underwater struggle that brought Britain and her allies closest to defeat. This was especially so during the periods of unrestricted submarine warfare after February 1915 and February 1917. Previously, and in the interim, U-boat commanders were expected to stay plausibly close to 'cruiser rules,' which required a belligerent to respect neutral vessels' right of passage but allowed them to be searched for contraband. If an enemy merchantman was to be sunk or taken as a prize the safety of its crew and passengers had to be assured. While reasonably practical for a surface raider these rules discarded a submarine's only edge and its main defence – invisibility. Moreover, the cramped space on board prohibited accommodating more than a very few non-essential personnel.

The overwhelming diplomatic motive for the policy of restraint was to keep America out of the war. The sinking of *Lusitania*, *Arabic* and *Hesperian* with US citizens aboard in 1915 had brought an abrupt end to the first campaign. The growing strength of both the U-boat arm and of British anti-submarine forces, combined with the apparent impotence of the High Seas Fleet, made a change of policy increasingly attractive toward the end of 1916.

Even so, many skippers were doing the best they could to preserve life within the existing rules. When HMS *Otway* boarded the Norwegian SS *Older* on 18th November 1916, she was found to be under the command of a mixed prize crew from *U-49* and *U-50*. She was due to make a series of rendezvous with the boats to pick up prisoners:

'Evidently the idea is that by using captured neutrals as dumping ships for crews of other vessels, "frightfulness" may be kept within

*such bounds as will render a strong protest from the United States
unlikely.*[50]

The second offensive created serious fears that losses would
overwhelm Allied capacity to replace them, to the extent that
Jellicoe warned the War Cabinet on 19th June 1917 that Britain
was in danger of losing the war before America's intervention
could take effect.

With the High Seas Fleet's options severely restricted after
the Battle of Jutland this was exactly Admiral Scheer's strategy.
The German Naval Staff predicted in December 1916 that the
loss of 600,000 tons of merchant shipping monthly for five
months would force Britain out of the war, and that France and
Italy would quickly follow.[51] Including Allied and neutral losses
the target was met on average from April to September 1917,
causing great consternation but no collapse.

Lack of prompt results did not dent many servicemen's faith
in the strategy. *Leutnant zur See* Richard Freude, a seaplane pilot
shot down in May 1917, chatted with his German-speaking
doctor in hospital and claimed,

*'The entering into the war of the U.S.A. is regrettable, but her Army
is of no account, and although the hostile activity of her Navy will be
a factor, it will not prove a very important one.*

*If Russia lays down her arms a rapid collapse of the allied cause will
ensue within a remarkably short space of time.'*[52]

While neatly summing up the official view, he might have done
well to recall the disdain heaped on the British Expeditionary
Force three years earlier. The report on *Kapitänleutnant* Freiherr
Spiegel von und zu Peckelsheim, commander of *U-93*, captured
in a clash with the Q ship *Prize* on 30th April 1917,[53] made the
comparison explicitly.

*'As regards America, his view was that (1) the Americans would
never raise an army; (2) that the army would be no good if they did
raise one, and (3) that they would never be able to transport even a*

make-believe army. It was amusing to note that his statements regarding America were almost word for word those which appeared daily in the German Press early in the war, when Kitchener's Army was still a very uncertain quantity. Spiegel, however, seemed quite unconscious of the parallel, and went on to say that the Germans had always known that the English were a great nation, and therefore were not surprised at our being able to raise an army of 3 or 4 millions during two years of war, but the Americans were of course quite a different people, and would never achieve such things.'[54]

By September 1918 the Americans had forcibly dispelled any illusion of their ineffectuality. Armand Denny, a former German naval stoker whose socialist views had seen him despatched to the front line, reported that,

'The advent of so many efficient American troops on the Western front has completely killed any belief in the decisive influence of the submarine warfare. Many of the troops express their agreement with v.Kühlmann's statement[55] that a military decision is impossible.'[56]

In eloquent testimony to the priority and value of Intelligence Division's interrogation reports, the Grand Fleet Commander-in-Chief had pre-publication typed copies sent to him and made up into a special volume of his Secret Packs.[57]

The interviews revealed urgently topical information, such as the Germans' orders to attack hospital ships in the belief that they were being used as 'false flag' troopships, in breach of the Hague Convention. Werner Fürbringer claimed that while serving as first lieutenant of *U-20* in 1915 he personally saw a ship, marked with the red cross, bound for Le Havre with her decks packed with armed British troops.[58] His captain at the time was *Kapitänleutnant* Walther Schwieger who had torpedoed three unarmed merchantmen without warning on 30th January 1915 (before the declaration of the unrestricted U-boat campaign), and took a pot-shot at the clearly marked hospital ship *Asturias* two days later.[59] In May he capped his notoriety by sinking the *Lusitania*.

By July 1918 Fürbringer was in command of *UB-110* when she was sunk off Hartlepool on her maiden patrol. His views had not changed.

> *'With regard to attacks on hospital ships, he expressed the opinion that such attacks are justifiable if a special order to sink these vessels is issued by the German Government, as the latter would not take such drastic measures without definite proof that the Red Cross was being abused. Pressed on this point, he stated that he himself would have been justified in sinking a 6,000-ton hospital ship off the French coast in the second half of 1917, as the vessel was certainly being used as a troop transport. On this occasion he saw about 300 troops on board. He was convinced that they were troops, as they were in uniform and, in his opinion, they "did not behave like orderlies off duty, but like troops on board a transport." He refrained from sinking the ship, as she was in a zone in which his Government had undertaken to respect hospital ships. He declined to state the position or date more precisely.'[60]*

Freiherr Spiegel of *U-93* accepted the allegations without question and repeated them in his influential book *The Adventures of the U-202*.[61] When his luck ran out, he was put on the spot by British interrogators.

> *'Questioned as to the evidence which the German Admiralty professes to have regarding the employment of Hospital Ships by the Allies for the purpose of transporting troops and munitions, Spiegel stated that the evidence consisted of the sworn statements of agents. When asked how much value he personally would attach to the sworn statement of an agent, he was at a loss for an answer. He merely said that he could not understand how the German Admiralty Staff could have been mistaken about such a matter.*
>
> *In his own book, one chapter describes the abuse of the Red Cross Flag by England. He admitted that the incident in question had been*

related by a brother submarine officer, and he himself could not vouch for it at all.[62]

HMHS *Anglia* was sunk with the loss of 164 lives on 17th November 1915, in a marked hospital ships' channel which had been deliberately mined. She was the first but not the last; at least sixteen British and Commonwealth hospital ships were torpedoed or mined by the German navy during the war.[63]

The reaction of U-boat captains varied: some certainly took the orders to heart, but many turned a blind eye. The crew of *U-81*, captured on 1st May 1917, were uneasy about the practice and quick to disclaim any part in it.

'Several of the prisoners were asked what they thought about the indiscriminate sinking of all vessels, and also of hospital ships. They said they had to obey orders, but did not appear to like it. They were all careful to lay stress on the point that "U.81" had never sunk a hospital ship.'[64]

We have already met *Kapitänleutnant* Kurt Tebbenjohanns of *UC-44*, sunk on 4th August, who put it like this:

'I have never attacked any hospital ships and I know that several submarine commanders have deliberately avoided attacking them in spite of orders to do so. On their return, the conduct of these officers has been privately approved by the Flotilla Commander. Such orders are most distasteful to submarine officers, and I hope that, under the new regulations, hospital ships will be immune from attack.'[65]

Even allowing for retrospective self-justification, Tebbenjohanns had to admit that such orders had been given. On the other hand, *Oberleutnant zur See* Kurt Utke, commander and sole survivor of minelaying submarine *UC-11*, was unabashed by the principle while taking care to deny any personal involvement.

'Lieutenant Utke made some remarks which prove how difficult it is for the German mind to discriminate between right and wrong, when the pursuit of the latter might be expected to confer some material advantage on the German State. It may be added that this officer did

*not make the impression of being a thoroughgoing Prussian, and was
certainly more modest than the majority of his class, even going out of
his way to minimize his own intellectual attainments as compared
with those of his brother officers, like Lieutenant-Commander
Wenninger.*

*When asked his opinion of the sinking of hospital ships, he admitted
that 'in itself' (an und für sich) the practice was reprehensible, but
stated that he would feel constrained to obey his orders, viz. to attack
all hospital ships met with inside the areas forbidden to them. He
urged the following pleas in justification:*

*(a) These vessels, on the outward passage, transport troops and
munitions. (He admitted that in this respect he simply had to take
the word of his superior officers.)*

*(b) On the return journey, in addition to the wounded, soldiers
proceeding on leave or important personages might be on board.*

*(c) It is a military necessity from the German point of view to sink as
much tonnage as possible. (This plea reveals a refreshing candour,
which sets at nought all distinction between right and wrong.)*

*Utke stated, however, that he himself had never actually carried out
or witnessed an attack on a hospital ship.*

*On the question of unrestricted submarine warfare in general, he
expressed the opinion that German submarines were entitled to sink
neutral merchant vessels:*

(a) Because the latter transport food and raw material to England;

(b) because, again, it is a military necessity to reduce tonnage.

*On the other hand, he considered that the British, if they decided to
attack neutral merchantmen trading to German ports, would not be
able to plead military necessity in justification, because neutral
shipping plied much more in the interests of England than in those of
Germany![66]*

By the time *U-110* met her fate on 15th March 1918 the policy
had changed. *Marine Oberingenieur* Bruno Schmidt, who had
access to his commander's operation orders, revealed that they

contained strict injunctions against sinking hospital ships. At that stage of the war the effect on neutrals' opinion was likely to outweigh any conceivable tactical advantage.[67]

In the 1921 Leipzig war crime tribunal *Kapitänleutnant* Karl Neumann of *UC-67* (the boat later commanded by Martin Niemöller) was put on trial for sinking the hospital ship *Dover Castle*. He was acquitted, as he was implementing a policy laid down from above. Ludwig Dithmar and John Boldt, two officers of *U-86* were charged for their part in sinking *Llandovery Castle* and firing on the survivors. Their sentence was quashed on appeal, on the grounds that they were following the orders of their commanding officer who had fled to Danzig and was not available to answer charges. Their commander, *Oberleutnant zur See* Helmut Patzig, was given a legal amnesty in 1931 and served again, mainly in staff roles in the Second World War.

The United Kingdom also listed the following First World War U-boat commanders as wanted war criminals, but few came to trial and none were convicted:[68] Where hospital ships, attacks outside the scope of 'unrestricted' operations, multiple passenger deaths or killing survivors were involved there was clearly a case to answer. There were however cases where the argument that Britain's increasingly sophisticated use of 'Q' (decoy) ships made hesitation fatal would have carried weight. In any case, most of these individuals were careful to change their identity or otherwise make themselves unavailable as soon as the war ended.

Commander	Boat	Ships alleged attacked/sunk
Wilhelm Kiesewetter	*UC-56*	Hospital ship *Glenart Castle*
Max Valentiner	*U-38*	*Glenby* and the passenger ship *Persia* sunk without warning
Wilhelm Werner	*U-55*	*Clearfield*, *Artist*, *Trevone*, *Torrington*, *Toro* sunk without warning; hospital ships *Rewa* and *Guildford Castle* attacked. Reduced to a charge of

Commander	Boat	Ships alleged attacked/sunk
		sinking SS *Torrington* and murdering the crew except the captain
Heinrich Jeß	U-96	*Apapa*, *Destro*, *Inkosi* sunk without warning
Hans Adam	U-82	Sinking passenger steamer *Galway Castle* (Heinrich Middendorff commanded U-82 at the time)
Hubert Aust	UC-45	Drifter *Golden Hope*, no casualties
Thorwald von Bothmer	U-66	*Mariston* (now believed sunk by U-45, Erich Sittenfeld)
Otto Dröscher	U-20	*Ikaria* and *Tokomaru* (sunk by U-20 under Schwieger's command)
Konrad Gansser	U-33, U-156	*Clan McLeod*, *Belle of France* (now believed sunk by U-21, Otto Hersing), *W C M'Kay*, *Artesia*
Carl-Siegfried Ritter von Georg	U-57, U-101	*Refugio*, *Jersey City* (now believed sunk by U-46, Leo Hillebrand), *Teal*, *Richard de Larrinaga*, *Glenford*, *Trinidad*, *John G Walter*, *Lough Fisher*; attacking *Arlington Court*. Acquitted of war crimes in 1923
Alfred von Glasenapp	U-91	*Haileybury*, *Birchleaf*, *Landonia*, *Baron Herries*, *Ethel*
Heinrich von Nostitz und Jänckendorff	U-151	Passenger steamer *Dwinsk*
Constantin Kolbe	U-152	*Ellaston*, *Elsie Birdett*; *Clan Murray*, attacking *Fernley* (the last two now believed sunk by UC-55, Theodor Schultz)
Claus Rücker	U-103	Fishing vessel *Victoria*
Otto von Schrader	UB-64	*Dartmoor* (now believed sunk by UC-50, Rudolf Seuffer)
Erwin Waßner	UC-69	*Addah*

Table 1: WW1 U-boat captains accused of war crimes.

Otto Dröscher may be on the list as a substitute for Walther Schwieger, who did not survive the war. Dröscher and Fürbringer both served under Schwieger in *U-20* when the latter started enthusiastically torpedoing merchant ships without warning before the start of the 1915 unrestricted campaign. His boat schooled future skippers in ruthlessness.

Twenty-five years later the defence, 'only obeying orders' was rejected at Nuremberg in a watershed for the concept of soldiers' personal responsibility. The perceived leniency of the Leipzig court's treatment of *U-86* and *UC-67* may have affected the approach taken toward *Kapitänleutnant* Eck and his fellow-accused of *U-852* in 1945.[69]

The Allied case, then and later, was complicated by the *Baralong* Affair. On 19th August 1915 HMS *Baralong*, a Q-ship (warship disguised as a merchantman) came across *U-27* in the act of stopping the liner *Nicosian*. *Baralong* approached flying the Stars and Stripes as a ruse, then raised the White Ensign and quickly despatched the submarine. With feelings running high after the sinking of *Lusitania* and *Arabic* German survivors in the water were killed, as were members of a boarding party on *Nicosian*. However, neutral American passengers witnessed the event which was widely reported. Outrage followed in Germany but Captain Herbert of the *Baralong* not only avoided any repercussions but was awarded a DSO for his action.

★ ★ ★

U-boats were routinely passing the Dover barrier of patrols, mines and nets which was supposed to keep them out of the Channel. The obstacle was intended both to protect precious troops and supplies crossing the Channel to France, and force submarines planning to attack trade in the Western Approaches to take the longer north-about route and so reduce their time on station.

A system of buoyed nets (later illuminated at night) covered by armed yachts and drifters backed up by destroyers was designed to force any U-boat attempting the passage to dive into a deep minefield. It was intermittently an effective deterrent but always permeable, and the lightly armed patrols with their exhausted crews were terrifyingly vulnerable to destroyer raids from the Flanders ports.

One problem was the difficulty of constructing a net that was light enough to suspend from a chain of buoys but robust enough to withstand both weather and a desperate U-boat's attempts to free itself. A survivor of *U-81* described one incident.

'One of the prisoners, who had served in "U.C.3", of the Flanders Flotilla, which he left in March 1916, stated that in that boat they had frequently gone down the Channel on the surface at night without being seen. They frequently passed destroyers or other patrol craft, and sometimes less than a cable off, without attracting attention. On one occasion, whilst "U.C.3" was running on the surface about 15 miles off Cape Griz Nez, they sighted two small steamers ahead. They dived to avoid notice, but ran into the net which these two trawlers were working. As soon as they found they were caught in the net, the captain ordered all tanks to be flooded, and the boat sank, tearing the net away, and eventually hitting the bottom in about 36 fathoms. The boat appeared to be undamaged, but when they tried to go ahead, the fuses of the main motors blew, and it was concluded that the net had fouled the propellers. The boat was then brought to the surface by blowing all tanks, and the oil engines started. These were powerful enough to free the propeller, and they returned to Zeebrugge. On examination, it was found that the boat was covered with net, which began at conning tower and went right along the boat to the after end. One part had got jammed between the rudder and one of the after hydroplanes; the bight had evidently got wound up on the propeller and brought the motors up standing; but the oil engines appear to have been powerful enough to part the wire. The

45

propeller was undamaged, and only slightly polished. No explosions of mines or depth charges appear to have been heard.'[70]

Some U-boats were fitted with external net cutters, but the trade-off between their effectiveness and their impact on the boat's performance and handling remained a matter for debate.

On 17th January 1917 at a conference to prepare for the unrestricted campaign, submarine captains were instructed to use the Channel whenever possible, taking advantage of darkness and bad weather to make the run on the surface undetected. Any boats taking the north-about route, on the other hand, were to be as conspicuous as possible to keep the Royal Navy guessing.[71]

Before accidentally stranding herself near Wissant on 26th July 1917 *UC-61* had followed a standard route, taking the commercial shipping channel through the South Goodwin Barrage on the surface at night. A submarine's low profile made detection difficult and, according to the captain, destroyers tended to keep to the middle of the barrage.[72]

An Intelligence Division analysis of barrier crossings for three months in 1917 gave a depressing view of its effectiveness.

Table 2: Passage of Dover Barrage March-June 1917[73]

Prisoners Mention	March (part)	April	May	June (part)
Passages	20	32	34	6
Patrols seen	14	8	13	
U-boats attacked			1	
Strong patrols in barrage		2		

This evidence ultimately contributed to the formation of the Barrage Committee in November 1917, and to the growing political pressure which culminated in Admirals Bacon (Commander of the Dover Patrol) and Jellicoe (First Sea Lord) losing their jobs.

Bacon's successor, Admiral Keyes, energetically renewed efforts to prevent the steady stream of U-boats passing through the straits. To little avail. *UC-75* was rammed on 31ˢᵗ May 1918 by ships of the convoy she was trying to attack after the captain misjudged his range. Survivors supplied a depressing insight into the barrier's ineffectiveness.

'(i) General.

On leaving Zeebrugge, the boat usually followed "Way A" which appears to lead roughly true West for 3 or 4 miles. A course was then shaped to pass outside all or most of the banks, and the boat usually proceeded on the surface until No. 4 buoy "off Dover" was picked up. This is presumably one of the buoys of the net barrage, but no reliable position could be obtained.

The time of leaving Zeebrugge was arranged so that the whole passage of the Straits of Dover could be made during hours of dusk or darkness; if possible, the boat passed through with *the tide.*

(ii) Mine Nets off Belgian Coast.

The prisoners generally appeared to be unaware of the existence of these obstructions. The commanding officer knew that they had formerly existed, but expressed the opinion that very little of them now remained. It is quite evident that these nets no longer act in the least as a deterrent, and no attempt is made to avoid them.

(iii) Net Barrage from the Goodwins to Dunkirk.

This obstruction likewise is regarded as innocuous. The boat always passed it on the surface and experienced no trouble from hawsers.

(iv) Deep Minefield.

The existence of this minefield is suspected, but neither officers nor men appeared to have any idea of its extent. They evidently realized that it was dangerous to dive in this locality.

With the exception of the (acting) navigating warrant officer they seemed to be under the impression that the "light barrage", as they called it, i.e. the drifters burning flares, was intended rather to reveal the presence of a submarine than to induce her to dive. This warrant officer, however, remarked: "I think they want to force us to dive." In practice, however, the drifters being a good distance apart and usually either moving slowly or entirely stopped, it was not found a difficult matter to keep clear of them and to slip past at full speed on the surface at a distance of 250-400 yards. The fact that the lights are apparently burnt on board all the drifters enabled the submarine always to locate the latter before she herself could be detected.'[74]

Interrogators probed the technical details of the U-boats and their equipment, prompted by Admiralty questions about (*inter alia*) German progress on wireless telegraphy, hydrophones, and torpedoes. They tried to keep track of how many boats had been built, where they were based, who was in command, and which had been lost. Tactics, routes, intelligence, communications were all explored for signs of vulnerability. Infuriatingly, evidence came to light suggesting that a German merchant ship in neutral Cadiz harbour was surreptitiously victualling U-boats, allowing them greatly extended time on station.[75] If true this was an ominous foretaste of Second World War practice.

In December 1916 an unnamed prisoner supplied the information that the latest long-range submarines (*U-81* to *90* and *91* to *100* classes) were to be fitted with a 4.1-inch gun, and that earlier boats would have their 22-pounders similarly upgraded as availability and the vessel's stability allowed. This weapon, which threw a 38-pound shell up to 14,000 yards, made them a dangerous opponent on the surface for anything smaller than a sloop.[76]

Hydrophones were increasingly fitted to submarines of both sides from about 1916 to allow them to listen for both targets and threats. The technology still left something to be desired. *UC-39* was sunk on her first patrol in February 1917. Survivors described the acoustic equipment fitted to this then brand-new vessel:

Sound Signalling.

No <u>sending</u> apparatus is fitted.

<u>Receiving</u> apparatus is as follows:-

3 microphones are fitted in the tanks between inner and outer hulls, one right forward, the two others one on either side amidships. By means of a 3-way switch each of the microphones can be connected in turn to a telephone head-set in the wireless cabinet, thus enabling the direction of vessels to be roughly determined.

By inserting a variable resistance in parallel with the circuit, interference due to sounds in the boat can be reduced, but the apparatus was said not to be really reliable unless the engines and all auxiliary machinery were stopped. The foremost hydroplanes were said to be particularly troublesome when listening.[77]

Captives from *U-48*, stranded and scuttled on the Goodwin Sands in November 1917, were usefully chatty about the limitations of the system.

'It was stated that very little use is made of the sound signalling apparatus, and that, as regards listening, almost as good results can be obtained by placing the ear against the pressure hull in the fore torpedo compartment as by using the apparatus. For this purpose, however, all noise must of course be stopped in the boat.'[78]

Intelligence Division had the previous month published a fifteen-page technical report on the type of German hydrophone fitted to their boat. The physical description, layout drawings and circuit diagrams may well have come from examination of wrecked boats but the sections on care, operation, maintenance, and fault-finding can only have been provided by crews familiar with the equipment.[79]

If both navies were struggling to develop the new technology of underwater sound detection, there were worrying suggestions that the Germans were ahead when it came to the application of wireless. Returning to *UC-39*,

> *A message sent during daylight hours by U.C.39 when abreast the Jade was taken in by the station at Bruges (distance about 240 miles). It was stated that another submarine could not have received the message at that distance. The wireless operator of U.C.39 said that he was able to hear Poldhu when at Kiel by using the amplifier which all submarines now carry.'*

Interrogators were probably unaware that this very advantage created the temptation for profligate communication which Room 40's cryptographers were simultaneously putting to such good use.

If submarine warfare was a new and disturbing feature of the First World War, so was the use of airships to raid inland cities. In October 1917 NID drew the Commander-in-Chief's attention to an interesting snippet from an enemy submariner:

> *'...all enemy submarines are fitted with a recognition mark which is to be displayed when in the presence of aircraft. This consists of a white ring painted half upon each of two plates of sheet iron, which are hinged together. One of these plates is secured flat upon the deck forward, the other one being folded down on top of it when in harbour or when it is desired not to display the recognition mark, and opened out at other times.'*

The commander of 10th Submarine Flotilla, based at Harwich, saw an opportunity. If enough information could be gleaned about the recognition mark something similar could be fitted to British 'G' class submarines (which looked passably like their German opposite numbers) and used to tempt a Zeppelin within range of their guns.[80] There is no record of this being done but the exchange of memos is an intriguing example of the ways in which the unique insights of prisoner intelligence were seized on for possible exploitation.

World War 1

Otto Launberg was the commander and one of two survivors of *UB-52* when she was torpedoed in the Otranto Strait on 23rd May 1918. He was rescued by his nemesis, HM Submarine *H.4*, and made some interesting observations on the relative state of submarine technology at that late stage of the war.

> *'Launburg expressed the opinion that British submarines had improved considerably of late, and were now as good as the German boats, except as regards their oil engines. He stated that the oil engines of some British 'E' boats which were sunk or captured in the Dardanelles had been salved and refitted in Constantinople, where they had then been run and compared with German Diesel engines. The results obtained were stated to indicate that the German engines were far superior to the British.*
>
> *Speaking of his experiences in H.M. Submarine H.4. the commanding officer of U.B.52 said that when he saw the British oil engines running, he was forcibly reminded of the German Diesel engines in use at the <u>beginning</u> of the war.*
>
> *He added that the W/T installation of H.4 was primitive in comparison to that of U.B.52, as it seemed necessary to stop all engines on board H.4 in order to communicate with the land.'*[81]

This corroborated intelligence from survivors of *U-48*, sunk in November 1917, who claimed that British submarines' exhaust was far too conspicuous and was often visible up to eight miles away.[82]

Worryingly, and prophetically for the next conflict, Launberg also referred to work on magnetic pistols (fuses) for torpedoes and turbine propulsion for submarines. The former were designed to explode under a ship's keel, breaking her back to cause catastrophic damage. Survivors of *UB-55* also described the pistols and were concerned at their unreliability and potential danger to the launching submarine. Advanced propulsion was hoped to give very high speeds both on the surface and underwater (24 and 16 knots respectively), giving the submarines a key tactical advantage against opposing warships.[83]

The report also noted that the *UB-52* survivors had already endured three interrogations in the six weeks it had taken them to reach London and formed a good idea of the questions they were likely to be asked. It concluded, '*Their statements must consequently be received with great caution.*'

Where the UC minelaying boats were concerned there was an extra imperative: to find out how many mines they had laid, and where, before they announced their presence explosively. Survivors of *UC-61*, sunk on 17th August 1917, stated that mines were, '*always laid at night, from the surface, and always after carefully marking the position.*'[84] Their claim of precise control may have been exaggerated. Acting Warrant Officer Bernhard Haack was left behind when *UC-32* had to dive suddenly as he was about to board a trawler in January 1917:

> '*Whilst laying their mines, they proceed either on the surface or submerged, according as our patrols are active or the reverse. In Haack's experience, the mines were always laid 50 metres (55 yards) apart. When laying mines on the surface, the U.C. boats usually proceed at half speed, about 6½ knots.*
>
> *The Navigating Warrant Officer is responsible for getting the boat into the position in which, according to her orders, the mines are to be laid. He is also responsible for plotting on the chart the positions in which the mines actually have been laid. It is needless to remark that the mines always appear in their appointed places; but Haack stated that he could rarely swear to their position within 300 or 400 yards, as there were no lights by which one could pick up one's position, and in some cases he was not able to obtain sights at all during the passage across the North Sea. The matter was further complicated by occasional chases of merchant vessels on the out journey, during which dead reckoning went to the winds. It may be added that, from*

Haack's observation note book, it would not appear that his sights were of very great value.' [85]

Kapitänleutnant Lafrenz (*UC-65*) flaunted his contempt for British mines by reminiscing how, while freeing himself from a submarine net off Flanders, he had taken two of the attached mines home with him and had them made into punch bowls. They were not always so ineffective; over time the British learnt to copy German designs which had themselves evolved from Russian patterns.

NID was able to keep track of the rapid U-boat building programme from late 1916 through the Germans' habit of insuring their vessels' engines and much of their electrical equipment with Swiss firms. The construction surge created a shortage of competent crews, especially acute among navigating, watchkeeping and engineering officers. This was met by recruiting partly from the largely idle ships of the High Seas Fleet and partly from merchantmen trapped by the British blockade.

For some crewmen in the High Seas Fleet the prospect of worthwhile action was a draw. For many, tales of the submarine service's relaxed discipline and better rations proved irresistible. Ratings' rations in the surface navy comprised 500g/day bread, turnip jam and cabbage soup. On Sundays they got one slice of meat, some potatoes and 35g butter. Submariners on the other hand had no meatless days and regular access to unheard-of luxuries such as butter, eggs, and real coffee. The submariners' better conditions and press coverage created an open rift with their former shipmates, who were dismissively called 'swabbing coolies' or 'armoured coolies'.

Merchant seamen were drafted into the U-boat service up to the age of 35, or with no age limit if they had a master's or first mate's certificate. Navigational skill qualified a recruit for accelerated training: entry as a leading seaman and rapid progress to warrant officer and beyond. They were known as 'War Pilots'.[86]

Not all crews thus thrown together achieved the seamless cohesion needed in a submarine, and fatal mistakes sometimes resulted.

The coastal submarine *UB-85* sank when diving hurriedly. Either the commander failed to secure the outer hatch, or the clips did not work. The lower hatch could not be closed because a cable had been run through it to a temporary gyro receiver. As the control room flooded an engineering petty officer compounded the problem by blowing only the forward ballast tanks, causing water to rush aft, gassing batteries and short-circuiting main motors. The crew surrendered to a nearby drifter, a much less powerful vessel.

In May 1918 *U-103* was trying to attack RMS *Olympic* (sister ship to the *Titanic*) when the skipper misjudged the range, the submarine was drawn under the ship's counter and mangled by her screws.[87]

Kapitänleutnant Ralph Wenninger of *UB-55*, mined and sunk in the Dover Straits on 22nd April 1918, acknowledged the problem. He,

> '...attributed the loss of a great number of submarines not so much to our counter-measures as to the fact that experienced submarine officers and crews are becoming very scarce. Whereas formerly a commanding officer could pick and choose his crew, and thus obtain efficient ratings, he now had to take those who were drafted to his boat.'[88]

The boats themselves were sometimes less than ready when they were thrown into service. *UC-39* had returned to the dockyard following very troublesome trials. She was handed back with the problems supposedly fixed in early 1917.

> 'Towards the middle of January, U.C.39 came out of dockyard hands and resumed her trials. The latter, however, were still

incomplete when, on 28 January, the boat unexpectedly received orders to proceed to Flanders. These orders were evidently given owing to the decision to commence 'unrestricted' submarine warfare. There was no time to get the boat cleaned up, and the necessary preparations for active service were made in the greatest haste.'[89]

Wenninger went on to offer a scathing assessment of 'dazzle camouflage,' often hailed as one of the great creative innovations of the war.

'The commanding officer of "U.B.55" was asked what he thought of "Dazzle Painting". He replied that he always wondered "why we wasted such an enormous amount of paint". According to him, submarine officers never pay much attention to the hull of a vessel when judging her course and speed, but base their judgement mainly on funnels and masts. They have also been instructed not to judge by a bow wave. He added that "Dazzle Painting" was of no use at all during the day time, but an inexperienced officer might be misled once or twice at night when attacking camouflaged vessels. He himself made an error of judgement once when attacking a ship at night, the bow of which was painted black and was against a dark background. This made the ship appear much shorter than she was in reality. He also mentioned another occasion, when a destroyer was painted on the side of a steamer. He at first believed that the destroyer was real, but soon found out his mistake and sank the ship by a torpedo.'[90]

His comments were echoed by *Kapitänleutnant* Robert Moraht of *U-64*, captured on 17th June 1918. He impressed his interviewers who described him as *'one of the best types of German naval officer'*. They reported some difficulty in persuading him to open up which may affect the credibility of this statement:

'Moraht appeared genuinely amused at the idea of the efficacy of dazzle painting, and did not consider that it assisted ships to escape submarine attack.'[91]

Crews of the ocean-going ('U') and coastal ('UB' and 'UC') submarines formed separate branches with little interchange between them.

The remorseless pace of operations took its toll, especially on the long-range U-boats whose crews were expected to busy themselves with repair and restocking while in port and sail again as soon as they were ready. Survivors attributed the rising loss rate to exhaustion. Despite buoyant morale while serving, once out of the war few were inclined to complain.[92] The following chart illustrates the grimly deteriorating prospects of U-boat crews as the conflict developed.[93]

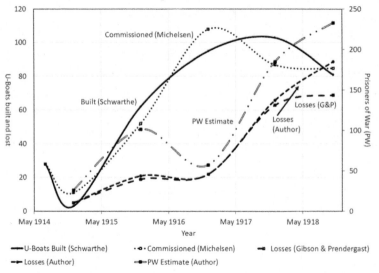

5: WW1 Annual U-boat construction & losses vs PWs captured.

Gibson & Prendergast's estimate of U-boat losses is based on German staff data updated with information received until 1922. The discrepancy with the author's 1918 estimate is probably because the latter includes boats scuttled during the surrender, and evacuation of occupied territory.

Successive prisoner cohorts gave a running commentary on the conversion of the seven surviving *Deutschland* class cargo submarines to 'cruiser' U-boats and subsequent production of long-range, heavily armed submarines specifically designed for the role. The survivors of *U-48* which went aground on the

Goodwin Sands on 24th November 1917 were especially informative.[94]

The initial adaptation of the class-leading *Deutschland* (re-designated *U-155*) involved fitting two 5.9-inch guns and their supporting magazines, converting much of her cargo space to oil bunkerage, and mounting six external torpedo launchers. The latter proved unsatisfactory, as torpedoes did not survive long exposure to salt-water, and she was far too slow to dive. A refit replaced the launchers with internal tubes, added two 22-pounder guns and addressed the diving issue. The lessons learnt were incorporated in later, purpose-built submarines.

Raiders in a Lost Cause?

In late July 1914, as the dominoes of interlocking treaties tumbled into the tombstones of global war, scattered units of the *Kaiserliche Marine* watched the world's inexorable stumble to conflict with mixed sentiments. They had trained for this and were confident in their skills and equipment, anxious to justify the Kaiser's trust and investment. But what if Britain did not stay neutral? Surely there could only be one outcome against the world's naval superpower?

Germany's global maritime interests were represented by the battlecruiser *Goeben* and the light cruiser *Breslau* in the Mediterranean, cruisers *Königsberg* off West Africa, *Scharnhorst*, *Gneisenau*, *Nürnberg* and *Emden* in the Far East, *Leipzig*, *Karlsruhe* and *Dresden* in the Americas. Additionally, like Britain, Germany had built many of her liners with strengthened decks for gun mountings, allowing their ready conversion to armed merchant cruisers (AMCs). Three (*Königin Luise*, *Kaiser Wilhelm der Grosse* and *Berlin*) ran the blockade from Germany while *Cap Trafalgar*,

Kronprinz Wilhelm and *Prinz Eitel Friedrich* were abroad at the outbreak of war.

Goeben and *Breslau* may have had the most profound effect on the war, their escape through the Dardanelles to Constantinople encouraging Turkey to join on the Central Powers' side. On 20th January 1918, the two ships were mined returning from a foray into the Mediterranean. *Breslau* (renamed *Midilli* in Ottoman service) sank with heavy loss of life while *Goeben* (*Yavuz*) had to be beached. *Breslau's* survivors were interrogated locally, and the NID covering memo was enthusiastic about the results obtained.

> 'This is the first reliable information which has been obtained from
> prisoners regarding Gunnery Matters in German Light Cruisers.
> With this as a basis upon which to work it is hoped to be able to
> augment our knowledge in this respect considerably in future.
> As the "BRESLAU" was. comparatively recently re-armed and
> fitted with fresh Control Instruments it is considered that the
> arrangements fitted in her may be taken as typical of all but the latest
> German Light Cruisers.'

On follow-up Bos'n's Mate Hermann Brückner, a gunlayer, yielded extensive information about rangefinders, fire control methods and instruments, local and remote aiming and firing arrangements, and the layout of turrets, shell rooms and magazines.

He gave an illuminating insight into the efficiency of German gunnery:

> 'When asked whether it was not extremely difficult to keep the
> crosswires constantly on the target, and what was the penalty if a
> gunlayer was unable to do so, or to fire within the prescribed time in
> individual firing, informant stated that any failure in this direction
> was punished by 5 days' cells and extra practices, and that if on three
> or four occasions a gunlayer failed, he lost his gunnery rating.

*Similar evidence has been previously given by a prisoner, and it is
thought that the harsh disciplinary measures used under the Prussian
system do, in practice, lead to a high degree of efficiency of the
personnel when performing the particular office allotted to each
individual.*

*This fact may account for the impression of officers in our ships which
have been in action, that director firing is carried out by all German
light cruisers and in some destroyers. The degree of efficiency in
German gunlayers in obtaining practically instantaneous salvoes
when firing by gong may well create the impression that the guns
were fired by a master firing key.'*

The reports anticipated that further examination by domain
experts would provide yet more insights into German fire-
control technology.[95]

The achievement is even more remarkable since the first
interviews with *Breslau* survivors at Mudros come over as inept.
Lacking the skills, patience, and documentary resources of the
central team in London the interrogators were inclined to accept
their subjects' insistence that they either knew nothing or were
honour bound to silence.

In an interesting aside a certain Lieutenant Karl Dönitz, then
serving in *Breslau*, published a propaganda leaflet about her 1914
cruise. A British diplomat in Bâle (Basel) picked it up and
translated extracts in 1917. The file copy has 'Ancient history'
scrawled over the cover.[96]

Von Spee's squadron comprising *Scharnhorst*, *Gneisenau*,
Leipzig and *Dresden* met and defeated Admiral Cradock's force
sent to find him off Coronel in Chile on 1st November 1914,
sinking the obsolete cruisers *Good Hope* and *Monmouth* in the
process. The shock of this humiliation so soon after *Goeben* and
Breslau's escape triggered an angry reaction. Admiral 'Jacky'
Fisher, just reinstated as First Sea Lord, ordered an
overwhelming concentration of force in the hunt for Von Spee,

including no fewer than three of the Royal Navy's precious battlecruisers. Against advice, von Spee attempted a raid on the Falkland Islands. He arrived just as most of the force sent against him was coaling there. His squadron was caught and annihilated.

In the world of 'might have been' it is intriguing to think that the absence of the forces sent to cut off von Spee brought the German High Seas Fleet and the British Grand Fleet as close to parity in the North Sea as they would ever be. The opportunity to force a surface fleet engagement on something like even terms was missed and would never recur.

This book does not try to track the raiders' fortunes in detail.[97] In general they tried to obey 'cruiser rules,' safeguarding neutral and civilian life and allowing free passage to neutral ships and cargo. They took advantage of the vastness of the ocean and poor communications, ensuring they were somewhere else by the time word of their latest strike reached the Royal Navy. One by one they were trapped by the need for frequent coaling and the deterioration of their ships and were either sunk or interned. The last was *Königsberg*, cornered and scuttled in Tanzania's River Rufiji on 11th July 1915.

Emden was trapped by the cruiser HMAS *Sydney* on 9th November 1914 in the act of raiding the important cable relay station on Direction Island. While *Sydney* was occupied with *Emden* and chasing down a collier due to meet her, the landing party under her executive officer Hellmuth von Mücke commandeered a small schooner, the *Ayesha*, and escaped. We will hear more of this group.

The loss of the entire raider force in less than a year posed a problem for the *Admiralstab*. Purpose-built warships were too precious to throw away yet converted liners were too vulnerable. They were fast, had prodigious need for coal and stokers, but did not have bunkerage for more than a few days' endurance. Unarmoured, their high sides made them easy targets and compounded the difficulty of transferring supplies and prisoners at sea.

Even so, the chaos and confusion the raiders had created in their short career was out of all proportion to their tonnage sunk and captured. Moreover, any chance to disrupt the trade of an enemy entirely dependent on maritime supply, far beyond the reach of U-boats, was not to be lightly given up.

The response was to pick out and arm several small, anonymous merchantmen from the dozens stranded by the British blockade. With bad weather, a bit of disguise and a modicum of luck they could sneak past the blockade and create havoc in the shipping lanes. If they were caught there was relatively little lost. This strategy was repeated with great success in the Second World War.

Among the most successful was *Wolf*, an inconspicuous former Hansa liner of 5,809 tons gross with two masts, a central deckhouse, and a single funnel. Her innocent appearance was wholly deceptive; it concealed two 6-inch, four 4-inch or 4.7-inch guns plus four smaller weapons, four torpedo-tubes, a seaplane, a rangefinder, two searchlights and a wireless which could probably be used for direction-finding. She also carried 500 mines when she left Germany on 30th November 1916. In a cruise lasting nearly fifteen months and taking in the Atlantic, Pacific and Indian Oceans she took fourteen ships as prizes and laid minefields which accounted for at least another fourteen.

One prize, the Spanish *Igotz Mendi* carrying prisoners and contraband, was not so lucky. She ran aground in poor visibility on 24th February 1918 and was boarded by Danish officials. They discovered her true nature, released the prisoners, and interned the crew. The ex-prisoners were interviewed by Intelligence Division and between them came up with an almost complete account of the ship's adventures. Later in the year the Division managed to obtain a copy of Captain Nerger's own narrative of the voyage.[98]

Jose Abad was an observant ex-captive who provided an information windfall. He was a Peruvian rating serving in the Norwegian barque *Staut Sandefieur* when she had the misfortune to run into the raider *Möwe* on 28th January 1917. He kept a record of his captors' movements and activities until they docked in Kiel on 21st March, along with an assessment of the ship's armament and a note of what was going on in Kiel. Having been freed with the other neutral citizens he signed on aboard another Norwegian ship and tried to negotiate a price for his information when it arrived in Lerwick.[99]

Later that year Paul Krause, a deserter who had been aboard *Möwe* at Kiel, confirmed Abad's technical description. In his anxiety to please he managed to describe the ship three times: twice under her own name and once as *Vineta*, a name she used for a series of short cruises in 1916.[100] Intelligence Division treated his evidence with scepticism, and in any case by the time it was available the ship's propaganda value outweighed its operational usefulness and it had been retired from active service.

A humbler example of the breed was the second *Kronprinz Wilhelm* a modern steamer of 1,800 to 2,000 tons taken up in October 1915 and based in Swinemünde (now Swinoujscie in Poland), the original raider of that name by then being interned in the US.[101] She was also known officially as Auxiliary Ship "K", but posed as *Maria of Flensburg* (possibly her original name) in harbour to mislead both neutral ships' crews and potential spies. All her mail was sent to that address. She was fitted with four concealed 4.1-inch guns, two machine-guns, six depth-charges, three or four smoke boxes and a hidden radio. She carried steel plates and a dummy funnel to disguise her profile and her lower deck was thought to be filled with barrels and sand to provide buoyancy and blast protection against torpedo attack.

Although equipped and crewed as a raider the ship was at first used to escort merchant traffic between Germany and Sweden. She was paid off in August 1917, but hastily recommissioned in October with a scratch crew drawn from trawlers and other vessels of the Commerce Protection Flotilla. Her commander, Julius Lauterbach, had been an officer on *Emden* and brought back one of her prizes, the *Ayesha*.

On 31st October *Kronprinz Wilhelm* set out for what may have been a shakedown cruise, venturing into the North Sea to steam around the Danish island of Anholt. On her way back, well inside the presumed safety of the Baltic, she sighted several destroyers which lookouts at first assumed to be German. The short, vicious fight which followed their disillusion left 37 survivors from a crew of about 86.

The captives produced enough material for a 21-page report, including insights into the forces available in the Baltic and anti-flash arrangements adopted by the German fleet. There was also more detail on the battleship *Bayern*, information on the development of high-speed remote-control explosive boats, and a detailed description and drawing of the type of depth charge carried by *Kronprinz Wilhelm*.

One survivor, *Zahlmeister Oberaspirant* (Assistant Paymaster) Sandhop, had the presence of mind to pocket the crew's and officers' pay which was in his care before abandoning ship. He tried without success to persuade his interrogators that the money was his own lottery win, and it was placed in the Prize Court.[102]

Another name reused was *Seeadler* (Sea Eagle), originally an old cruiser converted to a mine store which had the misfortune to blow up in Wilhelmshaven harbour on 19th April 1917 with great loss of life.[103] The name was picked up by a square-rigged, three-mast sailing vessel (formerly the American *Pass-of-Balmaha*, captured by a U-boat in 1915). She had been fitted with an engine, two 4.1-inch guns, machine-guns, a rangefinder, small arms, and a smoke generator. In her single eight-month cruise she captured and sank sixteen vessels totalling some 33,000 tons. There was little room for prisoners from her victims aboard, so some were transferred to one of her prizes (after ruining the cargo and radio and damaging the masts to slow her down). They passed on details of *Seeadler's* equipment and vulnerabilities when they finally reached Rio in April. Before that information could be used, *Seeadler* was wrecked on the coral island of Mopelia, about 300 miles west of Tahiti, on 23ʳᵈ August 1917. The captain, Count Felix von Luckner, with another officer and four seamen took to a motor launch and were captured in Fiji on 23ʳᵈ September. They were taken to New Zealand and interrogated there.

The rest of the crew hijacked a visiting schooner (the *Lutece*) to make their escape, leaving behind the remaining prisoners who were finally rescued on 6ᵗʰ October. They gave full details of *Seeadler's* raiding career since the previous December. As importantly, the navy now knew which ship to look out for.[104] The story stuttered to an end when *Lutece* herself (now renamed *Fortuna*) was wrecked on Easter Island in March 1918. The crew were brought to Talcahuano in Chile where a diplomatic spat ensued over their fate. Should they be interned as combatants or released as shipwrecked mariners? The wreck of *Seeadler* was rediscovered in 2022.

The *Kehdigen* was a steam trawler of 278 tons, originally fitted out as an outpost patrol vessel but upgraded with concealed armament in 1915 to act as a submarine trap or 'Q' ship. In that role she had two 22-pounder (88 mm) guns, one torpedo-tube, a searchlight, rangefinder, hydrophone, and smoke boxes. She did not fool any British submarine into an unwise approach but was used for cable-cutting, escorting U-boats and holding up neutral vessels. That career ended on the morning of 17th November 1917 when *Kehdigen* and another trawler were detailed to act as markers for minesweepers in the Heligoland Bight. As they were working a mixed force of British cruisers and destroyers loomed out of the mist causing a general scuttle for safety – a refuge which *Kehdigen's* slow speed gave her no chance of reaching. Twenty-two of the twenty-six crew survived, largely because many of the shells fired at the ship went straight through without exploding.

The prisoners seem to have been willing enough to talk but to have known little of value. They gave some updates on the strength, organisation and methods of the North Sea patrol, minesweeping, and special service forces. They also confirmed that the new minelaying cruisers *Brummer* and *Bremse* had been responsible for the devastating 17th October attack on a west-bound convoy from Norway. They claimed *Brummer's* captain had prevented any attempt to save life, and that he had since been relieved of command as a result. More significantly,

> '...the prisoners ascribed the unexpected appearance of the British forces to some leakage of information. This information, they thought, must have been wirelessed by a traitor German officer who was married to an Englishwoman. Even the sub-lieutenant in command shared this belief in treachery having taken place.'[105]

For those in the know, probably not including the interrogators, this must have been valuable reassurance that the *Admiralstab* remained blissfully unaware of Room 40's cryptographic success. *Kehdigen* had been caught in the middle of the Second Battle of Heligoland Bight, an intelligence-led attempt to trap and overwhelm the minesweepers' cruiser escort.

The converted merchantman *Greif* left Cuxhaven on 27th February 1916. She did not get far, meeting the British armed merchant cruiser (AMC) *Alcantara* near the Shetlands on 29th.

With the advantage of surprise *Greif* got in the first blow but *Alcantara* was quickly reinforced by the AMC *Andes*, cruiser *Comus* and destroyer *Munster*. *Greif* and *Alcantara* both sank in the short, bitter fight.

In March 1917 *Greif* survivors in Handforth prisoner of war camp produced a beautifully scripted and illustrated memorial leaflet to their ship, captain and fallen comrades. This, with the allegation that the British had continued firing after the crew had begun to abandon ship, provoked a furious reaction from the Admiralty.[106]

Although not strictly a raider the naval-manned auxiliary *Libau* deserves a place in this gallery of forlorn hopes. She was the former British SS *Castro*[107], 1,228 tons, prepared for her only voyage under her new role at Kiel. Her captain, Reserve Lieutenant Karl Spindler was the only one who knew her true mission in advance and was described by the interrogation report as, *'a pirate in the most literal sense of the word, and a most objectionable liar into the bargain.'*[108] The warrant officers had been asked to volunteer for 'an honourable undertaking' while the ratings were selected from the Wilhelmshaven patrol flotillas and given no choice. Almost all were unmarried and in above average physical condition.

Posing as the Norwegian *Aud* she set sail from Kiel on 9th April 1916. Her holds contained a visible cargo of enamelware, timber, and finished wood products. There was also a deck cargo of pit props. All were supported by manifests for Cardiff, Genoa, and Leghorn (Livorno) and backed up by a fictional log for a previous voyage to England.

The true reason for her voyage was packed under the hold cargo: 20,000 Mauser rifles, captured from the Russians, ten machine guns, a million rounds of ammunition and a quantity of explosives.[109] They were planned to synchronise with Sir Roger Casement's return and the Easter Rising in Ireland but, thanks to Room 40's cryptanalysts, the Admiralty knew they were coming.

Libau/Aud had difficulty *en route*, both with her engine and with badly stowed cargo shifting. Some unidentified cylinders, possibly smoke generators, were discarded early in the voyage and the deck cargo had to be jettisoned later. On arrival off Tralee Bay, she failed to make the planned rendezvous with Casement, was subsequently intercepted by the sloop *Bluebell* on Good Friday, 21st April and ordered into Queenstown (Cobh). Approaching port next morning Spindler ordered the crew to don uniform, had two German ensigns hoisted, set scuttling charges, and abandoned ship.

The crew were clearly terrified that they might be treated as spies or saboteurs rather than prisoners of war. Some of the ratings, especially, were less than pleased to discover the nature of their mission. Spindler himself chose a transparently false cover story.

'OBJECT OF THE VOYAGE.

Can only have been to land weapons and ammunition on the Irish coast. Spindler repeatedly stated that this was not the case, that he never wished to make the Irish coast at all, and that his real destination was somewhere in the neighbourhood of Madeira. He declined, however, to explain how his cargo could be of use there. He stated that he intended to mount guns on deck and had tools for that purpose. The Navigating Warrant Officer was also full of stories of the "LIBAU" being intended for a Raider; the small complement, however, rules this possibility out of court, even if there were not other evidence, as there was obviously no margin for prize crews. On leaving Kiel the vessel had on board 500 tons of coal which would have lasted for about 50 days. One man stated that he had understood from Spindler that they ought to be back in Germany before the end of May, but no confirmation of this could be obtained.'[110]

Spindler was subsequently interned in the Netherlands, when he formally alleged inadequate accommodation and brutal treatment during his stay at Cromwell Gardens. His claims were so exaggerated they were easily disproved.[111]

Whatever the reader's view of the Easter Rising, adding another 20,000 rifles to the mix could only have increased the slaughter on both sides.

'A Tide in the Affairs of Men...'

An intelligence officer could have no idea of the potential impact of the information he extracted – or, indeed of that he had missed.

On the night of 20th/21st March 1918 the torpedo-boats *A-7* and *A-19* were sunk during an operation to bombard Dunkirk, La Panne and Braye-les-Dunes. Eight survivors were picked up by the French, who were hastily joined by two British intelligence officers.

The results were only partly satisfactory. The British officers' arrival was delayed by fog, interviews were shared with their unwilling French opposite numbers, and the need to accompany the prisoners through a move disrupted the process. Nonetheless, useful information was obtained, if not followed up as well as they would have liked.

The interviewers were almost certainly unaware of the vital nature of the data they brought back. Part of the 'A' boats' routine job was keeping the approaches to Ostend and Zeebrugge clear of mines. The report included a detailed plan of Zeebrugge harbour. An appendix also listed the navigation buoys still in service and withdrawn, and the routes used by minesweepers.[112]

Barely a month later, on 22nd/23rd April, the Royal Navy raided those ports in a heroic (but ultimately unsuccessful) attempt to trap the Flanders Flotilla U-boats in their bases.

[1]   Michael Foley: *Prisoners of the British*. Fonthill, 2015.
[2]   TNA ADM 137/3881. P.168.
[3]   TNA ADM 171/87. Honour Sheets coded X 1-500 (various surnames).
[4]   The move probably saved his life. *Queen Mary* blew up at the Battle of Jutland with just 20 survivors from her 1,289 crew.
[5]   TNA ADM 137/3881, P.168-176.
[6]   TNA ADM 1/8446/15. NL 24619 (13/7/1916).
[7]   TNA ADM 137/3901. P.72.
[8]   *Papers of Bernard F Trench*. NMRN 2017/24/7-9.
[9]   Birch, Frank; Clarke, William F; *Room 40: German Naval Warfare 1914-1918*. Schaltungsdienst Lange o.H.G Berlin, 2009. P.xiii.
[10] Anthony Roland Wells PhD Thesis: *Studies in British Naval Intelligence 1880-1945*. King's College London, 1972. P.270.
[11] TNA ADM 137/3897. P.110-112.
[12] TNA ADM 137/3060. *CB 01400; UB81 – Interrogation of Survivors*. P.1.
[13] TNA ADM 137/1908. *Report of examination of survivors from "U.C.29", sunk on 7th June 1917*. P.3.
[14] TNA ADM 137/3060. P.368.
[15] Oil painting in the author's possession.
[16] TNA ADM 137/3060. P.366.
[17] Fürbringer, *FIPS*. P.120-128.
[18] Charles Herbert Lightoller, *Titanic and Other Ships*. P.401, 404.
[19] Utke went on to serve as Vice-Admiral in charge of torpedo development during the Second World War.
[20] TNA ADM 137/3060. P.333, 277.
[21] TNA ADM 137/1907, P.303.
[22] TNA ADM 137/3899, P.29.
[23] King-Hall, S. *My Naval Life*, P.128. TNA ADM 137/1907, P.598.
[24] Admiralty Confidential Interim Order 7266/1917 dated 23rd December 1917, in TNA ADM 137/3903.
[25] TNA ADM 137/3964. P.322-323.
[26] TNA ADM 137/3897. P.145-146.
[27] O.X.O. – standard header for classified reports.
[28] TNA ADM 137/3900. P.91-108.
[29] TNA WO 208/4970. P.2.
[30] TNA ADM 137/4808, P.57, 201.
[31] I shorten the contemporary terms 'Torpedo Boat' and 'Torpedo Boat Destroyer' to 'Destroyer' throughout.
[32] TNA ADM 137/3060, ADM 137/3879, P.65. UK Outward Passenger Lists 1890-1960. New York Passenger Lists 1920-57.

[33] TNA ADM 137/3060. *Report of Examination of Louis Jütte. UC65 – Interrogation of Survivors*. P.17.
[34] A letter criticising his treatment or mentioning sensitive information would not have been forwarded.
[35] TNA ADM 137/3060, *CB 01449; UC75 – Interrogation of Survivors*. P.11.
[36] Most German airships were supplied by the Zeppelin works, but a few were also bought from Schütt-Lanz.
[37] TNA ADM 137/3964.
[38] TNA ADM 137/1907, P.667-668.
[39] TNA ADM 137/3060. P.384.
[40] See for example TNA ADM 137/3060, P.52, 125. Roskill, *Naval Policy Between the Wars*, Vol 1. P.336.
[41] TNA ADM 137/1906, P.478.
[42] TNA ADM 137/1906, P.474.
[43] TNA ADM 137/4809, P.274.
[44] Ibid, P.277, 189. ADM 239/405.
[45] TNA ADM 137/1908, P.360. Minute dated 15th December 1917.
[46] TNA ADM 137/3874, 'U.B. 124' Interrogation of Survivors, P.24-27.
[47] TNA ADM 137/3060, *Report of Examination of Louis Jütte*, P.16. ADM 1371907, P.39.
[48] TNA ADM 137/3881, P.321.
[49] TNA ADM 137/1908, P.218-219.
[50] TNA ADM 137/1906, P.489.
[51] Scheer, *Germany's High Sea Fleet in the First World War*. P.248-252.
[52] TNA ADM 137/1907, P.192.
[53] *U-93* was reported to have stopped and then suddenly sunk, her disappearance accompanied by an 'explosion with black smoke.' Nonetheless she was later confirmed to have made it safely back to Wilhelmshaven.
[54] TNA ADM 137/1908, P.112.
[55] Richard von Kühlmann was Germany's Secretary of State for Foreign Affairs from December 1917 until July 1918, when a statement in a speech to the Reichstag that the war could not be ended by arms alone created a furore that ended in his resignation.
[56] TNA ADM 137/1907, P.663.
[57] TNA ADM 137/1908.
[58] Fürbringer, *FIPS*. P.6.
[59] Koerver, P.43.
[60] TNA ADM 137/3060. P.368. Baron Spiegel von und zu Peckelsheim, *The Adventures of the U-202*, in *U-Boat War 1914-1918*.
[61] Peckelsheim in Forstrerr et al, *U-Boat War 1914-1918 Volume 2*
[62] TNA ADM 137/1908, P.113-114.
[63] Dunn, *Securing the Narrow Sea*, P.100-101, 118.
[64] TNA ADM 137/1908, P.126.
[65] TNA ADM 137/3876, P.110-111.
[66] TNA ADM 137/3030, P.334-335.

67 TNA ADM 137/3060, CB 01431, P.17.
68 Gibson & Predergast, *The German Submarine War*. Appendix III.
    Uboat.net. All the COs listed were *Kapitänleutnant* rank at the time.
69 See Human Wrongs below.
70 TNA ADM 137/1908, P.126-127.
71 Ibid, P.254-255.
72 Ibid, P.202-203.
73 Ibid, P.253.
74 TNA ADM 137/3060, CB 01449, P.9.
75 TNA ADM 137/1907, P.222.
76 TNA ADM 137/1906, P.467-469.
77 TNA ADM 137/1908, P.62-63.
78 Ibid, P.418.
79 TNA ADM 137/3875, P.39-61.
80 TNA ADM 137/1907, P.848-849.
81 TNA ADM 137/3874, CB 01462, P.7.
82 TNA ADM 137/3060, CB 01398, P.9.
83 TNA ADM 137/3874, P.6. *CB 01437 OXO 'U.B.55' Interrogation of Survivors*. P.19.
84 TNA ADM 137/1908, P.203.
85 Ibid, P.35.
86 TNA ADM 137/3060, P.228, 292, ADM 137/1906, P.508.
87 TNA ADM 137/3060, P.267. P.283-4.
88 TNA ADM 137/3874, C.B.01437 OXO 'U.B.55' Interrogation of Survivors, P.20.
89 TNA ADM 137/1908, P.53-54.
90 TNA ADM 137/3874, CB01437, P.19.
91 TNA ADM 137/3060, CB 01464, P.15.
92 TNA ADM 137/3874, P.457-458 (*General report on survivors of U-48, 17th December 1917*).
93 Gibson & Prendergast, *German Submarine War*.
94 TNA ADM 137/1908, P.134-135, 218, 374-375, 393-399.
95 TNA ADM 137/1907, P.603-617.
96 TNA ADM 137/3896.
97 See Nick Hewitt, *The Kaiser's Pirates*, for an excellent treatment of the topic.
98 TNA ADM 137/3877, P.37-53, 1-36.
99 TNA ADM 137/1907, P.146-152.
100 Ibid, P.321-322.
101 There was also a battleship named *Kronprinz Wilhelm* (originally *Kronprinz*).
102 TNA ADM 137/1907, P.350-380.
103 TNA ADM 137/3881, P.98.
104 Ibid, P.221-253.
105 TNA ADM 137/3877, P.77.
106 TNA ADM 137/1629, P.263-275.

107 The *Castro* was caught in the Kiel Canal when war broke out in 1914.
108 TNA ADM 137/1906, P.241.
109 Modern sources, e.g. Ramsay, agree on this payload. The ID report suggests an unknown quantity of rifles plus a half-dozen 5 and 6-cm guns and explosives.
110 Ibid, P.247-248.
111 TNA FO 383/442.
112 TNA ADM 137/1907, P.546, 559.

Inter-War Intermezzo

As the 'War to end War' subsided Britain heaved a collective sigh of relief and set about rebuilding her shattered society – minus too many of the young men needed to do the building. The horrors of the last four years and the nation's desperate financial situation combined to create a strong pacifist impulse. Defence budgets were slashed repeatedly; with Germany on the ropes and under the diplomatic cover of the Washington Naval treaty (1922) and the follow-up London treaties of 1930 and 1936 it seemed safe enough. The government had adopted a guideline in 1919 that no major war was to be expected for at least ten years – the 'Ten Year Rule'. In 1928 Winston Churchill, as Chancellor of the Exchequer, made the rule self-perpetuating – it was to remain in force until cancelled. The Allied Control Commission in Germany disbanded in 1926 despite intelligence advice that the Germans had not only failed to complete the required disarmament but were covertly rearming.

If it was a hard time for the Navy as a whole, it was doubly so for Intelligence Division. Admiral Hall's unprecedented influence had made many enemies in Whitehall, who now turned their fire on a more accessible foe than the Kaiser. Hall retired on 3rd February 1919 and his division was rapidly filleted, both in scope and resource.

Prisoner interrogation had no role in peacetime. Worse, and almost unbelievably, copies of all interrogation reports were passed to Germany after the war. Similarly, the methods by which British prisoners had managed to escape or send covert messages home were published.[1]

Bernard Trench's time as port intelligence officer at Queenstown was followed by a succession of staff postings to the

East Indies and Africa stations, with a short break for study in France. He retired from a stultifying dull billet in Bermuda as a lieutenant-colonel in 1928 having concluded that his age and the number of officers ahead of him in the seniority list left no hope of further promotion. He marked his release with a walking tour starting in Perpignan and ending in Glatz, the site of his incarceration. He covered over 2,000 miles in 159 days wearing crepe-soled plimsolls.

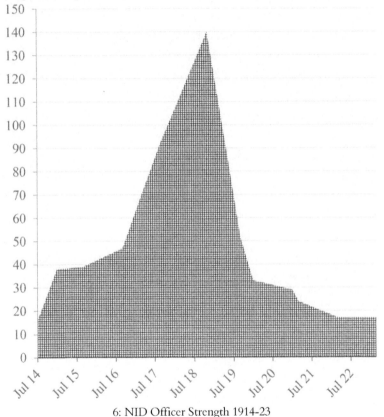

6: NID Officer Strength 1914-23

Source: TNA ADM 234/434 Appendix P

Vivian Brandon was awarded a CBE and Officer of the *Légion d'Honneur* for his work with NID, and later mentioned in dispatches for post-war mine clearance. He went on to perform valuable diplomatic service in the Persian Gulf before retiring in 1927 to take up a position as professional adviser to the Mercantile Marine department of the Board of Trade. He was recalled to the colours in May 1940 and worked with GCCS, the Bletchley Park codebreakers, until his death on 3rd January 1944 at the age of sixty-one.

Burton Cope was demobilised in November 1919 and found employment in the Paris office of the Cunard Line.

Intelligence Division's Movements Section, responsible for tracking British and foreign warships, foreign merchant vessels and compiling mercantile statistics still had three officers and six clerks in October 1920. By the end of 1928, its duties had been spread across other departments. One remaining officer had the job of answering queries about suspicious vessels as a subsidiary task (for which he retained the title 'Movements Officer') and a clerk elsewhere was responsible for watching foreign warships. Part time.

Stephen King-Hall, who we last met escorting a captive U-boat skipper and was now a lieutenant-commander, was posted to Intelligence Division for induction before taking up his appointment as Mediterranean Fleet Intelligence Officer in the mid 'twenties. His impression of the officers there was that they were passed-over, 'dead from the neck up,' and simply 'soldiering on for a pension.' They compiled geographical handbooks from data supplied by untrained ships' intelligence officers, much of which was of more use for goodwill tours than potential war fighting and could have been gleaned from a tourist guide. And then,

'The only other source of information were the British consuls who were told by the Foreign Office to do their best to fill up the naval questionnaires but that they must incur no expense in doing so.'[2]

In the words of the NID History,

"Elaborate questionnaires were sent out to Reporting Officers and were dutifully answered; paper poured into the Admiralty, but there were few to collate its contents. Masses of valuable information from all over the world, afterwards to be desperately sought for by the Inter-Service Topographical Department and by those who, when operations were being planned in 1942, were charged with providing Force Commanders with their Intelligence briefs, came into Whitehall on those far-off days and were not recorded."[3]

These 'Reporting Officers' were a worldwide network of Consular Shipping Advisers (CSAs) and Naval Control Service Officers (NCSOs) working under diplomatic cover to represent British interests in commercial and naval ports.

On the outbreak of war their role expanded exponentially. The Admiralty took control of all British merchant shipping on 26th August 1939, and the Naval Control Service staff were their eyes, ears, and hands around the world. They had to plan and brief convoys, counter enemy intelligence and sabotage efforts, organise defensive armament, and keep an eye open for potential blockade-breakers.

The CSAs, in particular, led a lonely existence, were unpaid for their reporting duties and sometimes had little concept of security or the needs of intelligence. With a naval background and, typically, employment in shipping or insurance they worked their contacts to keep an eye on comings and goings from their port of interest: which ship was carrying what where. Too often the local Naval Attaché had to smooth over the havoc they left in their wake, not making his diplomatic role any easier.

There were conspicuous exceptions. A draft history of NID begun in 1942 by Charles Morgan (in peacetime a novelist and playwright who worked part-time, possibly unpaid, for NID) singles out the Cherbourg Reporting Officer who, *"very frequently adds remarks which explain movements."*[4]

Already in 1935, Cope felt unable to visit his ailing father in Britain for fear he would not be allowed back into France.[5] This suggests his activities went further than representing Cunard-White Star interests.[6] His role there involved frequent trips to Cherbourg, looking after rich and influential passengers boarding and leaving transatlantic steamers. It is tempting to speculate that these trips provided an ideal cover to act as conduit or cut-out between the Reporting Officer and the Paris Naval Attaché – and perhaps even to do a little moonlighting for MI6.

The Spanish Civil War of 1936-39 threw a harsh light on the poor state of naval intelligence. When Italian submarines attacked Republican supplies and threatened British warships in 1937 the Admiralty found itself potentially in an undeclared war without the information needed to fight it. One positive outcome was the creation of a tiny Operational Intelligence Centre, whose first task was to try and identify and track the pirates. It set out to create a card index of the known movements of all German and Italian submarines, hoping by process of elimination to identify those which could have been responsible.[7]

The system started too late to help on that occasion but during the Munich Crisis this nucleus grew from four staff to about fifty in ten days, and it went on to play a key role in winning the Battle of the Atlantic.[8]

Other sources progressively dried up as peace evaporated. Karl Krüger, the invaluable agent based in the Netherlands, was betrayed, arrested, and executed. The arrest of Thomas Kendrick in Vienna threatened to blow the cover of MI6's resident 'Passport Control Officers'.[9] The Venlo Incident on 9th November 1939, in which the *Sicherheitsdienst* kidnapped British agents Sigismund Payne Best and Richard Henry Stevens, temporarily dismantled MI6's north European networks.

For a year before the outbreak of war NID sponsored covert air reconnaissance by a Mr Sydney Cotton in a civilian Lockheed Electra aircraft (which NID and MI6 had jointly helped him buy). Hidden cameras controlled by a switch under the pilot's seat brought back invaluable images of the Mediterranean, Red Sea, Heligoland, Bremen, and Wilhelmshaven. Using the Aircraft Operating Company's Wild A5 Autograph plotting machine he did much to develop techniques of air photography and interpretation, but the work ended abruptly with the outbreak of hostilities.[10] The RAF at that time had neither the equipment, the skills, nor the inclination for long-range maritime reconnaissance. The Admiralty and Air Ministry were locked in dispute over the allocation of photographic reconnaissance assets (and Mr Cotton's talents) at least until Admiral Godfrey's sacking at the end of 1942.

Moreover, it would be some time before Bletchley Park could make useful inroads into German naval cyphers. Despite heroic efforts and occasional 'breaks' it was mid-1941 before rapid, routine decrypts could be expected. The addition of a fourth wheel to naval Enigma machines produced a new blackout from February to October 1942. In the meantime, the German *B-dienst* was reading most British convoy codes and some naval traffic.

In January 1939 (then) Captain John Godfrey, newly appointed Director of Naval Intelligence (DNI), threw his prodigious energy and intellect into preparing the division for war. 'Blinker' Hall volunteered help and advice including the aphorism 'Boldness always pays' which no doubt fell on receptive ears.

By the end of the year, he was frustrated enough to write to the Deputy Chief of Naval Staff comparing his situation with Hall's:

'Before the Great War the Navy controlled its coast watching service; it was then the Coastguards. The Secret Service, Cryptography and aerial reconnaissance were non-existent. These were built up during the war and although the Secret Service was nominally under a separate head, in effect Admiral Hall had the disposal of the necessary funds and controlled his own system of agents abroad.'

…

The important [sources], the Secret Service, Cryptography, aerial reconnaissance and coast watching have been deliberately handed over to other Government Departments. We thus find ourselves in the position of being unable to do anything much to improve these services although they contribute vitally towards the success of Naval operations. We can ask them for information, we can criticise them and encourage them, but only by very indirect means and with the exercise of great tact can we arrive at any conclusion regarding their efficiency.

6. In the past the policy has been to make the best of a bad job and I have hesitated to draw attention to the shortcomings of the Secret Service until war experience gave us some lead. After three months of war I can confidently say that we are not getting the information we need, and as far as I can see under the present organisation there is little likelihood that we shall.

7. I find myself with deep regret unable to tell the Board anything of value about the German shipbuilding programme, or about the development of German weapons – the magnetic mine is a case in point.'[11]

To start with, prisoner interrogation would be the most valuable intelligence tool available. Agents, captured documents and equipment, escaped prisoners, refugees, air reconnaissance and above all cryptography and wireless direction finding filled out the picture as time progressed.

With no formal agreement in place Godfrey secretly visited Paris to discuss intelligence co-operation. He recorded,

"My mission … was to devise the machinery of collaboration with the French D.N.I. Rear Admiral de Villaine, and in the course of a cordial and co-operative visit we agreed to exchange information about intelligence centres abroad, and to make a simple cypher by means of which British and French Intelligence centres could exchange information chiefly about the movements of German, Italian and Japanese men of war and merchant ships. This involved revealing to the French our reporting system through British consular officers in foreign ports – a system of which they must have been conscious for many years."[12]

Regrettably, the fall of France the following year put paid to the nascent co-operation. Admiral Darlan had been a generous ally but issued an uncompromising order whose strict interpretation of Vichy neutrality prevented local commanders from joining the Allies, scuttling their ships in place, or removing them from the theatre of conflict as demanded by Churchill. This ultimately led to the Royal Navy opening fire on French ships in harbour at Mers-el-Kébir on 3rd July 1940. The incident still rankles.

As the timer ticked inexorably down to war in 1939 Godfrey scrambled to prepare a division so recently comatose for the challenges ahead.

It was impossible to requisition property until war broke out or an emergency was declared. As early as March 1939 the War Office therefore reserved space in the married quarters at the Tower of London for an interrogation centre, to be activated within 24 hours of hostilities starting. Preparations were also made with the Post Office for rapid supply of listening equipment. Two hundred beds were earmarked at the Royal Herbert Hospital, Woolwich, for prisoners requiring urgent medical treatment.[13] In the Great War Naval Intelligence had developed a sophisticated central interrogation facility, backed by detailed files. The army (and later RAF) had in parallel explored the use of microphones and stool pigeons in prisoner cages and internment camps.[14] Both made good use of captured documents and prisoners' letters. The next conflict would see these strands integrated in a breathtakingly successful intelligence gathering machine.

Executive officers would soon be rarer than gold dust. Moreover, in a severely reduced navy no attention had been paid to cultivating an interest or aptitude for intelligence work. As Morgan observed,

'An officer who specialises in Gunnery or Torpedo or languages adds to his prestige & his pay; an officer who takes a special interest in intelligence has no recognized specialization open to him. It follows that there is no body of men with recognizable qualifications from which the staff of N.I.D. may be chosen. In peacetime many officers were appointed who had no knowledge of intelligence organization, no experience of the work, and no inclination towards it. It was not surprising that some of them were concerned rather to rid themselves of papers than to digest them and were heartily glad when they returned to sea. The Division was not only understaffed but staffed haphazard, and in the Fleet intelligence work was little encouraged.'[15]

In June Godfrey wrote to the Chief of Naval Staff,

"With the object of releasing naval officers whenever possible, I propose to seek Board approval to engage a limited number of civilians at a suitable remuneration in peace time."[16]

This was a bold move, both because of its radicalism and because he had no budget. Morgan, again, was on the interviewing panel and observed,

"Men had come who looked as though they had been knitted by the blind but turned out to be people of astonishing learning who explained with embarrassment that they had no seamanlike qualifications but confessed to a native command of six languages, and eleven dialects. Others were travellers, yachtsmen, businessmen, schoolmasters."[17]

Three dozen civilians from a hundred and twenty or so applicants started work on the first day of the war. Most were later shoehorned into uniform. They were the pioneers of a large intake of RNVR Special Branch officers: men who did not necessarily need seamanlike qualities but possessed skills the navy would need in a fast-moving technological war. Basic training was kept to a minimum and they were regarded with lingering suspicion by executive officers. Tensions were bound to arise.

> 'The N.O. [Naval Officer] has an awful contempt for the civilian and will extend this to the Special Branch, however good they may be at their particular jobs.'[18]
>
> ...
>
> 'As regards R.N.V.R. officers (Special Branch), it should be remembered that they have practically no knowledge of the sea and therefore are unable to represent the sea-going point of view although clad in Naval uniform and having every outward appearance of a Naval officer.
>
> The 2nd Sea Lord has therefore ruled that, except in very special circumstances, R.N.V.R. officers of the Special Branch shall only be employed in appointments where they can be supervised by Executive Officers of the Royal Navy, and can appeal to regular officers for advice when questions involving maritime knowledge arise. This is not to say that many of them cannot, and do not, acquire a very full and adequate Naval knowledge which in due course will enable them to act independently of advice.'[19]

Most naval interrogators were Special Branch officers. Although it embraced a variety of disciplines the branch was widely associated with intelligence. For this reason, whether they worked in intelligence or not, many of its officers found it convenient to omit the green stripe worn between their sleeve rings. The branch was disbanded in 1959.

For their part, Special Branch recruits sometimes found naval bureaucracy stifling and the navy's rigid attitude to promotion frustrating. Advancement was strictly related to equivalent seagoing responsibility which, with RNVR lieutenants commanding submarines and small escorts, made anyone's case for promotion ashore difficult to argue. Naval officers were expected to hold their own by sheer force of personality against opposite numbers from other services who outranked them. This was emphasised in Admiralty and NID circulars CAFO 975 and NID 1755.

> 'There are so many cases where [seagoing] officers perform their duties in an entirely satisfactory manner in spite of lack of stripes and experience that it is extremely hard to make a satisfactory case for promotion merely because one's Military and Air colleagues hold higher ranks. In fact to claim a higher rank for such a reason is an admission of one's own failings, observing that the qualities that chiefly count and quite transcend any question of rank, are character and intellect.'[20]

It would take an unusually thick-skinned (or perhaps thick-skulled) officer to claim disadvantage in the face of such explicit official discouragement.

An early appointment alongside Morgan was a certain Ian Fleming, who became an invaluable aide and gatekeeper to the DNI, as well as an inveterate source of wild and sometimes suicidal schemes. His imagination served him well in later life.

Godfrey instigated several reforms to tighten the Division's professional discipline. Prominent among them he developed an intelligence classification system on a scale A1 to D5, the letter denoting trust in the source and the number the reliability of the source's information. A defector describing his own equipment might thus be rated A1, repeating dockside gossip about secret weapons his account might drop to A5. This permitted like-for-like integration of intelligence from different sources into a single, comprehensive picture. Rigorous segregation of hard intelligence from NID comment helped avoid the danger of what he termed 'wishfulness': the projection of what we would like onto what is.

In a separate development the Women's Royal Naval Service ('Wrens'), which had been disbanded after the First World War, was revived. The women of the service would play a vital part throughout the next conflict, including in NID. We will meet some of them later.

1   TNA ADM 223/851.
2   King-Hall, S. *Op Cit*. P.215-6.
3   TNA ADM 223/464. P.7.
4   TNA ADM 223/472.
5   Private letter, copy in the author's possession.
6   The companies merged in 1934.
7   TNA ADM 223/286. Denning note on Movements Section (25/1/38), P.18-19.
8   Roskill, *Naval Policy Between the Wars, Vol 2*. P.388. TNA ADM 223/297. P.25
9   Fry, *Spymaster*.
10   TNA ADM223/475. ADM 223/464.
11   TNA ADM 223/851.
12   TNA ADM 223/619. P.XXII.
13   Letter ref. 2625 (M.I.1) dated 23/03/39 in TNA ADM 1/10579. See *After the Battle* 70, 38-43 for a description of the Royal Herbert Hospital's treatment of wounded captives.
14   Heather Jones: *A process of modernization? Prisoner of war interrogation and human intelligence gathering in the First World War*, in Andrew & Tobia (Ed) *Interrogation*.
15   TNA ADM 223/473.
16   TNA ADM 223/467. P.48.
17   Ibid.
18   TNA ADM 223/297. P.14.
19   TNA ADM 223/467, P.72.
20   Both documents can be found in TNA ADM 223/467, endorsed by John Godfrey's post-war views.

SECOND WORLD WAR

"Total Germany"

At 11:00 on 3rd September 1939 a brief Admiralty signal launched the Royal Navy into existential combat for the second time in twenty-five years. There was no 'phoney war' or *Sitzkrieg* at sea: by the end of the day Fritz Julius Lemp in *U-30* had torpedoed and sunk the British liner SS *Athenia*, allegedly mistaking it for an armed merchant cruiser.[1]

The Admiralty's intelligence about the new threat was depressingly sketchy, both in the number of U-boats Germany could deploy and their capability. NID promptly issued a handbook summarising what it did know, but the preface frankly admitted that '...*the available details are rather meagre*' and that they were '*were supplied by the German Government under the late Anglo-German Naval Treaty and ... should not be regarded as completely reliable.*'[2]

Lieutenant-Colonel Trench was back in harness at the head of a new German prisoner of war section by 14th September, along with first-war veteran Lieutenant-Commander Edward Croghan.[3] Second-Lieutenant Frank Havard RM proved unsuitable for the work and was moved to the passport section. Another early reject was Commander Howard, 'transferred to other duties.'[4] Lieutenant Richard Pennell, a qualified interpreter, was initially seconded to NID for three months while his broken leg healed. Lieutenant-Commanders Ross Hallam and George Saunders also lent a hand. Others came and went in the churn of rapid mobilisation.

The tiny team was split between the Admiralty and prisoners' accommodation at the Tower, where they had a resource never used in the last war: cells were fitted with concealed microphones allowing eavesdroppers to listen in to their conversations from a so-called 'M' Room. 'M', when necessary, was given out as short for 'Map' to explain the strict access security surrounding the rooms.

Equipment was initially bought from the Radio Corporation of America (RCA) but subsequently sourced domestically from the Post Office Research Station at Dollis Hill, where Mr James F Doust moved mountains to develop and supply the kit the interrogators needed. This saved precious dollars and provided a shorter, more agile supply chain.

The original RCA equipment used pairs of microphones concealed above the ceiling. Apart from being more complex and expensive the fitting was easier to detect (and had been found by at least one inmate).[5] This vulnerability would later haunt CSDIC's US equivalent at Fort Hunt.

The replacement mono microphones were superbly concealed in light fittings, fireplaces and windows. Many prisoners suspected their presence on arrival, few if any detected all of them even after the most thorough search. Not unnaturally, the occasional paranoid inmate who found one bug tended to stop looking for others. This was a mistake. *Maschinenmaat* N209[6] boasted in 1940,

> *'We have a microphone in our room, built in above the fire-place. I unscrewed the lid.'*[7]

His bragging was recorded for posterity. The speaker is not identified but is probably Heinz Marticke of U-33. When the boat was sunk off the Isle of Arran the rotors from its Enigma code machine were distributed between crew members with instructions to drop them in the sea. One failed to do so, resulting in the capture of three rotors (two of them previously unknown).

Later captives' confidence was often enhanced by having discovered the bugs at sorting cages or Middle Eastern interrogation centres. *Matrosenobergefreiter* Lange of *U-264* was a case in point.

> *'N2247:   In the cell, at the racing stables where I was first of all, microphones were concealed in the pillars. They have them in the first you go to. They don't have them here.'*[8]

As was *Leutnant zur See* Fitz of *U-223*.

> *'N2401:   In the interrogation camp at ALGIERS there were microphones. There were two German officers who were probably stool-pigeons; we had to go on daily walks with them.'*[9]

Thus reassured, most relaxed, and assumed their talk was private. As late as 1945, after years of security drilling, *Leutnant zur See Banck* ridiculed his colleague's caution.

> *'PIPAL: We must be careful here in case they listen in!*
>
> BANCK: *Don't be silly; I have examined the place thoroughly – there's nothing.*
>
> PIPAL: *But it is an interrogation camp, which makes me suspicious. My father once worked in that sort of show.'*[10]

The listening team originally comprised six bilingual officers. By July 1942 it had grown to about forty, a mix of German and Italian speakers. As ever-growing need came up against the shortage of trained officers, it was supplemented by native German-speaking (mostly Jewish) refugees. The recruits were given instant promotion to sergeant and a terrifying security briefing on arrival. By 1944 the team was about a hundred strong.[11]

The first opportunities came quickly; *U-39* (*Kapitänleutnant* Gerhard Glattes) was sunk on 14th September while attempting to attack HMS *Ark Royal*. All 43 crewmen survived, arriving at the Tower on 17th. *U-27* (*Oberleutnant zur See* Johannes Franz) met her end on 20th September, *U-40* (*Kapitänleutnant* Wolfgang Barten) and *U-42* (*Kapitänleutnant* Rolf Dau) on 13th October.

There were 105 survivors from these boats, including all the commanders except Barten. Another three boats, *U-12*, *U-16* and *U-45* were lost in October with all hands, though the body of a *U-16 Steuermann* (helmsman) was later recovered with a useful notebook on his person. Trench discussed this gift horse with an Intelligence Division specialist in *ruses de guerre*, just in case. November added *U-35*. There were also a few deserters, refugees, and crews from merchant prizes to deal with. In an example of the evolving co-operation between the service branches at CSDIC the RAF prepared its own reports on *U-39*, *U-42*, *U-27* and *U-35*, apparently before NID.[12] Their information was incorporated into the final versions of the naval reports.

Glattes' crew made an unpromising start. He had time after capture to remind them of their duty to withhold information and, if possible, mislead questioners. The CSDIC report assessed them as generally stupid, thoroughly indoctrinated Nazis, indifferent to their circumstances and even their fate. Even so, recovery of the chief engineer's notebook provided useful data on fuel consumption and range, and interviews over three days brought out a few snippets.[13]

The crew of *U-27*, equally fanatical but pleasanter, had been kept segregated and yielded another notebook.[14] Both crews were pleasantly surprised at the good treatment they had received after capture, in contrast to the expectations created by Nazi propaganda.

In a foretaste of a future standard tactic, a couple of NID officers entertained captains Glattes and Franz to a slap-up lunch. Despite their enthusiastic pumping they learnt little on this occasion.

The Tower residency of *U-27*'s crew also saw the first recorded use of a stool pigeon, or informer, to try and gain intelligence from a supposed fellow-prisoner.[15] At this stage the candidate was probably a bilingual British officer who could hardly have helped revealing his ignorance of current conditions in the German military. The experiment probably did not deliver much of value.

By the end of October, the Admiralty could publish a table, derived from prisoner information, of U-boat underwater speeds against motor revolutions.[16] A submarine hunter needed to know four things to place his depth charges accurately: where was the target now, how deep, where was it going and how fast. This information helped him fill in one of the blanks. A more comprehensive document, largely based on the captured notebooks, summarised the technical information gathered to date about German U-boats.[17]

Details were also beginning to emerge about new German electrically propelled torpedoes which were cheaper and slower than conventional, thermal designs but left no wake. Lower speed was no drawback against a lumbering merchant ship whereas the element of surprise was a positive benefit.

Another innovation was a magnetic proximity fuse which, luckily for the *Ark Royal* and others, was chronically unreliable and tended to go off prematurely.

When drained of useful intelligence the captives were 'dumped' to conventional prisoner of war camps. At this stage there were only two: Grizedale Hall in Cumbria for the officers, and Glen Mill at Oldham, Lancashire, for the ratings. *Kapitän-leutnant* Glattes was for a while the senior German officer at Grizedale and made himself difficult, trying to intimidate the others into an attitude of non-co-operation. Matters eased with the arrival of *Kapitänleutnant* Werner Lott (*U-35*, sunk 29th November 1939) who was described by the commandant as '*a splendid type of officer*,' and had previously shown his character by taking on board the crew of his last victim (the steamer *Diamantis*) and landing them in Ireland.[18] The interrogation report for *U-35* finished with a coda which outlined the challenges faced by CSDIC and would become a recurring plea to executive commanders: segregate officers from petty officers and crew, and do *not* have a go yourselves.

> *'It is only in very exceptional circumstances that technical information can be obtained from prisoners of war by direct questions. Deserters, on the other hand, are willing to impart any knowledge they may possess and can be treated in a different manner.*
>
> *As a general rule prisoners of war are quite ready to discuss technical matters, provided they are let to believe the interrogator already knows the subject of enquiry. But directly their suspicions are aroused and they become aware of the particular item of information required from them, they usually decline to make any further statements.*
>
> *Thus it is a difficult matter to cover all the points contained in the questionnaires supplied by Admiralty Departments. Only by repeated examination, occupying several days, is it possible to piece together reliable information.*
>
> *More importance is attached to keeping prisoners segregated after preliminary examination before they are cross-examined, than in separating them immediately after capture. It is, however, important that officers should be kept apart from Chief Petty Officers and Petty Officers from the men.*
>
> *For this reason it is undesirable that interrogation should be carried out at the port of disembarkation, as it is impossible effectively to segregate prisoners during their transport to the examination centre.'*[19]

The point was driven home when most of the survivors from *U-49*, sunk in the ill-fated Norwegian campaign, were allowed to mix with U-boat prisoners who had already been examined. The interrogators' frustration comes through in their report's opening paragraph:

> *'The latter were thus able to warn the "U 49" crew and exhort them to maintain silence. The attempt to question a selected number of these "contaminated" men was made, but proved useless.'*[20]

U-49 did yield a chart showing the patrol areas of all U-boats stationed in the North Sea to support the Norwegian campaign.

It is a tribute to the self-control of interrogating officers, many of whom had relatives in Germany or the occupied countries or had lost close friends and family to enemy action, that they did not resort to violence when faced with the arrogance of dedicated Nazis. That is not to say they always observed the letter of the Geneva Convention. N189, *Bootsmann* Paul Galileia of *U-33* certainly felt he had heard something more than an implied threat on 19th February 1940:

> *'I've got a great respect for these fellows.*
> *"Well," I said "we didn't lay any mines." "Good" he said "if you*
> *had done so, you would have been treated as criminals, not as*
> *prisoners of war." ... I always think they want to put us up against a*
> *wall here.'[21]*

U-35's medic, theoretically a non-combatant and thus exempt from interrogation, was also interviewed at the Tower in December 1939.[22]

From 12th December 1939 to February 1940 the interrogation team decamped with their RAF and army colleagues to safer, larger, and better-equipped premises in a newly requisitioned country house at Trent Park near Cockfosters with twelve 'wired' rooms for prisoners. Admiral Godfrey, DNI, expected better results from microphones there that at the Tower where they had not proved satisfactory.[23] The phased move was constrained by the pace of fitting out.

Although it was a vast improvement, the limitations of the interrogators' new home quickly became apparent. It was within earshot of London's air raid warning system which bolstered the prisoners' morale and did not help the listeners focus on their conversation. In the twitchy atmosphere of 1940, when invasion seemed a daily possibility, its location began to look too vulnerable for comfort. Emergency evacuation was discussed.

Lieutenant Wilfred Samuel, formerly of the WW1 army Intelligence Corps had originally impressed NID by helping to debrief survivors of naval Zeppelin *L50* in October 1917.[24] He joined the team at the Admiralty in January 1940, on a one-month training appointment. His chatty nature quickly got on Trench's nerves, but the workload did not allow fastidiousness. The friction may however have influenced the decision to place Samuel permanently at Trent Park rather than Admiralty.

The Cockfosters team was strengthened further by the temporary secondment of Commander Charles O'Callaghan who was fluent in French, German and Italian, and RNVR Lieutenant Paul de Laszlo. The latter was a cryptographer whose expertise was useful when interviewing the wireless operators among the survivors.

The beginning of March saw the arrival of Lieutenant-Commander Philip Rhodes to take up the role of liaison with MI9(b), the military intelligence branch responsible for British prisoners of war.[25] He certainly had relevant experience, having been captured off the Belgian coast in 1915 and spent two and a half years in German camps before transfer to Switzerland for the rest of his internment.

As Trent Park was receiving its finishing touches Burton Cope's wife and daughter, who had been evacuated to Nantes, received an urgent summons back to Paris. They were getting out with whatever they could pack and ship quickly. The haste is curious, as this was months before the Hitler's assault on France. His daughter recalled being told that he was on a 'German list.' It is tempting to speculate that their flight was associated with the collapse of MI6's unofficial networks after the Venlo incident.

Returning to Britain, Cope strapped on his RNVR uniform – now several sizes larger after twenty years' fine dining – and presented himself at the Admiralty in February 1940. A broken arm prevented him from taking up his duties until 12th March, but a week after that he was fully briefed and working at Trent Park.

In June, the section was strengthened by a fourth permanent member, Richard Mansfield ('Dick') Weatherby, and a civilian assistant, Miss E R H Heath. Weatherby, a twenty-three-year-old alumnus of Winchester and Magdalen was a radically different recruit, of academic rather than military background and too young to remember the First World War. He set the pattern for what would become an increasingly eclectic mix as time progressed.

Meanwhile a steady drip-feed of U-boat survivors and a few others helped fill out the developing picture of the enemy's resources. Who was in command of which boat? How many submarines and other ships were being completed, how many had been lost, and could the supply of trained, motivated crews keep up? This was essential data for the Operational Intelligence Centre's plots and guesses. It also supplied Captain Talbot, Director of Anti-Submarine Warfare Division, with the facts he needed to refute Winston Churchill's wildly optimistic public statements about the number of U-boats still in operation. Talbot lost his job as a result.[26]

Then there was the engineering and operational data essential to tactical development: diving depth, fuel capacity and consumption, preferred routes, the need to recharge electric torpedoes, time needed to reload a torpedo tube and so on.

Prisoners' increased security-consciousness kept pace with the interrogators' growing experience. The introduction to the report on *U-32*, sunk on 30th October 1940, observed,

'It was again noted that the crews had been warned against disclosing any information which might be of value.

Previously it has been noticed that the policy of the German High Command was to maintain a high degree of secrecy by allowing all

officers and men to share only such knowledge as was essential to carry out their duties. The success of this policy was very noticeable in the case of the crew of "U 32." Various men knew the details of their own jobs only, and had no idea of the work of the other members of the crew.

…

They are all fanatical Nazis and obviously hate the British intensely. This attitude has not been so evident in the cases of prisoners captured at earlier dates.[27]

This boat carried a supernumerary officer, *Kapitänleutnant* 'Fritz' (Friedrich Wilhelm) Wentzel, who was a probationary U boat commander experiencing a war patrol as the final stage of his training. The report described him as 'rather pretentious' and expressed surprise at his statement that he would not hesitate to break parole and escape if the opportunity arose. He shared a room with Hans Engel, his contemporary and opposite number in *U-31*. They assumed the possibility of microphones and tried to keep their voices low during sensitive conversations. All to no avail. Wentzel was evidently the source of several snippets in the final report, which made his extended four weeks' stay at Cockfosters worthwhile. He supplied the information that *U-32* had not informed *U-31* of its encroachment into the latter's operational area, that Gestapo officers or 'deck parsons' were regularly slipped into destroyer crews (and were conspicuous by their incompetence), and that naval schools had been moved inland from Kiel and Wilhelmshaven to escape British bombing.[28] This was despite his only 'interrogation' being a stroll in the park with a British naval officer who, according to the former's memoir, raised a number of topics but didn't press the matter when he refused to answer. The walk no doubt spurred subsequent conversation in his cell. Even so, it is interesting that he appears in two consecutively numbered transcripts dated a week apart. This suggests that the eavesdropping process had not yet reached full maturity, at least on the naval side.[29]

At this stage, the captives coming through were almost without exception dedicated Nazis, convinced of a quick and successful outcome to the war. Some regarded the conflict with Britain as a regrettable interlude, to be got over with as quickly as possible. Others had taken the whole, sick dogma to heart. Twenty-six-year-old *Oberleutnant zur See* Egon Rudolph from *U-95*, sunk on 28th November 1941 was closeted with his cell-mate and evident soulmate *Oberleutnant (Ing)* Günther Gess of *U-433*. One of the more repeatable parts of their conversation went,

> 'N1050 [Rudolph]   *I hope the FÜHRER will grant us prisoners our wish and give each of us a Jew and an Englishman to slaughter;* …'[30]

There is a marked contrast with the mood eighteen months later after the hammer-blows of Alamein, Stalingrad, and the reversal of fortune in the Atlantic. The bigotry was still there but it was mixed with growing unease about consequences. The question '*If* we lose …?' was very rarely raised in 1941 but commonplace in 1943, often matched by the previously unthinkable '*When* we lose…'[31]

It was beginning to look as though CSDIC would struggle to keep up with the hectic pace of a technology-driven conflict. Most of the intelligence staff were Great War veterans and the younger members like Dick Weatherby were more familiar with tactics than engineering. It would be 1943 before the first professional engineer, Donald Welbourn, joined the team to provide a depth of technical knowledge that had been missing until then. At first his role was simply to advise and support the interrogation team, but he quickly developed a talent for the work himself.[32]

So far there was little sign of the U-boat service having to rely on conscription and the number of candidate commanders in the pipeline suggested that, on the contrary, there was still plenty of competition to enter the glamorous and well-paid branch. The one sign of stress was in the supply of experienced petty officers and officers, where training regimes were being shortened, promotion accelerated, and service commitments extended. Over time this would contribute to the vast difference in achievement between the 'star' captains and the rest.

In October 1940, the German-speaking interrogators were joined by Italian specialists Lieutenant-Commander William Rosevere and Lieutenant Edward Davies RNVR, to form a combined Section XI PW.[33]

By then stool pigeons, or informers, were starting to appear regularly in CSDIC transcripts. The idea may have been sparked by Lieutenant-Commander Croghan's visit to his French opposite number late in 1939. He reported that the French used harsher interrogation methods than he was comfortable with but made extensive use of stool pigeons.[34]

The first four 'professional' informers used by CSDIC were selected from 93 volunteer refugees and trained from scratch to impersonate members of the German armed forces – their attitudes, background and jargon. They were Stefan Georg Klein, Werner Teodor Barazetti, Josef Lampersberger and Georg Schwarzloh.

Their backgrounds varied widely but all came with strong anti-Nazi credentials and served until the end of the war. Schwarzloh was a former Hamburg policeman arrested in 1934 on unproven charges of high treason. Nonetheless he lost his job and ended up working for the Czech secret service, which he left under a cloud on an allegation of pocketing commissions from a firm he was investigating. Escaping to England he was interned, initially at Lingfield. By the time official consciousness had noticed his potential usefulness he had been moved to Canada and his wife interned on the Isle of Man. He was eventually retrieved and released on 30th July 1941.[35]

Lampersberger was a railway waiter, Catholic, and anti-Nazi activist. In 1933, warned that he was about to be arrested, he used his railway access to escape to Czechoslovakia. Continuing his political activities made him a target; he was arrested in 1935 just inside the Czech border, taken to Munich, and severely treated by the Gestapo. The international dimension of the incident meant they could not hold him for long, but his former comrades remained suspicious of him after his release. He escaped to Britain in March 1939, was interned in December but released again in April 1940. He appears to have mingled with and reported on Czech refugees before taking up employment with CSDIC. Intriguingly his connections with both Schwarzloh (who he disliked intensely) and Barazetti came out during interviews which emphasised the intense rivalry between émigré factions. Mutual denunciations cannot have made the security service's task any easier.[36]

Barazetti was a journalist, originally of Swiss extraction, working in Hamburg who was forced to move to Prague owing to his anti-Nazi views in 1936. In 1939 he escaped from Czechoslovakia with his wife and young son thanks to family connections with the late President Maseryk. Working at first with the British Committee for Refugees from Czechoslovakia he was suspected of lining his own pockets at refugees' expense. He was interned in May 1940 but released to serve with CSDIC from May 1941 to September 1945. After demobilisation he was convicted of stealing and receiving in 1947 but seems to have reformed his ways afterward. His successful application for naturalisation in 1957 included a typed testimony from Thomas Kendrick (head of CSDIC) to his wartime service.[37]

Klein was an Austrian citizen by birth and made the easiest transition to British nationality, achieving naturalisation in September 1946.[38] At the time he was still a 'Commissioned Officer in His Majesty's Forces'. There is little else known about him, but it is likely that he was the pervasive A713 who pops up in multiple guises throughout the World War II transcripts. He was the only one of the four who could have been in harness early enough to match A713's first appearances.

The role required confidence, courage, and acting ability. It did not always work. German prisoners who had been through Trent Park used to joke about meeting their roommate, a 'Kleinert' of variable rank and service. He was always discovered washing his socks, implying he had been there some time and giving him a ready-made excuse for curiosity about current developments.[39] The informers gained subtlety with experience and were progressively joined by genuine servicemen who, for various reasons, chose to throw in their lot with their captors.

The first stool pigeons started work at the beginning of December 1940. They were trained to impersonate aircrew and were not familiar enough with maritime technology and jargon to be very useful to Naval Intelligence. In a generally positive commentary on a CSDIC overview in February 1941 Admiral Godfrey observed, *'When the [stool pigeon] system develops and there is a naval element, it is anticipated that much improved value will be obtained, particularly on technical matters, which is perhaps the hardest type of information to obtain with any degree of reliability in other ways.'*[40]

Karl's Story

It took another year to grant his wish. 'Karl' (index number N1067) was a Boatswain's Mate, a survivor of a U-boat sunk in in December 1941. He had served three months in Papenburg concentration camp and a spell in prison for 'treasonable activity'. As a petty officer without obvious access to sensitive information he might easily have been 'dumped' to a standard internment camp without further ado, but the Trent Park interrogators evidently saw potential in him.

He had repeated conversations with a 'British Army Officer' between January and April 1942, some of which survive in transcript.[41] At first, he was encouraged to relate his experiences and accumulated resentment against the regime. It appeared that in 1934 he had been on watch during his merchant ship's visit to Rotterdam when some subversive literature had been smuggled aboard. From that moment he found his movements increasingly constrained until he was arrested by Dutch police and shipped to the border. He was tried and acquitted by a German magistrate but immediately re-arrested by the Gestapo and sentenced to three months in a concentration camp. While there he experienced casual brutality, witnessed floggings and prisoners 'shot while trying to escape'.[42]

On his release he was immediately thrown into prison again, with frequent interrogations trying to elicit a confession of communist subversion. It turned out that he had been denounced by a former school friend but, when it came to trial, could prove from his seaman's record book that he had been at sea when he was accused of distributing leaflets. The case was finally dismissed. Even so, although he was a trained merchant seaman, the only job he could get on his release was trimmer – the lowest grade of fireman (stoker).[43]

It is difficult, perhaps impossible, at this stage to tell how much of his tale is strictly accurate, how much exaggeration and how much perception. He certainly arrived at CSDIC with a burden of grievance which the Cockfosters staff did nothing to discourage.

As the conversations progressed, they were steered to the political situation and then to 'Karl's naval service. He candidly gave his views on the 'star' U-boat commanders Günther Prien (a 'monster') and Joachim Schepke (a jazz fan who cared for his crew's welfare and/but constantly played records on patrol). Both had died with their boats the previous year.

His wartime experience mainly under poor commanders, and of seeing the condition of soldiers back from the Eastern Front, did not improve his mood. At the last, when his boat was within seconds of being lost, the captain *'appeared to prefer to allow the boat to sink with her entire crew rather than risk capture by surfacing.'*[44] He was only dissuaded after a violent argument with the engineering officer, who subsequently shot himself.

This, with his enduring resentment of the regime, made him receptive to the team's blandishments. By July 1942, and perhaps earlier, he had changed sides and was working as a stool pigeon. He continued in the role for another year, by which time a steady drip of disillusioned defectors allowed him to retire to a safely segregated camp where there was no risk of him being recognised.

'Karl' illustrates many of the influences that commonly persuaded servicemen to change sides. Resentment of the regime, either from personal experience of its corruption and injustice and/or too-long suppressed ideological or religious opposition, was a strong driver. Experience of inept or brutal leadership nullified the team spirit that might otherwise have supported them through the disorientation of the interrogation centre. In another U-boat the captain was the first to abandon ship, tried to steal another man's lifejacket when his own would not inflate, then swam around shouting orders for the rest to scuttle the boat. While awaiting transfer to Britain the officers swindled the crew out of their cigarette ration. Unsurprisingly, this group yielded a willing convert.

As the war progressed and Germany's chances of winning faded, so did the appeal of a cataclysmic Wagnerian *dénouement*. Captives were increasingly inclined to question whether their natural loyalty to Germany and coerced allegiance to the Party and Hitler were the same thing.

For some, a tiny minority at first, physical imprisonment was a release from the mental stockade in which they had been living. N1558, an *Obermaschinenmaat* in a U-boat lost through its captain's incompetence and overconfidence, was sharing a cell with two other submariners. He was overheard saying,

> '*My dear man, when I get back to GERMANY, I shan't keep my mouth shut, you can rely on that. If, for instance, I meet my Flottillenchef in civil life, I shall give him such a sock on the jaw that he won't know whether he's coming or going. He was without any experience whatsoever but full of big talk. We were out near CASABLANCA and sailed around but didn't sink anything. When we got back he said: "One can tell by the length of your beards that your patrol wasn't a long one." The bloody fool!*'[45]

One of his earlier jokes would have been distinctly unwise at home.

> '*HESS is brought to LONDON and introduced to CHURCHILL. The escort says: "Mr CHURCHILL, this is the madman from GERMANY." HESS says: "No, I'm not the madman, but I am his deputy."*'[46]

This conversation took place in April 1943, after the German reverses at El Alamein and Stalingrad and as the Battle of the Atlantic was beginning to tilt in the Allies' favour. Many prisoners, like *Maschinist* Hellmuth Schlosser (N(Am)3) in the following extract, continued doggedly to claim faith in ultimate victory or at least to deny the possibility of defeat. N1558 was one of an increasing number who contemplated the alternative.

> '*N(Am)3:   When we go back we shall at least find our money waiting for us.*

N1558:   *If we will the war!*

N(Am)3:   *Of course we shall win the war.*

N1553:   *We no longer believe that.'*[47]

Note 'we'. The third man in the cell was N1553, from another boat lost in the same action. N1558, N1553, and N1553's shipmate N1552 would all defect and work successfully as stool pigeons. The latter was heard to say within four days of being pulled from the sea,

> '...*if all the English are as humane as this man (I.O.) here, it's more or less the same to me whether we win or lose.'*[48]

Sometimes a tentative overture ran into a brick wall. Stool pigeon N1485 may have thought his opposite number N1596, a wireless operator from the intercepted prize *Silvaplana*, was a possible prospect.

> 'N1485:   *Who do you think will win the war?*
>
> N1596:   *Really, what odd questions you ask!'*[49]

And on another occasion,

> 'N1485:   *National Socialism has proved a good thing in some ways, but the best form of government is Democracy, like here in ENGLAND.*
>
> N1535:   *You and I will never agree on politics.'*[50]

It took several months to talk 'Karl' around, but the process became slicker with time. Early 1943 brought in a wireless operator from a cornered tanker as well as the U-boat crew discussed above. 'Edmund', an *Oberfunkmaat* (PO Telegraphist) rescued later that year immediately volunteered information about short-code signals, even offered to serve in a British ship and do anything short of firing on his countrymen.[51] A survivor of a boat with a particularly inept and corrupt set of officers he was helping 'seed' conversations with his fellow-prisoners within a few days. February 1944 astonishingly brought a recruit from the tight-knit and highly indoctrinated band of survivors of the battle cruiser *Scharnhorst*. In the last year of the war CSDIC had more offers of help than it needed.

With a larger cohort of helpers and growing experience of managing them CSDIC began to introduce new tricks. A prisoner meeting persistent curiosity from a single cellmate might quickly become suspicious, so one stool pigeon was mixed with two genuine captives or two with one.

Stool pigeons in British centres (other than the original four 'professionals') received no pay or privileges apart from slightly better accommodation, and no promise of special treatment after the war. This was to ensure they were volunteering from a genuine change of heart. Their US opposite numbers who were known as 'gun dogs' fared rather better. Apart from the original four, who were primed with an 'escape word' if things got too tricky, they were unaware of the microphones which acted as a valuable check on their honesty.

It was vital to preserve an informer's security, both for his own safety and for his continuing usefulness. Mixing an army or air force stool pigeon with a naval survivor was a safe tactic, giving a ready-made excuse for the former's ignorance but limiting the depth of technical 'shop' they could discuss. An alternative was to adopt an identity from a U-boat sunk in a different theatre from that of the subject, minimising the chance that they would know anyone in common. It was essential that they came from different parts of Germany and that the subject was subsequently kept separate from genuine veterans of the informer's alleged boat. Both required careful record keeping and tracking of prisoners. Later, stool pigeons typically claimed to have served in boats whose survivors were interrogated in the USA, further reducing the likelihood of a subsequent chance meeting in a prisoner of war camp.[52]

Mechanikerobergefreiter Werner Drechsler's fate was a sobering reminder of the need for continuing care. Formerly of *U-118* he worked for seven months under two false identities at the Fort Hunt interrogation centre near Washington DC. When no longer needed he was returned to US Army custody with strict instructions that he must not be interned with other naval prisoners. By some oversight he was sent to a camp housing U-boat survivors. Within hours he had been recognised, denounced as a traitor, and hanged in a shower room. The perpetrators were later charged with murder, court-martialled, and executed.[53]

Not all volunteers were up to a task which demanded a rare mix of nerve and acting ability. In March 1943, an unnamed army prisoner was flagged as potentially suitable for the 'Y' (wireless interception) service. He was an enthusiastic recruit to the Allied cause and had been tried out by MI19 as a stool pigeon but rejected as 'lifeless and timid'.[54]

Most of the original four stepped back as defectors became available to take their place but one, index number A713, stayed in harness until mid-1944 and eventually gained enough skill and confidence to impersonate a U-boat captain while locked up with genuine submarine officers.[55]

Defectors' value was not exhausted when their career as stool pigeons was over. Some worked for Sefton Delmer's propaganda operation, others were kept in segregated accommodation and provided their expertise as needed to NID and the Admiralty's technical branches.

Given the increasingly extensive and sophisticated use of stool pigeons with German captives as the technique developed it is interesting that there is no evidence of their insertion into Italian cell conversations – at least on the naval side. Work continues to explore this facet of the interrogator's art.

Growing Up

As 1940 drew to a close the originally improvised shape of the interrogation section settled into something more permanent. Richard Pennell, whose three-month detachment had extended to a year, finally returned to Anti-Submarine Warfare Division. In February 1941 Wilfred Samuel was posted to Canada as liaison with DNI Ottawa. April 1941 saw the arrival of another Great War veteran, Commander Leonard Rideal.

The following month Ian Fleming, personal assistant to the DNI, brought in one Ralph Izzard, a six-foot-four former journalist who Trench described as 'rather a tough person,' on short-term loan. Izzard had been the *Daily Mail's* Berlin bureau chief before the war, had narrowly escaped capture when investigating the 'Venlo Incident' in which German intelligence kidnapped two British MI6 agents, and joined the RNVR as a gunner. His initial three-week CSDIC attachment ran on to 1944, when he transferred to (and led) the Forward Interrogation Unit closely integrated with Fleming's 30 Assault Unit (see Overlord and After below). In between he went to Washington to help the US Navy set up an interrogation facility and acted as CSDIC's link to the NID propaganda section, NID 17Z.

Entertainment was a key part of the softening-up process. It had several purposes: a carefully routed tour of London gave the lie to Goebbels' claims that the whole city was a smoking ruin, plentiful food and drink undermined belief in the effectiveness of the blockade, and alcohol just might loosen tongues. It was important not to overdo it though. Nicholas Rankin recounts one incident involving Izzard:

'In June or July 1941 Ian Fleming and two other NID officers, Eddie Croghan and Dick Wetherby [sic], took a pair of captured German sailors out to dinner at A L'Ecu de France in Jermyn Street, London, and then on to an MI5 safe house near Sloane Square full

of listening devices. The two Germans were Burkard Baron von Müllenheim-Rechberg, third gunnery officer on the battle-cruiser [sic] Bismarck, who had survived its sinking on 27 May 1941, and Hans Joachim Eichelborn, the chief engineering officer of U-110, which sank after the pinch by HMS Bulldog on 9 May. The interrogator Ralph Izzard later told John Pearson: 'The idea behind "mating" Rechberg with a U-boat engineer officer was as they both came from different branches of the navy they would be inquisitive about each other's experiences and thus talk usefully in a "bugged" cell.' Alas, in the event, everybody got very drunk and talked rubbish rather than secrets.'[56]

A later refinement was to have a group joined later by an officer who had been 'delayed' and was stone-cold sober.

As in WW1, the crews of rescuing ships sometimes made elementary mistakes such as failing to relieve survivors of papers in their possession. An unnamed *Leutnant zur See* (Sub Lieutenant), formerly commanding a prize crew from *Gneisenau*, was recorded saying,

'N576:   *There was electric heating in the cabin. Of course we burnt the papers. So stupid (of the English to let us).'[57]*

Once again, the team constantly and often fruitlessly struggled to prevent its subjects being spoilt by enthusiastic amateur questioning before they reached the interrogation centre. Interrogator Colin McFadyean summarised the problem in a post-war review:

a.   *'The untrained interrogator usually puts ideas into people's heads.*

b.   *He asks leading questions and unwittingly gets the answers he wants.*

c.   *He is unable to benefit by the knowledge of other interrogations and, therefore, does not necessarily know which questions to ask.*

> d. *Arrangements for segregation are bound to be inadequate and having once talked matters over between themselves, {ps/w} are unlikely to yield any further information that would be of value.*
>
> e. *Furthermore, having once been questioned, they are very chary of any further interrogation. They would be on their guard and the trained interrogator would not have a chance.*
>
> f. *There are bound to be mutual misunderstandings between prisoners of war and interrogators who cannot speak German and who do not understand German manners and modes of thought. These misunderstandings may lead to entirely false deductions being drawn.*[58]

The much larger RAF section placed a field interrogation officer with a partner from technical intelligence at each airfield, able to rush to a crash site and carry out a preliminary assessment.[59] The Air Force was selective in its choice of prisoners for detailed interrogation, whereas NID was clear from the start that it wanted to examine *all* U-boat survivors. Another key difference was that naval interrogators increasingly relied on listeners and stool pigeons for their results, whereas their colleagues in light blue preferred to trust direct interrogation.

> '73. *In the argument in favour of recorded conversations as a source of intelligence, such a [particularly valuable] prisoner should have been placed with a companion immediately and his utterances recorded without further ado; in the contrary argument this man night never talk under such conditions, whereas direct interrogation could produce all the results required. It is a fact that nearly all major intelligence scoops obtained by A.D.I.(K) were from direct interrogation.*[60]

Over time CSDIC built up a detailed card index about the personalities, places, vessels, and people facing them. This allowed an interrogator to walk into the room armed with such intimate information about his victim's life that it seemed to have come from a close colleague or spy. The surprise of an able seaman from the minelayer *Ulm* was typical of the way this approach could rock someone back on his heels and break down his resistance.

> 'N1266:   He (I.O.) told me more than I knew myself. Not only from the statements the others have made – it's uncanny the way they get hold of information. English espionage, their Secret Service is famous, it's the largest organisation of its kind that there is. We've also got our B-service on board, our listening service to listen in to the English W/T messages. He (I.O.) asked me about that, too. Then he talked about the F-boat and described the new type "S" mine chutes, although I've never seen one myself.'[61]

In-depth background information facilitated the exploitation of any rivalries or suspicions revealed by the microphones, allowing one captive to be carefully played off against another.

> 'N1891:   The other telegraphist (P/W) told him (I.O.) various things about it and said that I knew more about the thing.'[62]

The interrogator's carefully nurtured 'front' of omniscience was reinforced by his guest's conditioned respect for rank. A *Kapitän-leutnant* would be interviewed by a lieutenant-commander – or someone who appeared to be. Staff kept a selection of jackets for every occasion.

For an increasing number, as time passed, physical captivity was balanced by psychological liberation. A 1943 conversation between N1552, who later chose to work for the Allies, and *Mechanikersmaat* N1544 contrasted freedom of speech on the two sides of the conflict.

> 'N552:   In ENGLAND, in HYDE PARK, you can shout out: "CHURCHILL is a damn fool," and nobody does anything about it.
> N1544:   In GERMANY, if you said: "ADOLF HITLER is a damn fool"! (Laughter)[63]

Inevitably the team's workload, being driven by prisoner intake, swung wildly between feast and famine. It was vital to keep interviewees off balance, so neither staff nor guests got much rest in the initial scramble as a batch of captives arrived. When least productive and the worst influences had been identified and 'dumped' to internment camps the pace might settle somewhat, until the staff were satisfied there was no more useful information to be had and the final report could be typed up and sent to the printer. After that there was little to do until another U-boat or E-boat ran out of luck.

In March 1941 Lieutenant-Commander Rhodes and Sub-Lieutenant Evans of the Prisoner of War Interrogation Service (Home) were attached to Operation *Claymore*, the commando force setting off to raid the Lofoten Islands. They had their hands full on the way home, bringing back over 200 German prisoners, Norwegian quislings and more than 300 volunteers (including eight women) for the Norwegian forces in exile.[64] All had to be sorted and processed. By the time they landed they had boiled down the naval ranks needing CSDIC attention to seventeen individuals.

Convoy battles in March cost Dönitz three of his 'ace' U-boat commanders: Joachim Schepke of *U-100*, Otto Kretschmer of *U-99* and Günther Prien of *U-47*. Only Kretschmer survived. The interrogation team noted the loyalty and admiration he inspired in his crew, and were themselves impressed by his 'calm, quiet' demeanour and level-headed conversation.[65] Kretschmer on his part may have been put off his guard by the kind treatment he received both in HMS *Walker* and at Trent Park, where he had expected that '*they would bring us here in order to beat us with truncheons.*' Landing at Liverpool was a different matter: '*The women were the worst. If I'd fallen into their hands, they'd have torn me to bits.*'[66] Despite the easy-going impression he gave, Kretschmer chaired the illegal 'Court of Honour' at Grizedale Camp which convicted Bernhard Berndt, first officer of the captured *U-570* of cowardice and led to his death.

During 1941 the Naval Intelligence team was joined by Sub-Lieutenant David Williamson and John de Mussenden Carey, the latter to focus on reports. On 16th December it suffered its worst blow. Commander Edward Croghan, its most experienced Interrogation Officer, disappeared along with the four crew and two other passengers in a Hudson aircraft bound for Gibraltar. He was on his way to interview the survivors of *U-95* and was apparently shot down when it strayed too close to German shipping near Finisterre. This costly and painful event may have been the trigger for the later practice of flying selected survivors from remote theatres of war to the UK for rapid insertion to the interrogation system.

For Burton Cope the disaster spelt opportunity. His promotion to Temporary Acting Lieutenant-Commander had come through the previous March He now became the head of the Naval Intelligence team at Trent Park over the head of Commander Rideal, who had failed to impress Trench during the *Bismarck* interrogations and reverted to back-office duties.

At about the same time MI9 was reorganised with responsibility for enemy prisoners transferred to a new organisation, MI19 with effect from early 1942. Commander Rhodes stayed with MI9, taking charge of No 9 Intelligence School which trained allied servicemen in escape, evasion, secret correspondence and the use of improvised and smuggled-in 'toys'.

Latimer and Wilton

Trent Park remained CSDIC's only home until 15th July 1942. Its limitations had been apparent for some time. As an overt prisoner of war camp, it was liable to inspection at short notice by the 'Protecting Power' in the form of the Red Cross. Whenever this occurred the interrogation staff had to be evacuated for the duration of the visit. Being close to London the site was within earshot (and sometimes sight) of German air raids, which risked boosting internees' morale. Some *Luftwaffe* pilots were heard giving a running commentary on events overhead during the Battle of Britain.[67] Finally, as the throughput of captives grew, it was simply too small. The need for expansion had been foreseen as early as 1940. By January 1941 Admiral Godfrey was actively nagging Major General Francis Davidson, his opposite number in Military Intelligence.

With reference to our recent discussions regarding the development of Cockfosters and Wilton Park I have reviewed the results obtained from Naval Prisoners of War since the outbreak of war, and can unhesitatingly confirm that they are of such operational importance as to make it vital to develop this source of information to the full. Naval Prisoners of War have hitherto been captured in small numbers at irregular intervals, which renders it all the more important for me to ensure that nothing is missed when they do arrive. Consequently, from my point of view the increased accommodation in process at Wilton Park and the additional trained personnel necessary to operate the Centre at its maximum output are not only justified, but essential.

You will also appreciate that an additional reason for pushing on with Wilton Park is that the [anti-aircraft] barrage fire interferes considerably with the technique employed at Cockfosters, thereby justifying the location of the Centre in a quieter neighbourhood.

I regard this as of such importance as to override normal considerations of cost and I hope that you will be able to use every endeavour to see that this expansion is given absolute priority.[68]

Two properties were requisitioned, and construction started.

'Production-line' interrogation of German officers and other ranks moved to the newly commissioned, larger facility at

Latimer House in Buckinghamshire. The matching accommodation at Wilton Park, Beaconsfield, was not ready until December so Italian prisoners were processed in the interim by a mobile 'M' room at the reception cage at Newmarket racecourse. This was tested in August 1941, probably using the survivors of Italian submarine *Glauco*, sunk on 27th June, as guinea pigs. It worked well but the test identified a need for modifications. The bugged rooms (1-4 in the plan below) were close to the main camp thoroughfare, producing extraneous noise, and it was too easy for prisoners to spot or infer the microphone installation. A nearby airfield added to the noise problem. It was proposed to turn yard 'A' into a self-contained intelligence facility with the twelve horse boxes around it soundproofed and adapted for prisoner accommodation and interrogation – all wired.[69]

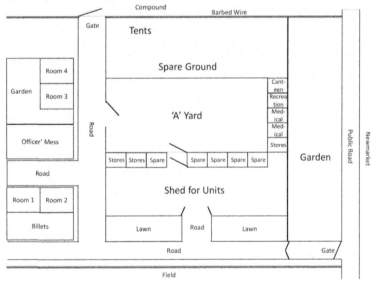

7: Newmarket Cage

Lieutenant Emmet's post-war review of CSDIC UK's Italian operation[70] refers briefly to stool pigeons but, intriguingly, the eavesdropping transcripts show no sign of their presence.

Trent Park had twelve 'miked' cells with maximum accommodation for sixty prisoners at the point of transfer; Latimer and Wilton Park each had thirty cells with room for 64 inmates and six interrogation rooms wired for sound, plus temporary holding accommodation for another thirty. By then the original six 'M' Room operators from the Tower of London had swelled to a staff of forty, a number clearly inadequate for the three centres by then operating. It was this expansion which prompted the recruitment of German and Austrian refugees from the Pioneer Corps.

The increased capacity of the new facilities required a larger interrogation staff. The old guard was reinforced by an increasingly eclectic mix of volunteer reservists from various backgrounds, with few preconceptions about how the job should be done. Inevitably some of them did not take to the work and were moved on in short order. In a tribute to their selection and training most seem to have adapted well.

John Marriner, an Australian journalist, arrived in January 1942. In November Dick Weatherby was joined by his elder brother John, an artist by training and inclination but freshly promoted to captain of Marines. Then came Charles Everett, a former SOE agent who had been operating under diplomatic cover in Portugal until declared *persona non grata*, and Brian Connell, another journalist. The following year Donald Welbourn, an engineer who had toured Austria and Germany before the war and seen the rise of Nazism at first hand, was recruited to strengthen the team's technical expertise. This did wonders for his life expectancy, as his previous posting had been experimental mine countermeasures work. He was quickly followed by Colin McFadyean, a convoy veteran whose talent for the work would see him promoted to head of German Prisoner of War section (NID1(P/W)) and thus Cope's superior. His handicap in the role was that his German wife had left the country shortly before war broke out, which left him out of the loop on some of the most highly classified information. 1944 brought Charles Wheeler, a Marine who would go on to be a well known television journalist. Later came Michael Reade, another experienced seaman with a DSC to his name, Harry Scholar, a Czech engineer, and Julius Lunzer, a Canadian of German extraction who had worked as a steward on Cunard liners. Lunzer barely had time to get his feet under table before joining Izzard and Wheeler in the Forward Interrogation Unit (see below).

From the opening of Latimer and Wilton the interrogators were increasingly supported by Women's Royal Naval Service (Wren) officers, fluent German speakers who integrated the intelligence from stool pigeons, secret listeners, and interviews, and produced the formal reports for the team's customers. Their contribution to the quality and pace of the naval group's output, and thus its credibility with its customers, is difficult to overstate. The officers certainly joined pub crawls with prisoners thought to be cooperative and, according to Evelyn Barron, also conducted interrogations to the consternation of their subjects.[71]

At the beginning of 1942 there was just one Wren officer (Esmé Mackenzie) attached to the section. By April 1943 there were four officers who, at the system's peak, were supported by five Wren petty officers, a Chief Wren, and several shorthand typists.

It is instructive to look at the contrasting careers of two of the Wren officers. Gwendoline Neel-Wall was born in 1897, making her by some margin the oldest member of the team. Her Jersey-born father was a master mariner, her mother German. Her husband, Liam Wall, served with the RFC and RAF during the first World War but little else is known about him. He is thought to have died before the outbreak of the Second World War. Her son Michael was lost with the submarine *Tempest* in February

1942 and her nephew Dennis Kumm with the anti-submarine trawler *Ullswater* later that year. From June 1940 to 1941 she oversaw the improvised Y (wireless intercept) station on Portland Bill. She joined CSDIC by March 1943 and left by October 1944, continuing to work for NID in different roles for the rest of the war. For part of her time with NID 24 (Documents section) she was seconded to NID 30 (30 Assault Unit) to help with '*drawing up supplementary target lists and making preparations for the disposal of captured material*'.[72]

Claudia Furneaux attracted national press attention as a student at Somerville College Oxford for her part in an all-female revue, *Under Twenty-One*, at the Fortune Theatre, London.[73] For someone who had been politically active the surrender of Marshall Pétain's government came as a thunder-clap. She later recalled,

'I was finishing my second year reading Modern Languages when news came of the fall of France. It may be difficult now to realise what an absolutely devastating blow this was, not only for the conduct of the war, but also for ordinary people like me who had to face the fact that France would now be occupied and completely cut off until the war ended.

At about the same time, I heard that the Admiralty was appealing for German speakers to work in Naval Intelligence. Many of the male students were leaving to join up and I decided to abandon my studies and join the Women's Royal Naval Service, known as the Wrens. I applied in London and was tested, investigated at length, and finally kitted out in a rather drab uniform and signed up as a Petty Officer (Special Duties).

When I told my tutor, Enid Starkie, she said "You could have got a First!" but of course we will never know.'[74]

She spent three years listening to German radio transmissions from various stations on the South Coast, finishing at the same improvised Portland 'Y' van as Neel-Wall. After this she was sent to an officers' conversion course at Greenwich, commissioned and posted to Latimer.

8: The NID Team at Latimer House, 1943.
Burton Cope is centre, standing. Richard Weatherby is at camera-right with Donald Welbourn and Ian Fleming next to him. Ralph Izzard is the tall officer at rear left. The Wrens in the front row are (from the left) Jean Flower, Evelyn Barron, Esmé Mackenzie, and Gwendoline Neel-Wall.

One of her more bizarre duties there was to help escort two U-boat officers on a pub-crawl to London – to reward them for good behaviour and no doubt to relax their tongues.

At CSDIC she met and married Harry Lennon, one of the American interrogators rotating through the site. After the war she returned with him to New York where she taught French in a Catholic girls' school and significantly broadened the reading list.

On the death of her parents, being already widowed, she returned to run the family farm in Essex until her own death in 2011. She never did complete her degree.

Trent Park now assumed a new role for the rest of the war, one in which it would make its greatest contribution. It became long-term accommodation for the most senior German captives where they were lulled into a false sense of significance and security. The first guests arrived during the North Africa campaign in 1942 and, until after the D-Day landings in 1944, they were almost exclusively from the German Army. Interrogators in the theatre of operations found them tricky to handle and passed them on as quickly as possible.

> *'P/W of General's rank were usually an embarrassment in the early days of the war, as no suitable accommodation had been planned for them. The mobile nature of desert warfare yielded a surprising number of senior prisoners. In order that the value of "X" sources should not be missed in the case of senior prisoners a marquee type of tent was fitted with "X" and served as mess room. Similar fittings were put into an "180 lbs" tent for sleeping quarters. In this way a tented compound was maintained behind wire for any senior officer prisoners, providing them with more liberty of action than was possible in the normal cell lock ups used for other P/W.*
> *Senior prisoners were always evacuated at the earliest opportunity to U.K. or INDIA, where proper accommodation was available.'*[75]

Direct interrogation of such high-ranking officers was unlikely to yield results. They were highly security conscious, loyal to their calling (if not necessarily to the Führer), and had such wide knowledge that, even if willing to talk, asking the right questions was problematic. Their heads were full of 'unknown unknowns'.

Nor was there any plausible way to introduce conventional stool pigeons, who would inevitably be too junior to win their confidence and could not stay long enough without arousing suspicion. A British intelligence officer (army Captain Ian Munro, aka 'Lord Aberfeldy') therefore lived on site in the guise of a welfare officer and interpreter.[76] The generals' suspicions were further lulled by ensuring that they were questioned before arrival, giving the impression that Trent Park was simply their accommodation (in a style befitting their rank) for the rest of the war. Brigadier Norman Crockatt, Deputy Director of Military

Intelligence, painted a dryly humorous thumbnail sketch of the scenario in a 1943 letter to C Jones of the US Prisoner of War Branch, MIS-Y.

'I want to refer to telegram No. 169 sent by Kirkman from Strong, in which is said "for morale of long trained interrogators here would be grateful for appetizer in form earliest despatch of some high ranking P/W."

I feel I should let you know our practice here in the case of Generals. These we do not send to C.S.D.I.C. nor do we interrogate them. Instead, they are met on arrival by Major-General GEPP, the Director of Prisoners of War (= your P.M.G. and G.1 combined), and go straight to a Senior Officers Base Camp. This Camp is a large country house in a fine park of its own. The fact that is happens to be "fitted" by us is just too bad. I tell you all this in case, should you intend to follow a similar procedure, you will have time to prepare a house for them before their arrival. You will probably want to consider the point that they will probably not re-act satisfactorily to the Fort Hunt atmosphere after the apparent liberty they have enjoyed in a Base Camp. Meanwhile we are pressing on with trying to get you a nice team of Generals who will mix well and re-act to one another satisfactorily. It is no good sending you chaps who won't talk to one another and it takes a little time to sort them out. But we should get you some off soon.

We are, unfortunately, having lovely weather, and these blasted Generals will spend a lot of their time out of doors instead of in their rooms. It makes our job much more difficult, and I pray nightly for rain.'[77]

CSDIC sent four generals and a colonel awaiting promotion to the United States in June1943, with more following as the war progressed. Only the first batch were housed, briefly, at a special interrogation centre (Camp Tracy in California). Unlike their British counterparts US interrogators did not give these senior officers special treatment or in-depth surveillance during the war but relegated them to standard internment camps. After the war they received much closer attention as the perceived threat shifted to the Soviet Union.[78]

After D-Day the generals at Trent Park were sometimes joined by naval colleagues captured as ports and headquarters fell. For example, *Konteradmiral* (Rear Admiral) Walter Hennecke, who had overseen the destruction of the Cherbourg harbour facilities, arrived on 1st July 1944. The DNI, Commodore Rushbrooke, interviewed him personally, with Lieutenant-Commander McFadyean helping, on 21st July. They found him in a state of depression which only deepened as the interview progressed. This was brought on by the sight of the Allies' overwhelming resources, and fear of Germany and the rest of Europe being overrun by Communism.[79]

Bernard Trench's World Tour

Global cataclysm was no reason to interrupt the daily internecine conflict at Admiralty. Neither Trench nor the DNI, Admiral Godfrey, were the sunniest personalities in the world and their abrasive relationship came to a head in 1942. Trench's diary records,

(2nd January)

'Campbell has played the dirty on me by making me responsible for the loss of some of our C.B.'s [Confidential Books] at the beginning of the war, which were then on his charge. A very sharp memo will reach the D.N.I. tomorrow on the subject.'

(4th January)

'Forwarded memo to D.N.I. & had an interview with him, during which he got very angry, said I was obstinate & mulish, which is quite correct, but he did not allow me to make any explanation. He said that he himself had received an expression of their Lordships'

displeasure. This I could well believe. The impression left on both our minds after the interview was that we both thoroughly disapproved of one another. In addition my feelings are that I have no pleasure in serving in the N.I.D. in this war, after having seen what a well organised & well run N.I.D. was like in the last war. I have now no interest in it & no enthusiasm for it. The D.N.I. has no capacity for instilling enthusiasm in his subordinates. A misfit, so very different from Sir William Hall.'[80]

Only one winner could emerge from such a clash of horns. There is no evidence of a direct link, but the diary entry four months later that the DNI *'wants me to go out to the Middle & Far East to advise on P/W matters'*[81] may be related.

The six-month trip would take him around the world. By the time he returned Colin McFadyean was firmly installed in his job and mainstream interrogation work had moved from Trent Park to the new centres at Latimer House and Wilton Park.

Ironically, by then Godfrey himself had fallen victim to inter-service politics and been succeeded by (then) Captain Edmund Rushbrooke.

Trench held a short and demure farewell gathering at his flat on 11th June. It was attended by nine favoured colleagues including interrogators Cope, Mitchell, Rosevere, McFadyean, Dick Weatherby and Williamson; Mrs Brown (his assistant at Admiralty), and Esmé Mackenzie, a Wren officer at Trent Park.

On 16th he travelled overnight to Glasgow where he met his companions for the trip and boarded the commandeered liner *Queen Elizabeth*. Observing the first boat drill he commented that, with ten thousand men and over eight hundred officers filling every space, a genuine abandon ship order would lead to disaster. The Cunard catering staff were however still there however, so the excellent food was some consolation.

The ship got under way around midnight on the 17th/18th June, initially steaming west with a strong escort at about twenty-five knots. Frequent drills made the evacuation process slicker, but Trench observed, '*I have not been allocated to a boat, so I am with the sinking party.*' The following day she discarded her escort and headed south, zig-zagging at high speed. She gained Freetown, Sierra Leone, in the early evening of 25th, carefully timing her arrival for high tide which was the only moment such a massive ship could enter the port.

They left the following day after taking on oil and water, giving Trench just enough time for a meeting on board with a local intelligence officer about prisoner interrogation. Arriving at Simonstown on 2nd July he discovered that any prisoners landed there were to be sent on to Durban for interrogation, so there was little point in loitering in the Cape area longer than necessary. With the outcome of the North Africa campaign still in the balance air transport was almost unobtainable, so he left by train on 6th, stopping at Johannesburg and Pretoria and arriving on 12th. Meetings at Pretoria and Durban produced material for his first reports.

Trench then arranged onward passage to Kilindini (Mombasa, Kenya) by flying boat. The luggage weight limit for the flight made him abandon his heavy uniform, and an overnight stop in Mozambique, a neutral Portuguese colony, forced him to travel in civilian clothes for fear of internment. He arrived at Kilindini on 16th July and spent ten days in meetings at Mombasa and Nairobi, including a lecture at the local Bletchley Park outpost which was mostly concerned with Japanese traffic.

In August 1941, the General Officer Commanding-in-Chief (GOC-in-C) West Africa had proposed setting up small interrogation centres with listening facilities at Accra and Freetown. Godfrey was initially sceptical, replying,

'With reference to your M.I.9(c)/FOL/42/3 of 25th August, I see no objection to the establishment of a unit in West Africa similar to the C.S.D.I.C. in the United Kingdom and Middle East, but I do not

think it desirable from the naval point of view that German naval Prisoners of War should be retained in Freetown or Accra for interrogation.

2. Since German naval prisoners who would be landed in West Africa would either come from U-boats, raiders, or supply ships, the information obtained from them is of greater importance to the Admiralty than to local authorities in West Africa. Therefore we would prefer that they should be sent to the United Kingdom for examination here, since all the information which serves as a background for interrogation is only available in the Admiralty.

3. Should the situation demand we would be glad to send out naval personnel for one or other of these centres, but meanwhile it is considered that our interests can be served by means of a watching brief held by S.O.(I) Freetown.'[82]

Nonetheless preparations continued, on the assumption that most prisoners would be Vichy French. The Post Office Research Station agreed to supply three of the latest listening sets within existing financial cover.

On 27th October 1941, with everything in train, MI9(c) sent a cypher telegram to the GOC-in-C West Africa confirming the arrangements. Crucially, this included a minimum staffing requirement of twelve intelligence officers, six technicians, five clerks and nine general duties infantry personnel. All but two or three key officers were to be found locally. This quickly produced a reply to the effect that it was impossible to find the staff from his authorised strength. The equipment supply was cancelled, and the project stood down. A letter from Major-General Davidson to Godfrey and Air Vice Marshal Medhurst in February drove the point home.

'This is to the effect that, whilst the experts advised that small static units could be set up at Freetown and Lagos Accra involving an increase of but two technical other ranks over existing establishments, the scheme must remain in abeyance for the present, since even the

small increase in European personnel entailed cannot be accepted, in view of the limitations imposed by the ceiling figures and of the priority needs of other requirements.

If you agree, therefore, I propose to drop the matter for the time being.[83]

The case for a permanent centre in West Africa was difficult to argue, though in practice interrogators were flown from Cairo for preliminary interviews of survivors landed in Freetown.

From December, however, war with Japan and the quick succession of defeats in South-East Asia made a compelling case for better intelligence in the Indian Ocean. Although the Deputy C-in-C Eastern Fleet, Vice-Admiral Peter Danckwerts, was sceptical about the chance of having any prisoners to deal with, Trench's reports added new impetus to work in progress on a CSDIC near Mombasa. A house and grounds were requisitioned at Nyali about six miles away. The plan was that the building would house staff and the M Rooms while tents provided prisoner accommodation and interrogation rooms. Experience in Egypt had shown that their low reverberation gave a much cleaner acoustic environment than permanent buildings, and they had the added advantage of making it easier to move the equipment if necessary.

Colonel Charles Lamplough RM (Deputy DNI) summed up the situation in a memo from Admiralty to MI19 dated 21st October 1942:

'According to a report from Colonel Trench, it appears that the construction of a camp at Mombasa may have been commenced, and he suggests that two rooms in this camp should be equipped with special listening apparatus and accommodation provided for the following Naval prisoners of war:- 5 Officers, 10 Chief or Petty Officers, 40 men. He recommends the Naval Interrogation Staff should consist of 2 Japanese-speaking Naval Officers, 1 German-

speaking Naval Officer, 1 lady clerk, if possible with a knowledge of Japanese.

3. Interrogation of prisoners is robbed of a great deal of its value without the use of listening apparatus, but Trench in his report states that 1 Japanese-speaking Military Officer is expected shortly (report dated July 1942) and 3 or 4 more are to come later. I presume, therefore, that these Officers will be available to man the special apparatus.'[84]

German-speaking interrogators would be flown from Cairo if required, while Mombasa's Japanese speakers could reinforce the Indian centre. The twenty-five ratings then undergoing intensive Japanese language instruction in London were not expected to be of much value.

A MI19 minute of 26th October also refers to *'the centre now being formed at MOMBASA.'*[85]

On 26th July Trench set out by flying boat on the two-day journey to Cairo, with overnight and refuelling stops on Lake Victoria and along the Nile. While there he visited the prison camp cum interrogation centre at Al Maadi, where he met Lieutenant-Commander Gustav Rodd to discuss the upgrades needed at Mombasa and received enthusiastic co-operation. While memos of escalating bewilderment flew between Admiralty and MI19 in London Rodd quietly got on with the job, visiting the site in September to plan the installation. At the beginning of November, acting on the principle that it is better to ask for forgiveness than permission, he sent a cypher telegram stating simply, *'Captain Hayward and two signalmen leave today for Mombasa to install centre. Request approval.'*[86]

In the event it seems likely that the Kilindini centre was completed but not routinely used. Commander (Retired) Stephen Lushington, a fluent Japanese speaker, was posted from Trade Division to NID Kilindini on 1st September 1943 as 'Officer i/c Language Personnel' with no-one visibly reporting to him. By October 1944 he led a substantial CSDIC and SEATIC section at Kandy in Ceylon (now Sri Lanka), which was the location first intended for a South-East Asian naval intelligence centre.[87] Survivors of *U-852* (sunk 3rd May 1944) were however brought to East Africa (presumably Kilindini) for preliminary interrogation.[88] Eight, including the captain, were flown directly from there to the UK. Prisoners in both centres admitted the boat's part in the massacre of *Peleus* survivors (see Human Wrongs below), which sealed the fate of three of their officers.

Trench left on 4th August, again by flying boat, on the four-day trip to Delhi. The eventful journey involved an overnight stop at Kalia on the Dead Sea, where the resort manageress spoke only German and was suspiciously curious about Trench's movements. The aircraft was repeatedly plagued by engine trouble which culminated in an extra stopover at Karachi while the offending motor was changed.

On arrival in Delhi Trench made his way to the imposing Red Fort, which housed India's CSDIC. This section had been created recently, when proposals to set up a facility in Singapore and then Burma had been overtaken by the incredibly swift Japanese advance. The equipment destined for Singapore had therefore been diverted to India. Japanese language skills were a major constraint, and it was thought that it might be possible to identify suitable Japanese-speaking Chinese refugees.[89]

There he met an interrogator and the senior available officers, most of whom did not impress him. Meetings the next day with the Directors of Personnel Services and Military Intelligence were enough for him to conclude his business and write up his report.

There were six Japanese army prisoners in residence at the time and Brigadier Cawthorn, the Director of Military Intelligence, was anxious to add naval expertise to his interrogation team.[90] Trench identified three officers in the Royal

Indian Navy who were fluent Japanese speakers and suggested they could be trained as interrogators.

The CSDIC India War Diary for June 1945 records that *'Early in the month the special segregation rooms and the D.I. rooms were completed.'*[91] This implies that the Red Fort did not have a functioning M Room at the time of Trench's visit. There is an intriguing suggestion that some of the senior German officers captured in North Africa may have been sent to India, but I have found no corroboration.[92]

> Trench's state of mind was bleak. He confided to his diary, *'The Russians seem to be retreating still and everything seems to be going in favour of the Axis. We are doing nothing, waiting for the Russians to be defeated, so that Germany can concentrate on us. I have no confidence at all in our Government – ostrich like they bury their heads in the sand. There seems no prospect of the Allies winning the war; the only hope is that we may avoid losing it, but in any case we shall lose most of our empire.'*[93]

On 13th August Trench set off by an extraordinarily convoluted route for his eventual arrival in Australia. It first involved a return to Cairo by air, then by stages to Durban where he boarded the independently sailing merchantman *Desirade*, about 12,000 tons. Her maximum speed of about 11½ knots ensured a leisurely passage, arriving at Sydney on 27th September.

On arrival he went to the Naval Headquarters on Garden Island and met Admiral Muirhead-Gould, who had formerly been naval attaché in Berlin and was later Flag Officer Western Germany until his untimely death in June 1945.

Trench then travelled overnight to Melbourne, discussing prisoner interrogation with intelligence officers there from 2nd to 5th October. Returning to Sydney, he flew to New Zealand on 8th. While there he observed the interrogation of an army prisoner at Featherston camp, about 41 miles from Wellington.

He then received instructions from the Admiralty to co-ordinate his onward travel with Lieutenant-Commander Ralph Albrecht, USN, who was not due to arrive at Brisbane until about 7th November. This gave him time for a little sightseeing before his return to Australia. Trench had met Albrecht earlier, facilitating his visit to Britain in April 1942 when he had been shown around Trent Park, inspected HMS *Graph* (formerly *U-570*) and the preparation of the Latimer and Wilton Park sites.[94]

Trench flew back to Sydney on 30th October, spent a couple of days there writing up his report, then travelled by train to Brisbane (site of Australia's central interrogation facility at Indooroopilly) on 5th/6th November. Albrecht arrived on 8th. The next few days were spent in further report writing, planning their programme, and in discussions with senior naval, intelligence and political figures.

Trench and Albrecht finally left on Monday 23rd November. They island-hopped across the Pacific, flying via New Caledonia, Fiji, Palmyra Atoll and Honolulu (Pearl Harbour), where they spent five days in further talks and arranging onward transport. They arrived at San Francisco on Wednesday 2nd December, just having time to visit the West Coast interrogation centre at Camp Tracy, Byron Hot Springs before catching an evening train to Washington via Los Angeles and Chicago.

They reached Washington on Monday 7th December and were met by Albrecht's wife and son. Trench dined with the family that evening and spent the next few days meeting British and American naval officers including Albrecht's superior, Commander John Riheldaffer. He also visited Fort Hunt, the recently opened US interrogation centre near Washington.

On 11th December Trench said his farewells and boarded a train to New York where he boarded the SS *Westerland* the next day. Never the most 'clubbable' of people he expressed little gratitude for the open-hearted hospitality he had received in Washington.

Westerland sailed with a slow convoy of about a hundred ships on 13th. The next day, in an unnerving few hours, she was forced to stop and repair a steering gear failure, then put on her unimpressive best speed to catch up with the convoy. A straggler was every U-boat skipper's dream.

The rest of the voyage was uneventful, and Trench arrived at Greenock on 28th, caught the overnight train to London where he found tenants still occupying his flat. He therefore reported directly to the Admiralty where he was informed of a proposal that he should become Deputy Director of Naval Intelligence – Prisoners of War (DDNI(P/W)).

Subsequent events suggest this 'promotion' was more like a palace coup. Colin McFadyean had been promoted (over Cope's head) to Trench's former Admiralty desk NID1 (P/W), and Trench's diary suggests that his official duties took up much less of his time from this point onward. In deteriorating health, he was allowed to retire in December 1944.

At about the same time as Trench's homecoming Major D McMillan, normally based in Cairo, returned from a technical tour of C.S.D.I.C. installations in India, Australia, and America. His experience informed the design of mobile eavesdropping units for use in North Africa, Burma, and Australia. He noted that US-designed equipment was 'very inferior to that developed for use in this country'. Later practical experience found that an American portable tape recorder worked better in tropical conditions than British disc recorders.[95]

McMillan is not mentioned in the Trench diaries so, despite treading the same ground at roughly the same time, it is unlikely their paths crossed.

The Mediterranean Club

On 23rd June 1940 Admiral John Godfrey, Director of Naval Intelligence, sent a memo to his army opposite number Major General Beaumont-Nesbitt, copied to Air Commodore Boyle. It began,

> *As we are now taking numbers of Italian prisoners from all three of their Services, and, in view of the valuable information we obtain from Cockfosters, I feel it is desirable to have a similar institution in the Middle East.'*

Though phrased as a suggestion, Godfrey made it clear that he was already looking into the naval staffing requirements.

By 1st July, the proposal had been agreed in principle by the three services in Britain and by the Commander-in-Chief Middle East. A paper dated 13th July outlined the proposed staffing and equipment needs (three naval, four RAF and thirty army interrogators, supported by ten listening positions with two recorders each) and anticipated the need for skilled technical support to cope with the very different environment. British GPO recorders would be procured instead of the American RCA equipment originally rushed into the Tower, both to minimise the overall cost and to preserve precious foreign currency. The Cairo area was selected as the best location, and a memo explaining the plan in more detail was forwarded to the C-in-C Middle East.[96]

Despite having instigated the project, Godfrey had second thoughts. Retired Engineering Lieutenant-Commander William Rosevere arrived for interview from his home in Belfast in July, while the DNI claimed to be searching for suitable officers to staff the Cairo centre. Rosevere's command of Italian, German, French and Spanish seemed perfect for the role, but he was immediately told there was no work for him at Admiralty and no need for him in the Mediterranean.[97] His commission was eventually reactivated in October. It is unclear whether he made an unfavourable first impression, or Godfrey was torn between the benefits of rapid processing in theatre or shipping prisoners back to Britain for in-depth examination.

On 19th July, the sinking of the Italian cruiser *Bartolomeo Colleoni* and rescue of over five hundred prisoners brought the matter to a head. Lieutenant-Commander (Retired) Gustaf Rodd, a former Assistant Naval Attaché in Rome, left for Egypt in August. RNVR Lieutenant William Nussbaum and Sub-Lieutenant Richard Long (both of whom knew Italy) went with him. As the workload grew the section would be strengthened by Rosevere, Lieutenant Edward Davies and Heneage Emmet, who would contribute a post-war paper on the subject.[98]

The first centre went live at Al Maadi near Cairo in December 1940, with a capacity to handle about sixty prisoners at a time. The fluid nature of war in the Middle East theatre, the army's dominant role, the long distances involved and the urgent need for short-term operational intelligence quickly imposed a different approach from that used by CSDIC UK.

Prisoners were interviewed at division and army level before reaching CSDIC, to try and capture ephemeral intelligence while it still had value. This contrasted sharply with the UK's care to avoid any risk of priming CSDIC's subjects about the gaps in their interrogators' knowledge. As Charles Mitchell later observed,

> '...they laid great store by forward interrogation units, with mobile microphone equipment, etc., keeping pace with a fluid campaign. The results (as seen from the Admiralty end) were disappointing, largely because interrogators in the field lacked the necessary information for cross-checking from other sources: in other words, the idea of mobile interrogation units is based on the false assumption that one source of intelligence is of value without others to supplement it.'[99]

Mitchell's point reinforced the lesson that technology was no substitute for the elaborate confidence trickery developed in the First World War and based on a comprehensive filing system. When Forward Interrogation Unit went into action alongside Assault Unit 30 in Normandy and North-West Europe in 1944 its interrogators did not bring microphones with them – but did have access to relevant background information for all kinds of tactical interrogation.

Intelligence officers were accompanied in both forward and rear areas by Political Warfare interrogators, looking for anti-Nazi captives whose experiences could be quickly turned around in propaganda leaflets.[100]

As in the UK the listeners were originally bilingual officers, but they were replaced from October 1942 by NCOs, usually Jewish refugees from Palestine, who were native Italian or German speakers. In a sharp departure from British practice some of them met (and spoke with) the prisoners under observation to help with voice recognition. This was arranged by presenting them in catering or welfare roles. In 1942 some of them went further, joining a Special Interrogation Group (SIG) formed to operate behind enemy lines at immense personal risk to its members.[101] This was a precursor to the Forward Interrogation Unit which provided such valuable service in the 1944-45 North-West Europe campaign.

In mid-1941 CSDIC took over the field interrogation duties previously carried out by general service intelligence officers, releasing the latter for army staff work. CSDIC interrogators rotated between central and field work. Inevitably this increased the section's emphasis on the army's needs at the expense of the navy and the air force.

Another consequence of haste was that direct interrogation assumed much greater prominence compared to covert listening and stool pigeon reports than it did in the UK. As a later report by the Office of the Assistant Chief of Staff G-2 put it,

'Prisoners that reached the U.K. were not required to give operational intelligence. By the time they reached the U.K. their operational information was old. Such information as they had to give was of a long term nature and usually of the highly technical kind. Patience and accurate recording of "X" source [covert listening] was the only technique possible. In the Mediterranean theatre operational intelligence had priority over any other intelligence; thus the Centre concentrated first on direct interrogation for operational intelligence, and at the same time made selections for long term intelligence in the U.K.' [102]

Conversations later overheard between prisoners in Britain suggest the pressure for quick results sometimes prompted measures which stepped well over the Geneva Convention line. They supposedly included fifteen-hour interrogations by questioners working in shifts, and prisoners ordered to dig what they were told were their own graves. [103] The allegations are strenuously denied in the official history of CSDIC Mediterranean, which notes:

'Many complaints of ill-treatment of P/W were received by the Protecting Power as alleged to have taken place at the Interrogation Centre. Most complaints were easily disposed of by the very nature of the complaints themselves, which were so obviously tendentious, also because the complaints could not have been supported by independent or even enemy witnesses. These complaints were nevertheless an embarrassment and a careful record of P/W processing was kept in order that the complaints could be refuted. Every interrogation of a P/W was duly recorded on the P/W's personal card, with the name of the interrogator, so that records of the interrogation reports, which included a short description of the mental attitude of the P/W towards interrogation, could be turned up and checked. An accurate record was also kept of all other P/W with whom a prisoner had been in

contact during his stay at the Centre. No violence or man handling was tolerated under any circumstances.'[104]

The microphone and recorder equipment sent out from the UK at first proved too fragile for the climate and physical conditions of Egypt. Field modifications mitigated the problem, but the kit always needed a higher level of skilled maintenance than in more temperate areas.

Subsidiary interrogation centres with microphone-equipped rooms were set up in Omdurman (December 1940), Rehovot (Rehovot?) in Palestine (July 1941), Baghdad (March 1942) and Bethlehem (June 1942).

Conversations and evaluation visits between March and July 1941 about setting up a CSDIC in Malta were not followed up at first. A cipher telegram to Lieutenant-Colonel Crockatt in charge of MI19 on 18th July read,

'H.E. [His Excellency, the Governor] has ruled that (2 groups undecipherable) expenditure involved does not justify the installation of an "M" centre in Malta for small number of prisoners available.'[105]

Another setback occurred when ship carrying the first set of equipment to Malta was sunk in transit. A small installation eventually opened in March 1943 and operated until October, supporting the landings in Sicily.

As the Eighth Army advancing from the east and the First Army from the west met in May 1943 a joint Anglo-American centre with six bugged rooms was set up in Birkhadem, a village about six miles south of Algiers. The intelligence team were late on the scene with the result that the best accommodation had already been 'bagged' by other units. The official history describes the premises as 'profoundly unsatisfactory' and the results as 'only just about good enough.'[106] More worryingly, there are indications that the microphones were inadequately hidden. N2401 (*Leutnant zur See* Spitz, *U-223*) told a cellmate when he got to Britain,

> 'In the interrogation camp at ALGIERS there were microphones. There were two German officers who were probably stool-pigeons; we had to go on daily walks with them.'[107]

While the naval and air force interrogation teams used stool pigeons the army, who managed the Middle East centres and relied almost exclusively on direct interrogation, did not. One consequence may have been less careful attention to their insertion and cover story. Junior officers from *U-450* and *U-223* compared notes about their experience in Algiers after they reached the UK.

> 'N2402:   There was an 'Oberleutnant' from the GAF [German Air Force] in the camp at ALGIERS who was most certainly a stool-pigeon. He was very talkative. He said amazing things about a weapon for reprisals etc. He had black hair and a round face.
>
> N2343:   Yes, he was in my room, but as a captain. He had dark eyes, hadn't he?
>
> N2402:   Yes. I wrote on the window there: "Look - out, stool-pigeon"!'[108]

Every cloud has a silver lining. On arrival in the UK, they seemed to have no suspicion of the subtler use of microphones and stool pigeons at the CSDIC centres there.

A theatre-specific innovation was the development of 'binaural' or stereo microphones which could be hidden in tent poles. These, combined with the lack of reverberation in a tent and the silence of the desert, allowed listeners in mobile units to 'steer' the microphones' reception by adjusting their volume and thus discriminate between several different voices. They did not have stereo recorders, so the mobile units relied entirely on listeners' shorthand. The experience gained with 'binaural' microphones later (from July 1944) proved useful in static installations which did not always have the luxury of a quiet environment, as in the UK.

Reports from CSDIC Middle East condensed what the interrogating officer felt were the most relevant passages from each conversation into a summary covering several days and topics. Worse, at least from a historian's perspective, they appear to be dated when the record was typed up and not when the conversation took place. This is apparent from transcripts bearing dates after the subjects must have embarked for the UK.

The mobile units were introduced in May 1942 to bridge the gap between forward intelligence teams who could only give captives the most cursory attention and the 'cages' at Cairo and Algiers. Five were set up to provide timely information at army level and are of little relevance to the naval focus of this book.

Following the invasion of Italy, the British staff at Birkhadem moved forward to a new site in the village of Portici near Naples, which proved equally unsuitable for their needs. In June 1944, the unit took up residence in much better accommodation with seventeen 'miked' rooms at Centrocelle near Rome. In parallel, a unit staffed by Italian officers was set up to screen refugees from the occupied north of the country.

The American unit at Birkhadem moved to southern France in September 1944 following the success of Operation *Dragoon*, the Provence landings, in August.

A small, static unit was set up at Alexandria in June 1944 to assist with the interrogation of Greek mutineers. It operated for only a few weeks and closed as soon as its temporary purpose was achieved.

From a naval perspective the achievements of CSDIC Mediterranean may be less spectacular than those of the pioneering home unit, but only in the context of the Battle of the Atlantic and of the mine menace. The team's work was hampered by an organisation oriented toward quick results and by a degree of inter-service and inter-Allied friction not met in the UK.

A reorganisation in early 1944 divided the Mediterranean theatre into three areas for interrogation. CSDIC AFHQ (Armed Forces Headquarters) at Algiers was responsible for the North African coast west of the Tunisia-Tripolitania frontier, plus Corsica, France, and Spain. CSDIC CMF at Naples was responsible for interrogation in Italy, the Adriatic, the Balkans, and Central Europe. CSDIC ME (Middle East) at Cairo covered the African coast east of the Tunisia-Tripolitania frontier plus the Levant, Greece, Romania, and Bulgaria. It reported to C-in-C Mediterranean. Each centre was to concentrate on the enemy order of battle affecting its area. There were lively debates about how best to apportion resources and work between them, the UK, and the US.[109]

A further complication was the desire of the Free French to get involved. Since the enemy recognised only the Vichy French government the Free French would not be deemed to have ratified the 1929 Geneva Convention. It was feared that any allegation of mistreatment by their officers would rebound on Allied prisoners. Moreover, participation there might lead to demand for access to British centres, which was completely unacceptable on security grounds and best avoided before it arose. The question was escalated to the Joint Intelligence Committee (JIC) in London. Despite pleas from local commanders the reply was clear.

'THE SUB-COMMITEE had before them a Memorandum (M.I.19(a)/CC/250/7 dated 8th April, 1943) by the Director of Military Intelligence, stating that an offer had been received from the Head of the Polish Intelligence organisation of the services of a Polish Intelligence Officer now in Algeria, for the purpose of interrogating Axis prisoners of war of Polish origin captured in North Africa. The Memorandum also referred to a proposal put forward by the Chief

Intelligence Officer at Allied Force Headquarters for the employment of a number of French Officers in the Combined Services Detailed Interrogation Centre in North Africa. ....

THE SUB-COMMITTEE were reminded that we and the Americans were responsible under the Geneva Convention for the treatment accorded to prisoners of war detained by us respectively. Many of our Allies were not parties to the Convention. Their methods of interrogation might not conform with the rules laid down in the Convention or with our standards. It was highly undesirable that we should lay ourselves open to criticism as regards the treatment of prisoners of war in our hands. It would not be feasible for Allied Officers to carry out the detailed interrogation of prisoners of war under supervision.

It was, however, suggested that we might well agree to Allied Officers interrogating prisoners of war a good deal further forward in the battle area at, for example, the prisoners of war interrogation sections at Army Headquarters.

THE SUB-COMMITTEE: -

Instructed the Secretary, in consultation with Brigadier Crockett, to prepare a telegram to the Chief Intelligence Officer at Allied Force Headquarters, giving the Sub-Committee's reasons for refusing to agree to the suggestion that selected French Officers should be employed in the C.S.D.I.C. in North Africa, but suggesting that such Officers might take part in the interrogation of prisoners of war further forward.' [110]

The French response was to interrogate their own prisoners and pass them directly to their own internment camps, with consequent loss of intelligence sharing. Under protest from local commanders, who pointed out that their separate prisoner handling prevented any chance of controlling their treatment of captives, JIC modified its view. Four named French and one Polish officer were allowed to work at CSDIC Algiers under supervision. JIC was adamant however that there was to be *no* French access to the UK CSDIC sites.

Despite their political and environmental difficulties, the Mediterranean CSDIC teams gave early warning in early 1944 of the equipment, personnel, organisation, and tactics of the 'small battle units' which could have caused a major headache off the Normandy beaches (see below). Their results, combined with those of their UK colleagues, kept the C-in-C Mediterranean informed of the U-boats which had attempted the perilous passage of the Straits of Gibraltar, who commanded them, and how many survived. By the end of September 1944 there were none left. A retrospective (army) evaluation commented, '*The successful development of anti submarine warfare was mainly due to P/W interrogation and "X" source [microphones] work.*'[111] Captives also gave valuable information about coastal defences in southern France – indeed, some who had worked on the Atlantic Wall were hastily shipped to Britain and drained of their topographical knowledge in preparation for D-Day. The urgency and importance of the need can be gauged by AFHQ's success in persuading the Air Priorities Board to increase its allocation for prisoner transport from twenty to 40-50 per month.[112]

Overlord and After

In the run up to the Normandy landings, codenamed *Overlord*, Naval Intelligence staff had two principal concerns: doing all in their power to ensure their success and planning how best to exploit the foothold once gained. The experience of sudden surges like that in January 1944, when the survivors of five vessels arrived almost simultaneously, showed that the methodical processes they had developed for extracting high quality intelligence would not cope with the expected flood of new clients.[113] Moreover, experienced interrogators would be needed further forward. Something had to give.

As a first step CSDIC produced a distilled summary of the U-boat intelligence acquired up to June 1944.[114] This signalled that they would not produce such detailed reports in future, unless there was important new intelligence to convey. Instead, their efforts would focus on questionnaires produced (and sometimes hastily scribbled) to meet the information needs of the Allied Expeditionary Force.

As preparations gained pace the service reoriented to meet the challenge. Detailed planning was under way from February 1944 on the working assumption that 2,000-2,500 prisoners per day would arrive at British ports,[115] from which 100-250 per day would be selected at a reception camp for further questioning, and 15-25 for detailed interrogation at CSDIC. It was accepted that many would be interrogated in the field before embarkation in the search for urgent operational intelligence.[116] Trench was acutely aware of the strain that such a volume would place on the finite resources available. Chairing an Anglo-American planning meeting on 9th February 1944 he added the following pre-emptive defence to the minutes.

'4. General remarks regarding Interrogation.

a) it must be clearly understood that no one unless trained can interrogate usefully. Training takes several weeks.

b) The Naval Section of the C.S.D.I.C. must not be considered as a pool from which trained interrogators can be drawn on demand.

c) During invasion the Naval Section of the C.S.D.I.C. will be fully occupied in interrogating Prisoners of War sent back and with those Prisoners of War in hospitals or cages near the disembarcation [sic] ports to which interrogators may have to be sent.

d) Therefore interrogation staff for A.N.C.X.F[117] must be specially appointed and earmarked for this duty and trained at the C.S.D.I.C. beforehand.'[118]

In the agreed scheme landing ships returning from the beaches deposited prisoners, mainly at Southampton for those taken in the British sector and Portland for those in the American sector. Their first stop after that was a reception 'cage' at Kempton Park and Devizes respectively for delousing, sorting, and preliminary interview. From there, those thought to have no relevant information were sent straight to camps whence they might eventually find their way to internment in the US or Canada. Those with limited intelligence value were sent on to Lingfield Park (UK) or a second Devizes camp (US). Those who turned out either on first or second look to be more interesting (which still included all U-boat survivors) were sent on to CSDIC at Latimer or Wilton Park. Ordinary prisoners were then 'dumped' to base camps while senior officers, having completed (as they thought) their interrogation made their final transfer to the comfort of Trent Park.[119]

In a further refinement the Political Warfare Executive, based on its experience in North Africa, planned to base a small team at Lingfield Cage. Its job would be to identify and filter off a few articulate, anti-Nazi prisoners to write and appear in propaganda broadcasts and leaflets. The Executive had already recruited at least twenty disaffected captives who had been flown from North Africa in March and April, along with a steady feed of volunteers and former stool pigeons from other sources.[120]

At about the same time residents of the original Number 1 Camp at Grizedale Hall, which was by then a retirement home for stool pigeons and propagandists who had outlived their usefulness, were moved to a segregated compound at Ascot. This overcame a developing capacity problem and kept them more accessible in case the intelligence community needed to pick their brains.

As *Overlord* finally launched there were eight naval interrogators still working at CSDIC. Ralph Izzard, Julius

Lunzer and Charles Wheeler were detached to the Forward Interrogation Unit (see below).[121] Michael Reade and John Wilkinson (an NID staffer who does not appear on the formal CSDIC strength) took up residence at Lingfield Cage, and Charles Everett at Kempton Park.[122] In December 1944 Burton Cope left to mobilise Naval Party 1735 (see Naval Parties below) and Bernard Trench, whose role had been largely bypassed, was finally allowed to retire. This left a skeleton naval staff at the core CSDIC sites. Dick Weatherby and Harry Scholar were at Latimer, Donald Welbourn and Stuart Marriner at Wilton Park. John Weatherby's location is uncertain, and some reports are attributed to a Segner, apparently at Wilton, who may have been a US intelligence officer on secondment.

The Italian naval section in the UK was largely redundant, as the *Regia Marina* almost entirely ceased to be a threat after the armistice of 1943. William Rosevere, the former section head, was preparing to go to Germany with the occupation forces when he was run over by a tram and died in March 1945.

Prisoners had already given up valuable information about the location, design and manning of coastal defences which could be used to plan the preparatory bombardment. Even more pertinently from the navy's perspective they described the standing orders which applied to the still-potent forces in the Biscay bases – Brest, St Nazaire, La Pallice and Bordeaux. On receiving the invasion alert every seaworthy U-boat was to sortie against the Allied fleets. In the event thirty-five attempted to get through the wall of anti-submarine ships and aircraft across the Western Approaches. Just five made it back. The vulnerable destroyers and torpedo-boats did not even try.

In the Channel the defenders were increasingly forced to rely on 'small battle units'. These were hastily developed mini-submarines, human torpedoes, or explosive-packed speedboats with crews whose training was equally rushed. In theory they were *not* sent on suicide missions. In theory.

The National Archives has a photograph taken on 6th July 1944 on the beach at Courseulles. Lt Cdr Ralph Izzard is interviewing a human torpedo pilot who looks like a petulant child, dwarfed next to Izzard's 6-foot 4-inch frame.[123] The lucky survivor had run into one of the small Forward Interrogation Unit (FIU) team attached to 30 Assault Unit (30AU). Charles Mitchell, who was himself involved with FIU, observed,

> *'...the forward interrogation units (which did <u>not</u> have or need microphones) attached to A.N.C.X.F. after the invasion of the Continent were a resounding success, not only because they were staffed by some of the best British and U.S. interrogators trained in C.S.D.I.C's, but because at that time the relevant background information of all kinds for tactical interrogation was in the hands of A.N.C.X.F. [Allied Naval Commander Expeditionary Force] rather than in Admiralty. But even then, arrangements were made to get prisoners sent back very quickly to C.S.D.I.C. for detailed interrogation.'[124]*

30AU, a brainchild of Ian Fleming, was a mixed group of marines and intelligence specialists briefed to go with (or sometimes ahead of) front-line troops and grab anything or anyone of naval interest. It arrived with a typed list of locations, equipment, and people likely to be relevant. The list had known shortcomings: an introductory caveat read,

> *'3. The intelligence contained in this document should not be graded higher than C. Further, it should be carefully borne in mind that all pinpoints and localities listed as possible targets may alter as a result of bombing or evacuation. Interrogation of prisoners in the field and up-to-date aerial photographs will probably be the only reliable cross-checks.*
>
> *4. The latest date of intelligence contained in this edition is 15th April, 1944.'[125]*

The intelligence targets were prioritised according to the standard NID classification, with the appropriate level of effort and risk matched to each. So 'A1' justified 'the mounting of special operations and the incurring of heavy casualties on the part of 30 Assault Unit,' 'B1' was worth 'crossing the enemy's line, subject to no extraordinary risks being taken,' whereas 'B2' and 'C' were to be seized in cleaning-up and guarded until specialists arrived respectively.

'A1' material included any code books, encryption machines and their components. Ominously, the briefing notes went on,

'The necessity for avoiding or eliminating witnesses to successful action and for the demolition of any building or ship's cabin and which has yielded results and which is likely to be re-occupied by the enemy is emphasised.'

Specific details in the brief, such as 'In the case of ST. NAZAIRE it is reported that the secret books are kept in a light metal chest in an office in the pens: the door is marked only with the name "Oberschreibersmaat Fritz Frank" without reference to his employment' can only have come from someone familiar with that highly secure environment – most likely a prisoner of war.

The only other 'A1' target was 'Any mine working on a new principle used in the invasion,' which illustrates the continuing urgency of this topic (see 'The more there is of mine …' below).

Thanks to advance intelligence and the help of Resistance guides a 30AU column in unarmoured vehicles was able to reach Paris 24 to 48 hours ahead of the general advance and go straight to the U-boat headquarters and Torpedo Arsenal West in the Bois de Boulogne. Prisoners who had been on courses there helped fill out details of the nature and location of the vast complex, encouraged by stool pigeons building on partial information. In May 1944, our friend A713, by now impersonating a U-boat skipper, encouraged Leutnant zur See Mertsch of U-448 to describe his experience.

*'N2446:   …He (IO) kept on wanting to know where my
course was. I didn't tell him, because I believe its whereabouts interest
them very much and that's why I haven't told them.*

N/A713:   Not in the Place de la Concorde?

N2446:   No.

N/A713:   Not at the BdU either?

*N2446:   No, it's a new place, you wouldn't know it. No-one
con get in, it's a military prohibited area.*

…

N/A713:   Where did you stay?

*N2446:   The first time we were put up in the BdU's house, an
enormous palace out by the "Bois de Boulogne", "Rue Général de
……", one of the five ROTHSCHILD palaces, not far from the "de
la Pompe" metro station.'*[126]

A torpedoman from the same boat helped fill out more detail.

'(cf S.R.N.3595)

N/A713:   Whereabouts in PARIS were you?

*N2440:   It was at the beginning of February of this year. We
were there only for three days, with Oberleutnant BAST. I don't
know what the place was called. At first we lived in the BdU house
and then we went out to the shelter down there. It's right under the
ground. Admiral DÖNITZ had formed a new torpedo school.*

N/A713:   Near VINCENNES?

N2440:   I believe that was the name. It's a very large shelter.

N/A713:   You drove from the BdU house –

*N2440:   We went by bus southwards, it took about thirty
minutes, you have to go over the SEINE. It's been formed quite
recently, it's only for these instructional courses.*

N/A713:   Were you billeted in the BdU house?

N2440:   Yes.

N/A713:   At the Porte de la Mouette?

N2440:   Yes.

…

N2440:   We drove to the SEINE and then round beyond the SEINE and then for some distance along the left bank of the SEINE. I believe we turned off to the left afterwards. I don't know it very exactly, I have only driven that route three times.

N/A713:   I believe that is at VINCENNES.

N2440:   Yes, that was written on our ...... paper. We didn't pay any particular attention to it.'[127]

This and other snippets gave the marines and technicians of 30AU the precise directions they needed to overrun the vast underground bunker before the garrison had time to recover from Resistance sabotage operations. The intelligence take was immense, including intact torpedoes, fire control and GSR equipment, and a fine haul of research and administrative documentation.[128]

With the help of intelligence received both from 30AU and from the flood of prisoners taken after D-Day the target list was re-issued as a revised, expanded, and professionally printed pocketbook in December 1944. Most of the team returned to Britain after the fall of Paris to rest, reorganise and digest the results so far. They were now girding their loins for the Rhine crossing and final assault on Germany.

The UK interrogation teams had to cope with a vastly increased flow of prisoners after D-Day, and with the loss of some of their most experienced officers to the FIU and teams being set up for the planned occupation of Germany. When Cope joined the exodus on 7th December 1944. Commodore Rushbrooke, the Director of Naval Intelligence, gave him this parting tribute:

'During five years of war the interrogation of prisoners of war has been developed from an incidental source of Intelligence to one of unique value; the Royal Navy and other Services have become reliant upon it; and this result is largely due to the persistent and imaginative effort of yourself and your team at Cockfosters and Latimer.'[129]

[2]   TNA ADM 234/994.
[3]   Croghan died in an air crash on his way to Gibraltar in December 1941.
[4]   TNA ADM 223/464. P.23.
[5]   GPO 1, 24/8/1940.
[6]   The speaker is not identified in the report but is probably Heinz Marticke of *U-33*. When the boat was sunk off the Isle of Arran the rotors from its Enigma code machine were distributed between crew members told to drop them in the sea. One failed to do so, resulting in the capture of three rotors (two of them previously unknown).
[7]   TNA WO 208/4141. SRN 32 (14/3/40).
[8]   TNA WO 208/4200. Extract from SR Draft No 2062 (2/3/44).
[9]   Ibid. Extract from SR Draft No WG 951A (10/4/44).
[10] TNA WO 208/4200. Extract from SR Draft No WG 586/45 (13/3/45)
[11] TNA WO 208/4970. Appendix E, P.2-3.
[12] TNA AIR 40/2394.
[13] TNA ADM 186/805, P.7-13. NB: Many reports in ADM 186/805 are superseded by later versions, which I have not yet tracked down.
[14] Ibid. P.17-28.
[15] The meal and stool pigeon, along with many useful dates, are recorded in his diary from Diary 11/2/38-29/11/39 (NMRN 2017/24/27), in the National Museum of the Royal Navy, Portsmouth, Library (NMRNP).
[16] TNA ADM 1/9777. P.4.
[17] TNA ADM 186/805.
[18] TNA ADM 1/10069. Letter from F R Cobb, Commandant of Grizedale Hall, dated 25/12/39.
[19] TNA ADM 186/805. P.18.
[20] TNA ADM 186/805. P.3.
[21] TNA WO 208/4141. SRN 15 (19/2/40).
[22] Bernard Trench diary 30/11/39-14/9/41 (NMRN 2017/24/28); entry for 11/12/39.
[23] TNA ADM 1/26868.
[24] TNA ADM 223/464. P.25. ADM 223/257. February & December 1940. ADM 137/3964. P.220.
[25] At this time there were two divisions of MI9: MI9(a) to interrogate captives in British hands, and MI9(b) to support British and allied servicemen captured by the enemy.
[26] Roskill, *Churchill and the Admirals*, P.94. Trench Diaries (NMRN 2017/24/28), 21/4/40.
[27] TNA ADM 186/805. P.290.
[28] Ibid. P.319-320.
[29] See Wentzel, *Single or Return?* P.26-34; TNA WO 208/4141; SRN 97 (2/11/40), 120 (13/11/40), 121 (20/11/40).
[30] TNA WO 208/4143. SRN 720 (25/12/41).
[31] See my *Castaways of the Kriegsmarine* for more on this topic.
[32] Welbourn, *An Engineer in Peace and War*, Vol 1.

[33] Engineer Lt Cdr William Henry Rosevere (1877-1945) became one of Trench's closest confidants. He was run over by a tram and killed on 28th March 1945, when about to be posted to Germany as a technical specialist on the Control Commission.

[34] TNA ADM 1/26868; Interrogation of PoWs.

[35] TNA KV 2/3767.

[36] TNA KV 2/2690.

[37] TNA HO 405/3688.

[38] TNA HO 334/164/19474.

[39] Kendal Burt & James Leasor: *The One that Got Away*. P.66, 73.

[40] TNA WO 208/3455 CSDIC UK Survey, 3/9/1939 – 31/12/1940; Memo from John Godfrey dated 11/02/41.

[41] TNA AIR 40/3106. Special SR 13, 14, 34-36. The interrogation of a naval captive by an army officer, recorded in an air intelligence file, is an excellent example of the CSDIC approach.

[42] See TNA WO 208/4143, AIR 40/3106.

[43] In merchant service 'fireman' but I use the more familiar term 'stoker'.

[44] TNA ADM 186/807; CB 4051(36). P.5.

[45] TNA WO 208/4145. SRN 1683 (23/4/43).

[46] Ibid. SRN 1667 (21/4/43).

[47] Ibid. SRN 1664 (23/4/43).

[48] Ibid. SRN 1512 (15/3/43).

[49] Ibid. SRN 1658 (20/4/43).

[50] Ibid. SRN 1492 (20/2/43).

[51] TNA WO 208/5158.

[52] In a curious exception to this practice, stool pigeon N1878 once claimed to be a survivor of *U-281*, which remained in service until the end of the war. (e.g. TNA WO 208/4151. SRN 3525, 30/4/44).

[53] Moore, *Getting Fritz to Talk*. III.

[54] TNA WO 208/5158.

[55] See for example TNA WO 208/4151. SRN 3594-6.

[56] Rankin, *Ian Fleming's Commandos*. P.124-125.

[57] TNA WO 208/4142. SRN 285 (19/4/41).

[58] TNA ADM 223/475. P.2-3.

[59] TNA AIR 40/2636. P.5-6.

[60] Ibid. P.11.

[61] TNA AIR 40/3102. Special extract from SR Draft No 3707 (12/9/42).

[62] TNA WO 208/4163. SRX 1868 (19/9/43).

[63] TNA WO 208/4145. SRN 1589 (6/4/43).

[64] TNA WO 165/39. March 1941.

[65] TNA ADM 186/806, P.74.

[66] TNA WO 208/4141. SRN 178 (21/3/41).

[67] See for example TNA AIR 40/3070. SRA 429 (30/8/40), 441 (2/9/40).

[68] TNA WO 208/5621.

[69] TNA WO 208/3518.

[70] 'Italian Naval Prisoners of War' in TNA ADM 223/475.

71   Fry, *The Walls Have Ears*. P.50. This facet of their work is not however mentioned in McFadyean's or Charles Morgan's papers or in surviving M Room transcripts and is contradicted in Claudia Furneaux' reminiscence.
72   TNA ADM 223/257.
73   *Sketch*, 26/6/1940, P.405; 10/7/40, P.59. *Evening Telegraph*, 24/6/1940, P.5. *Press and Journal*, 25/7/40, P.2. *The Bystander*, 3/7/40, P.26.
74   Interview by Jill Hamblin in *Somerville Magazine*, 2011, P.12-13.
75   TNA WO 208/3248. P. 9.
76   See Helen Fry, *The Walls Have Ears*, for more on this topic.
77   TNA WO 208/3461. Crockatt to C Jones, Col Gatesby (29/5/43).
78   Mallett, *Prisoners of War-Cold War Allies: The Anglo-American Relationship with Wehrmacht Generals*.
79   TNA ADM 223/475.
80   NMRN 2017/24/29: Trench Diaries 15/9/41-3/12/43.
81   Ibid. (24/5/42).
82   TNA WO 208/3453. Godfrey memo P.770 (31/8/1941).
83   TNA WO 208/3453. Memo ref. MI19(c)/C/111 (1/2/42).
84   TNA WO 208/3452. Memo Lamplugh/Crockatt (21/10/42).
85   TNA WO 208/3453. Minute BM MI19(a)/CC/252 Sheet 1 (26/10/1942).
86   TNA WO 208/3452. Signal 290240 from Rodd to MI19A cc COC-in-C E Africa (1/11/42).
87   TNA ADM 223/257.
88   TNA ADM 223/355, DNI Note for 15/5/1944.
89   TNA WO 208/3453. Memorandum for JIC, *Formation of a Combined Services Detailed Interrogation Centre in the Far East* (2/1942).
90   Trench Diaries, 8/8/42.
91   TNA WO 166/17838 (June 1945).
92   TNA WO 208/3248. P.9.
93   Bernard Trench Diary 15/9/41-3/12/43; entry for 10/8/42.
94   Albrecht report to J L Riheldaffer (22/4/42) viewed on www.uboatarchive.net.
95   GPO Research Branch Secret War Diary, Vol.1, P.171; 'ATIS Interrogation Techniques' in Dunn, *Allied Translator and Interpreter Section*.
96   TNA WO 208/3453.
97   Trench Diaries NMRN 2017/24/28: 11-12/7/1940.
98   See TNA ADM 223/475.
99   Ibid.
100 TNA WO 208/5617.
101 Jellicoe, *George Jellicoe*. P.68.
102 TNA WO 208/3248, P.3.
103 TNA WO 208/4200. SR Draft No WG 837 (26/3/1944).
104 TNA WO 208/3248, P.11.
105 TNA WO 208/3453. Signal GL 1530/41 (18/7/1941)
106 TNA WO 208/3248. Appendix I, P.3.
107 TNA WO 208/4200. Extract from SR Draft No WG 951A (10/4/44).

[108] Ibid. Extract from SR Draft No 3346 (12/4/44).

[109] See TNA WO 208/3454, WO 208/5629.

[110] TNA WO 208/3461. Extract from minutes of JIC Meeting 13/4/43.

[111] TNA WO 208/3248, P.12.

[112] TNA WO 208/5629.

[113] See my *Castaways of the Kriegsmarine* for details.

[114] TNA ADM 186/809, P.266-331.

[115] The average for the first 36 days of the campaign was 1,413 per day (TNA WO 208/5158).

[116] TNA WO 208/3439.

[117] ANCXF: Allied Naval Commander Expeditionary Force.

[118] Ibid.

[119] TNA ADM 223/475.

[120] TNA WO 208/5617.

[121] They were joined at some point by Charles Mitchell, a civilian officer normally working at the Admiralty.

[122] TNA ADM 199/2478. The interrogation reports later in the file include the IO's name and, sometimes, location – itself a new departure.

[123] TNA ADM 202/599. P. D9, Photo No 969856.

[124] TNA ADM 223/475.

[125] This and following quotations are from TNA ADM 223/501.

[126] TNA WO 208/4151. SRN 3595 (4/5/44).

[127] Ibid. SRN 3612 (7/5/44).

[128] See TNA ADM 223/214.

[129] Original document in the author's possession.

SOME YOU WIN...

Cassandra, tell me what I want to hear

There were times when the team must have felt like legendary prophetess Cassandra, fated to speak truth yet never to be believed. They repeatedly came up against the impenetrable presumption that 'If we can't do it, they can't either.'

It was clear from prisoner conversations in 1941 that the latest Type VII U-boats were designed for a depth of 200 metres and could go deeper in an emergency. The interrogation report on *U-100*, sunk on 17th March, observed that the boat had managed 230 metres (albeit not deliberately). Similarly, *U-70* (7th March) and *U-138* (18th June) had exceeded their design criteria.[1]

This was a problem: British depth-charges could not reach that far. The Navy started the war with 1918-vintage 'Type D' charges which had a maximum firing depth of 280 feet (85 metres) and a sinking rate of 10 feet (3 metres) per second, giving a canny commander time to steer out of the way. The later Mark VII reached 500 feet (152 metres).

Worse, U-boat crews knew about the limitation. In July 1941, an able seaman from *U-138* was heard to say, '*They wanted to drop the depth charges (to explode) under us. They can't drop them (to explode) deeper than 170m.*'[2] At about the same time a *U-556* artificer explained to colleagues from the supply-ship *Alstertor*, '*I estimate it to be 160 at the deepest, but that is the very lowest depth to which they go (can be set).*'[3]

Admiralty experts were sceptical of the evidence until the capture of *U-570* (later HMS *Graph*) in August 1941 and its subsequent evaluation removed all doubt. Once the message sank in the standard Mark VII charge was modified for deeper settings and a faster sinking rate, to the chagrin of *Leutnant zur See* Friedrich Gassauer, *U-607*:

> *'A(Am)103:   Can't you submerge out of range of the depth charges?*
> *N1694:   Not at the moment. Up to now it had always been the*
> *case that the enemy had not set his depth charges so deep, so that we*
> *were always far below the depth charges, but now he has found out*
> *somehow how deeply we can submerge and has changed the setting of*
> *his depth charges.'[4]*

The successes of the Bletchley Park cryptanalysts against supposedly invulnerable German machine cyphers are well known and justly celebrated. Naval Enigma had been the toughest nut to crack until the capture of *U-110* and *U-570* in 1941, which also gave Allied boarding parties valuable clues about where to look for secret material in future 'pinches'. All went relatively smoothly until February 1942, when the *Kriegsmarine* added a fourth rotor to its Enigma machines. The resulting blackout cost the Allies dearly in ships and men and lasted until the sinking of *U-559* that October yielded a sample of the new machine. By the beginning of the following year U-boat crews were noticing the difference and guessing at the cause. *Leutnant zur See* Wolfgang Verlohr (*U-175*) commented to two fellow-officers,

> *'The January successes were very poor. And do you know why?*
> *Because (convoys) managed to avoid all the U-boat packs. We made*
> *patrol sweep after patrol sweep, but (the English) avoided them all.*
> *Strict instructions came out in January to the effect that Flotillas were*
> *no longer to write operational reports. Only an officer was to be*
> *allowed to use the codes etc. They are very strict instructions and*
> *nothing whatsoever that concerns U-boat warfare may be transmitted*
> *over any other wave-lengths, not even from GDYNA or somewhere*
> *like that; our code documents have been withdrawn from everyone.*

Only the Flotilla has the code documents for…….. That was DÖNITZ's first measure.'[5]

The need to protect the secret of cryptographic ('special') intelligence from all but the select few indoctrinated officers at Admiralty created an immense amount of work for them. The source of good intelligence had to be disguised and false information filtered out without revealing why. Prisoner intelligence presented a problem, as Admiral Godfrey recalled.

'Many papers prepared by the Sub-sections had to be elaborately scrutinised in order to exclude statements which were known from Special to be false or which, as often occurred in Prisoner of War reports, might accidentally arouse suspicion of the existence of Special'[6]

It is less appreciated that for much of the first half of the war the code-crackers of the *Kriegsmarine's B-Dienst* had at least as good an insight into British codes as those of the Government Code and Cypher School (GCCS) did into theirs. The German bureau, led by veteran Wilhelm Tranow, never dispersed after the First World War, and by the outbreak of the second had penetrated British commercial and some naval codes. Tranow's analysts were helped by the Admiralty's reliance on manual encryption: new code books took time to print and distribute in the quantities needed, so limited the frequency of changes. This disastrous situation was not finally corrected until spring 1943.[7]

It need not have been so. An eavesdropped conversation involving two U-boat radiomen in March 1941 contained the following snippets from two unidentified speakers, the more informed of whom was probably *Funkmaat* Hermann Bruhn of U-70:

'?   (re B Service) We heard by W/T that we were to arrive at the end of March ………. It is astounding how well organised it is.

?   By the Germans?

?   Of course.

...

?   Our "B" service knows everything; (they know) where every ship was etc.'[8]

The formal interrogation report on *U-70* contained a brief reference to *B-Dienst* and a statement that,

'"U 70" had also been warned by the B.d.U. of the approach of convoys. Detailed information had been provided of the estimated time of arrival, course, number of ships, and escorts.'[9]

It would seem the significance of this gem was missed. If that was perhaps a little subtle and understated, the same cannot be said of a warning issued that August:

'N842 – Obermaschinenmaat (artificer in the PINGUIN – 'Raider 33') Captured 8.5.41.

P/W stated that:-

Our Merchant Navy code is known to the Germans. Armed merchant cruisers listen in to our ships when they announce their arrival at a port, asking for fresh vegetables, etc. and thus find out their position, intercept and sink them. Our Naval code is not known to them.'[10]

Telegraphist N871, also from *Pinguin*, was quite specific in his conversation with stool pigeon A713.

'A713:   The U-Boat people told me we have got the code used by the English.

N871:   Yes, but not the one used for transmission to warships; we cannot de-code those messages, unless we (Germans) now know more about it. But we had the code for merchantmen, we were able to crack that. We had the necessary data, the code group books which have the meanings of the various code groups, we worked out the substitution tables for ourselves. That is not so difficult, as there are so many W/T messages and the more W/T messages you have, the easier it is to work it out, as so many code groups are frequently repeated as they are encoded with the same substitution table. The English of course always made their messages up in the same way.

But in our code, for instance when a text is set up, it always begins differently. Sometimes we start off with the signature - i.e. "From the Naval authorities (Seekriegsleitung) to ship E or to ship A", or it is put the other way round: "To ship E from the naval authorities". The Naval authorities are of course in BERLIN. We do that just as we like. It is left to the discretion of every W/T operator as to how he does it. But he must not do it systematically always the same way. The English, however, always send the message in the same way. The messages for all the ships we got started with: "From Admiralty for –" then came the name of the ship. With the new substitution table which had just come out, we always got the first two or three groups, as we knew what represented "From the Admiralty for –". And the last group was also known – it was always "Ends".[11]

Funkmaat Franz Atsamski of the captured *U-570* was even more explicit when prompted a little later by the ubiquitous A713, posing as a downed fighter pilot.

A713:   *Can we decode the English naval code?*
N894:   *Yes.*[12]

These notes had extremely limited distribution (eight or ten copies, entirely within the naval and air intelligence community). Even so, at least some warnings were issued. A raider alert sent out by the DNI in January 1941 included the sentence, '*Efficient D/F [direction finding], compromisation [sic] of Merchant Navy Code and agents in neutral and British Empire ports provide accurate knowledge British shipping.*'[13]

Another clue came in a conversation that October, involving the captain of tanker *Ketty Brövig*. A note at the top of the SR report (eavesdropping transcript) warns that the German text was obscure, but it was still clear that raiders were effortlessly reading instructions sent to British merchantmen.[14]

Ordinary Seaman N1294 of the minelayer *Ulm*, sunk on 16th October 1942, described how they had been spotted at the very start of their last voyage.

'N1294:   …We decipher all the English W/T messages. We still couldn't see the aircraft, but he'd already seen us. He wirelessed. "Probable German ship; we presume mineship is putting to sea from TROMSÖ." We deciphered that word for word. Afterwards came: "Will attempt to attack the ship." So then we knew for certain that an attack would follow, and we were waiting for him to arrive of course; we gave him a warm reception. We hadn't seen the aircraft at all, but we knew that the ……… were after us.'

Even more frighteningly, this suggested that by then not even British naval codes were safe. As a non-specialist he may not however have been fully informed. His shipmate *Mechanikersmaat* (PO Artificer) N1265 informed A713, by now a 'bomber pilot' since they were closeted with a real fighter jockey, that *Ulm* had embarked no fewer than eighteen telegraphists to listen in to British transmissions. He seemed to think they depended more on traffic analysis and direction finding than decryption for their information.

A713:   Don't the English transmit in code?
N1265:   What's the good of that? You can always make something out from it. They've already got such experience and routine in it by this time. They don't find out everything, but at any rate you know from the W/T messages how far away they are and from how many miles away they are being transmitted.'[15]

In February 1943, a conversation at Trent Park between Generals Crüwell and von Thoma gave renewed cause for concern.

'General CRUEWELL:
All our communications with JAPAN are by W/T. All the things we hear when the English are using their W/T are startling when they are worked out. They don't worry about it at all. Of course they may be doing it purposely.
General VON THOMA:
No, no.
General CRUEWELL:

I don't know, perhaps they aren't doing it any more. At any rate it was quite amazing up to the time that I was taken prisoner. At that time our successes were partly due to that, otherwise it wouldn't have been possible at all. BAYERLEIN and I actually gave our orders accordingly. Not exclusively, but at any rate it was very important information for us.'[16]

Later that year newly recruited defector N1878, a wireless operator, was shown or told about a signal from Control to *U-523*. A note recorded his reaction:

'The chief interest to the Funkmaat in this was that they had not made the report themselves to Control, as they had not had time and he therefore presumed that the Germans must have our code.'[17]

The time needed to break cyphers, decrypt messages, and convert the intelligence into operational orders meant that the gaping hole in Allied security was not always as damaging as it might have been. Nonetheless many more lives were lost before this 'open book' finally snapped shut.

No-one underestimated the criticality of breaking into the Germans' naval Enigma cypher. The first year of the war saw little progress on this which, compounded by patchy direction finding (D/F) and poor air reconnaissance, meant the Royal Navy was too often fighting a sighted enemy blindfold.

It seemed a breakthrough might be in prospect when *Funkmaat* Erich May, a *U-35* survivor, arrived in London on 3rd December 1939. Trench went for a walk with him at Trent Park and found him 'quite a pleasant person.' Pennell was then sent hotfoot up to Bletchley to prepare for a further interview with May on 1st January.[18] Meanwhile Erich was subjected to the full charm offensive. On 23rd December he described being taken out by a naval officer:

'He invited me alone to his house, where he is living for the time being only with his butler. His wife is on the west coast. He has a number of country estates, one in the West of England and another in

South Africa and his fine house in London. We had a very good
meal and drank only champagne and port, he is a fine fellow. I
believe him when he said that he only has a personal interest in me
and has no connection with the other officers. He also told me that he
always has great difficulty in coming to see me here, and that it is as if
there were a great table between us, he also gave me to understand
that if I needed anything here I should write to his wife who would
willingly send me whatever I want.'[19]

While most of the naval officer's story was undoubtedly fiction, thickly laid on to impress his guest, the reference to South Africa suggests he might have been Edward Croghan who was born in Johannesburg.

Pennell continued chatting with May well into January, extracting details of operating procedure, plugboard settings and wheel changes by pretending that British submarines also used Enigma machines and 'comparing notes'. At one point his report observed, *'(I hope the listeners in got it, as I can't remember.)'[20]* May's evidence probably helped Alan Turing and Peter Twinn make the first break of naval Enigma, the most secure machine code used by the German armed forces.[21]

May was sent to Oldham prisoner of war camp with the rest of the non-commissioned crew, and thence to Canada for the rest of the war. He eventually died in Neuss, Germany on 27th March 1993.

The need to support Bletchley's efforts and cope with the intermittent prisoner surges led to the occasional use of co-opted specialists from outside the team. There are interrogation reports on file authored by Lieutenant Paul de Laszlo RNVR, Major-General Leonard Forster RMA and Commander Charles O'Callaghan (retired).[22]

Although the Bletchley cryptanalysts knew early on the essential details of how the Enigma coding machine worked, the tricky aspect was finding out which combination of wheels and plug-board settings was in use at any given time. This was much easier if an entire machine or relevant documents could be 'pinched' from an enemy ship or submarine, which was done on several occasions. Since the vessel in question was usually sinking the boarding party had little time and needed to know exactly where to go. Which was where CSDIC came in. This conversation between N1568, 2nd Officer Hans Falkenhahn in blockade-runner *Regensburg*, and two U-boat officers illustrates the approach.

> 'N(Am)2:　We couldn't send any more short signals – with us everything had broken loose – the entire R/T apparatus.
> The codes are kept in the keel locker.
> N1538:　Yes – you have to open three locks – you can get nothing from the R/T table.
> N(Am)2:　You have to open three locks and the panelling
> ....
> N1568:　We merely had one locker in the Captain's cabin.
> N1538:　Yes – inside, behind a steel door.
> N1568:　Hm.
> N(Am)2:　With us it was substantially bigger – a nice locker on rollers – which went down(?) immediately ....'[23]

★ ★ ★

In 1942 it was several months before Admiralty experts believed prisoner evidence about the *Pillenwerfer* acoustic decoy (see Underwater developments & dodges below), and it took even longer to work out what it did.[24]

Stories that the German Narvik class destroyers had gun armament roughly equivalent to a British light cruiser had been circulating for some time before they were confirmed by survivors of *U-461* in September 1943 and endorsed by the crew of E-boat *S-96* in November.[25] These powerful ships carried five 150mm (5.9-inch) guns in one twin and three single mountings. The information was frankly disbelieved until a brief, brutal fight involving the destroyers in Biscay on 28th December 1943.[26] Some authorities struggled to accept it until a Narvik was captured after D-Day.

Human Wrongs

'*You can no more humanise war than you can humanise hell*'. Admiral 'Jacky' Fisher's cynical observation from half a century earlier was demonstrated in the unrestricted U-boat campaign and the industrial slaughter on land of the Great War. The 'Twenties and 'Thirties were marked by a sustained diplomatic effort to ban, or at least reduce, the tools of warfare and restrict the ways in which they could be used. The net result was that despotic regimes with no visible scruples about international agreements were best placed for the next conflagration.

★ ★ ★

The horrors of the Holocaust are well known. It is less appreciated how widely awareness of the camps (*Konzentrations-lager*, KZ or KL) spread among the ordinary military of all ranks. Several had first or second-hand experience of brutal incarceration themselves. Being Jewish was the quickest and surest route to the wrong side of the barbed wire but there were many others. Sadistic cruelty and casual murder were common, though few involved systematic extermination. While it was a rare prisoner who admitted to atrocities himself the widespread post-war claims of ignorance should be treated with caution.

One of the first pieces of firm evidence came from N610, a petty officer navigator in the captured U-boat *U-110*.[27] The interrogation report notes a rating alleged to have communist leanings and continues,

An even more astonishing fact was the inclusion of a man who had been in a concentration camp and had suffered appalling cruelty at

the hands of the Nazis; this man was entrusted with important and responsible duties, although he must have been classed by the German Naval authorities as an "irreconcilable" in view of his and his family's sufferings. While he was somewhat taciturn on the subject of his past, other members of the crew discussed the conditions in concentration camps. This man had been a merchant service officer and was carried for navigational duties; he was graded as a Petty Officer and would have automatically become a temporary commissioned officer after eighteen month's [sic] of service. He gave the impression of being a good type of German and was a man of considerable experience gained in many parts of the world.'

The report details some of the treatment meted out to camp inmates.

'Unspeakable cruelties were practised, such as forcing the prisoner to lie down on a floor covered with broken glass; any attempt to push aside the glass was discouraged by flogging with riding whips.

…

In the Oranienburg [Sachsenhausen] Concentration Camp, 1,200 Social Democrats and Communists were made to lie flat on their backs side by side and then S.S. men in field boots and full equipment goose-stepped over the prostrate bodies.

…

Relatives of interned men were sometimes told to come and fetch their relations home, and on arrival were handed an urn containing the prisoner's ashes.'[28]

N610 had been incarcerated for nine months in 1934. When he was finally released the legal system had one final kick in store for him.

'When I got out of the Concentration Camp the 'Kapitän' said to me: "You have so and so much money due to you. At last you have been acquitted and the money must now be refunded to you. There is justice in the Third Reich". It took nine months for them to discover how, when and where I had been born. But it did not take three days

before I got a letter from BERLIN to say that owing to being
suspected of racial pollution (lit: "incest") I had no claim against the
state. I showed that to the 'Kapitän' and said: "Here, Herr Kapitän,
so much for your justice!"[29]

On the same day, chatting with fellow prisoner N538, he described some of the excesses he had heard about in the Battle of France.

'N610:   The S.S. "Verfügungstruppen" did not take any
English prisoners; they killed them all. They took reprisals. They had
shot German airmen who were baling out. The others, of course, said
it was parachute troops that they had shot. That was a ghastly
business in FRANCE. People told me themselves how they (had
shot) Englishmen from morning till night. They took no more
prisoners.

N538:   Now they seem to have come to some arrangement
about prisoners, as they have the Hell of a lot of our people, too.'[30]

After interrogation N610 was assigned to Sefton Delmer's propaganda section where he was treated, and paid, as an officer until the end of 1943. With his value there exhausted he was transferred to the former officers' camp at Grizedale Hall, which by then was a segregated refuge for anti-Nazi prisoners.[31]

As a torpedo training school Libau (now Liepāja in Latvia) was a familiar posting to many German naval crews. They could hardly help knowing about the systematic murder of the city's Jewish population. *Maschinengefreiter* Kurt Liedke, rescued from *U-845* in March 1944, graphically described the mass shooting of hostages in reprisal for an incident at a brothel in 1942.[32] *Obermaschinist* Fritz Kornmeier was the senior survivor of E-boat *S-53* in 1942 and described being invited to watch a mass execution.

'Nearly all the men there were interned in large camps. I met a fellow
one evening and he said, "Some of them are going to be shot
tomorrow. Would you like to see it?" A lorry went there every day

*and he said, "You can come too." The Kommandeur of ..... execution
there belonged to the Naval Artillery. The lorry arrived and stopped.
In a sort of sandpit there was a trench about twenty metres long.
There was a man there ..... they threw him out and he called out in
broken German that he wasn't one and so on. I didn't know what
was happening until I saw the trench. They all had to get into it and
were hurried into it with blows from rifle-butts and lined up face to
face; the Feldwebel had a tommy-gun ..... there were five of them,
they (shot) them one after the other. Most of then fell like that, with
their eyeballs turned up, there was a woman among them. I saw that.
It was in LIBAU.'[33]*

In view of the explicit invitation Kornmeier's claim that he did
not realise what was about to happen is difficult to credit. Others
were less equivocal. *Maschinenmaat* Albert Creuzmann of *U-517*
was open about his views.

*'It says in the newspaper that the Nazis intend to shoot all the Jews
in EUROPE. That would be quite good, but we haven't got enough
ammunition. What an outcry they are making here, just because a
few Jews are shot.'[34]*

Karl Völker was a *Fähnrich (ing)* (Engineering Midshipman) late
of *U-175*. He too was violently antisemitic, repeating the libel of
Christian blood sacrifice. He concluded,

*'I now have no mercy. We shot them all mercilessly. There certainly
will have been some innocent ones among them, but there were some
guilty ones too. It doesn't matter how much good you do, if you've got
Jewish blood, that's enough!'[35]*

Maschinenmaat Werner Wiezorek of *U-744*, captured in March
1944, described atrocities in Lithuania. He evidently found the
experience distressing, but perhaps not outrageous.

*'These Jewish persecutions in LITHUANIA weren't pleasant.
There was a large-scale massacre on the beach, the ...... had to dig
their own graves. The soldiers could go and watch or take part in the
shooting themselves.'[36]*

Paul Osmy, a *Bootsmannsmaat* (Bo'suns Mate 1st Class) from the minelayer *Ulm* was clearly being led by stool pigeon N1067 but did not seem to relish the atrocities he described.

'N1067:   *In FRANCE a lot of people are being shot.*

N1286:   *Yes. At CHERBOURG a small store — of M.G. and rifle ammunition — was blown up. In revenge the S.S. seized a hundred people at random from the street and mowed them down.*

N1067:   *Dreadful things are going on in CZECHO-SLOVAKIA.*

N1286:   *And in the BALTIC STATES. A fellow I know told me that at six o'clock every evening they used to shoot up a lot of Jews. They simply threw a bit of sand over them and rolled a tank over them.'*[37]

This conversation between N731, a sub-lieutenant from the supply ship *Egerland* and N733, a U-boat *Kapitänleutnant* (both dedicated Nazis) shows the depth of indoctrination even among some of the more educated guests.

'N733:   *The British have quite the wrong idea about German aims. What nonsense they talked about politics on board the destroyer. They say HITLER wants to subjugate EUROPE and that he wants to attack AMERICA. All this talk has been put into circulation by the Jews. The British understand nothing about continental policy. Their senses are blunted by the press. It makes you furious to hear them talk about POLAND and LUXEM-BOURG. We attacked the Poles because the Poles kept the Germans down. The population of LUXEMBURG is not a foreign one, but German. ENGLAND herself has always broken her word and let her allies down.*

How "old Fritz" (Frederick the Great) used to curse the British!

N731:   *Yes, and rightly so. I have been so angry with the British that I have given up being angry.*

N733:   *They have quite the wrong impression of us.*

*N731:   They have quite the wrong idea of the Gestapo! They
do not understand that the Gestapo is necessary for the transition
period. If even a tenth part of what the British say about the Gestapo
were true, GERMANY would have no right to be in the world.*[138]

When it came to the lower deck, interrogators too often found
themselves up against young men who had been fed a steady diet
of National Socialist ideology during their formative years, who
were physically fit and could trot out the slogans all day but were
mentally armoured against any form of enquiry or debate. The
interrogation report's comment on *U-556* was scathing.

*'The ratings were the usual propaganda-fed, sheep-like Nazis of
about 19 to 22 years of age; many were typical products of the
"Hitler Jugend" organisation, had joined the Navy because they had
been attracted by clever propaganda, and had been drafted without
option to U-Boats. Some were men of poor brain and had lived the
simplest peasant lives until they found themselves, almost to their
surprise, in the Navy.*[139]

It is important not to paint the entire German armed forces in
the same bloody brush strokes. Some individuals, as we have
seen, bought the whole, sick, ideology of the regime they served.
Others ranged through the entire spectrum from active
detestation to various, often inconsistent, levels of scepticism
about Hitler, the Party, its policies, and its officials. For example,
Maschinenmaat Theodor Averkamp of *U-91* (captured February
1944) had lost whatever faith he had had in the Party but would
not hear a word said against its leader.

*'I'm no Nazi either, but what ADOLF has done: "Not for myself
but for the people," and if anyone talks against him, he should be
shot!'*[40]

It is worth repeating a conversation between *Kapitänleutnant*
Heinz Hungershausen (N2364) and *Oberleutnant zur See* Kurt
Böhme (N2344) who were former commanders of *U-91* and
U-450 respectively. Böhme had become strongly anti-Nazi,

though no fan of democracy either, and was a family friend of Pastor Martin Niemöller (who at this point in 1944 was beginning his seventh year in concentration camp). He described his disillusion as follows:

'It is all very well if you consider the government as a collection of idealists, but, as experience has shown up to now in the history of the world – and one of the greatest disappointments of my life has been that I thought the National Socialist Government <u>was</u> such a government – experience has shown that as soon as it has come into contact with the small temptations of life, it has proved just such a conglomeration of petty people – except for the FÜHRER himself – as any other one in history.'[41]

Hungershausen claimed to have been thrown out of the Hitler Youth on account of his views. CSDIC staff nonetheless felt that any independence of thought had been knocked out of him since. The interrogation report noted that, *'He impressed his interrogators rather favorably [sic] as a man of some education and considerable personal charm. His mind, however, had succumbed to Nazi doctrines and through consequent lack of use, had become vague and unreliable.'[42]*

The two of them were locked up together for some time and had long political discussions with each other and with interrogators.

'N2364:   Since 1939 my father-in-law has spoken about HITLER'S being insane.

N2344:   When I read in the newspapers that HIMMLER calls any man who doubts the victorious outcome of the war a defeatist and a traitor, I almost wish that the allies would win the war.

N2364:   If a collapse comes, it will be catastrophic; there will be starvation and expropriation. If only we could be in GERMANY then, so as to protect our families.

Wouldn't you on principle carry on a war as long as you possibly could?

N2344:   *Yes, but if it's completely hopeless?*

N2364:   *Well, what do you mean by "hopeless"?*

FREDERICK THE GREAT went on fighting, too. One must go on fighting until one is actually beaten.

N2344:   *Well, what will "beaten" mean for us? That the whole of GERMANY will be reduced to rubble and a further million will lose their lives.*

N2364:   *The ENGLISH are hypocritical devils. all they want is a weak EUROPE under their control.*

N2344:   *Power is no sort of an ideal.*

N2364:   *I don't know about that. Just think, if GERMANY really had come into power. It would be best of all for GERMANY if she were to continue national-socialist but without the Party. That is to say, the Party's programme without its organisation.*

N2344:   *You would have mayors instead of "Gauleiters"?*

N2364:   *Yes, that's about it.*

N2344:   *That would call forth a lot of opposition.*

N2364:   *I don't know about that. Nobody wants the Party Bigwigs, but the Party's programme could be retained. The racial laws and that sort of thing would be kept on.'*[43]

Böhme had come to his views partly through a fundamental clash between his Lutheran upbringing and the Nazi view of human beings as, essentially, livestock.

'I know, for example, from my sister-in-law in the Labour Service, where they were asked "Who among you will present the FÜHRER with a child?" that twenty-two out of thirty-five volunteered, that things were arranged accordingly and that it was said: "Two women" (to one man). I've often heard it said "That can be justified from every point of view because we have lost so many men." Thank God I've not yet seen the effects of it. In accordance with that view the

woman is no longer a being with whom you share your life,
physically and spiritually, but just a piece of flesh.'[44]

His evidence was corroborated by several accounts of state-sponsored breeding programmes for 'Aryan' children. One or two might have been hearsay but the accumulated weight of evidence had to be taken seriously. For example, *Maschinenmaat* Josef Hellmanns of *U-643* passed on a tale he had heard from his fiancée when on leave.

'*She said that institutions have been opened where lustful young women go; only SS men are allowed there and these places are for the purpose of producing children. The women get free board, they don't need to work or anything, they get their food for nothing, and if they give birth to a boy they get a bonus of RM.50 – the child is taken away from them after three months. They don't get anything for a girl.'[45]*

Oberleutnant zur See Günther Schramm, the senior survivor of the torpedo boat *T-25*, placed at least one such 'home' at Wannsee near Berlin and described yet more abuses.[46] *Leutnant zur See* Karl Seiferth of *U-131* told of a shore-based colleague who had been ordered to seduce and impregnate unattached, widowed or separated young women to 'maintain the birth-rate'.

'*He was absolutely astounded, and all he could say was: "What do you take me for?" "What we take you for has nothing to do with it, this is a national necessity." Then he said: "You can get somebody else, I won't stand for it."'[47]*

Such tales were not calculated to improve the morale of men posted away from home indefinitely.

Böhme's distaste was reinforced by the daily corruption and injustice of Party officials.

'*If a man comes to the court and says that he is an old Party Member, from that moment they can't do anything against him.'[48]*

He struggled to overcome the scepticism and disbelief of Hungershausen, whose faith in German justice had so far survived unscathed. Böhme laid out his evidence: a man sentenced to death for openly doubting the propaganda about reprisal weapons, Niemöller tried, acquitted then immediately rearrested and sent to concentration camp, and his own brush with military authority when the first questions asked were whether he was a Party member and had been in the Hitler Youth.

Another controversy was over how a submarine should treat the survivors of a merchant ship it had sunk. The impracticality in this case of 'cruiser rules', under which an attacking warship must take adequate measures to ensure the safety of the victim's crew, had been demonstrated in the First World War. A submarine simply does not have space for passengers. With a few conspicuous exceptions this was not attempted in the Second. Leaving survivors in the water, sometimes with a gift of supplies or a raft if it could be spared, was common practice. Deliberately killing them was not.

Funkobergefreiter Lucian Seeger of *U-353* was understandably concerned when he and his captain, *Oberleutnant zur See* Wolfgang Römer, ended up as guests of the British. On 12th October 1942 *U-353* and *U-133* had jointly sunk a small steamer in the Atlantic.

'N1324:   *If they knew here that our Captain sailed through the debris and put the engines twice at three-quarters speed! (The survivors of) the crew were swimming about there, they hadn't a single lifeboat. They were just swimming about in the water with life-jackets, without a spar or anything.*

N1067:   *Was none of them saved?*

N1324:   *No. That (the fact that there were no survivors) is the one thing which will save him (the Captain). He was standing here on the bridge and the Brückengäste (?) said, when they were relieved, that one man was quite near the U-boat. He could almost*

have climbed on board but he (the Captain) turned the boat away,
and the man was dragged down by the suction astern.[49]

He was talking to a stool pigeon as well as to hidden listeners, so there was no chance of Römer's behaviour staying secret. The interrogation report noted his callousness toward survivors, but no further action was taken.

The most egregious example of a post-sinking war crime, and one where CSDIC played a key part in gathering evidence, was *Kapitänleutnant* Heinz-Wilhelm Eck and *U-852*. Ordered to the Indian Ocean in a large Type IXD boat, he had been warned before departure that this class was among the most vulnerable in service. On 13th March 1944 he sank the small Greek freighter *Peleus* in the South Atlantic. Nervously conscious of the marker he had left in his wake he spent five hours attempting to sink the ship's life rafts with machine guns, anti-aircraft cannon and grenades, finally leaving the scene in the small hours of the morning. Most survivors of the sinking were killed but three were picked up on 20th April. Eck had not only lost precious time that he could have used to make himself scarce, but he had also completely failed to eradicate traces of the ship's sinking. He had assumed the rafts had hollow floats, but they were buoyant and did not sink. A wreck also leaves copious quantities of floating oil, wood and cork which are conspicuous from the air.

U-852 herself was damaged by air attack on 2nd May off Somalia and beached the following day with seven casualties and 59 survivors. Eight, including the captain, were flown to Britain for interrogation. Prisoners interrogated in the UK and in East Africa admitted the massacre, while the captain of *U-1059* interrogated in the US claimed Dönitz had issued a standing order that, "*In future, as part of the total war, following sinking of enemy shipping all survivors are to be exterminated.*"[50]

CSDIC faced a quandary in dealing with the issue. SR reports of atrocities were carefully preserved but no-one could be sure at that time whether they would be admissible in a future court case. In the event the question was never tested. If the fact of eavesdropping on prisoners would not have surprised anyone the extent, organisation and success of the Allied operation was considered too secret to reveal after the war.

U-852 survivors' unguarded conversations provided plenty of material about the *Peleus* affair, but in formal interviews they remained nervously tight-lipped. Interrogator Donald Welbourn recalled,

'We laid on what was made out to be a court of enquiry, with three naval officers sitting at a table. Hovering behind them was our RM officer in his khaki uniform with a red Military Police arm-band round the sleeve, apparently representing the Secret Service charged with looking into war crimes.[51] We made it clear that if they did not tell us nice Naval types all that they knew, they would be handed over to him and his like. We started with the man whom we thought was probably the weakest link, and gradually built up the whole story.'[52]

On 6th June 1944 Eck was formally interviewed by a British naval officer and a legal representative from the Admiralty. He was confronted with statements by two lookouts that they saw machine guns being fired, and with a written statement made earlier by his engineer officer *Kapintänleutnant (Ing)* Hans Richard Lenz. As an English speaker Lenz had been detailed to question a *Peleus* survivor about the ship's identity and destination before the massacre. His affidavit, produced under interrogation at Al Maadi, was something of a 'smoking gun' for two of his fellow officers.

'N1878:   The IO said that someone from your boat had thrown hand grenades at the survivors.
N2531 [Lenz]:   Yes, I told the IO in CAIRO that HOFFMAN (PW) fired and threw a hand grenade and that the ship's surgeon fired.'[53]

Leutnant zur See August Hoffmann was the second watch officer and had joined Lenz for the interrogation of the *Peleus* survivor and the subsequent conference with Eck. He was now in serious trouble, but nothing like as serious as was building up for *Oberstabsarzt* Walter Weisspfennig the ship's doctor. U-boat medics were known to stretch the limits of their non-combatant status by, for example, helping to operate SBT acoustic countermeasures in emergency. Picking up a gun was of a different order entirely. Lenz himself, despite his formal objection to the order, and lookout *Matrosenobergefreiter* Wolfgang Schwender had taken part in the shooting during the second watch.

Under a certain amount of pressure – he was given an hour's thinking time instead of the day he requested – Eck stated under oath that he did not wish to contradict any of Lenz' evidence and that he had not acted under superior orders.[54] He outlined his reasoning in a separate conversation with the captain of *U-550* on the same day.

> 'I searched my conscience in that moment – I mean, one doesn't do that kind of thing cold-bloodedly, and I said: "It's got to be."
> I shall tell the IO what my attitude was, namely, that, if we had saved the crew they would have operated against us again. I would naturally have taken the people prisoner, if it had been possible, but it wasn't possible.
> It's obvious that I can't drag in the High Command. I can't say we had orders ......'[55]

Eck may not have realised that he had been doubly incriminated by his failure to destroy the boat's *Kriegstagebuch* (KTB) or war diary, which had been retrieved from the wreck.[56]

Nothing more happened until five months after the end of the war. Eck, Hoffmann, Weisspfennig, Lenz and Schwender were then moved to the Altona prison in Hamburg and charged with war crimes. The first of the two charges brought, that they

had sunk the *Peleus* in violation of 'the laws and usages of war' –
i.e. not observing 'cruiser rules' – was successfully dismissed by
the defence as not reflecting the realities of modern warfare. The
second charge concerned the killing of the surviving crew. The
facts of the matter were not in dispute. Eck's defence relied on
'operational necessity' – the need to preserve the lives of his own
crew and/or prevent the survivors continuing hostile action. The
others could only claim they were obeying Eck's orders.

The court disagreed. All five defendants were convicted
despite a rather diffident attempt by the defence to invoke the
Baralong and *Laconia* cases (see below) as precedents. Eck,
Hoffmann and Weisspfennig were sentenced to death and
executed by firing squad on 30th November 1945. Lenz and
Schwender received lengthy prison sentences which were
reduced to a further seven and six years, respectively. These five
were the only U-boat crew convicted of war crimes in the
Second World War.

It must be acknowledged that killing survivors was not
confined to the Axis record. On the night of 9th July 1941
Lieutenant-Commander Anthony Miers in command of HM
submarine *Torbay* ordered machine-guns to be turned on the
rafts of shipwrecked German soldiers after their vessels were
sunk. In January 1943, the US submarine *Wahoo* under
Lieutenant-Commander Dudley 'Mush' Morton opened fire on
survivors of the Japanese troopship *Buyo Maru*. Miers received a
mild reprimand, Morton a commendation. It might have made
a difference to the commanders concerned, though not to a
civilian court, that the survivors were servicemen who could
have reached land and resumed hostilities.

On 12th September 1942 *Kapintänleutnant* Hartenstein's
U-156 torpedoed and sank the liner RMS *Laconia* carrying
civilian passengers, military material and personnel, and a large
consignment of Italian prisoners of war. Seeing the scale of the

catastrophe, and perhaps influenced by the presence of allies in the water, Hartenstein sent a radio message in clear calling for a humanitarian truce and set about rescue operations. He was joined by *U-506*, *U-507* and Italian submarine *Cappellini*. The four of them set out for shore with as many survivors as possible inside, decks packed, and towing lifeboats. On 16th September *U-156* was spotted by a US Liberator aircraft whose pilot radioed for instructions and was ordered to attack, forcing her to cut the lifeboats loose and dive. An attack on *U-506* followed the next day. A war crime? Probably. In the brutal arithmetic of the time the untold harm an intact U-boat could do outweighed the lives of *Laconia*'s survivors.

A smaller and even more problematic incident occurred on 25th November 1944 when the submarine HMS *Sturdy* sank a small coastal cargo vessel in the Java Sea using gunfire and then demolition charges. On reaching the vessel the leader of the boarding party discovered there were still women and children aboard. Informing his captain, Lieutenant William St George Anderson, of the fact he was ordered to proceed. One member of the party had examined the cargo and believed it was rice, not oil as later stated. He refused to take part in subsequent boardings, believing he had witnessed a war crime. He expected punishment for his stand but heard no more about it. If his version is accurate, aspects of a 1988 statement to Parliament by Roger Freeman, Under Secretary of State for the Armed Forces, are not.[57]

The drugs of war

On the outbreak of war in September 1939 NID found itself strapped for sources of information. There was no guarantee that the euphemistically named Government Code and Cypher

School (GC&CS) at Bletchley Park would repeat the spectacular insights of the Admiralty's Room 40 cryptographers in World War 1. The Admiralty's use of a private contractor (Sydney Cotton) for air reconnaissance ended abruptly with the start of hostilities. A clash of service priorities caused great difficulty in persuading the RAF to step into the breach when it lacked both suitable aircraft and crews trained for long range maritime reconnaissance.[58]

Initially relations with the Secret Intelligence Service (SIS or MI6) were no better. Even before the 'Venlo Incident' in November 1939 crippled the entire SIS network in western Europe the organisation had lost credibility with NID by passing on rumours of German submarine operations and secret bases in the South Atlantic, and U-boat construction beyond the numbers permitted. All were treated with scepticism and later proved false. One NID staffer's damming assessment was that there was an,

'almost complete lack of useful information from CX [spies] … such information as reached him was worthless and frequently so evidently worthless as to provoke laughter…'[59]

The quality of the information provided by SIS and the relationship between the organisations improved over time, but in the first months of the war prisoners were one of the few reliable sources of information available to NID. Unsurprisingly, every possible trick to maximise the yield from that source was assessed. Direct interrogation had been brought to a fine art in the first war and was revived by the same practitioners. Eavesdropping through hidden microphones, explored but never used in the earlier conflict, was in place from the beginning. The first, tentative steps had been taken in the exploitation of stool pigeons and entertainment. The former, at this stage German speaking British officers, were too easy to see through. The latter relied on alcohol, the oldest truth serum in the business, which had the unfortunate side effect of reducing coherence as fast as inhibition. What else was there to try?

Perhaps inspired by fiction, Admiral Godfrey picked up a suggestion that a combination of drugs and hypnotism might work where other measures had failed. A drug called Evipan, a barbiturate derivative, would render the subject helpless to resist interrogation and susceptible to hypnosis, which would then erase the incident from his memory. It was vital to prevent him having the least suspicion, then or later, of what was being done to him as it was a clear breach of the Geneva Convention.

In a precis dated 12th December 1939 of two meetings Godfrey notes two possible ways of covertly administering Evipan. It could be done under the pretext of determining the subject's blood group by taking a sample, or by surreptitiously giving him amphetamines to make him ask for something to counter sleeplessness.

Godfrey recognised the potential moral, legal, and political dimensions but concluded,

'9. *The conclusions which I reach are that the method is justified provided that*

(a) *the doctors are satisfied that the technique is one which can easily be carried out, and which will have no permanent effect on the patient's health;*

(b) *the information which it is desired to elicit is of vital importance, and the preliminary experiments show that the patient is likely to respond favourably to the interrogation.*

10. *If these two conditions are fulfilled, the objections on moral and legalistic grounds should be accepted.*'[60]

Trench was briefed on 14th December and brought into a further meeting on 2nd January, which also involved two doctors and John Flügel (Professor of Psychology at University College, London).

The following week a diplomatically worded memo from NID Section XIV, the DNI's Secretariat, did not say in so many words that this was a crazy idea but pointed out the potential drawbacks.

'I think the conclusions summarised the bedrock of the situation, viz.
  (a) The strong professional feeling of doctors. Also:-
  (i) The fear of being struck off the register if the matter leaked out.
  (ii) The doctor who has no scruples over this might be unscrupulous in other ways, and talk from malice or negligently.
  (b) Restriction of the method to cases where the information was vital.

If I were in the Cabinet I would not agree to the method, as, if by bad luck it leaked out, there would be such widespread popular agitation about it that it would become a first-class political scandal.'[61]

Despite this discouragement Trench, Croghan and Mitchell, all in plain clothes, drove out to Stanborough Park Hospital in Watford (then a psychiatric unit) on 1st February 1940. Mitchell voluntarily submitted himself to the treatment, which was a complete failure as he remained perfectly normal throughout.[62]

This was not a fully representative trial, as Mitchell was aware of its purpose. Still, that was the end of it. As McFadyean wrote in a post-war paper,

'Early in the war the use of drugs was carefully investigated and it was found that apart from the difficulty of administering them they did not have the desired effect, experiments were in fact made on a civilian officer in N.I.D.'[63]

If NID abstained from the technique on practical grounds their reluctance was not universal. In September 1940, a captured *Abwehr* agent, codenamed Tate, was undergoing preliminary interrogation at MI5's Camp 020 (Latchmere House near

Richmond). A visit by Lieutenant-Colonel Scotland, head of the London District Cage, disrupted the process. The diary of Guy Liddell, head of the MI5 section responsible, takes up the story.

> 'I have just been told that the officer from MI9 who was present at the interrogation of TATE yesterday [i.e. Lieutenant Colonel J Scotland] took it upon himself to manhandle the prisoner without saying anything about it to Stephens, Dick or Frost. The interrogation broke off at lunchtime, when [Colonel] Scotland left the room. Frost, wondering where he was, followed him and eventually discovered him in the prisoner's cell. He was hitting TATE in the jaw and I think got one back for himself. Frost stopped this incident without making a scene, and later told me what had happened. It was quite clear to me that we cannot have this sort of thing going on in our establishment. Apart from the moral aspect of the thing, I am quite convinced that these Gestapo methods do not pay in the long run. We are taking the matter up with the DMI [Director of Military Intelligence] and propose to say that we do not propose to have that particular MI officer on the premises any more. I am told that Scotland turned up this morning with a syringe containing some drug or other, which it was thought would induce the prisoner to speak. Stephens told Scotland that he could not see [+++++++] TATE, who was not in a fit state to be interrogated. Actually there was nothing seriously wrong with [+++++++] TATE.'[64]

'Tate' (real name Wulf Schmidt, later known as Harry Williamson) became a successful double agent.

The ones who got away

German servicemen had been given a simple code, involving the first letter of each word, to be used in letters home if they were captured. The initial letters represented Morse code dots, dashes or breaks depending on their position in the alphabet; A-I were dots, J-R dashes, and the rest of the alphabet breaks. This was broken in March 1940, which led to a rapid review of letters already passed by the censor to see what information might have leaked back. From then on Trench or one of his senior colleagues scrutinised every prisoner's letter home; and only interfered with those containing seriously harmful intelligence. The Germans did not discover that the code had been compromised until 1943, allowing the Allies to foil at least two attempts to rescue prisoners from Canada and the United States by U-boat. The code remained in use until early 1944.[65]

February 1941 brought the unit's first major scare. *Oberleutnant* Franz von Werra, a serial escaper, finally made it across the US border after jumping from a train window in Canada. While a prisoner of war he had been fruitlessly exposed to every interrogation technique in the British armoury and it was feared that the knowledge he brought back to Germany would invalidate the secret process so carefully assembled. Prisoners were immediately segregated into 'X' and 'Y' categories depending on whether they had been taken before or after von Werra's return.

In the event the precaution was unnecessary. Von Werra's report did inform strengthened counter-interrogation training, but this was accompanied by such lurid stories of the treatment to be expected at British hands that when the latter proved unfounded the former was often discounted as well. Later, seamen were treated to a play in which three 'captives' were subjected to mistreatment including baking in an overheated room, drugs, and eyestrain from bright lights. The depiction of interrogators using stool pigeons and the shock of superior knowledge in the play was accurate, the rest not.[66]

A more serious outcome was that the *Luftwaffe's* interrogation centre at Oberursel incorporated many of the lessons he had learnt and became by far the most effective of the German prisoner intelligence resources.

In Britain, the 'X' and 'Y' categories were retained but used to separate prisoners who had and had not enjoyed the full CSDIC experience.[67]

A less famous but perhaps even more influential escaper was Kurt Reich, *Maschinenmaat* (Engine Room Artificer) from *U-63*. He staged a daring break from the transport steamer taking him to Canada, as described in the following year's interrogation report on *U-70*:

'It was obvious that increased security-consciousness had been systematically instilled into these men.

This development is believed to be due to the fact that prisoners of war interrogated some months ago have escaped and have passed on to the German authorities details concerning the British interrogation methods, centres and personnel.

This is confirmed by the fact that the German Government has recently made a request to the Swiss Legation in London to pay a visit to the camp where interrogations are conducted.

In September 1940, a Petty Officer who had been captured on 25th February, 1940, at the sinking of "U 63," and who had been interrogated by naval officers, escaped from a transport ship in the St Lawrence River. On the voyage from Great Britain he trained for this escape in the ship's swimming bath. He swam ashore, procured the necessary clothing, and reached the United States where he placed himself under the protection of the German Consul, who subsequently sent him back to Germany via Japan and Russia.

It is obvious that the escape of this man was assisted by other prisoners of war who will have primed him with all the details and complaints they may have nursed; he will certainly have been most thoroughly examined on his return to Germany by naval intelligence officers, to whom he could have given much valuable information

*about the fate of "U 63," the subsequent interrogation of the crew and
their imprisonment.*

*It seems obvious that the German Naval Authorities would not
neglect to warn U-Boat and other personnel of the details and pitfalls
of British interrogation.'*

Subsequent interrogations revealed that crews based at Kiel had
received the enhanced security briefing, whereas those operating
from Lorient had not.[68]

Unable to resist gilding the lily, Nazi propagandists coached
Reich into making unfounded allegations of ill-treatment in
captivity. These were wild enough to have limited traction at
home and to be actively counter-productive among those who
had experienced the reality. N610, a petty officer navigator from
U-110 captured on 9th May 1941, observed,

> *'Someone from a U-boat escaped from captivity in CANADA, and
> somehow got back to GERMANY. The broadcasting people
> somehow got hold of him and insisted that he should say he had been
> badly treated by the English. They really went too far. My
> "Kommandant" was very vexed about it. Such things introduce a
> quite unnecessary rancour into the war.'[69]*

Not only rancour. A *Bismarck* survivor suggested that false fear
of atrocities had caused needless loss of life.

> '?:   *Many who were swimming in the water shouted after us:
> "Come away, the English are shooting at us!" They actually swam
> away from the English ships. And they (the English) had made all
> preparations for rescuing the men!*
>
> ?:   *That is a triumph for our propaganda!!!'[70]*

According to Trench's diary *Oberleutnant (Ing) Rottman of U-33*
and another engineering officer also managed to escape from
Canada in March 1941.[71] This achievement, if it happened, has
left no impression on published records.

British prisoner-of-war camps in North Africa offered an
escaper the chance of making it to the Spanish enclaves of Ceuta

or Melilla, whence a home run was a good prospect. The second watchkeeping officer from U-593 and his opposite number from U-73, for example, removed themselves by hiding in a latrine while two petty officers took their place at roll call.[72]

A further, and continuous, risk of information leakage came from the repatriation under the Geneva Convention of prisoners unfit for further service. First there was the mechanics of transfer – how to arrange their passage without giving away the safe route through minefields. Then there was the knowledge of those selected for transfer. They might be unsuitable for active service but well-qualified to train the next generation, they often did have up-to-date experience of British interrogation methods and personnel (including stool pigeons). Prisoners due to appear before the mixed medical commission, which reported directly to the Protecting Power (Switzerland) and had the authority to repatriate, might thus suddenly find themselves transferred to a different camp or on a ship heading for Canada. In the confusion of the time the Prisoner of War Information Bureau (PWIB) could not possibly keep its records fully up to date![73]

Inevitably, there were mistakes. *Oberleutnant* Jakob Häusermann of *U-660* spent two weeks as a guest of CSDIC in November and December 1942 and was repatriated on 14th October 1943. On his return he helped produce a security film giving full details of what captured seamen could expect.[74] *Leutnant zur See* Arnold Rehburg (*U-744*), captured in 1944, told his stool pigeon cellmate,

> 'N2332:   A Kapitän zur See MEISSNER, holder of the Oak Leaves, who was exchanged, reported that they used microphones to a very great extent.'[75]

On another occasion an interrogator relaxed too much with one of his 'clients', an E-boat officer, and let slip a tactical vulnerability which was exploited as soon as the latter was repatriated. This probably prompted the following reminiscence by captured *Seehund* (midget submarine) pilot *Leutnant zur See* John in April 1945.

> '*Charlie MÜLLER could speak English extremely well, was for that reason given the post of interpreter in this camp, and was also taken to that English Admiral. This admiral showed him everything, and gave him a detailed description of the English E-boat defences in the CHANNEL. He visited him daily in his room in the camp, and took part in everything that went on. Of course he knew about everything, so they didn't want to exchange him. By some accident – some clerk must have messed things up somehow – he actually was exchanged, and was then able to pass on a good deal of information to us.*'[76]

Another senior E-boat commander who was anti-Nazi and had been very helpful was accidentally repatriated. His extensive knowledge of CSDIC would have been very damaging had he not chosen to remain silent for his own reasons.

In a 'state of the nation' review before his departure for the US in January 1942 Admiral Godfrey was forced to concede,

> '*The interrogation of German prisoners of war, originally a relatively simple process, has now become highly complex due to the steps taken by the enemy to increase the security-consciousness of their ships' companies. This will undoubtedly involve a slowing-down of the interrogation results which must, I am afraid, be accepted.*'[77]

---

[1]   TNA ADM 186/806. *CB 4051(19) "U 100" Interrogation of Survivors*, P.13; *CB 4051(18) "U 70" Interrogation of Survivors*, P.12; *CB 4051(25) "U 138" Interrogation of Crew*, P.12.

[2]   TNA WO 208/4143. SRN 577 (22/7/41).

[3]   Ibid, SRN 588 (24/7/41).

[4]   TNA WO 208/4163. SRX 1840 (17/7/43).

[5]   TNA WO 208/4145. SRN 1770 (7/5/43).

[6]   TNA ADM 223/297. P.2.

[7]   Kahn, D: *Hitler's Spies*. Chapter 13.

[8]   TNA WO 208/4141. SRN 238 (30/3/41).

[9]   TNA ADM 186/806. *CB 4051(18) "U 70" Interrogation of Survivors*. P.13.

[10] TNA WO 208/4196. SP/F/85 (12/8/41).

[11] TNA AIR 40/3102. Extract from SR Draft No 2741B (29/8/41).
[12] Ibid. Extract from SR Draft No 2865 ((16/9/41).
[13] TNA 199/725 quoted in Hore, *Sydney*. P.60.
[14] TNA WO 208/4143. SRN 681 (31/10/41).
[15] TNA AIR 40/3102. Special Extract from SR Draft No 3625 (10/9/42).
[16] TNA WO 208/5158. Transcript dated 3/2/43.
[17] Ibid. Note re signal from Control to U-523 0540/23.8.43.
[18] Trench Papers: *Diary 30/11/39 – 14/09/41*. Entries for 03/12/39, 16/12/39, 30/12/39, 01/01/40.
[19] TNA WO 208/4141. SRN 1 (23/12/39).
[20] TNA WO 208/5158.
[21] Boyd, *British Naval Intelligence*, Note 19 to Chapter 21.
[22] Vienna-born Temporary Lieutenant Paul Leonardo de Laszlo RNVR (Special Service) 1906-1983, seniority 29th March 1940, signals branch seconded to NID, was a barrister in civil life. Major-General Alfred Leonard Forster DSO 1886-1963 was ADNI in early 1940 but in poor health. Commander Charles O'Callaghan DSC (retired) 1894-1969 was a Jutland veteran, former submariner, and qualified interpreter in French, Italian and German.
[23] TNA WO 208/4145. SRN 1707 (26/4/43).
[24] TNA ADM 223/464. P.253.
[25] TNA ADM 186/808. P.597, 756.
[26] See my *Castaways of the Kriegsmarine* for a more on this.
[27] Possibly *Steuermann* (Chief Quartermaster 2nd Class) Heinz Nehmer.
[28] TNA ADM 186/806. P.170, 198-199.
[29] TNA WO 208/4142. SRN 352 (21/5/41). See also SRN 341 (20/5/41).
[30] Ibid. SRN 351 (21/5/41).
[31] TNA WO 208/3442, WO 208/3527.
[32] TNA WO 208/4150. SRN 3319 (5/4/44).
[33] TNA WO 208/4143. SRN 852 (11/3/42).
[34] TNA WO 208/4144. SRN 1387 (24/12/42).
[35] TNA WO 208/4145. SRN 1767 (8/5/43).
[36] TNA WO 208/4150. SRN 3321 (6/4/44).
[37] TNA WO 208/4144. SRN 1075 (14/9/42).
[38] TNA WO 208/4142. SRN 539 (11/7/41).
[39] TNA ADM 186/806. P.297.
[40] TNA WO 208/4150. SRN 3299 (2/4/44).
[41] Ibid. SRN 3309 (1/4/44).
[42] ADM 186/809. *CB 04051(100): U.257, U.91, U.358 & U.744 Interrogation of Survivors*. P.6.
[43] TNA WO 208/4150. SRN 3229 (24/3/44).
[44] TNA WO 208/4151. SRN 3382 (8/4/44).
[45] TNA WO 208/4147. SRN 2300 (13/10/43).
[46] TNA WO 208/4164. SRX 1952 (23/2/44).
[47] TNA WO 208/4143. SRN 775 (26/1/42).
[48] TNA WO 208/4151. SRN 3191 (20/3/44).

[49]   TNA WO 208/4144. SRN 1256 (10/11/42).
[50]   TNA ADM 223/355. *Most Secret Notes for DNI, 29/5/44*. P.4. *Oberleutnant zur See* Gunter Leupold, when interviewed, said that he and all other commanders he had discussed the order with had expressed equal indignation.
[51]   The Royal Marines officer was probably either John Weatherby or Charles Wheeler.
[52]   Welbourn, P.189.
[53]   TNA WO 208/4200. Extract from SR Draft No WG 1407 (5/6/44).
[54]   TNA WO 208/4198. Extract from SR Draft No WG 1419 (6/6/44).
[55]   TNA AIR 40/3104. Extract from SR Draft No WG 1417 (6/6/44).
[56]   Messimer.
[57]   Letter (undated) from R A Watters to Mr Anderson (son of Sturdy's CO) in NMRN *Submarine Boat File P248 – Sturdy*. Statement by Mr Freeman to Parliament in Hansard, 9/6/1988. 'Inhuman' submarine commander sacrificed civilians, *The Times*, 7/5/1988. Demand for answers on Navy killing of civilians, *The Times*, 9/5/1988. TNA FCO 15/5366.
[58]   See TNA ADM 223/475, Roskill, *The War at Sea 1939-45*: Vol 1.
[59]   TNA ADM 223/851.
[60]   TNA ADM 223/475.
[61]   Ibid. The signature is indecipherable but could be Ian Fleming's.
[62]   Trench Diaries.
[63]   TNA ADM 223/475.
[64]   TNA KV 4/186. P.23-4.
[65]   TNA ADM 223/475. Paper '*P/W Interrogation 1939-45*', P.61. ADM 223/355. Briefing note for 10/4/44.
[66]   TNA WO 208/4198. Special Extract from SR Draft 2560/45 (16/3/45).
[67]   TNA WO 208/3443.
[68]   TNA ADM 186/806. P.42, 73. Admiral Godfrey identifies Reich as the escaper in a memo in ADM 223/475.
[69]   TNA WO 208/4142. SRN 398 (10/6/41).
[70]   Ibid. SRN 440 (25/6/41).
[71]   Trench Papers: *Diary 30/11/39 – 14/09/41*. Entry for 22/3/41.
[72]   TNA WO 208/4200. Special Extract from SR Drafts Nos 865 & 844, ADM 186/809 P.57 (CB 04051 (95) P.1).
[73]   TNA ADM 223/475. Paper '*P/W Interrogation 1939-45*', P.68.
[74]   TNA AIR 40/3104. Special Extracts from SR Drafts Nos WG 111 & 112 (6/1/45).
[75]   TNA WO 208/4200. Extract from SR Draft WG 855 (26/3/44).
[76]   TNA WO 208/4198. Special Extract from SR Draft No WG 731/45 (10/4/45).
[77]   TNA ADM 223/472. NID 004766/42: *Current Developments in NID*, 23/01/42.

THE STRUGGLE AT SEA

The Sealion's bark

'Never in the field of human conflict was so much owed by so many to so few.'

Winston Churchill's oratory of 21st August 1940 echoes down the decades. The previous months had seen France, a military superpower, vanquished in weeks and other countries topple in days. The tattered remnants of the British Expeditionary Force were retrieved without their weapons, and the Norwegian campaign was an unmitigated disaster. As 'The Few' faced the *Luftwaffe* assault overhead, the Admiralty was ringed with barbed wire and Marine guards were posted outside. Bernard Trench drew a steel helmet, revolver, and ammunition, and visited Trent Park to discuss evacuation. As early as March he had confided to his diary, *'I really think that it would be better to make peace before it becomes impossible & we end in defeat.'*[1] It seemed there was nothing to prevent Operation *Seelöwe* (Sealion), the German invasion, rolling over Britain.

And yet there was. There were twenty miles of restless salt-water, vicious tides, unpredictable weather, and a factor to which the Nazi planners had no answer so chose to ignore. The Royal Navy.

In 1974 the Royal Military Academy at Sandhurst conducted a wargame which exercised the German invasion plan against the British defence plan. The three German and three British umpires unanimously concluded that the initial landings would succeed, but the assault would peter out even before reaching the first hastily improvised 'stop-line' owing to the *Kriegsmarine's* inability to protect cross-Channel traffic for reinforcement, resupply and eventually evacuation.

This in no way understates the contribution of the RAF: only silent skies could have allowed the *Luftwaffe* to counteract the overwhelming British superiority in surface warships, especially after half the *Kriegsmarine's* destroyers had been sunk in Norway. The planned assault and supply by strings of converted river barges, painfully hauled by slow-moving tugs was terrifyingly vulnerable.

The obstacle was no more apparent to German than to British casual observers at the time. *Leutnant zur See* Willi Koch of *U-63*, captured in February 1940, did not expect to be kicking his heels for long.

> '*N203:* *We must have patience till the 1st April. If HOLLAND is taken by the end of March then one reckon to clean up here (in England) by the end of May. It must happen suddenly. They've got no trained troops here in England, they've sent their best troops to France.*'[2]

In June, with the Battle of Britain raging overhead, an unnamed *Maschinenmaat*, probably from *U-13*, was equally sanguine, and apparently clairvoyant.

> '*N273:* *...I know for certain I'll be back in Germany on 22nd September as sure as my name is N273. You can see in my diary that I always knew ahead when anything was going to happen. I foretold when NORWAY and DENMARK were going to be occupied. Hermann has said that peace with England will be made on 22nd September. I also know when England will be attacked: On the 9th June, exactly a week from now. In July and August peace negotiations will take place and in September we'll be at home.*'[3]

The forty-eight survivors of *U-26*, sunk on 1st July, were sure their stay would be a short one. This exchange between the skipper *Kapitänleutnant* Heinz Scheringer (N316) and engineer

Leutnant (Ing) Herbert Freund (N317) seemed unusually precise.

'N317:   *I imagine the attack will start between the 15th July and the 1st August.*

N316:   *They think our present air attacks are big things; they'll have a rude awakening!'[4]*

As each dawn threatened to bring a sky filled with parachutes and echoing to the sound of church bells tolling, German prisoners were conscious of the punishment awaiting them on their return if they had given too much away.

Yet July, August, September passed, and assault troops were spotted moving away from the embarkation ports. The onset of autumn seemed to have lifted the threat. For now.

A months-long drought of new naval prisoners ended when *U-32* and *U-31* were sunk within days of each other on 30th October and 2nd November.[5] It quickly became clear that seagoing crewmen were treating the setback as a delay, not a cancellation. *Kapitänleutnant* Willfried Prellberg of *U-31* confidently expected an invasion in March 1941. N415, an *Obermaschinist* from the unlucky *U-31* and N441, a *Maschinenmaat* from E-boat *S-38* discussed the prospects.

'N415:   *…The English officers treat us very well.*

N441:   *We're well-treated, I have the impression that they're treating us well because they're afraid of reprisals when our troops land.*

I think we'll still be here at Christmas.

N415:   *It's possible that we'll be here another year. I travelled right across ENGLAND on my way here; they still get meat to eat everywhere.*

N441:   *I wonder if the invasion will happen soon.*

N415:   *The idea must have been given up.*

N441:   *When I was in KIEL negotiations with ENGLAND were still in progress. I don't know what the outcome*

was. The English naval officers on board the destroyer that saved me,
came and shook hands with me and were very friendly. The English
don't want to continue the war, it's only that little clique round
CHURCHILL that wants to carry on with the war.
N 415:   I've noticed, too, that the English don't want war.'[6]
Meanwhile Prellberg got into an argument with *Kapitänleutnant*
Hans Jenisch of *U-32* over what should happen to the British
after conquest. The former's argument for (relative) moderation
fell on deaf ears.
    'N 364 [Jenish]:   ENGLAND must be absolutely cleared out.
It must be as if the island did not exist.'[7]
It was *Kapitänleutnant* Otto Kretschmer (N481) of *U-99*, one of
the top-scoring U-boat 'aces', who introduced a note of realism.
He was captured in a convoy battle that killed the notorious
Joachim Schepke on 17th March 1941. To cap a triple disaster the
infamous Günther Prien, who sank the battleship *Royal Oak* in
Scapa Flow, had perished a few days earlier. Kretschmer
explained to Horst Hesselbarth, a trainee commander who was
with him to gain experience,
    'N481:   …more difficult than in NORWAY. We have talked
too much about the invasion. It can no longer come as a surprise. If
we had not talked so much about it, we could just lead them up the
garden now. But it's rotten now. …?… it is impossible to effect a
landing.
    N482:   But surely they are practising the crossing and landing
operations in HELIGOLAND.
    N481:   Yes, I know that – I have heard that too. I think that
if they invade at all they'll do it in the late autumn. At home they are
training naval troops (marines?) night and day in landing
operations. The navy was not … looked after. You must bear in
mind the (enormous) difference in the strength of the British and the
German navies – oh hell! You must remember that all our naval
manoeuvres, which we've carried out in the last few years, have never

been directed at the English fleet but always against the French. In
that respect our fleet was organised on entirely wrong lines.'[8]

In May *Leutnant* Helmut Ecke, a war correspondent who had
been riding with *U-110* was heard to observe,

'The possibility of a successful invasion keeps getting more and more
remote. It can't be done with ships and the G.A.F. is not enough.
However gallant the individual soldier may be, he can't advance
against an English tank. Even if 30,000 men could be landed by the
G.A.F. – 30,000 men against the English home army of 300,000
men with all sorts of motorized vehicles, artillery, tanks, etc…!'[9]

A month later Germany turned on her Russian ally. About four
million soldiers crossed the frontier on an 1,800-mile front. The
Wehrmacht had a track record of lightning victories, while the
Soviet army had failed to subdue tiny Finland in the Winter War
of 1939/40. What could possibly go wrong?

Hitler's armies, unlike Napoleon's, held on through two
grim winters before von Paulus' defeat at Stalingrad turned the
fingerposts firmly back westward. With no evidence, Military
Intelligence chiefs meanwhile continued to insist there was an
uncommitted German army of twenty divisions held back for
the invasion of Britain.

The army may have been imaginary, but the potential threat
was not. Agents' and reconnaissance reports in autumn 1941
suggested renewed invasion craft construction. These were reinforced by captives' stories.

'Prisoners stated that a large number of passenger ships had been
collected in Hamburg and had had part of their bows cut away, in
order to facilitate the landing of troops. It could not be ascertained
whether these ships were for use against England or Russia.'[10]

NID commentators hedged their bets, but prisoners seemed
convinced the target was Britain. Much of their invasion talk at
this time sounds like whistling in the dark, but now and then
someone seemed to be speaking at least from plausible rumour.

Bootsmannsmaat Friedrich Huffmeyer of *U-434* was overheard saying,

> *'N1095 was telling me that there are a lot of factories near his home (Neuendorf, Saxony), and in one of them gliders are built. They're like flat triangles, and are towed either by three bombers or by a 'Ju'. They can carry a big tank, with the crew and everything.'*

Equally *Maschinenmaat* Konrad Lorenz of E-boat *S-53* spoke with apparent confidence of tanks able to crawl up to fifteen metres under water.[11] The underwater tanks, at least, were real but did not come close to operational use. Neither lead was thought worth including in the relevant formal report.

The topic never quite died down. In March 1942 *Leutnant* Hans Opitz of *U-93* theorised that the assault would happen that autumn or the following spring, while Japan took care of India and the Far East. That May A1024, a bomber air mechanic, was overheard saying,

> *'Just wait until the S.S. gets busy here, then the tears will flow. They'll do exactly the same here as they did in POLAND.'*[12]

N1699, a *Matrosenobergefreiter* (Able Seaman) from *U-506*, told two stool pigeons in July 1943 that he had seen more troops in France than ever before, and paratroopers carrying out intensive exercises. His statement was collated with several others in a July 1943 report, which seemed to confirm work in progress on new heavy gliders but left open the question of whether it was offensive or defensive. The report's preamble stated,

> *'Since the cancellation of the former "Seelöwe" operation of September 1940, the possibility of another attempt at invasion was only very rarely mentioned by P/W until a few months ago. P/W from U-506 and U-607 captured on 12 and 13 Jul 43 have, however, made a number of references to this possibility, and their statements and those of other recently captured P/W are summarized below.'*[13]

As late as 1944 there was real concern that an airborne invasion, however futile, might be attempted to forestall the D-Day landings.

Bismarck, Hood, and Tirpitz

On 27th May 1941, the fearsome *Bismarck* sank after a long, brutal chase in which the Royal Navy lost the battlecruiser *Hood*, and the brand-new battleship *Prince of Wales* was damaged. Seventy-five of the 110 survivors rescued by the Royal Navy[14] were selected for interrogation, arriving at Trent Park on 8th June. It is clear from Trench's diary that the staff struggled with the scale of the task; the report was eventually sent to the printer on 21st July.

Crippled by a lucky torpedo strike on her steering gear, *Bismarck* had fought to the end against British battleships *King George V* and *Rodney*. She had somehow remained afloat under unimaginable pounding until, reduced to a helpless, blazing wreck, the combined effect of more torpedoes and her own scuttling charges sealed her fate. Yet it was a close-run thing. Admiral John Tovey's forces were running dangerously low on fuel, *Bismarck* was approaching the point where she could expect shore-based air support, and the battle was entering the U-boat danger area. And her sister, *Tirpitz*, was still an intact and ever-present threat. It was vital to understand how these capital ships seemingly outclassed the Royal Navy's best – and what could be done about them.

Over two thousand seamen died in the wreck. More might have been rescued but for propaganda-induced fear that survivors would be shot at (see The ones who got away, above).

There were probably not too many tears shed for the unfortunate *Bismarck* crew left in the water, as the navy and the nation were still reeling from the traumatic loss of the 'Mighty Hood' due to a magazine explosion after just a few German salvoes. An ordinary seaman gunner's boasting made uncomfortable listening but gave some insight into the loss.

'The 'HOOD' was at a nice distance, 23 Kilometres. An armour-piercing shell only has its best effect from a distance of 23 Kilometres, because they drop almost vertically. There was a running fight on the port side. The 'HOOD' opened fire on us, got the range at once and hit us in the bows. The 1st Gunnery Officer was standing on the foretop and the 2nd Gunnery Officer was at the forward gun control tower. Before opening fire the 1st Gunnery Officer said: "I'd certainly like to know what ship that is". The 2nd Gunnery Officer said: "That isn't a cruiser, it's a big ship. Just look at the superstructure, Herr SCHNEIDER. Surely you know which ship in the English navy has that superstructure; it is none other than the battle-cruiser 'HOOD'!" Who of us had ever thought that we would have got mixed up in a naval battle, we were only thinking of commerce raiding.

.... range-taking was proceeding. He was calling out "23 Kilometres, 23 Kilometres" .... they were calling out (the figures for) C/D battery – "C/D Battery" "Central (? control)" Bang! "Short" "Up 200 metres" .... you see, no, they were firing 4 (? with a 400 meter bracket) .... The 1st Gunnery Officer gave .... "Over" from the foretop .... second, the next one fell. That was short. "Short" .... that is to say just in front. That .... up 200 metres. With this elevation put on .... should give a straddle. "Straddle" he shouted. The fourth salvo comes down "Enemy on fire". The fifth salvo goes flying into the air, and she put another (salvo) across. "Enemy sinking" .... The 1st Gunnery Officer immediately gave the order: "Now swing to the left and on to the 'KING GEORGE'".[15] Then by direct fire control, we all fired the first salvo into the upper part of the 'KING GEORGE'. I mean the guns were trained by direct observation. Then the brute turned away!

That was a bit of bad luck! She would have met the same fate as the 'HOOD'.[16]

Hood was under construction at the time of Jutland in 1916. The lessons learnt from that battle led to considerable strengthening of her side armour, but there was not enough reserve buoyancy to do the same for her deck armour. This caused her fatal vulnerability to plunging fire from a more modern battleship. Listeners did at least have the consolation of knowing that her first rounds had been on target. Later evidence suggests that they caused a critical oil leak which slowed *Bismarck*, made her easier to track and narrowed her options.

That left *Tirpitz*. Following the Washington, Geneva, and London arms limitation conferences of the 'Twenties and 'Thirties capital ships were limited to a maximum 35,000 tons displacement. This was supposed to constrain the mixture of speed, armament, and armour they could incorporate. Thus, the British *Nelson* class packed a massive punch with their nine sixteen-inch guns but were relatively slow with a maximum speed of 23 knots. The newer *King George V* class were a good five knots faster but limited to fourteen-inch main armament. Treaty limits relied on builders telling the truth. A conversation between two *Bismarck* artificers suggested otherwise.

A: *The largest and most modern battleship in the world, 35,000 tons, and she goes down like that!*
B;   *Do you know what our real displacement was?*
A: *Hm?*
B: *50,000 tons.*
A: *I don't believe it.*
B: *Someone told me that a long time ago.*
A: *Hm?*
B: *It's true.*[17]

The interrogation report, when finally published, was cautious about taking the claim at face value but suggested that the builders had economised with the truth by calculating the vessel's weight largely empty.

'Amongst prisoners there was a divergence of opinion as to "Bismarck's" tonnage, although the majority insisted that this was 35,000 tons. In accordance with the Washington Treaty the standard displacement should have been 35,000 tons, excluding oil fuel and reserve feed water but with ammunition.

One prisoner, who had been a considerable time in the ship during building, stated that the declared tonnage of 35,000 tons was considered by the German Authorities to exclude fuel, feed water, domestic water and stores, and included only half the ammunition. If this basis can be accepted it seems probable that the loaded or deep displacement was not far short of 50,000 tons. This figure is naturally dependent on the oil fuel storage capacity (See VII, 21), regarding which there is some doubt, and which has been estimated at 8,500 tons. Many British officers, who had taken part in the operations, considered "Bismarck" to be of at least 50,000 tons, and statements from some prisoners tended to confirm this figure for the deep displacement.'[18]

This was perhaps the first concrete evidence that the Germans had systematically lied about the size of the ships built in their rearmament programme since 1934. In 1936 the German Embassy had told the Foreign Office that Battleship F (which would become *Bismarck*) would have a length of 241 metres, beam of 36 metres and draught of 7.9 metres to stay within the Washington and London Treaty limit of 35,000 tons. On this basis the Admiralty's Plans Division assumed the ship was intended for use in the Baltic and therefore aimed more at Russia than Britain. In fact, her draught was 9.3 metres. Both the vice-consul in Hamburg who was present at her launch and Muirhead-Gould, an earlier Naval Attaché in Berlin were sceptical but ignored.[19] A 1938 German document captured post war gives a table of actual and declared characteristics for

Scharnhorst, *Bismarck*, and three planned ships which were never built. The commentary makes it clear that there was nothing accidental about their excess size.[20]

The captured survivors included four officers, whose knowledge helped CSDIC to produce a 59-page report covering the ship's construction, armour, machinery, electrical equipment, armament, optical and radar sensors, damage control and many lesser details.

Kapitänleutnant Wunderlich, late of the supply ship *Gonzen-heim*, had been chatting with a *Bismarck* survivor and passed on his cellmate Herbert Wohlfarth, formerly commander of *U-556*.

> 'N719:   *The English did not sink the BISMARCK in the way they imagine, thank goodness.*
>
> N794:   *Well, that is obvious.*
>
> N719:   *That is wonderful for the TIRPITZ, isn't it, because they have no idea what they are up against. The next time they will not take so much trouble, they will think........'[21]*

The Admiralty's conclusion was that if *Tirpitz* ever left her Norwegian lair it would take three *King George V* class battleships to subdue her. On this basis her mere existence tied down an unreasonable part of Britain's military strength. Regular reconnaissance was needed to check that she was still there, and enough ships ready to intercept her in whichever direction she might go. The slaughter of Arctic convoy PQ17 in June 1942, ordered to scatter just on the fear that she might be out, was reminder enough of the looming effect that ship could have British plans without ever weighing anchor.

Early in 1942 Admiral Godfrey therefore invited ideas for dealing with *Tirpitz* from anyone who thought they could help. He received plenty – over thirty-five submissions, many with several options. They ranged from almost practical to verging on the insane, and most would have been near suicidal for the poor souls asked to carry them out.[22] Nonetheless the exercise

produced enough useful concepts to be worth repeating, and
some bore startling resemblance to the trick which lured
Scharnhorst to her death the following year.

Just 36 *Scharnhorst* survivors made their way to Britain in the
first days of 1944. One was a stretcher case and there were no
officers among them. By then the CSDIC information factory
was so finely tuned that it could produce a 96-page draft report,
including a nearly complete compartment map, from this
unpromising raw material by the end of February. More
relevantly, some had previous experience of *Tirpitz* and described
the low morale aboard the 'prison ship.' One had been present
during the midget submarine attack the previous autumn and
described the extent of the damage and progress of repairs.
Between them they provided intelligence on the strengthened
anti-submarine and anti-aircraft defences at her anchorage,
which must have been valuable in planning the subsequent air
attacks. Five naval and three RAF missions between April and
November 1944 repeatedly delayed her readiness for sea and
eventually sank her.[23]

Capture Me if you Can

A damaged submarine, if it reaches the surface at all, tends not
to stay there long. This was doubly so for U-boats whose
commanders had been indoctrinated with the principle that their
boats must not fall into enemy hands, even at the cost of their
own and their crews' lives.

There are exceptions to every rule. The first was Fritz-Julius
Lemp, who had opened hostilities on the first day of the war by
sinking the liner *Athenia*. By May 1941 he was the popular,
experienced, and respected skipper of a newer boat, *U-110*.
While attacking a convoy he was cornered and depth-charged by

three escorts and forced to surface. Assuming the boat was doomed the crew abandoned ship and most (not including the captain) were rescued by the corvette HMS *Aubretia*. They landed at Scapa Flow and were taken to Trent Park with no idea of subsequent events at sea.

Another of Lemp's attackers, HMS *Bulldog*, sent over a boarding party led by Sub-Lieutenant David Balme. They retrieved everything they could including, critically, an intact Enigma machine and the current set of code books and cipher settings. *U-110* was taken in tow but sank on its way to Iceland.

At Trent Park N702 *Bootsmaat* Willy Brohm was closeted with N640, an opposite number from *Bismarck* for whom the high casualties after the sinking still rankled. Brohm clarified the brutal priorities of Atlantic war.

'N640: *On board the destroyer the English told me that they would have rescued still more people, but were prevented from doing so because a German U-boat had fired a torpedo at the destroyer. I don't believe that a U-boat would interfere with rescue work.*

N702: *It certainly would. A destroyer is worth more than the few men who would have been saved.'*[24]

The boat's crew included two interesting and unusual members. One was Helmut Ecke, a twenty-three-year-old war correspondent from the *Propaganda Kompanie* (PK) given the nominal rank of *Leutnant zur See*. He had never seen a U-boat before volunteering for this cruise. For some reason he was taken to Brixton Prison on arrival in London and given prison clothes to wear, an indignity which he felt very keenly, and which had to be talked through before he would volunteer any information. A conversation with watch officer Ulruch Wehrhöfer confirmed that neither of them had any idea the boat had failed to sink.

'N637 [Ecke]: *That [destroyer] is the one that took us to SCAPA. I thought that the Kommandant had died of his own free will, as I had not seen him at all in the water. I thought that perhaps*

*he had remained on board, had shut himself in and sunk the boat
with (flooding) vents.*

*N609 [Wehrhöfer]:   The L.I. [Engineer Lieutenant] and 1st
W.O. thought that too, because we had been together all the time and
he certainly did not get to (the corvette). When I went overboard and
was afterwards swimming in the water, the U-Boat was already
under water aft as far as the conning tower. The L.I. was washed
over the U-Boat again and could no longer get a foothold in the stern.
When the U-Boat went down, we were 400 miles from Iceland in
the middle of the Atlantic.'[25]*

The other odd catch was navigation petty officer N610, who we
met before in Human Wrongs. The inclusion of N610 and two
ratings of known Communist views may reflect Lemp's
willingness and ability to build and keep an able team around
him.

The report on *U-110* makes no mention of the boat's capture
and the interrogators themselves were probably unaware of it.
There was no chance of keeping the next gift under wraps. Three
months later, on 27th August 1941, *U-570* was just three days into
her first cruise when *Kapitänleutnant* Hans Rahmlow gave the
order to surface. He came up almost directly below a patrolling
Hudson aircraft which immediately attacked, straddling the boat
with four depth charges. With the boat taking on water, batteries
giving off chlorine gas, multiple breakages, and a panicky crew
Rahmlow aborted his crash dive and returned to the surface.
Squadron Leader Thompson overhead ceased his attack when he
saw a white flag but carried on circling warily.

The stand-off lasted twelve hours, during which Rahmlow
informed Dönitz of his predicament then disposed of his
Enigma machine and confidential papers. No fewer than six
British and Canadian ships arrived over time and, with
difficulty, towed *U-570* to Iceland where she was beached on
29th August. She was re-floated on 5th September and, after a

hasty survey and repair, sailed to Barrow-in-Furness under her own power from 29th September to 3rd October.

Secrecy was impossible. Apart from the captain's own signal the boat was surveyed in Iceland by US officers who were still neutral at the time and arrived at Barrow in a blaze of publicity.

An Admiralty order to refrain from hasty interrogation either did not reach the ships at sea or was ignored. Luckily, Lieutenant Ryan in HMCS *Niagara* transporting 31 prisoners to Iceland was a former policeman and knew what he was about. When they arrived, they may have met Charles Mitchell, a civilian member of NID staff, who flew out on 30th August and returned on 4th September well pleased with the information and documents he had harvested.[26] The prisoners themselves landed Clydeside on 13th September. In early November NID interrogators were sent to Barrow in relays to inspect the submarine and get a feel for her layout, so they could better relate to their guests. When she was recommissioned as HMS *Graph* later that month, they were probably expected to get in some sea time with her.

There was no question in the minds of the officers who surveyed the boat that a more experienced and competent crew could have repaired enough of the damage to dive the boat out of danger during the night. First officer *Oberleutnant zur See* Bernhardt Berndt seemed, in retrospect, to agree.

'The disaster came about because we were in a position where we couldn't help ourselves, thinking we should be shot afterwards if we tried anything on. But, of course, that was a false impression. It would have been the best thing for us if we had been depth-charged and not bombed from the air. The trawler which took off our wounded placed an armed prize crew on board us at once, and they said: "Three officers must go across now. We have to stay here as a prize crew." It was all up then. The accumulators had run down and there was no current. Nobody went below again. It occurred to me

afterwards that one could have done some damage to the U-boat by means of the diver's emergency hatch (Tauchernotluk). They towed the U-boat the whole day long. We were hoping that she would somehow sink through the action of the tide. It is amazing what that U-boat stood up to.'[27]

For Berndt there was a fatal postscript. On arrival at the officers' internment camp at Grizedale Hall he was summoned before a prisoners' kangaroo court, or 'Council of Honour' chaired by Otto Kretschmer. Convicted of cowardice he was ordered to escape, make his way to Barrow, and destroy the boat. He got away but was recaptured. Rather than face whatever 'justice' his peers had in mind he made a futile run for it and was shot by the Home Guard.

On 4th June 1944 *U-505* encountered a task group centred on USS *Guadalcanal*, which had been directed to the boat's approximate position by signals intelligence. After a brisk fight which left the abandoned boat circling on the surface and taking on water a boarding party managed to secure her. She was recovered complete with code machine and documents and is now displayed outside Chicago's Museum of Science and Industry. The crew were kept incommunicado at Camp Ruston in Louisiana to prevent the seizure of secret material leaking.

These were the only U-boat captures. *U-559* was sunk in the eastern Mediterranean on 30th October 1942. Before she went down a boarding party from HMS *Petard* had time to pass out her code machine and cipher books. Sadly, two of the party perished in the process.

There were other cases of surface vessels being apprehended either in the normal course of events or deliberately targeted to 'pinch' their cypher documents and equipment. CSDIC staff were deliberately kept ignorant of the cryptanalysts' work so one example will serve to illustrate the point. In the constant struggle to keep up with the changes to German codes Harry Hinsley, a

Bletchley codebreaker, suggested that weather and supply ships might be a fruitful source. This was proven on 7th May 1941 when the weather ship *München* was taken by surprise and her code material captured. The crew arrived in London on 12th and were interrogated, but there is no report on record.

Viva Vigo

The Admiralty's recurring nightmare was that Axis powers might gain access by force, diplomacy, or subterfuge to the remaining neutral ports. Britain had occupied Iceland, with its strategic mid-Atlantic location, at the same time as the Nazis marched into the Netherlands and Belgium. That left Sweden, the Republic of Ireland, Spain, Portugal, and Turkey as principal headaches, all of whom at least expected a German victory if they were not actively sympathetic to German aims.

Spain and Portugal, in particular, were dictatorships which commanded strategic locations. Portugal's Atlantic coast and ownership of the Azores could have allowed Dönitz' U-boats to envelop the critical convoy routes. Spain commanded access to Gibraltar, and thus the Mediterranean, as well as having her own Atlantic and Mediterranean ports. Both countries were the scene of intense diplomatic and covert manoeuvring to tilt their favour one way or the other.

A reader familiar with the book, film, or TV series *Das Boot* may remember the scene in which the protagonist refuels and resupplies at night in the shadow of a German merchant ship in the Bay of Vigo. This really happened. We have already met Friedrich Huffmeyer, one of three surviving *Bootsmannsmaate* (Boatswains Mates) from *U-434*, who inadvertently gave the game away.

*'N1112: We had already been at sea for six weeks. I took stock
of the provisions and told the commander that we could only last out
for another five days. He said: "I must have an official report from
you about that," to which I replied: "Yes." We entered VIGO by
daylight, submerged, and lay submerged there the whole day. At
night, when it was dark and the traffic had stopped, we surfaced near
a Spanish cruiser, which lay about 200 metres off the jetty. There
was a German steamer there. Everything was ready. Then came the
hose pipes for water and fuel. And then we took on case after case.
You could hardly move about on board, with all those cases. All our
provisions were in wooden cases – tin lined – the tinned stuff was in
them.'[28]*

Moreover, a list of stores taken on board was captured with the
survivors.

Apart from enjoying a few hours of safety and fresh air (albeit
with strenuous physical work) the submariners were sometimes
allowed to board the depot vessel, Neptun Lines' MV *Bessel*.
N1180 (Günter Flörecke), a *Mechanikersmaat* from *U-581*, took
the opportunity to write home.[29]

The situation could hardly have been kept secret from the
Spanish authorities: their naval ships regularly visited the bay,
Bessel's crew had frequent runs ashore, her captain was alleged to
be in close touch with the Gestapo and certainly had constantly
to scour Spain for supplies in the transparent cover of a corn
chandler. *Bootsmaate* N1067 from *U-574* and N1097 from *U-131*
summed up the British dilemma:

*'N1067: You mustn't say anything about VIGO. We were
there too. We were to return to port and then they sent us a message:
"Take provisions and fuel on board at VIGO, there is a German
ship there." We took provisions and everything on board there. That
was at the end of our second cruise.*[30]

N1097: They probably know that too.

N1067:   Yes, they know that too. Now if an English submarine goes in and sinks this ship, it will naturally have sunk, not a German ship, but a neutral one and of course that will be very awkward for the English.[31]

N1067's shipmate N1068, a *Funkmaat* (telegraphist), elaborated on the system.

'The "HAPAG" ship previously mentioned is lying at anchor in the Bay of VIGO and U-boats go in and make fast alongside at night. Their boat [U 574] came in after midnight and left at 5 a.m. the same morning. The crew of the supply boat is allowed ashore, but unless having night passes must return by the last tender leaving VIGO pier at 2330 hours.'[32]

There was more evidence in 1943 when *U-536 Funkgefreiter* Heinz Kern was chatting with stool pigeon N1552.

'I know of one boat which was in SPAIN for a fortnight, they got ammunition and then sailed again. A fellow told me that, who afterwards joined the "505". I believe it was the "163".[33]

MV *Bessel* remained at Vigo until the end of the war, when she was surrendered to the British Government. She continued in merchant service under a variety of owners until 1972.

Nor was this the only convenient Spanish myopia. The *Abwehr* maintained an observation post in Algeciras whence they could report on British naval and air movements to and through Gibraltar. Also, at Algeciras, Italian special forces set up shop in the hulk of an interned tanker, *Olterra*, from which they sortied through an underwater hatch on manned torpedoes to attack shipping in Gibraltar harbour. Supplies had to be smuggled in, so it is possible the authorities were unaware of this almost insanely brave enterprise. They had no such excuse in the Canary Islands where they actively co-operated in the conversion and use of stranded German merchantmen as naval supply ships and blockade-runners.[34]

We can sympathise with the frustration of intelligence officers faced by clear evidence of Spanish abuse of neutrality but unable to do anything about it. Their suppressed fury comes through in this extract from the history of NID Section 20.

'*N.I.D. fought a long battle to prevent the enemy from using Spain for their own purposes. They accumulated evidence which should enable the Foreign Office to protest to Spain against German infringement of the laws of neutrality, but, though such protests were made from time to time and were of some effect, our Ambassador was reluctant to press Spain too hard and firmly resisted any eagerness by N.I.D. or C. [the head of M.I.6] to take an unneutral leaf out of the German book. The enemy did continually what we were not allowed to do and in all our counter-activities we had one hand tied behind our back by diplomatic caution.*'[35]

The risk of driving an already sympathetic fascist government into open alliance with the Axis powers was simply too great.

---

[1] Trench Papers: *Diary 30/11/39 – 14/09/41*. Entry for 18/3/40.
[2] TNA WO 208/4141. SRN 25 (4/3/40).
[3] Ibid. *SRN 1-240*. SRN 69 (7/6/40).
[4] Ibid. SRN 75 (11/7/40).
[5] *U-31* had the distinction of being sunk twice: once on 11/3/40 by air attack in the Jade Bight with the loss of all hands, and again after being raised and put back into service, with 2 dead and 44 survivors. 31 was an unlucky number.
[6] Ibid. SRN 135 (24/11/40).
[7] Ibid. SRN 151 (7/12/40).
[8] Ibid. SRN 148 (30/11/40), 182 (22/3/41).
[9] TNA WO 208/4142. SRN 349 (20/5/41).
[10] TNA ADM 186/806. CB 4051 (29), *Interrogation of Survivors from Raider 33 (PINGUIN) and of other Raider Prisoners*. P.48. This was based on a conversation between two *Pinguin* survivors on 22/8/41 (WO 208/4143, SRN 635).
[11] TNA WO 208/4143. SRN 766 (24/1/42), SRN 805 (23/2/42).
[12] TNA AIR 40/3102. Extract from SR Draft No 1392 (25/5/42).
[13] Ibid, SRN 870 (11/3/42). WO 208/4196. SP/F 119 (19/7/43). WO 208/4198. *Invasion of Great Britain*.
[14] About another hundred were picked up by a German weather ship.
[15] The target was *Prince of Wales*, another *King George V* class battleship.

16 Ibid. SRN 436 (21/6/41).

17 Ibid. SRN 387 (6/6/41).

18 TNA ADM 186/806. P.238.

19 McLachlan, *Room 39*. P.136-142.

20 TNA ADM 199/443.

21 TNA WO 208/4143. SRN 566 (20/7/41).

22 TNA ADM 223/473.

23 See TNA WO 208/4149. SRN 2710 (10/1/44), 2735 (11/1/44), 2755 (13/1/44), 2751, 2752 (17/1/44), 2819 (21/1/44), 2831(22/1/44), 2800 (23/1/44), 2047 (24/1/44), 2033 (26/1/44).

24 TNA WO 208/4142. SRN 397 (9/6/41).

25 Ibid. SRN 343 (20/5/41).

26 Waller, *The Surrender, Capture and Recovery of U-570*, P.6-7. Trench Diary 30/11/39-14/9/41 (NMRN 2017/24/28).

27 TNA WO 208/4143. SRN 668 (8/10/41).

28 TNA WO 208/4144. SRN 807 (23/2/42).

29 Ibid. SRN 886 (16/3/42).

30 This was on or about the night of 13th-14th December 1941.

31 Ibid. SRN 741 (10/1/42).

32 TNA WO 208/4196. SP/F/96 (31/12/41).

33 TNA WO 208/4148. SRN 2494 (28/11/43).

34 Juan-José Díaz-Benítez: *German Supply Ships and Blockade Runners in the Canary Islands in the Second World War*. Mariner's Mirror 2018 P.318-329.

35 TNA ADM 223/487. P.90.

MEASURES AND
COUNTERMEASURES

The more there is of mine …

The benefits of a joint-service approach were amply demonstrated by information obtained from *Luftwaffe* prisoners about air-laid magnetic mines. As early as 20th November 1939 Bernard Trench confided to his diary, *'Hitler has got the Admiralty properly fussed over his magnetic mines, which we don't seem able to sweep up,'* and that he had been tasked with producing a report about them.

The *Kriegsmarine* started offensive mining by submarine, destroyer, and disguised merchant ship on the first day of the war. Three ships were mined off Orfordness and Flamborough Head within a few days, the last despite the area having been 'cleared' by sweeping. A leading seaman from *U-27* provided the first confirmation that influence mines were being used.

> *'The mines, it was stated, are impossible to sweep up by ordinary methods. …the only method of clearing them would be, as he humorously described it, by allowing them to detonate under a ship, or by using a magnetic rod ("stange"). Such a method of sweeping would be very clumsy, and for this reason there was a device to render the mines inoperative after a period of 4 to 5 months.'[1]*

In a separate development German naval and *Luftwaffe* aircraft began to drop mines fitted with parachutes to slow their descent and a secondary fuse to detonate them if they landed on a hard surface. A prisoner later revealed that experiments with air-dropped magnetic mines had begun as early as 1934.[2]

209

Tricky night navigation and equipment failure led to a stroke of good fortune on 23rd November 1939, when two unexploded mines were recovered from the mudflats of Shoeburyness. Reverse engineering their mechanism allowed the British to develop degaussing technology for their ships, and a magnetic influence sweep.

That was not the end of the story. Trench wrote to Lieutenant-Colonel Kendrick, Commandant of Trent Park, in February 1940 urgently requesting more details about mines (and especially their markings) from overheard conversations. He was alarmed by an M Room report of 3rd February which referred to an even newer development: acoustic mines which incorporated variable activation delay and a ship counter, and could be dropped on land as well as water.[3]

CSDIC's resource triptych: direct interrogation, stool pigeons (SPs) and microphones, was brought to bear on the problem. We have met stool pigeon A713, who comes over as skilled, inventive, and nerveless. He served almost throughout the war and convinced a wide variety of captives that he was one of their own. A711 was another. Bit by bit, the snippets of information started to come in.

A702: (After interrogation on mines)
He (I.O.) also asked about mines which only explode after a certain time. There are such mines. They are set in advance. (They have) either time fuses so that they explode only after say 6 or 7 days or else they are set in such a way that the mine explodes only after a certain number of ships have passed over it. A steamer can pass over it for instance without anything happening and then a convoy comes along and the thing explodes. We have laid mines which only become live after 7 days.[4]

Ship counters and arming delays were among the first of the tricks employed in the constant battle of wits between mine and countermeasures specialists. The first allowed several ships to pass safely over the mine before it detonated, the second inserted a time delay before it armed. Either (or both used together) might lull minesweeper commanders into believing a channel was safe when deadly munitions simply lay dormant on the seabed. *Maschinengefreiter* Schneider of *U-517* explained the principle to stool pigeon N1067.

'N1067:   *More ships are likely to strike the mines (you laid).*

N1526:   *Yes. We laid some in January – they are said to have had a terrific effect, that's the good thing about them, you can pass over them twenty times and at the twenty-first time they explode.*

N1067:   *Time setting?*

N1526:   *We don't know ourselves how they were set. It's a good thing that the mine artificer hasn't come here with us – he left the boat when we put into the shelter. We left again afterwards and he wasn't there.*

N1067:   *Were they proper round mines?*

N1526:   *Like aircraft bombs with tail fins and everything.'*[5]

Other mine types embodied fuses designed specifically to kill disposal officers, which made it imperative to know what each version looked like and what markings it carried. Prisoner conversations, helpfully prompted by stool pigeons, gradually filled out a catalogue.

'A 711:   *But surely it can happen that you mix the mines up if they all look the same?*

...

A 707:   *The acoustic mine is the green mine, and is also called "L.M.B. Stern" a/c mine B.Star. The white mine is the "L.M.A." and the yellow mine is the "L.M.B.", the green one being the "B.Star".'*[6]

★ ★ ★

'A 707:   *He (I.O.) had a sort of operational report. There it said: "L.M. Green", the marking is V.H.4, that is that L.M.B. Green Star. That is the acoustic one. I said it was the magnetic one.*

But it is the other way about. "L.M. Blue" is a special mine with a long-delay fuse. I said that it could be dropped on land …

A 711:   *A marine mine, too?*

A 707:   *Hm.*

A 711:   *But it isn't.*

A 707:   *Yes. He (I.O.) does not know for certain about that.'*[7]

He does now.

These and similar transcripts provided the kind of intelligence that could only be obtained from the heads of the people who knew or, very expensively, by trial and error while trying to defuse live mines.

German technological and tactical innovation continued throughout the war but never again achieved the nasty surprise of 1939. A year after these events, for example, in March 1941 an interrogator from the RAF section at Trent Park telephoned Ashe Lincoln of the Department of Torpedoes and Mines Investigation Section (DTMI) about a particularly arrogant *Luftwaffe* pilot's boast that a new type of magnetic mine would destroy Britain's merchant fleet, that it didn't need a parachute (allowing it to be dropped with greater stealth and accuracy) and could not be swept or made safe. Further enquiries yielded only its name, BM1000, which was enough to infer its weight (a metric tonne) and that 'BM' might stand for *Bombemine*, meaning that it functioned both as a bomb and as a mine.[8] Then the secret listeners played their part.

'A777:   *He (I.O.) wanted to know something about the B.M.1000. I told him I knew nothing about it.*

A817:   *I'm in the happy position of not knowing anything.*

A777:   *It is a thing that can be dropped on land or in the sea. If it drops into water to a greater depth than 12 m., it explodes like a bomb. If it drops less than 12m. down in the water, it does not explode but remains at the bottom and acts as a mine.'*[9]

★ ★ ★

'A807:   *Yes, it is very secret, I have given lectures about the B.M.1000. From the outside it looks exactly like a 1,000 kg. bomb, it has, however, no "Spritzring" and a tail unit of (some) compressed substance .... The disadvantage is that they can recognise it easily; but the time-fuse ....(?) And when it drops without exploding it has a fuse which becomes live (?) if it is opened. In any case it explodes - anyone who opens it .... It may only be dropped from aircraft which have that bomb switch (?) (Bombenamfschalter) in which the releasing current and the fuse current are coupled so that the release current can never function without the bomb having been made live – that is to say without the fuse current. That was not the case formerly: you had the fuse switch box and the R.A.B. It was possible to release a bomb and if one had forgotten to connect the switch box the bomb was not live. The release current was there but not the fuse current, and now these two are coupled on one switch. Only those machines are allowed to drop them, so that the danger of their dropping the bombs blind is quite small (except when using) the jettison lever.*

A777:   *Does this bomb act like a mine if it falls in the water?*

A807:   *Yes. Up to 12 metres, between 6 and 12. That sound measurer is only there to control the instrument. It is called a "Radappel" (?), for that is the "R" as far as know. It always goes at certain intervals and only makes one movement.'*[10]

This conversation illustrates a limitation of the M Room system: the pace of technological progress quickly outran the listeners' knowledge and made it difficult for them to produce sensible transcriptions. The problem was later addressed by recruiting stool pigeons from serving German technicians, and interrogators with an engineering background. Nonetheless, the effort evidently bore fruit, for a follow-up in May read:

'During the last few weeks there were progressive indications that the enemy was about to make an alteration in his mining attack.

2. Officers responsible at the Admiralty were put in touch with Wing Commander Felkin and the Staff of the C.S.D.I.C. who took the keenest interest in the subject and the greatest pains to appreciate its technicalities and to understand what to look for and what would be useful.

3. As a consequence, matter of the greatest importance was transmitted to the Director of Torpedoes and Mining, enabling him to form in advance a remarkably accurate picture, to recognise the new object directly it arrived and have an officer on the spot without any delay, and to issue warning and guidance at home and abroad.

4. Since this result has been achieved by close co-operation between all three Services and with the resources of the C.S.D.I.C. it is desired to bring to your notice the satisfactory results achieved, and to request that you will convey an expression of appreciation of their valuable work to the Staff of the C.S.D.I.C. and particularly to Wing Commander Felkin.'[11]

Such close co-operation between services and later between allies, though not perfect, was an integral part of the model from its inception. It was the key to CSDIC's advantage over totalitarian regimes, where vicious inter- (and sometimes intra-) service rivalry was the norm.

On 11th April 1941 CSDIC reported a reference to the new mine, by then known as 'Type G'. This was followed up well enough to create an almost complete reconstruction of its design and issue detailed warnings before its first use on 5th May. It was however left to the DTMI to discover the nature of the booby-traps built into the fusing mechanism.

The Directorate of Torpedoes and Mining observed:

'In view of the complex nature of this weapon and the effect it has had upon our sweeping material and technique, the warning received has been of the utmost importance to the course of the war.'[12]

In an infuriating footnote, full details of the BM1000 were passed to the Russians in a spirit of Allied co-operation, along with a warning that the Germans were unaware that the information had been compromised and a request to keep the matter secret. In marked contrast to Soviet paranoia about their own secrets, full details of the weapon were subsequently published in *Pravda*.[13]

Torpedoes

The Kriegsmarine had high hopes at the start of the war for a secret new design of torpedo 'pistol' or detonator, which was triggered (like a magnetic mine) by a ship's magnetic signature. Not only did this not require a direct hit but, if the warhead exploded beneath a ship's keel, the back-breaking damage that resulted was much worse.

Kapitänleutnant Glattes' *U-39* discovered the flaw in this theory on the boat's first and only operational patrol, when she fired two torpedoes at the aircraft carrier *Ark Royal* on 14th September 1939. The crew heard an explosion, leading them to believe that they had achieved at least one hit. In fact, the torpedo's warhead had detonated short of the target and done nothing more than attract the escort's attention. Four days later Glattes and his disconsolate men were trooping into the Tower of London. They were disconcertingly tight-lipped subjects, but the interrogation report noted, '*It seems fairly certain that magnetic pistols (M.Z.) are being used.*'[14]

The captain of *U-42* (sunk 13th October) admitted the magnetic pistol had been unsatisfactory but claimed that it had been modified and was now very good.[15] NID expressed scepticism which was borne out in practice. While interrogators learnt more about the system U-boat captains' trust in it deteriorated. By the time the crew of *U-55* (sunk 30th January 1940) arrived at Trent Park their faith in it had evaporated.

'It is almost certain that the Germans have a non-contact pistol that works on the vertical component of the ship's magnetic field. On account of the complications that such a pistol entails it is probable that U-boat captains prefer to fire to hit.'[16]

The interrogation report on *U-63*, sunk 25th February 1940, summarised the state of knowledge about German torpedoes at that time. Information was graded according to its reliability, with the magnetic pistol given top billing.[17] The mechanism had to be calibrated for the earth's magnetic field at the latitude where it was used, and this was difficult aboard a submarine. Prisoner N189 (probably *Bootsmaat* Paul Dachner of *U-63*) explained the problem to his cellmate and the eager listeners.

'They are attracted by the ship's magnetism. And then the things are always set; so the magnetic currents run across up to 100 metres. Beyond that there are other magnetic fields. In Germany each of our boats was given a square (on the map); only in that may you shoot and when you get out of this square, into another square, you must change everything ("umstellen").'[18]

A torpedo petty officer from *U-76*, sunk on 5th April 1941, mentioned that magnetic fuses were no longer used. This was confirmed by survivors from *U-651*, sunk in September, who all agreed that they were unsatisfactory in several ways, but especially as they were prone to explode prematurely.[19]

Work continued, and by the time *U-175* met her fate in April 1943 the bugs seemed to have been eliminated. According to *Mechanikerobergefreiter* (Artificer 1st Class) Josef Rosencrantz,

'Up in NORWAY, where so many missed their mark, it was always the pistol which was at fault, but now with the new pistols ....
they (the English) wind a cable round about as often as they like, and send a strong current and so on through it, but the torpedo can't be deflected; the torpedo is now – because – .... intensify or weaken the magnetic .... field, the torpedo (?) is always detonated

(?) .... just like a magnetic mine, it reacts to the increase and decrease of the (magnetic) field.[20]

The interrogation report summarised this and clues from other crew members under the note, *'Prisoners have made obscure references to a new type of pistol.'*[21] While some statements were garbled and contradictory, they agreed that the new fuses were magnetically actuated, did not need to hit the target to explode, and that torpedoes were therefore set for an increased running depth. The technology would come into its own when combined with acoustic homing (see below).

Another development given high confidence in early reports was the use of electric propulsion for torpedoes. Although slower than the alternative combustion engine (no drawback against lumbering merchantmen) electric motors had the advantages of being cheaper and leaving no tell-tale wake. They had originally been trialled in the First World War and not forgotten in the meantime.

A *U-76* survivor produced one of the first straws in the wind about a worrying new development in April 1941.

An officer prisoner stated that experiments were being carried out on a torpedo which would react to sound, so that after being fired in the direction of a ship it would be attracted to its target by the sounds made by the ship, which could therefore not save itself by changing course. According to this prisoner, the "acoustic" torpedo might involve only a relatively slight alteration in the design of torpedoes as a whole, the normal method of propulsion being retained.[22]

At almost the same time Commander Ashe Lincoln of DTMI observed the Trent Park interrogation of a *Feldwebel* (sergeant) whose father was a foreman at the Eckernförde torpedo research plant. This cheerfully open interviewee admitted to knowing and caring nothing about torpedoes but mentioned that his father had brought him along to watch night trials at which the weapon's track could be followed by an upward-shining light.

He described a snaking course which could only be explained by some form of built-in correction.[23]

By the end of 1941, the threat was beginning to look urgent. Stool pigeon N1067 asked *Bootsmannsmaat* Friedrich Huffmeyer of *U-434* straight out,

'Have you got these acoustic torpedoes?'

'Yes'[24]

The interrogation report on *U-210*, sunk in August 1942, noted,

'Experiments are being made with acoustic torpedoes, partly because the British are suspected of using them. This suspicion is due to the large number of instances where British torpedoes have hit the after part of the target – as in the case of "Bismarck." This causes the German authorities to think that British torpedoes are guided by propeller noises.'[25]

These clues were enough to prompt the development of acoustic noisemakers, codenamed Foxer in Britain and FXR in the US, which were designed to be towed behind a ship and distract the torpedo away from the sound of the vessel's screws. They were manufactured in quantity and stored until the expected outbreak of ships being torpedoed in the stern should indicate that homing torpedoes were being used in earnest. Then nothing happened. For quite a long time. Had it all been an expensive false alarm?

At about 0500 hours on 20th September 1943 *U-270* torpedoed HMS *Lagan*, a River class frigate escorting convoy ON 202 in the Atlantic. The severely damaged ship was towed to the Mersey where she was deemed beyond repair and eventually broken up for scrap. One officer and 28 ratings were killed or missing. In the torrid few days that followed the escorts HMCS *St Croix*, HMS *Polyanthus* and HMS *Itchen* were sunk along with six merchant vessels at a total cost of over 440 lives.[26]

The unfortunate *Lagan* was the first ship lost to the new T5 *Zaukönig* (Wren, or 'Gnat' to the British) acoustic homing torpedo, itself derived from the T4 *Falke* (Falcon), of which only about 100 were made and 30 used. It created a new tactical option – to go after the escorts first and leave the convoy defenceless.

Just too late for *Lagan*, *Kapitänleutnant* Werner Pietzsch (N1899) of *U-523* was overheard chatting to the ubiquitous A713. He confirmed that at the time of his sinking in August the T5 was ready for imminent deployment and gave it a name.

'N1899:   *My flotilla had already received secret instructions about ...... I myself know nothing whatsoever about the torpedo.*

A713:   *It hasn't arrived yet?*

N1899:   *No! The instructions are already there ...... the torpedoes will be used operationally in the near future, I don't know how they work, nor do I know how fast they are ......*

A713:   *I suppose they are magnetic or acoustic?*

N1899:   *Yes.*

A713:   *What actually is the secret part?*

N1899:   *......I haven't seen the drawings of the torpedo yet. I can't say how it's constructed – there are so many different types of torpedoes, my dear fellow. "G.7A", "G.7E" and "T.1", Torpedo "I", TII, TIII, and Pi.I which is the impact pistol and Pi.II which is the magnetic pistol: they're continually being altered and given new designations.*

A713:   *What is the name of the new one?*

N1899:   *I don't know, it's got a code name.*

A713:   *What do you call them? That's not giving anything away.*

N1899:   *No, I'd rather – well they're said to be called (?) "Zaukönig".*

A713:   *The little bird?*

N1899:   *Yes.*'[27]

A conversation between stool pigeon N1558 and *Maschinenmaat* Josef Hellmanns of *U-643* in October 1943 cast more light on the tactical use of the new weapon.

'N1929: …The other boats were able to attack the night before. We didn't get near enough. Three weeks before we were in the operational square, the pack which we relieved (sank) ten destroyers and 43,000 gross register tons in one night.

N1558: That's not true!

N1929: Ten destroyers.

N1558: I simply can't imagine it.

N1929: The weapons were only for use against destroyers.

N1558: I should think that if you could sink a destroyer with a torpedo, then you could also sink a merchant ship.

N1929: No, not with that weapon, they can't sink a merchant ship with that.

N1558: I'll tell you something, If I have a torpedo, it doesn't matter how complicated it is, merchant ships or –

N1929: You can't …… that torpedo, it can't be used, it won't work. It only works against a certain ship. I can't explain it to you exactly. But …… at least at first, you mark my words, we shan't hear anything now, but later on we shall hear something. A new apparatus with new torpedoes, – now there is new apparatus in them ……'[28]

In fact, the T5 worked perfectly well against merchant ships. It was just expensive. U-773's first officer explained the attacking boat's dilemma in a post-war interrogation.

'…orders were always to attack primarily Merchant Ships but as escorts became stronger, particularly on the Russian Route, it became necessary to attack them, in order to weaken the screen. Even if success in this was achieved, it was usually too late by then to attack the convoy itself. The introduction of the "Gnat" also made it easier to attack escorts, particularly fast ones, than it had been previously.'[29]

Although effective the Foxer/FXR countermeasures had an unfortunate drawback. Without knowing the exact frequencies which the T5 used for homing they had to broadcast noise over a spectrum covering the whole range of ships' propeller noise.

This unavoidably interfered with the escorts' own sonar and made their work more difficult. CSDIC therefore kept an alert ear open for anything that would refine the Admiralty's understanding of the weapon.

The interrogators struck lucky with *U-73* and *U-593*, both sunk in December 1943. A Torpedo Petty Officer from each boat had recently attended a short course on the T5 at Gdynia and was able to fill in some of the missing detail.

They gave the weapon's speed and range as 24½ knots and 5,000m – both slight underestimates but near enough – and the safety run-out before the homing mechanism was enabled as 300 to 400m. It was claimed to detect sounds within an arc ±45° of straight ahead in the 'supersonic' band (NID doubted this as it was also said to be impervious to Asdic transmission). It steered toward the loudest noise using full left or right helm, or straight ahead. There were separate settings to attack an approaching or receding target, along with one to disable homing when it was not required or not working, and a safety mode for maintenance. With the torpedo nose now occupied by the homing system's hydrophones a different way of triggering the warhead had to be found from the previous impact pistol. A combined inertia and magnetic fuse was set into the top of the weapon, which allowed it to detonate under the target's keel – far deadlier than a direct hit against the ship's side.

Maintenance was finicky: T5s needed regular greasing like all torpedoes but with much greater care: the nose and a strip along the top had to be kept clean and polished. Scratches and dents were to be avoided at all costs and the nose and screws were extremely delicate.

In use the torpedo was fired from periscope depth as normal and had to approach within 300 to 400m of the target to detect it. In the meantime, the firing submarine had to proceed for one minute at 'dead slow' to avoid the risk of the weapon homing on the boat that fired it.[30]

A full understanding of the weapon had to await the painstaking reassembly of its homing unit from parts recovered during the liberation of Normandy and the capture of almost intact equipment following the fall of Paris.[31] CSDIC had however produced enough information, soon enough, to draw the teeth of an innovation that might otherwise have tilted the Battle of the Atlantic in Germany's favour.

9: T11 torpedo homing unit on display at Birkenhead

Post-war analysis showed that of 640 T5 torpedoes fired operationally just 6% hit their targets. Over 2,500 were fired in development, an extraordinary technical achievement for the time, again presaging the direction of later research.[32] But for the timeliness and detail of the information provided by CSDIC the butcher's bill would certainly have been far higher. The weapon's psychological impact was nearly as important as its tactical value. Several U-boat prisoners subsequently reported escorts turning away from them despite their blatantly showing a couple of feet of periscope.

Prisoners also mentioned trials carried out in the Baltic of blind firing acoustic torpedoes against sonar bearings (in fact related to the development of the Type XXI U-boat) and an improved homing weapon, they thought faster. In fact, the T11, as it became, embodied improvements including reduced self-noise, variable enabling range, better countermeasure resistance and the ability to launch from greater depths. It arrived too late to make any difference: only thirty-eight were made, and three of them were aboard when *U-534*, disregarding Dönitz' order to surrender, was sunk by aircraft on 5th May 1945. The salvaged boat and one of its torpedoes are now on display at the Woodside ferry terminal at Birkenhead.

U-boats also carried conventional thermal-powered straight-running torpedoes and another electrically driven design: T3, known as Curly. This was a pattern-running weapon designed to attack a convoy's merchantmen. After launch it turned onto a pre-set course to port or starboard (so the submarine did not have to point directly at its target) and could then be set to proceed in a weaving series of linked semicircles, or circle continuously to port – the circle in either case having a diameter of 75 metres. The idea was to maximise the chance of it hitting something when let loose among the stately, regular lines of a freighters.

On occasion the torpedo's rudder stuck after the initial course change, so that the weapon circled unnervingly over the submariners' heads.[33]

The Germans studied or developed over fifty torpedo types including wire-guided, hydrogen-peroxide fuelled, alternative homing technologies and, in increasing desperation, some frankly weird physical configurations.

Underwater developments & dodges

The Royal Navy had been fitting Asdic (active sonar) underwater detection sets to its warships since the nineteen-twenties in the confident expectation that this would solve the submarine problem. At first, German survivors agreed. *Bootsmannsmaat* Willy Brohm (N702) of *U-110* tried to explain the concept to his cellmate, a *Bismarck* survivor.

> 'N702:   *They hear the U-boat with certainty. They get every third U-boat. In one month we have lost six new U-boats –*
> *PRIEN, N481 [Kretschmer], SCHEPKE, FIEDLER, N534*
> *[von Hippel] – all first-rate 'Kommandanten'.*
> N640:   *Do they really see them (the U-boats)?*
> N702:   *No, they have a searching device. Acoustic. Exact soundings (onto the U-boat). Like an 'Echolot' [echo sounder]. Transmits rays to the bottom of the sea, then they are reflected back and show on an indicator. That is first rate! …*
> -----------------oOo-----------------
> N640:   *The U-boat arm is finished. Absolutely finished. What use is it to us if …… is sunk (in) 6 days? We have sunk 350,000 tons but the (U)boat is finished!*[34]

In fact, they were overly pessimistic. It took a skilled and experienced operator to tell the difference between a submarine and marine life or oceanographic anomalies. Asdic looked ahead of the ship but depth charges were launched astern (until the development of forward-firing throwers), meaning that the operator lost sight of the target in the vital last seconds of the attack. And, critically, it was useless against a U-boat on the surface which, trimmed down for a night assault, was almost as difficult to see as when submerged. The solution to that had to wait for radar.

Prisoners repeatedly spoke of attempts to develop anechoic submarine coating, which could absorb Asdic transmissions.

'N1120:   It can't be done. How would you do it? There is a means, to be precise it's a sort of rubber layer which covers the boat entirely (including) each propeller – have you ever seen a boat like that? The Asdic beams glance off it, without being reflected, but then they can listen for us.'[35]

In the event the rubber covering proved tricky to get right. It did not work very well, and in any case tended to peel off almost as soon as the boat went to sea. N1899 *Kapitänleutnant* Werner Pietzsch, commander of *U-523*, explained the problem to stool pigeon A713.

'N1899:   No. Something has already been tried out once, whereby the U-boats are enveloped in a kind of rubber covering, but it all peeled off again, it is a kind of rubber which was actually tried out by I.G. FARBEN, and which was very good. Before the experimental U-boat was covered with it, one of our officers went to I.G. FARBEN; he was taken into a room like this, the door was closed, and they had a conversation in there. But as soon as they began to speak — they talked about all sorts of things but they couldn't understand a word because all the sound was immediately absorbed.

A713:   By the rubber?

N1099:   Yes, by the rubber. Then they coated a U-boat ...... *after a month it had all come off again.*

A713:   The rubber came off again?

N1399:   Yes, owing to the salt water etc., it wasn't proof against salt water; and apart from that there are too many pipes on the upper deck, and too many corners and it all peeled off again.'[36]

Nonetheless the engineers persisted. After three problematic trials with retrofitted anechoic tiles (codenamed *'Alberich'*), *U-470* and *U-480* were built in summer 1943 with them fitted from new, an approach which solved the main problems.

U-470 discovered a limitation of the system on her first North Atlantic patrol in late 1943. Stool pigeon N1552 challenged one of the two survivors, *Mechanikerobergefreiter* Gerhard Tacken, to explain how the miracle coating had failed to protect them.

> '*N1552:* The rubber works all right and yet you were D/F'd all the same?
>
> *N1963:* Yes, by an aircraft, when on the surface.'[37]

Surprised on the surface, the captain decided to fight it out rather than risk diving while under attack. This quickly turned into a hopeless situation when the first Liberator to spot him was joined by two more.

In March 1944 N1552, again, continued exploring the topic with *Matrosenobergefreiter* Georg Kugler of U-264:

> '*N1552:* Did you ever see those rubber-covered U-boats, "470" – "480"?
>
> *N2243:* They don't have those any more. "480" is still operating, but without the rubber covering.'[38]

He was mistaken. *U-480,* returned to a previously fruitful hunting ground in the Channel on or after 29th January 1945. She ran into a minefield probably laid for her benefit and was lost with all hands. The wreck is still there and apparently cannot be spotted by fish-finding sonar.

A few later boats were built with the technology, but all were either sunk with all hands or survived the war so CSDIC's information relied on hearsay. The system was never deployed in volume.[39]

After the D-Day landings Assault Unit 30 was briefed to look out for any continuing work on submarine insulation or noise reduction (see *Overlord and After* above).

A more promising approach was the SBT (Submarine Bubble Target or *Pillenwerfer*). This acoustic decoy was discovered almost by accident when interrogator Lt Ralph Izzard was in Washington helping the US Navy set up and train its equivalent of CSDIC in 1942. SBT comprised canisters of 'pills' which could be ejected through a special tube and effervesced on contact with water. There were two kinds of pill in the same canister: one made a noise to attract hydrophones and the other created a bubble cloud which gave a strong Asdic return. The DNI's report for 20th July 1942 summarised the discovery:

'A chance reference in a letter from Lt. Izzard in America to some un-usual bubbles rising from the wreck of U 701, followed up by Lt. Willouby [sic] at Cockfosters, has resulted in the collection of enough evidence concerning the Pillenwerfer on which to base an out signal to the Fleet.'[40]

Some knew more than others. Ordinary Seaman N1198's questioning on the topic was followed up by stool pigeon N1067 to no avail – the shrugging shoulders are almost visible in the transcript, *'At any rate I don't know it.'*[41] Sustained picking at the topic yielded occasional titbits of information, until later that autumn when the unusually chatty captain of *U-353* gave an almost complete description of the system and its use.[42] The standard tactic was to deploy several while making sharp turns in alternate directions between each one. It remained effective and popular, but its value was severely degraded by the fact that Allies were now aware of it. It had the drawback of confirming the presence and recent location of a submarine, and critically gave no Doppler shift – it did not move. By May 1944 *Obermaschinen-maat* Fricke of *U-473* was distinctly cynical about its value.

'The worst thing there is the S.B.T. Firing that is the worst thing you can do. Through that they can fix your exact position.'[43]

From June 1940 U-boat captains began to experience aircraft pouncing through thick cloud, and ships emerging from night or mist to attack them. Inevitably a crashed, radar-equipped bomber soon revealed how far British technology had advanced, and a receiver (named 'Metox' after the French firm that made it) was hastily adapted to warn of nearby transmissions. It was not perfect – the antenna had to be rotated by hand and manhandled down the conning-tower before the boat dived. It could not take a bearing, struggled to pick up short transmissions, was easily confused by other emissions and – worst of all – emitted a strong and theoretically detectable signal itself. This made the decision to use it a matter of balancing risk. Still, finding U-boats became harder.

Once again it was the garrulous crew of *U-353*, one of the early boats fitted with what the British dubbed GSR (German Search Receiver), who gave the game away. Engineer *Leutnant* Rolf Holtz was heard explaining the system to a colleague from *U-464* in October 1942:

> *'We could see as soon as it was properly in the instrument – it gives all the frequencies straight away, so that you can see straight away who has detected you, whether it's an aircraft, or a destroyer or a cruiser or what. Every frequency is included. The Funkmaat read it off and reported the frequency to the Captain: "We are in .... at such and such a time." Then he said; "Stand by to dive." Then we submerged. We surfaced again after an hour, put out the instrument, one man went below and listened: "all clear"'*[44]

All three stool pigeons then available: A711, A713 and N1067, were set to work on the topic and produced a comprehensive range of survivors' views from which NID was able to distil an accurate picture of the equipment. From then on captured radiomen, already treasured for their knowledge of codes and cyphers, were guaranteed even closer attention from stool pigeons and secret listeners.

Early in 1943 new microwave radars operating in the 3,000 MHz range (ASV Mk III and Type 27x) began to find their way into service, the former in the face of intense competition between RAF Bomber and Coastal Commands for the precious sets. Surprise attacks began to rise again. *Kriegsmarine* confusion was helped by a captured RAF officer who, with great presence of mind, claimed in his interrogation[45] that they could home on

Metox emissions from up to 90 miles from a height of 1,000 metres. A steady stream of captive radio operators confirmed that paranoia about GSR emissions ranged from caution in its use to outright prohibition.

> 'N1884 [*Mechanikerobergefreiter Rudolf Gerke, U-468*]: I don't know how well Radar works, I only know about the G.S.R. That's why we got a W/T message at the end: "Switch off the G.S.R!" The fellows D/F'd the G.S.R. beams. We sent out beams from our apparatus too. They picked them up. Without locating us they knew: "Aha, there's a U-boat there." A lot were sunk by this means in the BAY of BISCAY.
>
> N1553 [a stool pigeon]:   Isn't anybody allowed to use the G.S.R. there now?
>
> N1884:   No. In the BAY of BISCAY not at all.'[46]

A later version of Metox came with a permanent antenna installation which did not have to be recovered before diving, to the immense relief of the bridge watch. Improved search receivers – Wanze G1 and G2 followed by Borkum – solved the emissions problem but still did not detect the new radars. The later Naxos receiver began to fill the gap, but allied radar technology remained one step ahead until it was far too late to make a difference, so long as production and allocation kept up with the need.

There were two unfortunate issues. RAF Bomber Command had first call on the precious airborne microwave radar sets, to the despair of Coastal Command. Pilots learnt to compensate by leaving their radar in search mode rather than switching to track when they found a target and reducing the power as they closed to give the impression that they hadn't spotted the target. Others went back to visual search, no doubt sparing some submariners' lives. On the surface, the Royal Canadian Navy lagged well behind the Royal Navy in gaining access to the equivalent shipborne equipment.

A skilled U-boat operator and captain could also use GSR offensively. For example, Purkhold's *U-260* tracked convoy ONS 154 through the foggy night of 27/28 December 1942 while a wolf pack assembled. The convoy lost fourteen ships for the destruction of one submarine. Purkhold and his crew were never interrogated so Naval Intelligence may not have realised until later what had happened. Admiral Dönitz, on the other hand, realised the potential of the tactic. In March 1943 he tried to counter the Allies' radar edge by instructing U-boats to follow a convoy at long range by observing its smoke or using their search receivers to track the escorts' radar. They could thus build up enough information to get ahead of their prey for an underwater attack.[47] In September Gerhard Kluth (*U-377*) tried using the technique in fog to regain a convoy he had already attacked but was driven away before getting anywhere near it.[48]

Equipment	*f* (MHz)	*Manufacturer*	*Introduced*
FuMB 1 Metox 600 and 600A	120-240	Metox & Gardin	Aug 1942
Wanze G1	200-250	Hagenuk	Aug-Sep 1943
Wanze G2	200-250	Hagenuk	Aug-Sep 1943
Borkum	100-400	NKV-Telefunken	Late 1943
Samos	90-470	Rohde & Schwarz	Late 1943
FuG 350 Naxos 1 FuG 350a Naxos 1a	2,500-3,750	NKV-Telefunken	Sep 1943
FuMB 26 Tunis	1,300-15,000		June 1944
FuMB 35 Athos	1,300-15,000		Early 1945

Table 3: GSR Equipment
(*f* – Range of frequencies the equipment could detect)

U-406, sunk on 18th February 1944, yielded a fine snapshot of the current state of GSR technology in the person of *Kapitän-*

leutnant Dr Regierungsrat Greven, a specialist riding with the boat to look after no fewer than 24 pieces of equipment combined into five systems with coverage ranging from 5cm to 40cm (6 GHz to 750 Mhz).[49] *U-473*, sunk on 6th May had a similar fit and two telegraphists with specialist training. *Mechanikergefreiter* Grüner boasted to stool pigeon N2175, '... *the IO [Interrogating Officer] here doesn't know anything about this apparatus.*' He was wrong about that but correctly identified one of the tactics aircrew used against the receiver, '... *They can switch off the apparatus and then switch it on again, but then they may already be nearer.*'[50]

The apparently 'silent' approach of aircraft fitted with centimetre-band radar had created suspicion that the Allies were using some form of infra-red detection. Some crews reported seeing red lights in the sky (possibly cockpit instrument lights) just before a surprise air attack. Such reports led to confused instructions and reactions typified by that of *Oberleutnant zur See* Wolfgang Römer, in command of *U-353*.

> 'I did once get a warning to look out for air attacks when going through the BAY OF BISCAY, and that those would be preceded by a sort of dark red searchlight, a sort of dark red splash of light in the sky(?). That had happened recently to U-boats and it was reported immediately; they had been attacked at night without any warning: we concluded from this that that was due to some sort of radio-location set, amounting roughly to an infra-red searchlight .... and that they sweep the area with infra-red rays, or with ultra(-violet) rays, I don't know, and then, one sees a splash of red light.......'[51]

The anti-infra-red paint used in response made vessels *more* conspicuous to radar.

This fear was the more plausible because some boats carried *Seehund* (Seal) infra-red telescopes, which crews had mixed feelings about. It was fragile and added to the bridge clutter having to be removed before crash-dive.[52]

U-boats also carried Radar Decoy Balloon (RDB or *Aphrodite*) floats, each of which flew a balloon trailing several foil reflectors and which could be thrown overboard to distract radar-equipped aircraft or ships when the submarine dived. This must have looked like a great idea from a desk on shore. Most skippers deployed them seldom or never and some crews used the balloons as footballs.[53] A captain whose stock-in-trade is stealth and unpredictability tends to resist putting up a big, shiny sign saying, 'I was here.' The scepticism was not however universal: Carlsen on *U-732* used them to decoy a convoy's escorts after an attack in the Caribbean.[54]

An even more doubtful idea was the Radar Decoy Spar-Buoy (RDS), a floating timber construction about 27 feet long by 12 feet high with reflecting metal strips attached. They were supposed to be laid in large numbers across the Biscay killing ground to confuse Allied aircraft. They took up much-needed space in the boat, were awkward and time-consuming to assemble and launch and of no practical use whatsoever. The only one recovered is said to have been spotted visually.[55]

Finally, an officer from *U-593* mentioned having seen trials with wire netting stretched around submarine conning-towers to break up their radar signatures. Several configurations were tried with towers mounted on rafts. None worked. If the netting was stretched far enough from the structure to work, it made the boat unwieldy and threatened to tear away in the first heavy sea.[56]

The turning point in the Battle of the Atlantic came between March 1943, a dismal month for the Allies, and May. Over those two months the availability of new escorts, microwave radar, high frequency direction finding, long-range Liberator patrol aircraft and new anti-submarine weapons decisively tilted the odds against the wolf packs. Losses reached a pitch that forced

Dönitz to withdraw his forces while promising a new assault with revitalised equipment.

Attempts to develop a radar small enough for in U-boats had delivered variously unsatisfactory derivatives of the *Seetakt* shipborne set from 1941 onward. By late 1943 few U-boats were so fitted, but prisoners later that year revealed that, in a revival of interest, some boats were getting modified aircraft sets codenamed *Hohentwiel* and operating in the 50 cm (600 MHz) waveband. A *U-73* telegraphist had done a course on the equipment.

The next development was thanks to RAF Bomber Command. An aircraft shot down near Rotterdam on 3rd February 1943 gifted German researchers an intact cavity magnetron, and with it the secret of microwave radar. The German equivalent was naturally enough christened 'Rotterdam,' or in the productionised version 'Berlin.' NID was fully aware of both these evolutions and keeping an eye on them, as this May 1944 conversation between stool pigeon N1485 and *U-473 Funkgefreiter* Spindler demonstrates.

> 'N1485:   Did the "Hohentwiel" prove a success?
>
> N2508:   ...... They(?) kept contact with the convoy all the time.
>
> N1485:   Do you think they'll equip all boats with it?
>
> N2508:   I don't know.
>
> N1485:   I wonder whether the "Rotterdam" will prove a success in U boats?
>
> N2508:   What's the good of Radar ......
>
> N1485:   Well, but you saw they did maintain continuous contact with it.
>
> N2508:   What's the good of maintaining contact but not firing? At best as a contact-keeper, but as soon as soon as you make a signal they've got you...'[57]

Designing the equipment was one thing, delivering it in an increasingly resource-strapped economy was another. CPO (Navigation) Truhn of *U-765* told stool pigeon N1878 about having to put to sea with an incomplete torpedo load, and went on,

'N1878:   *Did you have Radar?*

N2484:   *No. You don't get it any more. They haven't got the*
sets.

N1878:   *Weren't you a new boat?*

N2482:   *Brand new.*'[58]

Even when radar was available, often sharing a mast with the GSR antenna, only the most brazen skippers had any interest in using it. The Germans were not the only ones with detectors. Paul Strickner, a radioman from *U-643* explained the dilemma to stool pigeon N1878.

'N1938:   *Yes, 7 to 10 km in good weather [range of U-boat*
radar]. But if you D/F with radar and you are at a distance of 20
km from another boat then she can detect you with the G.S.R.
without any trouble, and you can't see her at all. That's the
damnable part of it. For that reason I say get rid of the radar. If I
were in a position of authority I should build in a G.S.R. three times
as large and throw out the radar. And as well as that I should take
one member of the U-boat crew and train him as a G.S.R. observer
who would only have to bother about that one thing.'[59]

The interrogators did not always get it right. An able seaman captive in the US laid a convincingly false trail with a detailed but entirely imaginary description of anti-escort mines which could be discharged by a U-boat under attack to float in the path of the chasing destroyer. This migrated from a US Spot Item to the NID weekly report, was promulgated by C-in-C Western Approaches and caused alarm and despondency among the ships under his command. Meanwhile CSDIC interrogators and stool pigeons tried fruitlessly to confirm their existence. In December

1942 *U-660* survivor *Bootsmaat* Adolf Reinboldt seemed to confirm the fear.

'(Re periscope mines)
They don't know what periscope mines are. They call them
"tumblers" (Stehaufmännchen) .... The mine has a proper
periscope. When waves wash over it, it rights itself again, and the
mine is attached to it underneath. The destroyer sees the periscope
.... dashes towards it .... the mine explodes.'[60]

Despite repeated picking at the topic no further details or confirmation were forthcoming. By early 1944 it seemed clear this self-evidently mad idea had been a false alarm.

'N 2203:   There is now also an apparatus of which he (IO)
said, that it looks like a periscope on top, and a mine is attached to it
underneath.
N 2385:   I haven't seen that yet.'[61]

Secret Weapons

There had been rumours for some time of German preparations for gas warfare. Some were wilder than others. It is difficult to imagine this bomber pilot's assertion from December 1940 being taken seriously.

'A 677 said that GERMANY has a new gas, which will be sprayed
from the air over LONDON and render everyone except
CHURCHILL unconscious.
Thia gas is comparatively harmless for the first 48 hours, apart from
rendering everyone unconscious, and during this time HITLER will
ring up CHURCHILL and arrange a peace. As soon as this is
done, further a/c [aircraft] will be sent over spraying an antidote and
all will be well.
If no peace is agreed upon, the people, after having been unconscious,
die.

When pressed as to how exactly CHURCHILL would retain consciousness, he shut up, saying: "Oh! I have already said far too much."[62]

In May 1943 *Fähnrich* (Midshipman) Karl Völker of U-175 described going on a gas course, anti-gas capes issued to troops and vast dumps of shells ready for use.[63]

Günter Schramm told a stool pigeon how ordnance officers he knew well would clam up when gas ammunition was mentioned, leading him to believe it was planned for deployment. A three-way conversation with a coastal artillery gunner mentioned empty shells from 10.5 cm upwards, bombs and sprays from tanks or aircraft – the last being impractical because of the immense number of planes needed to contaminate an area. His T-25 shipmate *Feldwebel* Diessel admitted the possibility of gas shells but said he had never seen any.[64]

A common theme was that Germany would never stoop to first use, not least because of the immense resource disparity between the two sides. *Matrosengefreiter* Wolfgang Blumenberg of U-386 put it in a nutshell.

'N 2189:   I know for certain that preparations for gas warfare have been made, not defensive ones, but offensive. But I don't believe the Germans will do it as they haven't an air force left and the English would be able to retaliate a thousandfold, and they know it.'[65]

Allied troops preparing for D-Day still had to have unpleasantly realistic anti-gas training.

Blumenberg was also susceptible to some of the wilder tales about new weapons. A mix of half-knowledge, distortion and wishful thinking produced a blizzard of snowballing rumours: a wall of noise from which analysts had to pick out the music of genuine intelligence.

'N 2189:   (Re new gas-bombs): There is a liquid in then which is ejected on impact and the moment it touches human or animal flesh it produces an effect of boiling liquid and if it touches the ground it turns into a gas. The heat of the body doesn't turn it into gas, it's [sic] effect is similar to 'Lost'(?). When it touches the ground it turns into gas and sweeps along the ground and wherever it comes – grass turns black, everything is burnt up. And that ground can never again be cultivated. It is the same as if you were to burn some field, the ash is completely useless. If a human being is sprayed by it, the effect is the same as if you had held him in boiling water and pulled him out again. You could peel of [sic] his skin, just like that. That is the effect of that stuff. Wherever it touches, nothing more will grow. The amount they have in readiness is enough to make a whole section of the earth practically disappear. However, the man who told me this said that, on <u>express</u> orders of the FÜHRER, it was kept in readiness <u>only</u> in case the other side should start with it first.'[66]

This and stories of 'liquid air' bombs that could ravage vast areas were pure imagination, but the V weapons were real enough.

Despite some barely credible rumours beforehand the first clear warning that Germany was developing long-range missiles came in a conversation between Generals von Thoma and Crüwell at Trent Park on 22nd March 1943. Von Thoma's eye-witness account focussed interest on the work under way at Peenemünde. The eyes of Air Intelligence photographic interpretation unit at RAF Medmenham turned in that direction and the ears of CSDIC's secret listeners sharpened for any mention of the subject.[67]

The junior ranks passing through Latimer and Wilton did not have their seniors' privileged access but had often picked up snippets of information which could be added to the mix, if with caution. Rumour, exaggeration, propaganda, and wishful thinking all contributed to the distorted picture, and that was before considering the possibility of ideas being 'planted' by inept interrogation.

In April experienced stool pigeon A713, now using the prefix 'N/A' because he was impersonating a third engineer from the blockade runner SS *Regensburg*, used scepticism to try and separate a bomber pilot's knowledge from guesswork.

> *A1193:*   *I told people (here) that we have all sorts of plans; they don't seem very happy about it. I've already told you that the Kommandeure were very optimistic about the immediate future here – all sorts of things.*
>
> *N/A713:*   *Did they say it was to start this summer?*
>
> *A1193:*   *Yes, it was to start in June.*
>
> *N/A713:*   *With what?*
>
> *A1193:*   *He didn't say. At any rate, with various new things, rockets etc. rocket ammunition and I don't know what else. New aircraft.*
>
> *N/A713:*   *In spite of the fact that they've not yet been tested? I don't believe it can start this June; in time they will doubtless do something of the sort, but I don't believe it will be this summer*
>
> *A 1193:*   *That is very doubtful of course.*[68]

Oberleutnant zur See Jeschonnek, commander of *U-607*, had been on a coastal inspection trip despite his relatively junior rank, perhaps because his late half-brother, a *Luftwaffe* general, was rumoured to have originated many of Hitler's 'intuitions'. He had visited the Baltic coast on leave and noticed the constant procession of high-ranking visitors passing through the tight security cordon. In August 1943 he found himself chatting with A713, now posing as a downed bomber pilot.

> *A713:*   *This rocket business is a new idea, isn't it?*
>
> *N1693:*   *It has proved successful. I know that the experiments have been successful for the first time, and that they wanted to start the thing sooner, but in some way they could not get sufficient quantities, and so it had to be postponed.*

A713:   And it's to be used against ENGLAND?

N1693:   Yes. From the CHANNEL coast.

A713:   But the things are not yet assembled on the CHANNEL coast, it is on the BALTIC?

N1693:   That's merely an experimental station ......

A713:   If they had fired the rockets when you were there, you would have seen them in the air.

N1693:   You wouldn't necessarily see them. It's a very long way away. The whole district is a restricted area, you can't get to within kilometres of it. KOSEROW is fairly far off. Bad KOSEROW is the first resort on the island which has been made open to the public.

A713:   And PEENEMÜNDE is restricted?

N1693:   Yes. PEENEMÜNDE has always been restricted.'[69]

On the same day *Leutnant zur See* Egon Horsmann, another survivor of *U-607*, was closeted with Gerhard Braun, his opposite number from *U-454*. He had been shown photographs of the new weapon at CSDIC.

'N1694 [Horsmann]: He showed me photographs here of the shells as they were lying on the ground.

N1760:   What do they look like?

N1694:   They are tremendously large things. About as long as a torpedo, but of a larger calibre.

N1760:   With what do they intend to fire them, then?

N1694:   They are fired from a barrel. They must be (?) about 70 cm. .... (probably sketching) and behind – that is the real shell – behind comes the rocket. That comes behind, there are barrels like that. There is a gyroscope in it too, those are kind of steering surfaces, real steering rudder and hydroplanes. They want to build in a kind of F.A.T[70]. ...... Neutral observers! Who can have photographed it? Only the Swedes can have done it. In fact, that must be so, because it is being tried out in the BALTIC; they must have (photographed) it from over there.'[71]

Horsmann was struggling to describe something completely new in terms he could cope with and was equally thrown by lack of a scale reference. Nonetheless it sounds as though British Intelligence had managed to obtain photos of a V2 or an early technology demonstrator for the concept.

Remarkably the *U-607* interrogation report makes no mention of these insights. They may have been reported through a separate, highly classified route.

A713 was still on the case in October, working on *Kapitän-leutnant* Hans Speidel of *U-643*. The interrogation report described this security-obsessed commander as a perfect Nazi or, more graphically, 'a complete swine.' He was too much on his guard for a questioner's usual tricks to work but relaxed when chatting with a supposed companion in misfortune.

A713:   *I have never been to PEENEMÜNDE.*

N1926:   *I haven't either. The best way of finding out about PEENEMÜNDE is to ask barbers in BERLIN.*

I once met a meteorological expert from PEENEMÜNDE when going from HALLE to KIEL, and from the security point of view, he spoke somewhat irresponsibly. He said that from the point of view of calibre, range and target, everything was quite ready. Naturally, you mustn't (?) do it just for five minutes, you need a whole week.

A713:   *A whole week for what?*

N1926:   *So that, let's say, a target like LONDON –*

A713:   *In order to destroy it. People I know say it's a thing weighing six tons and the range is supposed to be 160 km.*

N1926:   *Considerably greater, he said 200 and more.'*[72]

At this stage Germany was losing the conventional war on all fronts and there was little Goebbels could do to disguise the fact. Whatever hope the loyal core retained of survival and perhaps ultimate victory depended on technological rabbits being pulled from the Führer's hat. At sea there would be new weapons and submarines; elsewhere the 'miracle' secret weapons which would make their suffering and endurance worthwhile. *Obermaschinenmaat* Otto Heydt of E-boat *S-96* summed up their expectations.

> 'N1915: It has always been the case that if the capital falls, the whole country collapses too. You just see what happens when they blast LONDON to bits with those rockets.'[73]

A CSDIC staff psychologist took quarterly snapshots of prisoners' views on (*inter alia*) the regime, Hitler and the outcome of the war.[74] Counter-intuitively, morale improved in the second half of 1943 despite the reverses being experienced. It is difficult to imagine any reason for this other than the promises of miracle developments just around the corner. As 1943 became 1944 faith in the new weapons and their effect began to sound almost like a catechism, at least in the words of *Leutnant zur See* Kurt Heinemann (*U-593*).

> 'N2182: The new weapon will certainly work. That'll shake them. If that were not so, then things would be quite different in the GAF [German Air Force]. After all, we haven't been sleeping for two years. The new weapon is going to win the war!! I believe in it.'[75]

Funkobergefreiter Hans Ewald of *U-264* seemed to go even further, drifting into the realms of fantasy in his conversations with stool pigeon N1485.

> 'N2254: They want to wipe out the whole of ENGLAND; not with aircraft, but with rockets, "Dödel". The things are said to weigh twenty tons.'

★ ★ ★

> 'N2254: (Re Dödel): It will come like a flash of lightning. I heard that they intend firing only <u>four</u> of these rockets on LONDON. That will destroy the whole town.'[76]

Was this pure fantasy, or had he heard garbled reports of the German nuclear project?

Despite the intense secrecy, some rumours had certainly got out. *Oberleutnant zur See* Gunther Schramm, an anti-Nazi survivor of the torpedo-boat *T-25*, had picked up surprisingly accurate (if, to him, incomprehensible) information from a friend.

> 'N2074:   *On the other hand, although I really don't know, there must be some fantastic plans in existence; I heard from an old school friend of mine who, after he had passed his "Abitur", went in for chemical research and whom I met again quite recently on leave in HAMBURG. He told me some really interesting things about modern developments in splitting the atom – goodness knows, he gave me a very lengthy talk, of which, of course I understood very little. He was also very careful how he expressed himself, so he certainly didn't go to the root of the matter, but all the same it's a question of the minutest bodies. Probably atomic weights of the order of those described in that novel by DOMINIK: "Atomic Weight 500" ("Atomgewight 500"), which can be steered from great distances and after a quite definite time, i.e. after a time which can also be controlled – can cause destruction at the chosen spot; (it is likely) that experiments were being carried out all over the place, i.e. in his own district, and that he was taking part in those developments.'*

With further prompting he suggested Dresden as a possible centre for the work. The conversation then turned to V-weapons.

> 'A713:   *What do you think about the rocket things from PEENEMÜNDE? If only we could get over the technical difficulties of control!*
>
> N2074:   *They have practically been got over already, through these "Nebelwerfer" things.*
>
> A713:   *Through the "Do"-Geräte?*
>
> N2074:   *Yes. But then there's the difficulty of control, accurate control, with a certainty of hitting the target.'*[77]

With the start of the V1 assault just months away the drumbeat of new evidence accelerated in early 1944. *Kapitänleutnant* Gerd Kelbling commanding *U-593* commented to one of his officers while in the Algiers interrogation centre,

'*N43/1578: I don't really care whether they send me to ENGLAND or not; the only thing is, it won't be exactly a picnic there when we start our reprisals.*'[78]

Even so the risk of accepting fantasy as fact, or inadvertently leading witnesses, was constantly at the front of interrogators' minds. CSDIC transcribers were cautious enough to add the caveat, '*N2407 was interrogated by RAF officers in ALGIERS and it is therefore possible that the information contained in this report was injected*' to the following.

'*N2407:   If just one of those things, weighing thirty tons, is fired, the GULF OF DANZIG –*

N2353:   Thirty tons? How far is it supposed to travel then?

N2407:   They fired it from SWINEMÜNDE into the GULF OF DANZIG. I didn't want to believe it either.

N2353:   Then they could smash up the whole of ENGLAND, firing from FRANCE.

N2407:   I can only say what the Air Force man told me.'[79]

On 13th June the first V1 missiles landed on London in an assault that would last almost to the end of March 1945. But for the efforts of CSDIC the V1 flying bomb, V2 rocket and V3 long-range gun would have been operational earlier and used in far greater quantities. The potential effect is difficult to contemplate.

---

[1]   TNA ADM 186/805. P.27.

[2]   TNA AIR 40/3070. SRA 23 (5/2/40).

[3]   TNA WO 208/4123. SRA 1221 (03/02/40) WO 208/4121. SRA 933 (16/11/40). WO 208/4122. SRA 1238 (6/2/41).

[4]   Ibid. SRA 1301 (19/02/40).

[5]   TNA WO 208/4144. SRN 1484 (18/1/43).

[6]   TNA WO 208/4123. SRA 1302 (19/02/40).

[7]   Ibid. SRA 1337 (23/02/40).

[8]   Lincoln, *Secret Naval Investigator*. P.72-73.

[9]   TNA WO 208/4123. SRA 1617 (30/04/41).

[10] Ibid. SRA 1561 (24/04/41).

[11] TNA WO 208/3460. Letter from B F Trench to T Kendrick dated 6th
      February 1941, referencing SRA 1221 (03/02/41) and SRA 1230
      (31/01/41). Letter from J M R Campbell (for Director of Naval
      Intelligence) to Major-General F H N Davidson DSO, MC and Air Vice
      Marshall C E H Medhurst CBE, MC (24/05/41).

[12] TNA ADM 223/475. DTM Minute 27/10/41 appended to DNI Note
      25/10/41.

[13] Lincoln, *Op. Cit.* P.95.

[14] TNA ADM 199/805. P.10.

[15] Ibid. P.73.

[16] Ibid. P.127.

[17] Ibid. P.167.

[18] TNA WO 208/4141. SRN 47 (17/4/1940).

[19] TNA ADM 199/806. P.119; P.330.

[20] TNA WO 208/4145. SRN 1759 (7/5/43).

[21] TNA ADM 186/808. P.362-3.

[22] TNA ADM 199/806. P.119.

[23] Lincoln, *Op. Cit.* P.140-160.

[24] TNA WO 208/4143. SRN 767 (25/1/42).

[25] TNA ADM 186/807. P.366.

[26] TNA ADM 223/475. Memo from ACNS (UT) to Commodore
      Rushbrooke (DNI) dated 23rd October 1943 and Godfrey's reply dated
      28th October. Offley; *Turning the Tide*, P.378.

[27] TNA WO 208/4147. SRN 2232 (22/9/43).

[28] Ibid. SRN 2302 (14/10/43).

[29] TNA ADM 1/17685. Report 24/6/45 Encl. No 1.

[30] TNA ADM 186/809. P.46.

[31] Lincoln, *Op. Cit.* Ch 13. TNA ADM 223/214 paragraph 105.

[32] Kirby, *A History of the Torpedo Part 3* P.85.

[33] For example, this happened to *U-73* during her final attack on convoy
      GUS 24. See TNA ADM 186/809, P.59; WO 208/4148, SRN 2588
      (31/12/43).

[34] TNA WO 208/4142. SRN 395 (8/6/41).

[35] TNA WO 208/4143. SRN 782 (4/2/42).

[36] TNA WO 208/4147. SRN 2226 (21/9/43).

[37] Ibid. SRN 2399 (6/11/43).

[38] TNA WO 208/4149. SRN 2976 (3/3/44).

[39] Later U-boats believed to have had *Alberich* coating include the Type
      VIIC boats *U-485*, *486* and *1105-1107*, Type XXIII *U-4704* and *4708*
      (*Deutsches U-Boot Museum*). U-1105 and U-485 took part in comparative
      Admiralty trials with an uncoated boat (U-1171) after the war.

[40] TNA ADM 223/352.
[41] TNA AIR 40/3102. Special Extract from SR Draft No 2085 (25/7/42).
[42] TNA ADM 186/807. P.463-464.
[43] TNA WO 208/4152. SRN 3700 (18/5/44).
[44] TNA WO 208/4144. SRN 1166 (20/10/42).
[45] Interrogation on 13/8/1943. See Mallman Showell, *Dönitz, U-boats, Convoys. n*.P.180.
[46] TNA WO 208/4147. SRN 2216 (14/9/43).
[47] Dönitz, *Memoirs*. P.334.
[48] Mallman Showell, *U-Boats*. P.87.
[49] uboatarchive.net. *CB 04051(99) "U 406," "U 386" and "U 264" Interrogation of Survivors*. May, 1944.
[50] TNA WO 208/4152. SRN 3733 (18/5/44).
[51] TNA AIR 40/3102. Special Extract from SR Draft No. 4924 (10/11/42).
[52] TNA WO 208/4149. SRN 2985 (28/2/44).
[53] TNA ADM 223/142. Summary No 42 for week ending 19/9/43.
[54] TNA WO 208/4147. SRN 2437 (12/11/43).
[55] Mallman Showell, *Dönitz, U-boats, Convoys*. P.184.
[56] TNA WO 208/4149. SRN 2895 (4/2/44).
[57] TNA WO 208/4152. SRN 3723 (18/5/44).
[58] Ibid. SRN 3689 (17/5/44).
[59] TNA WO 208/4147. SRN 2318 (14/10/43).
[60] TNA WO 208/4144. SRN 1315 (5/12/42).
[61] TNA ADM 223/144; Summary No 66, for week ending 11th March 1944. ADM 223/475; Paper *PW Interrogation 1939-45*, section D(c); *No Interrogation in Ships effecting Capture*. WO 208/4150. SRN 3178 (24 /3/44).
[62] TNA WO 208/4196, SP/F/9.
[63] TNA WO 208/4196; *SP/F 1-142*. SP/F/116 dated 6th May 1943, SP/F/117 and SP/F/118 dated 8th May 1943.
[64] TNA WO 208/4149; SRN 2781 dated 17th January 1944, 2722 dated 11th January 1944. WO 208/4163; SRX 1897 dated 10th January 1944.
[65] TNA WO 208/4149; SRN 2979 dated 3rd March 1944.
[66] ibid. SRN 2965 dated 3rd March 1944.
[67] See Fry, *The Walls Have Ears*, Ch 9.
[68] TNA WO 208/4163. SRX 1754 (27/4/43).
[69] TNA WO 208/4146. SRN 2071 (11/8/43).
[70] Pattern running – this was pure speculation.
[71] Ibid. SRN 2070 (11/8/43).
[72] TNA WO 208/4147. SRN 2376 (29/10/43).
[73] Ibid. SRN 2290 (13/10/43).
[74] See my *Castaways of the Kriegsmarine* for more on this.
[75] TNA WO 208/4149. SRN 2851 (25/1/44).
[76] Ibid. SRN 3014 & 2989 (3/3/44).
[77] TNA WO 208/4163. SRX 1897 (10/1/44).
[78] TNA WO 208/5508.
[79] TNA WO 208/4151. SRN 3379 (20/4/44).

STEEL COFFINS

Bodging the Boats

Between March and May 1943, the Battle of the Atlantic tilted decisively in favour of the Allies. The workhorse Type VII medium range and Type XI long range U-boats which had served the *Kriegsmarine* perfectly well so far were becoming too vulnerable. Both stop gap and long-term solutions were needed.

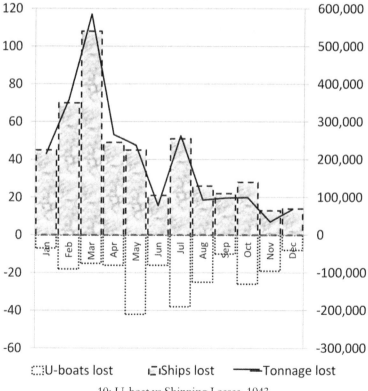

10: U-boat vs Shipping Losses, 1943

One option was ready to hand in the form of the *schnörkel*: a pre-war Dutch invention which fed fresh air to a submarine's engines and carried the exhaust away through a mast projecting above the surface. The first indication of its use came from *Boots-mannsmaat* (Boatswain's Mate) Friedrich Huffmeyer of *U-434* as early as February 1942.

> '*N1112:   Yes. They are building U-boats now – for instance the big Dutch boat – which can travel under water on their Diesels.*
> *They have a ventilation mast (Luftmast), just like a periscope, which they can push up. I know about it because a pal of mine is Obersteuermann on board it. I was once on board it myself.*'[1]

At the time there seemed no case for the expense of fitting the equipment generally. A year later anything that might reduce a U-boat's vulnerability was worth a try. *U-264*, believed to be the first boat so equipped, was sunk in an Atlantic convoy battle on 19th February 1944. Karl Heinz Stadtler, *Mechanikerobergefreiter*, explained the principle to stool pigeon N1878.

> '*N1878:   Is it on the port side, forward on the right?*
> *N2261:   Yes, on the port side. It is quite simple. Do you know the ball-cock of a WC? When the level is up, the ball-float goes up and shuts off the water. This also has a ball-cock, and when a wave comes, so that water would be sucked in, the ball-float rises and keeps the water out.*
> *N1878:   How long is the tube altogether?*
> *N2261:   As long as the periscope.*
> *N1878:   12 m?*
> *N2261   Well, yes, it may be ...... 12 m.*
> *N1878:   Can it be worked from below with air?*
> *N2261:   It is worked hydraulically, with oil pressure.*
> *N1878:   Can the mast be kept in place hydraulically?*
> *N2261:   Yes, and move it up and down. There are two tubes*
>
> ......
>
> *N1878:   So the air intake is circular. And in the intake there are two tubes?*

N2261:   *Yes, that is the two tubes, only they are covered. On the first patrol we submerged ...... they started the Diesel running, the Diesel exhaust came into the boat and then they had to surface as quickly as possible and ventilate the boat. You have no air. The first boat that tried it out in the BAY OF BISCAY, the ATLANTIC; that was us. But with the dockyard manager ...... specialists from the BdU and the FdU. We were out for about five days. Only us.*

Because we were the first boat to get the extensible Diesel air intake.'[2]
As the crew of *U-264* discovered, the innovation had to be used carefully. If the air intake dipped below sea level the boat's engines would suck air from the interior, causing a sudden and painful drop in pressure. As well as skilful depth keeping the technique required an alert periscope watch: the *schnörkel* left a surface wake and a tell-tale smoke trail. *Maschinenmaat* Blume, one of the eleven survivors of *U-765* sunk on 6th May 1944, let slip the useful information that the *schnörkel* mast obscured the periscope's view to port (left).[3]

Nonetheless it was widely adopted and remains a standard fitting on conventional submarines today.

The next, and more difficult, step was to improve the submarines themselves.

Diving below the reach of British depth charges had proved effective in the early stages of the war, so why not repeat the tactic with a stronger hull to outwit the better weapons now in use? This thinking led to the development of the deep-diving Type VIIC/41 and later 42 versions of the medium-range workhorse, identical except for a stronger pressure hull with lighter machinery to compensate. *Obermaschinist* Heinz Hamm (*U-468*) gave stool pigeon N1821 a useful, if inaccurate, description in September 1943.

    '*N1882:*   *There are now boats which have a double pressure-hull, and they are supposed to submerge to a depth of over 300 metres.*

N1821:   *Have you seen them already?*

N1882:   *I haven't seen them but they talked about them at the*
base.

N1821:   *Where are they built?*

N1882:   *They must be built in GERMANY.*

N1821:   *What do they look like?*

N1882:   *They are exactly the same type of boat as ours only*
they have double pressure hulls.'[4]

CSDIC continued following up the thread, and a few months later Kurt Böhme, commander of *U-450*, gave another stool pigeon an update.

'N1878:   *Then there is "VII C/42", what is that?*

N2344:   *They can tell you about that here; that is a boat which*
can submerge to 400 metres. It is the same boat as the "VII C" boat,
but it can do one or two knots more submerged, as it has a slightly
larger battery and the steel of the pressure-hull is different. It is
thicker, it has a thicker pressure-hull.'[5]

As some crewmen pointed out it was all very well to escape to an invulnerable depth, but a U-boat had to come back up again to do its job. Ninety-one Type VIIC/41 boats were built but the VIIC/42 programme was abandoned to divert resources to more advanced types.

Another Type VII derivative was the lengthened Type VIIF, of which only four were built. Two were used to transport torpedoes out to U-boat flotillas in the Far East and two for operational patrols in the Atlantic, where they achieved little. They entered service in mid-1943. Both the operational and one of the supply boats were sunk during 1944, by which time CSDIC listeners had gathered detailed knowledge about them. This conversation between stool pigeon N1878 and *Funkmeister* Zwemke (*U-550*) is just one of several examples.

'N1878:   *What was she doing then? You say she was ...*
definitely a torpedo supply boat?

N(An)50:   *She was taking torpedoes to JAPAN.*

N 1878:   *Was she as large as your boat?*

N(Am)50:   *No, she was quite a different shape. A completely new shape. She was much wider at conning -tower level, but otherwise had the shape of a 500-ton boat; I said now that she was a 500-ton boat, but specially constructed as a torpedo supply-boat. The conning-tower is differently constructed, and wider.*

N1878:   *The conning-tower is wider?*

N(Am)50:   *No, not the conning-tower. Below it the pressure hull. She is no ...... boat.*

N1878:   *Well, has she got outboard tanks?*

N(Am)50:   *Yes.*

N1878:   *Those are already the Type VII-F boats. I haven't heard yet that they are so wide below on the conning-tower.*

N(Am)50: *It's not the conning-tower but the pressure hull below the conning-tower amidships. At any rate it looked to me like that because of the outboard tanks."*[6]

1943 also brought an innovation to mitigate the danger for U-boats crossing the Bay of Biscay from their French bases to their Atlantic patrol areas. Being within easy reach of Allied aircraft based in Cornwall and South Wales, this was a perilous run. The U-Flak looked like a possible answer. This was a standard Type VII boat with longer conning tower to take greatly upgraded anti-aircraft armament. It could escort standard boats on the surface. If attacked their charges would dive while the U-Flak stayed behind and gave the enemy pilot the surprise of his life.

The tactic worked – for a while. Its effectiveness fell off rapidly as surprise was lost, and it had already been compromised by *Fähnrich zur See* Zupke (*U-439*) who told a cellmate in May,

A completely new thing that will surprise the English – a Flak U-boat. It is primarily for the BAY OF BISCAY and is merely a 500 ton U-boat. Quite a lot of boats are being convered [sic] in the SCHICHAUER dockyard. Everything remains the same with the

exception of the conning-tower, which is being lengthened. ......
other Flak U-boats with 3.7s etc.'[7]

Seven U-Flaks were ordered (not all were completed). The survivors were converted back to standard Type VIICs by the end of the year.

As the aircraft threat became more lethal increasing numbers of U-boats were equipped with 37mm cannon behind the conning tower in either a single or twin mount, as well as twin or quad 20mm cannon on the two 'bandstands' behind the tower. With the increased armament came orders to stay on the surface and fight it out unless the plane was spotted far enough away to make a deep escape a realistic option.

> 'N1514: *An order has come out that that the U-boats are not to submerge when they see an aircraft, but they are to defend themselves. Aircraft are now so fast and employ such a variety of tactics. When they approach at low level, the U-boat hasn't got time to submerge, if the alarm has not been given. If a state of alarm already exists, she submerges immediately, but the aircraft can still drop depth-charges and the U-boat is defenceless when submerged. Therefore, she remains on the surface and can fire with her 3.7 – our boat had a 10.5 above, then a 3.7 – she can fire with her 3.7, she can fire with her 2 cm and also has two movable M.G's. And then, of course, two more M.G's can be put up, making four M.G's, and I think that is enough armament for a small boat like that. If an aircraft comes, it is no easy matter for it to hit the U-boat.'[8]*

Opinions varied as to the relative value of the twin and quad mount 20mm – the latter was more intimidating but took longer to bring into action and needed a larger crew, so more people to count back in for a crash dive. This armament was enough to give a captain a sporting chance of at least putting a pilot off his aim and buying enough time to dive while he turned for a second pass – if it worked. After prolonged immersion in saltwater this was not a given.

'N2254 [Funkobergefreiter Ewald, U-264]:   *A destroyer is not such a danger to us as an aircraft. They have removed our four-barrelled guns again because they are not a success. They are all right on land, but for us, who are continually proceeding submerged, they are no good.'*[9]

Oberleutnant zur See Kurt Böhme, commander of *U-450*, helpfully gave stool pigeon N1878 a complete run-down of the U-boat types then in service on 14th April 1944. This must have helped NID compile a consolidated report on the current state of the threat that June.[10] It set a baseline which allowed them to focus on new and evolving threats, particularly as they affected the Normandy and North-West Europe campaigns.

Since early on the interrogators had been trying to decipher garbled, conflicting accounts of wholly new developments: super submarines that would change the rules of the game entirely. Over time these resolved themselves into three distinct classes. There were midget submarines and manned torpedoes ('Small Battle Units'), fast 'Walter' boats driven by Professor Hellmuth Walter's air-independent propulsion, and the Types XXI and XXIII Electro boats. There was, too, a fourth initiative which may have passed them by. We shall come to this shortly.

Small Battle Units

Following unconfirmed reports that the Germans were building very small submarines NID and the Department of Naval Constructors carried out a feasibility study in 1939, looking into the kind of threat the navy might encounter. They concluded that self-destructing submarines of about 25 tons towed or carried to the target area by a mother vessel, or miniature submarines of 50-100 tons, would be practical ways to attack ships in harbour. Moreover, they would be difficult to detect.[11]

Interrogators were probing rumours of mini-U-boats at least from 1941. Their task was not made any easier by the sheer variety of concepts explored by the *Kriegsmarine*, which were inspired by Italian human torpedoes, Japanese midget subs and by captured British equipment (X-craft and Welman mini-submarines, and 'chariot' human torpedoes). Rumours and garbled eyewitness accounts described boats with crews ranging from two to eighteen men which might or might not be the same as 'Hanomag' high speed semi-submersibles and might or might not be carried to their target area by a parent ship or submarine. In the event none of these early concepts seem to have reached active service.

An early lead was provided by *Mechanikerobergefreiter* N501, probably Wilhelm Helling, a survivor of Kretschmer's *U-99*. He denied all knowledge of the subject when questioned, but the experience left it at the top of his mind.

> *'What do you think of the small U-boats with a crew of 3 - 4 men – "Kommandant" – old KRUGEL (?) (KRUG ?) with a depot ship? (the crew of the small U-boat consisting of) "Kommandant", torpedo mechanic, a man for the motor and a "Steuermann".'[12]*

The sinking of *U-210* and supply boat *U-464* in August 1942 added a little more evidence.

> *N1254 [Matrosengefreiter Werner Grimm, U-464]:   They don't know here that two-man U-boats exist.*
>
> *N1222 [Mechanikergefreiter Kurt Gerhardt, U-210]:   He (I.O.) asked me, "Do you know that sort of commando boats are being built in GERMANY?" Then he told me to give him some information. They had seen something flashing through the water, they had only seen a wave, nothing more. Those are the new E-boats, but I said nothing.*
>
> *N1254:   He asked me that too. You can't see anything at all and can't tell what it is.[13]*

CSDIC staff felt this, in combination with the other evidence available, was worth a guarded statement in the *U-464* report.

A prisoner from "U 464" (sunk 20.8.42) said he had seen three or four two-man U-Boats doing trials off Kiel-Wik in July, 1942, but did not describe them beyond saying that they still flew the Blohm and Voss house-flag.

A prisoner from "U 353" (sunk 16.10.42) said he had seen two-man U-Boats in Kiel. ("U 353" sailed from Kiel on 22.9.42.)

(N.I.D. Note: Previous interrogation reports (see C.B. 4051 (48), Section X (x) and C.B.4051 (49), Section IX (ii)) have referred to Two-man U-Boats, but there is no other evidence supporting the existence of these boats.)[14]

Obermaschinist Max Schmitz from *U-464* seemed to think the project involved a semi-submersible torpedo boat and had been abandoned.

'N1263:   Were those two-men U-boats which we saw in HELA?

N1251:   No, E-boats.

N1263:   Are they no longer being built?

N1251:   I don't believe so.

N1233:   Are E-boats no longer being built?

N1251:   This new type – in which only the turret [sic] projects out of the water.'[15]

Rumours persisted. *Funkmaat* Heinrich Weigel of *U-660* told a stool pigeon on 11th December 1942,

'They have built a two-man U-boat at HELA. Nobody was allowed in where they were building. No photographer could get near it. They tried one out there. What do they intend to do with them? They might perhaps sail on the ALSTER, or do they have to be carried in another U-boat?'[16]

In early 1943 an E-boat survivor, *Matrosenobergefreiter* Arthur Maack of *S-71*, seemed to confirm that the idea was no longer being pursued.

'*N1067:   They (I.Os) asked me about those HANOMAGS –
the E-boats with an underwater pressure-hull*
N1526:   I don't know them.
N1067:   I've seen some at KIEL.
*N1526:   That's the boat which they've built as an experiment.
There's only one about, which is the one at KIEL. It's like a U-
boat, with only the bridge sticking out. She takes a crew of six. They
are not being used operationally…'[17]*

Another *U-464* crewman mentioned ten-man U-boats, but
again without corroboration. Although this initiative came to
nothing a minelayer officer captured in August 1942 put his
finger on the key advantage of what would become known as
Small Battle Units: cheapness and expendability.

'*The two-man U-boat is not at all a bad weapon. For one thing they
can be put together quickly. Then the loss of one of those U-boats
doesn't much matter, if only two men are lost.*'[18]

Allied landings in Sicily, Italy and France forced Germany to
fight defensive battles on its own metaphorical doorstep, and
where its opponent had overwhelming air and sea superiority.
Range was no longer an issue. The crisis sparked renewed
interest in Italian, Japanese and British experience with human
torpedoes and midget submarines.

The Italian *Decima Flottiglia MAS* pioneered the use of
manned torpedoes, assault swimmers and explosive motorboats
between 1940 and armistice of 1943. During that period, they
succeeded in sinking or disabling the battleships *Queen Elizabeth*
and *Valiant*, the heavy cruiser *York*, two destroyers, two
submarines and several merchantmen in various harbours.

The Imperial Japanese Navy (IJN) built five classes of midget
submarine which had limited operational effect, though one
succeeded in damaging the battleship *Ramillies* at Diego Suarez
in May 1942. Five took part in the Pearl Harbour raid. All were
sunk although one may have succeeded in firing its torpedoes

either at a cruiser or at Battleship Row. Towards the end of the war the IJN developed the *Kaiten* human guided torpedo. This was a lengthened Type 93 weapon with larger warhead, extra fuel, pilot's compartment, and oxygen supply. Unlike the Italian, British and German equivalents, once launched the pilot's death was certain.

The British learnt quickly from their suffering at the hands of the *Decima Flottiglia MAS* and designed their own human torpedoes or 'chariots'. Development of midget submarines was already under way and resulted both in the successful X craft, which among other exploits seriously damaged the *Tirpitz*, and the less successful Welman. The Germans captured examples of both designs.

Their programme suffered from a late start, desperation, lack of resource and time along with the constant risk of intelligence compromise and air attack. This inevitably meant their operational history would be a tale of half-trained crews using half-developed equipment in what were only theoretically *not* suicide missions. Some pilots aborted their missions because of navigational or equipment problems; many were sunk, captured, or simply disappeared without trace; some made unverifiable claims of success. A very few achieved concrete results and lived, at least for the time being, to tell the tale.

German opinion of Italian military skills was often dismissive to say the least. However, the bravery of their assault swimmers and charioteers in attacking British harbours demanded respect. *Matrosengefreiter* Otto Weis of *U-517* described their technique.

> '*N1398:*   (re Italian submarines) On the upper deck they have large containers, and they have small assault torpedoes with one man inside them – one-man torpedoes. The man gets inside and the torpedo is pushed overboard.*
> *N1451:*   And what happens to the man?*

*N1398: He presses a knob and is ejected by means of
compressed air – maybe he has a rubber thing round his waist, which
is used as a sort of small rowing-boat with two oars lying alongside it
– then he rows off. He is either taken prisoner or he gets back
again.'[19]*

The first German effort was the *Neger* (N*****), a modified
torpedo in which the pilot sat with his head in a transparent
bubble, with a conventional torpedo slung underneath. It could
not submerge, launching and aiming were difficult, reflection
from the canopy and wake made it easier for an alert lookout to
spot the *Neger* than for the pilot with his eyes at sea level to find
a target. Breakdown and accident prevented many from even
starting their missions and casualties were horrific among those
that did.

Fähnrich zur See Walter Schulz was a lucky survivor of the first
attack, on the Anzio beachhead in April 1944. Forty *Neger* were
assigned to the operation, thirty-seven made it to the launch
point, twenty-three successfully launched and just ten pilots
made it back. Despite the crowded roadstead and harbour the
force did not achieve any confirmed results. One *Neger* was
captured intact with the pilot dead at the controls. Schulz, picked
up by a US patrol boat, was one of four pilots taken prisoner and
turned out to be quite talkative.

'*N1878: You said that you carried out the operation with thirty-
five or thirty-six of the things, what happened to the others?
N2465: The others dropped out when we were on the journey
down. Three of them dropped out while being transported there, and
another two dropped out down there later, or rather one, a
"Bootsmaat", who was drowned, and the other fellow stuck on a
sand-bank right at the beginning, and as he couldn't get away from it
he got out there. That was the fifth(?) one. The battery of one fellow's
torpedo with warhead exploded ...... One fell over while being
transported down there – that one too was smashed up completely.'[20]*

With no room to move, attending to the call of nature was out of the question. Later in the conversation Schulz explained how this dilemma was dealt with.

> 'N1878:   Suppose you are inside the thing for twelve hours, how do you manage to last out?
> N2465:   We had such wonderful food during the preceding days that we could easily hold out even longer if necessary.
> N1878:   Surely this other diet must be particularly harmful to you?
> N2465:   Yes, it is sometimes. You get only macaroni, no potatoes, a great deal of fat and white bread and biscuits, no peas or beans.
> N1878:   No vegetables?
> N2465:   Yes, vegetables didn't matter. We have a special doctor to supervise it all. Actually it ought to start four days beforehand. This is how they worked it out, biscuits and rolled oats and a thick milk-soup in the morning.
> N1878:   That would gradually promote constipation.
> N2465:   We tried it out beforehand.
> N1878:   Yes, and then can't you eat anything during those twelve hours?
> N2465:   After eating three tins of Choko-Kola, you are quite replete. There are three tins, each containing another two layers, so you've got six little packets of five slabs. Nobody ate as much as that en route. When I was taken prisoner I had eaten only half a box of Choko-Kola. The damned Americans took away the two-and-a-half tins that I had left.'

The pilots' stamina was further reinforced by tablets called DIX, which comprised a mixture of Eukodal (a narcotic), cocaine and Pervitin (a methamphetamine). It is a reasonable guess that their long-term welfare was not a consideration.

Matrosengefreiter Figel, pilot of *HT-93* was captured on the same raid and discussed the shortcomings of the *Neger*, and of their briefing, with stool pigeon N2203.

'N2468:   *... The steering gear was continually breaking down. If you were at sea you thought: "Hell, what's the matter?" You could no longer steer: the steering was broken....*

N2203:   *And no WT installation or wireless of any kind?*

N2468:   *Nothing. You are entirely on your own, you are your own CO. Once you're in the water you don't take orders from anyone. They told us that if we couldn't get away we were to give ourselves up. It's damnable; when you're inside it, you're as helpless as a frog.*

...

One thing was damnable: we wanted to attack by night, but there's no shipping at all at ANZIO during the night. The blighters arrive by day and clear off again in the evening, those LST's, large 3000-ton landing boats.'[21]

On 5th July 1944 twenty-six *Neger* attempted an attack against the Allied supply lines to the Normandy beaches. Two aborted with motor trouble, the rest sank three ships between them. Ten *Neger* were lost. The following night an operation by twenty-one *Neger* claimed two victims, but none of the raiders returned.[22] Sporadic missions continued into August on the same pattern: multiple human torpedoes launched (sometimes accompanied by speedboats and/or E-boats), perhaps one or two ships sunk, horrific losses among the attackers.

The shortcomings of the hastily improvised *Neger* prompted the development of an improved version, *Marder* (Marten). Visually similar – a torpedo with a man in it carrying another torpedo underneath – its main advantage was the ability to submerge.

Surviving pilots were re-equipped with *Marder* and sent back to the Mediterranean, where nineteen-year-old Wolfgang

Hoffman's luck finally ran out in December 1944. Despite his youth he was by then a veteran but lost his way and accidentally beached his weapon in Allied territory. Both he and his *Marder* were captured, giving interrogators a complete picture of the equipment and its use.[23]

Our chatty friend *Fähnrich zur See* Schulz also added to NID's knowledge of the *Linsen* (Lens) explosive remote-control speed-boats. This came in two variants, a three-man command boat which controlled two one-man explosive boats. The concept was that the explosive boat pilots would approach the target as close as they dared, then bale out. Two of the command boat crew would direct the final attack by radio, the third piloting the command boat itself. Afterward, all being well, they would pick up the attack boat pilots.

The system was developed on Lake Constance from 1942, based on an idea explored in the First World War, and was intended to be used in the same offensive as the ill-fated *Neger* attack on the Anzio beachhead. Lake and sea conditions are not the same, however, and the mission was stillborn. Schultz was unaware of the problem.

> *'N2465:   We have other things as well – remote controlled things. This one thing that has come from the BRANDEN-BURG(?) "Division" is already making good progress and can be put into operation shortly, if the opportunity arises, that is to say, if they invade somewhere. I am certain that they are standing ready with remote-controlled devices. Not these remote-controlled light E-boats; that is something else. This is a boat that does thirty knots and carries the explosive charge in its bows. It is remote-controlled and is directed straight to the target. There is some sort of arrangement so that it doesn't go off until it is at a depth of 2 or 3 m., so that the target is hit and holed below the water-line. Not a bad thing, either! I have seen them going along and they move at a hell of a speed!*
> *N1878:   How large are the boats?*

N2465:   *They aren't big – from here to the wall. (Dimensions of room: 12. ft. 6 by 9 ft 6)*

N1878:   *Are they broader?*

N2465:   *Yes.*

N1878:   *Do they travel on the surface?*

N2465:   *Yes.*

N1878:   *The boat is directed to a certain point and does it then sink?*

N2465:   *Yes, then it sinks – it can probably be set in different ways – then it explodes. Moreover it's so small that it's impossible ......* [24]

Schultz went on to describe what can only have been the *Biber* (Beaver) single-crew assault submarine.

'*N2465:*   *I have seen the one-man U-boats, they are operated by officers, also by "Fähnriche", "Oberfähnriche" and "Oberfeldwebel". It requires rather more intellect and training.*

N1878:   *Can you only take one torpedo with them?*

N2465:   *Two torpedoes.*' [25]

By the end of 1944 thirty-one *Biber* had been lost in return for one merchant ship sunk. The 128 days of European hostilities in 1945 saw eighty-two *Biber* losses (including accidents in port) from ninety-five sorties for no result. There was also an ineffective attempt to use them against the critical bridges at Nijmegen, which remained in Allied hands after the daring but unsuccessful Operation *Market Garden* ('A Bridge Too Far') in September 1944.

Name	Type	Crew	In Service	Remark
Neger	HT	1	Apr 44	
Marder	HT	1	Aug 44	
Hai	HT	1	N/A	
Delphin	Midget		N/A	
Seeteufel	Midget	2	N/A	Tracked, for sea-bed crawling

Steel Coffins

Name	Type	Crew	In Service	Remark
Schwertal	Midget		N/A	Walter powered
Biber	Midget	1	Aug 44	
Molch	Midget	1	Sep 44	
Hecht	Midget	3	May 44	Training use only
Seehund	Midget	2	Jan 45	
Linsen	Speedboat	1/3	Apr 44	Explosive & control versions

Table 4: Small Battle Units
(HT – Human Torpedo)

The most successful German miniature submarine was the *Seehund* (Seal) or Type XXVII B5 which, confusingly, shared its name with an infra-red telescope mentioned previously. This seventeen-ton craft had a crew of two and carried two torpedoes. A total of 285 boats were built; between January and April 1945 they made 142 sorties, sank eight ships, and damaged three. Thirty-five were lost.

'Walter' Boats

As far as Professor Hellmuth Walter was concerned the answer to most questions was High Test Peroxide or HTP, a concentrated solution of hydrogen peroxide in water. It can be induced to decompose rapidly into water and oxygen, releasing a great deal of heat in the process and is thus suitable – if handled carefully – for use as an air-independent fuel. Its drawbacks are high cost, noise, and inherent safety issues.

The first mutterings of a revolutionary submarine propulsion system began to emerge as early as 1941. A *Maschinenmaat* from *U-556* couldn't help showing off his knowledge to two crewmen from the tanker *Alstertor*.

'N802:   *There is a U-boat with a crew of six. It has a turbine, and this turbine is said to be a unit which works under water and on*

263

the surface. It is true it is worked by a gas which is so dangerous that you have to wear rubber gloves and leather clothing. It is a sort of liquid air which is completely consumed without leaving any residue. They tried it out in KIEL where a firm completed one or two boats in its own dockyards. We can take them with us on a battleship – a crew of six – or on an auxiliary cruiser.[26]

This must refer to the unarmed prototype Walter boat *V80*, built at Kiel in 1940 and used for trials until 1942. It was followed by small, armed, experimental Type XVIIA/B boats, two examples each of which were built at Blohm & Voss Hamburg and Germania Werft Kiel respectively. *Maschinenmaat* Dehler, late of *U-489*, was probably thinking of them when he told stool pigeon N1558,

'The GERMANIA shipyard at KIEL and the DEUTSCHE WERKE at HAMBURG have been working on a new U-boat, with a speed of 25 knots on the surface and 20 knots submerged. They are small boats, carrying only two torpedoes, and can go to sea only in company with supply boats. They run on some stuff like gas, have only turbines and the exhaust gases are collected in bottles. They proceed on that both on the surface and when submerged; they don't need any batteries.'[27]

Some witnesses' garbled accounts conflated the programme with the small and midget submarine experiments happening in parallel, leading to a confusing variety of physical descriptions. An E-boat stoker who had seen one clarified the matter.

'N2189:   You've seen the "Walter" boats, haven't you; what do they look like? Do they actually look like ordinary U-boats or are they somehow different?

N2480:   They look just like ordinary ones.'[28]

In March 1944, an overheard conversation between an able seaman from *U-744* and a stoker from the tanker *Charlotte Schliemann*[29] suggested that the new submarines, if they worked, could be a real headache.

'N2279:   *The new "Walter" boats can easily do thirty knots.*
(High pressure, hot steam?)
N2349:   *...... something else too. The boats have turbine*
installations.
N2279:   *Yes, turbine installations and ......*
N2349:   *That's something different ...... A destroyer*
proceeding ahead of a boat like that ...... that would be
something!'[30]

The normally reliable Kurt Böhme, commander of *U-450*, gave two apparently contradictory views on the same day, 12th April 1944, in conversation with stool pigeon N1878.

'N1878:   *Where are the "Walter" boats supposed to be produced*
in quantity?
N2344:   *In my opinion BLOHM & VOSS must be*
producing them in quantity.'

----------oOo----------

'N2344:   *"Walter" boats aren't being built at all. .... is*
another type of boat, smaller, somewhat similar to the VII C boats,
only smaller and with several times the battery capacity. Accordingly
it can proceed submerged for a longer period and at greater speed. The
boats are supposed to do twelve knots submerged and twelve knots on
the surface – the same speed in both cases. ...'[31]

The second version he described was almost certainly the Type XXIII 'Electroboat' (see below); a small, conventionally powered submarine which saw some service in the closing months of the war.

Rumours persisted but the Electroboat was clearly a safer, quieter, cheaper, and more practical development route. The proposed operational Walter boats, Type XVIII, were never completed. The research boats were scuttled at the end of the war but the Royal and US navies each retrieved one. The British Type XVIIB, *U-1407*, was refitted, renamed HMS *Meteorite*, and tested to evaluate its potential. The trials showed enough promise, in the eyes of the Admiralty if not the crew, to commission two purpose-built HTP submarines: HMS *Explorer* and *Excalibur*. Noisy and lethally temperamental, their crews nicknamed them *Exploder* and *Excruciator*. The initiative was not pursued further (see Occupation, Reparation below).

Electroboats

Revolutionary new propulsion methods were all very well, but the *Kriegsmarine* needed something that could be made to work quickly and reliably and produced in wartime. The workhorse Type VII and IX boats had largely been chased from the sea in the second half of 1943. The desperate measures adopted since – better electronics, armament, diving depth, countermeasures, 'stealth' coating, *schnorkel* – could only do so much. *Oberleutnant zur See* Kurt Böhme (*U-450*) put the issue graphically.

> *'Seven knots, three-quarters speed or maximum speed, and you can't hear yourself speak in the conning-tower because there's such a noise set up outside by conning-tower fairing and all those things, guns and 2 cm. – the flak that's standing up there and all that sort of thing, it all vibrates. The protective plates on the quadruple mounting move to and fro, the vibration is terrific. Just imagine what it would be like when doing twelve knots submerged! A cod is streamlined, and a U-boat must be likewise. Nothing should protrude, there must be no corners.'*[32]

The plea for streamlining anticipated one of the design criteria for a new generation of 'electroboats'. Sleek exterior combined with massively increased battery capacity and motor power to give high underwater speed and endurance. Sonar and fire-control upgrades matched with pattern-running torpedoes allowed the new boats to carry out an attack without showing any part of themselves above water.

Another innovation was a revolutionary approach to construction: 'section build'. Hull sections were manufactured in remote locations and brought to the coast where they could be welded together to form a complete submarine relatively quickly. From laying-down to commissioning was said to take ten weeks. *Maschinenmaat* Blume of *U-765* described the process to stool pigeon N2392 on 17th May 1944.

> 'N2482:   ...*Take HAMBURG, for example. The majority of the boats aren't actually built there, they are sent there from the interior half-completed, and then they just assemble them.*
>
> N2392:   *But the pressure hulls are surely constructed at HAMBURG, aren't they?*
>
> N2482:   *Yes, but even the parts of the pressure hull are made in the interior.'[33]*

Garbled prisoner accounts tended to confuse different development streams. There were several reports of fast, eighteen-man submarines with two torpedo-tubes which had to be loaded from outside – on the face of it a concise summary of the Type XXIII (see below). However, they often featured novel drive technology or were mixed up with other ideas which never saw production.[34]

Perhaps the first concrete information about the new boats came from a Bletchley Park decrypt of a despatch from the Japanese ambassador to Berlin. This diplomat had privileged access to a great deal of information and wrote usefully informative reports. His alarming update on the Type XXI ocean-going and Type XXIII coastal electroboats was summarised in the Director of Naval Intelligence's secret weekly report for 2nd October 1944.

> '*Type XXI: (250 ft. long). The final assembly yards for this type are Blohm and Voss, Hamburg; Deschimag, Bremen, and Schichau, Danzig. Particulars: It has a high underwater speed in the region of 15 knots, and has a peculiar streamlined hull and conning tower*

structure. It has 6 bow tubes and no stern tubes. There is a strong suggestion that it is intended to fire torpedoes, with the aid of a new hydrophone fitted in the bows called Balcon at depths possibly over 160 ft. Schnorkel is fitted. Production: About a dozen of this type are already commissioned, and it is estimated that over 60 may be ready to operate, if not already operating, by the end of the year. None is yet at sea, but a few may well come out shortly.

N.I.D. Comment: a) Until recently it was estimated that the Germans might have 25-30 of this type ready to operate in December, 1944.

b) Most recent reconnaissance evidence, however, suggests that about 60 may be ready to operate in December, 1944.

c) The Japanese Naval Attaché has stated that the German plan is to complete 30 a month by December, 1944. A.1.

This is higher than the figure (16+ per month) anticipated in current recco evidence, but the Germans may well accelerate their present rate of production.

Type XXIII: (110 ft. long). The final assembly yard is at Hamburg-Finkenwaerder. Particulars: Like the larger type the Type XXIII has a high speed submerged and streamlined construction. It has two bow tubes only, and no reload torpedoes. Production: Up to a dozen have been completed and commissioned. None is yet at sea, though a few may come out any time.

Note: Time for trials for a normal 500-tonner is 5-6 months, but it is expected that this time will be drastically cut for the new types. (Source: Japanese Naval Attaché, and notebook from Toulon). A.1.[35]

Sixty small (234 tons surfaced) Type XXIII boats were built. Almost all the space inside was taken up by machinery, leaving just enough for a crew of fourteen to eighteen men and two torpedoes, which had to be loaded from outside. Six made operational patrols between January and May1945, sinking a total of four ships. Seven were lost to various causes, only one of which was enemy action.

Oberleutnant (Ing) Striezel was rescued from *U-1003*, a Type VIIC U-boat, in March 1945. Despite serving in a by-then obsolescent model he had previously been assigned to a Type XXI boat and was keen to share his enthusiasm for the new technology with the two stool pigeons in his cell.

'*STRIEZEL: The new boats (Type XXI) were supposed to have been ready by Christmas. But it didn't come off. To start with the Allies smashed half of them at HAMBURG and at BREMEN. There was a heavy air-raid just on the factories of BLOHM & VOSS and DESCHIMAG and they smashed half of them then. Some are out – a certain number of the new boats are in use already. I had the nineteenth.*

37Z: Are the new boats much better?

STRIEZEL: Even the English have said: "The design is good, after the war we will take it up." At the moment, of course, they are experiencing teething troubles, a thing like that can't be produced just out of a hat. They are incredible things. Six torpedo tubes forward – (sketching) The large depth-gauge indicates up to 400 m.'[36]

The delay no doubt explained Streizel's continued service in a Type VIIC. He went on to describe the new boat's tactical edge when attacking a convoy.

'*42Z: CNEUSS(?) told me you can fire from a range [depth] of 50 m. Is that a fact?*

STRIEZEL: Yes. You get underneath the convoy and then the Captain says: "Let's fire six torpedoes!" You don't need to worry any more about periscope depth and being spotted or the 'snorter' head being located etc. Nothing like that any more. They are now working on it so that they can fire the torpedoes from 80 m. I didn't get that, but the 50 m. range was already laid down in the instructions.'[37]

Rushed development, wartime conditions, systematic bombing of the assembly yards, and a workforce less than motivated for the task combined to make section build, already stretching the industrial technology of the time, a forlorn hope. For example, the design allowed for a tolerance of plus or minus 4 mm in the diameter of hull sections. In practice they arrived with a variation of plus 17 mm to minus 12 mm which, since the demands for rapid throughput precluded rejecting any, required 'bodge' fixes in the dockyard.

> *'STRIEZEL: But the kind of people they had working on them! A mixture of nations was working on the Type XXI, Ukrainians, French PW, Russians, concentration camp prisoners under strong escort, German dockyard labourers, naval detachments and our own men had to help as well. On SCHNEE's boat they caught an English agent among the workmen!*
> *It was two years from the first stroke of the pen to the first completed boat. That boat was constructed at the conference table. It was rumoured in GERMANY that HITLER had locked up the technicians and said: "Right, now you've got to lay down a boat, whether you like it or not."'[38]*

No fewer than a hundred and seventeen Type XXI U-boats were built. The scale of the design's problems can be judged from the fact that just two of them made operational patrols, in which they achieved nothing (though *Korvettenkapitän* Adalbert Schnee in *U-2511* made a dummy attack on HMS *Suffolk* after the surrender order).

There is little question that if this design, which did not need any ground-breaking new technology, had been reliably available two years earlier the Battle of the Atlantic might have looked quite different. Without a largely uninterrupted logistic train across the ocean from late 1943, would D-Day have been feasible? Would the outcome of the war in western Europe have looked the same?

All the victorious Allies studied and learnt from the Type XXI U-boat, arguably the first designed as a true submarine rather than a submersible torpedo boat. The Soviet class known to NATO as 'Whiskey' and its derivatives were very closely modelled on the design.

Underwater Diesels

As time passed an increasing number of hints emerged about U-boats with uprated diesel engines. Typically, they involved the larger types and fast-running engines normally used in E-boats (motor torpedo boats). The advantages claimed were speed (though this was implausibly exaggerated) and the ability to run under water. Few if any of the informants had seen the equipment they described, so intelligence officers faced a greater than usual challenge to make sense of their evidence. *Obermaschinist* Willi Klose (*U-464*) produced one early account in October 1942.

> 'N1263: He (I.O.) wanted to know about U-boats with E-boat engines. They now have containers for exhaust and waste (?) gases. They can proceed submerged for a certain length of time using their Diesels.*
>
> N1251: A definite or indefinite length of time?
>
> N1263: It's controlled by the exhaust containers. Did you know about it already?
>
> N1251: I've never heard about it at all.
>
> N1263: It isn't 100 per cent satisfactory yet.'[39]

Klose's knowledge was worth further investigation. Twelve days later, now closeted with a colleague from *U-353*, he seemed to have dropped the theme of storing exhaust gases in favour of feeding the engines with bottled air.

> 'N1263: They wanted to know something about this under-water Diesel engine.
>
> N1315: I know nothing about it either.

N1263:   ....in bottles. And during a dive there are exhaust gases so the exhaust pipe is just above the surface of the water. But in my opinion there is not much point in that. The use of bottles limits the length of time it can be used.'[40]

Leutnant zur See Wolf Danckworth, first lieutenant and sole survivor of *U-224* seemed to know more. Prompted by previous questioning he discussed the topic with his opposite number from *U-187*.

'N1536:   He (I.O.) spoke of 1200-ton U-boats with E-boat engines. There is one, isn't there?

N1495:   I don't know.

N1536:   I've seen it.

N1495:   Where – at KIEL?

N1536:   No, at HELA.'[41]

The interrogation report observed that fast-running engines would need much more maintenance than the medium-speed plant usually fitted to U-boats. It inferred that the boats so equipped must be operationally constrained, as a submarine's cramped quarters limited both access for repair and spares storage. The builders aimed to get around the problem by fitting more engines. *Funkobergefreiter* Robert Fisch of *U-523* told stool pigeon N1485 how the system worked but remained sceptical himself.

'N1485:   … What sort of diesels have the 1200-ton boats got? Nine-cylinders?

N1888:   It has six Mercedes-Benz-engines, E-boat engines. There must be something in them, but they don't get far, they don't work well with this fuel.

N1485:   Then why are they not built in everywhere?

N1888:   It was apparently no good.

N1485:   Why hasn't it proved to be any good?

N1888:   I don't know.'[42]

What the crewmen did not know was that fitting fast diesels to a few large Type IX boats was a trial run for much more ambitious project. As early as 1918 Germania Werft had explored the possibility of a closed cycle engine that did not need to breathe air from outside. The research was resumed in great secrecy from 1939 using the Daimler-Benz engines evaluated in operational conditions as a base.

The next step of the programme was to install a functional closed cycle propulsion system in an experimental Type XVIIK U-boat using the Daimler-Benz engines, and a smaller version using a truck engine in a modified *Seehund* midget submarine. This phase was well advanced when the war came to an end.

The main motive was an insurance policy, in case either the Walter boats failed to live up to expectations or they could not be used because of disruption to the HTP supply. It appears the Allies had little idea of this development until Lieutenant Schilling, USNR, interrogated two of the engineers involved at Eckenförde after the war.[43]

---

[1] TNA WO 208/4143. SRN 805 (23/2/42).
[2] TNA WO 208/4149. SRN 3045 (2/3/44).
[3] TNA WO 208/4152. SRN 3695 (17/5/44).
[4] TNA WO 208/4147. SRN 2201 (15/9/43).
[5] TNA WO 208/4151. SRN 3361 (14/4/44).
[6] Ibid. SRN 3519 (29/4/44). The N(Am) index number denotes a captive taken by US forces.
[7] TNA WO 208/4145. SRN 1838 (21/5/43).
[8] Ibid. SRN 1495 (3/3/43).
[9] TNA WO 208/4149. SRN 3011 (2/3/44).
[10] TNA WO 208/4151. SRN 3360 (14/4/44). ADM 186/809, P.266 *sqq*.
[11] TNA ADM 1/10176.
[12] TNA WO 208/4141. SRN 218 (28/3/41).
[13] TNA WO 208/4143. SRN 1012 (1/9/42).
[14] TNA ADM 186/807. P.393.
[15] TNA WO 208/4144. SRN 1122 (4/10/42).
[16] Ibid. SRN 1341 (11/12/42).
[17] Ibid. SRN 1457 (19/2/43).
[18] Ibid. SRN 1070 (12/9/42).

19   Ibid. SRN 1325 (6/12/42).
20   TNA WO 208/4151. SRN 3597 (4/5/44).
21   Ibid. SRN 3566 (3/5/44).
22   Paterson, P.41-47.
23   TNA WO 208/3258. CSDIC (Mai) CMF/N/16 (5/1/45).
24   TNA WO 208/4151. SRN 3512 (3/5/44).
25   Ibid. SRN 3557 (3/5/44).
26   TNA WO 208/4143. SRN 585 (26/7/41).
27   TNA WO 208/4146. SRN 2131 (14/8/43).
28   WO 208/4152. SRN 3667 (14/5/44).
29   HMS *Relentless* caught *Charlotte Schliemann* attempting a U-boat rendezvous southeast of Mauritius on 9th February 1944. 41 survivors were first landed in Mombasa where they underwent preliminary interrogation by Lt Burnett RNVR, who flew there especially. One was then sent to CSDIC Middle East for further interrogation, the rest direct to the UK.
30   TNA WO 208/4150. SRN 3105 (15/3/44).
31   Ibid. SRN 3347, 3338 (12/4/44).
32   TNA WO 208/4150. SRN 3338 (12/4/44).
33   TNA WO 208/4152. SRN 3698 (17/5/44).
34   See for example TNA WO 208/4146. SRN 2091 (5/8/43).
35   TNA ADM 223/357. DNI Note for 2/10/44, P.4-5.
36   TNA AIR 40/3104. Special Extract from SR Draft No WG 683/45 (30/3/45).
37   Ibid.
38   Ibid.
39   TNA WO 208/4144. SRN 1140 (8/10/42).
40   Ibid. SRN 1178 (20/10/42).
41   TNA WO 208/4145. SRN 1586 (5/4/43).
42   TNA WO 208/4147. SRN 2219 (15/9/43).
43   Combined Intelligence Objectives Sub-Committee, CIOS Target No 12/246 (August 1945).

POST WAR

Naval Parties

With the war's end in sight, if not necessarily in range, the Navy began to look at what should come after. Several naval Port Parties were preparing for the end of hostilities, even as 30 Assault Unit was limbering up for its new deployment. One of them was Naval Party 1735, destined for Wilhelmshaven which had twice built and launched fleets against Britain. Twice was enough.

Burton Cope was posted to Naval Party 1735 on 7th December 1944 as one of its core members, responsible for planning and mobilisation. He would become Staff Officer (Intelligence) serving under Captain Edward Conder, formerly Executive Officer of the battlecruiser HMS *Renown*.

At almost the same time Bernard Trench achieved his long-held ambition of final retirement. His legs had been giving him pain for some time and, following an Admiralty reshuffle, his grand-sounding title of Assistant DNI (Prisoners of War) offered little employment and less satisfaction.

High-level planning for the initial occupation of Germany, between ceasefire and the establishment of civilian government, had started as early as 1943. The practicality now, as far as the Navy was concerned, would be to take over naval ports as promptly as possible, confiscate and preserve all secret and warlike material, prevent any continuing hostile action, dismantle Nazi Party machinery and laws, and replace them with a working administration. In the chaos of a collapsed state, and with over a decade of indoctrination to undo, this was no trivial task. Officers of Naval Party 1735 were given simpler guidance:

'...take such physical action, destructive or constructive, that in your judgement will be most effective in preventing German children from fighting English children when they grow up.'[1]

What did this mean for a town which existed solely to build, support, and operate warships? There was no clear idea yet. Both in Britain and in the USA, there was a strong public feeling that Germany should be thrown back centuries, to a purely agrarian economy.

The naval parties were not going in completely blind. Air reconnaissance supplied a certain amount of information about the physical destruction they had to expect, but more important were the briefing notes gleaned from prisoners, refugees and deserters over the preceding months and years. They provided a gazetteer of key Nazi functionaries, the officials they had displaced, the location of their offices and their organisational relationships. This information would be an invaluable aid to separating the sheep from the goats in the coming days.

Naval Party 1735 set off on the unpropitious date of Friday 13th April 1945, as fully staffed and prepared as possible in the time. Rumours that fanatical Nazis would make a final stand on the East Frisian Islands meant there was no time to lose in securing their command structure. After an eventful run from Ostend through the chaos of countryside recently liberated or still fought over, the advance party entered Wilhelmshaven with units of 1st Polish Armoured Division on 6th May.

While the Poles took the formal surrender of the city naval teams secured key points in the naval base and dockyard, and a reconnaissance party including Conder and Cope in three jeeps raced ahead to the secret communications headquarters at Sengwarden. The wireless, phone and teleprinter links in this intact and highly secure complex could talk to any part of the German high command. In the last weeks of the war all German naval operations had been run from there.

11: NP1735 at Enschede *en route* for Wilhelmshaven

The party defused a tense situation by ordering lunch, and shortly afterward a parachute regiment arrived to make the surrender official.[2]

12: Surrender at Wilhelmshaven
Lt Cdr Cope at far left is reading the surrender terms to British and German officers present.

The designated Flag Officer in Charge, Admiral Muirhead-Gould, his opposite number Admiral Erich Förste and the latter's Chief of Staff *Vizeadmiral* Kleikamp either could not be traced or did not arrive in time, so Captain Conder and *Konteradmiral* Kurt Weyher undertook the formal handover negotiations. The atmosphere was strained at first – Conder knew about conditions in the nearby Bergen-Belsen concentration camp – but the two gradually built a good working relationship.

A party from Assault Unit 30 entered Wilhelmshaven on the same day.[3] The FIU interrogator attached to this group was none other than Cope's old colleague Ralph Izzard. It is entertaining to speculate what the two might have had to say to each other.

Two days later conditions were settled enough for a 'splicing the mainbrace' session in Sengwarden barracks.

13: 'Splicing the Mainbrace', Wilhelmshaven, 8/5/1945
Admiral Muirhead-Gould is facing left in the foreground. The tall officer behind him is Ralph Izzard.

The serious work of occupation now began. For the Naval Party this meant finding and making safe, removing, or destroying warlike stores, organising the removal of land and sea mines (German technicians had both the skills and expendability for this work), and dispensing food, security and justice. Seaworthy warships and U-boats were concentrated at Wilhelmshaven awaiting agreement on their distribution between the victorious powers.

The occupiers were constantly on their guard lest the German skeleton crews should take it into their heads to commit one final act of sabotage and scuttle their charges. The memory of the High Seas Fleet's scuttling in 1919 was still fresh. On Sunday 16th December 1945, an early-morning raid by a mixed force of naval, marine and army personnel secured all the ships in port under a secret plan codenamed Operation *Silver*. Two days later the sailing crews of the vessels destined for the Soviet Union returned to their ships and were informed of their destination, their new commanders for the voyage, and reassured that any who did not volunteer to stay would be brought back and discharged on their return. The remaining ships were transferred, under guard, to the USA and Britain between December 1945 and early summer 1946.

Cope was fully involved in the effort: tracking down wanted men and missing equipment, interviewing crews to ensure that the individuals most likely to give trouble were separated, talking to freed prisoners and forced labourers to identify the most committed Nazis. With the team still building up to full strength it was an incredibly stretching time for all involved. He still maintained desultory correspondence with Bernard Trench, now retired and living in Wales.

Apart from Cope's work on de-Nazification there was the lively social life of the Naval Party – now named HMS *Royal Rupert* – to keep up with. This included entertaining visiting dignitaries. Some like his former team-mate Colin McFadyean (now head of Naval Intelligence Prisoner of War section) had a professional interest. Mary Churchill, stationed with her ATS unit near Hamburg, came to lay the foundation stone for a cinema named after her father. Then there were the 'tourists' who were difficult to refuse, such as Field Marshal Montgomery's party in November 1945.

14: Cope greeting General Horrocks at Wilhelmshaven
Probably November 1945

Cope left Wilhelmshaven in uniform for the last time on 12th April 1946. Captain Conder's parting assessment stated,

'He has carried out his duties as an intelligence officer with great precision, common sense and ability. He has been principally responsible for excellent work in de-nazifying this area. He is loyal, zealous and hardworking. His German, Dutch and French are perfect & he is excellent at office work.'[4]

That was not quite the end of the story. He was discharged from naval service in June 1946 and awarded a Military OBE in the same month. By September he had taken up employment with the Control Commission and continued his de-Nazification work in the Hanover area, including at least some time in the former Bergen-Belsen concentration camp. Around this time, he got to know John Bingham who was on secondment from MI5 and would later form part of the model for John le Carré's protagonist George Smiley.

His employment with the Control Commission finished at the end of 1947. He was not entitled to a naval pension and unable to secure re-employment or a pension from Cunard, so took a low-paying job with Cook's tourist bureau in London. It is unclear how long he was able to sustain this in the face of his declining health. He died in April 1952.

Occupation, Reparation

In the chaos of the collapsing Third Reich British and Canadian forces hurried to occupy the north and east of Germany. This both secured the British zone as agreed at the Yalta and Potsdam conferences and pre-empted a feared Russian occupation of Denmark. It also put most German naval infrastructure in the British zone of influence.

One team from Ian Fleming's Assault Unit 30 (AU30), after following several false leads, found themselves at *Schloss* Tambach near Coburg in Thuringia on 25th April 1945. The castle held the entire German naval archive, from 1870 to date, largely intact. The enormous find, said to weigh about three hundred tons, was secured and progressively shipped to London where it was divided between the US Embassy and the Admiralty. Translators were wheeled in from wherever they could be found – including CSDIC – to help process the files to which NID allocated PG ('Pinched from the Germans') references.

On 4th May another AU30 team entered Kiel and made its way directly to *Walterwerke* engine plant, where Dr Hellmuth Walter was living on site. This discovery attracted an immediate crowd of interrogators, technical specialists and military investigators closely followed by a constant procession of actual and aspirational VIPs. Walter himself was brought to the UK where he was interviewed by a panel of experts from 24th-30th May.[5] It seemed that whatever question Dr Walter was asked the answer was high test peroxide or HTP (also known as 'Ingolene'). Walter's projects applied this highly reactive and dangerous substance to,

- Submarine propulsion.
- Surface, underwater and air-launched torpedoes.
- Steam-generating plant for long-range rockets.
- Assisted take-off and climbing aids for conventional aircraft, also a fuel additive for increased performance.
- Rocket and jet-propelled aircraft.
- Powered glide bombs and free-fall bombs.
- Remote-controlled explosive tanks.
- Air-independent drive for underwater tanks.
- Rocket or jet-propelled anti-aircraft and artillery shells.
- Jet brake for air-launched torpedoes and mines.
- Jet-propelled explosive assault boats.
- Aircraft and V1 catapults.
- Self-propelled mines.
- Explosive beach hurdlers.
- Long-range and liquid-propellant guns.
- Infantry anti-tank weapons.
- Acoustic minesweeping.

The contents of his cocktail cabinet do not bear thinking about.

One of the more successful developments using his technology was the Messerschmidt 163 rocket-propelled fighter which, however, had an unfortunate tendency to blow up on landing. An even more lethal idea which never made it into service was the *Natter* manned anti-aircraft rocket.

> *'In a final attempt to master the Allied air attacks, a weapon known as the "Natter" was devised. This was … in the form of a manned flak rocket. Some alterations were required … to allow vertical firing …. When under a flight of bombers the unfortunate operator was intended to release four powder driven smaller rockets on to the target. He then should come down by parachute. Only one manned trial was carried out, the luckless victim soard [sic] heavenwards, and evidently reached it quicker than he intended, as he did not return.'*[6]

Staff at the plant were generally co-operative, though with disturbing reminders of how things had been before liberation.

> *'About three hundred Russian slave workers had been employed in the plant. Walter said that whereas they had arrived like wild beasts, they had now become respectable members of community. They caused little trouble, except one day they demanded to have a bath en masse, and on another occasion shot one of the German guards dead. After June they all dispersed.'*[7]

Where they went is not recorded.

Wilhelm Otto Gottfried Blume was an engineer who had worked on the Walter project from January 1943 until just before the war's end. He was then employed by the Russians at Blankenberg, where they had removed as much of the relevant equipment as they could salvage. In July or August 1946 he took the opportunity of a visit to his wife and children in Berlin to defect and was interviewed by Lieutenant-Commander Donald Welbourn (engineer and former CSDIC interrogator) who came out from the UK for the purpose. Welbourn felt Blume's real practical skills were undermined by poor theoretical knowledge, though he did provide an insight into Russian efforts to poach engineers already working in the western sector. He and his family were brought out and rehoused, but it was thought too dangerous to try and recover his personal possessions.[8]

In a further coup for NID Paul Kanis, director and chief engineer of the Brückner-Kanis enterprise in Dresden, decided in February 1947 that work in the Russian zone was not to his taste. He decamped, with key members of his team and such microfilms and documents as they could hide in their effects, to the British zone where Welbourn and B Norton interviewed them. Kanis brought with him more insights into the development of Walter technology but pointed out that *'the real brains behind the original design are in fact in the British zone.'*[9] Their real value was the skills and knowledge locked up in their heads.

The British tested the concept of HTP-powered submarines with HMS *Explorer* (1956-65) and *Excalibur* (1958-68). Noise, safety, endurance, and cost compared to the emerging nuclear technology sealed its fate. A parallel attempt to develop an HTP-fuelled torpedo ended in disaster when the result, a Mk 12 (code named Fancy) exploded in the torpedo tube of HMS *Sidon* while alongside in Portland. The boat sank with the loss of thirteen lives, and it was a long time before the Royal Navy equipped its submarines with another thermally propelled weapon. Sweden and Russia, however, persisted with the technology, which in the latter case contributed to the loss of the submarine *Kursk* with all hands. British engineers continued work on HTP as a rocket fuel, and it is still used for that purpose by some private firms. Carefully.

Apart from the scramble for the Third Reich's intellectual and physical property there was the urgent question of what to do about millions of formerly mobilised and now suddenly unemployed people. The risk that the flames of Nazism had merely been damped down, not extinguished, could not be ignored. Nor could the perception, articulated by so many prisoners, that the injustice of the 1918 Armistice combined with the brutal recession that followed set the fire of extremism in the first place.

Former prisoners of war were progressively repatriated according to their assessed level of political indoctrination. Those who convinced their captors they were anti-Nazi were allowed home first, the unrepentant had to undergo an extended course of re-education.[10] The British also used former prisoners in agricultural work and on reconstruction projects as informal reparations. It was several years before they all found their way home – but even so they were far better off than those left to the tender mercies of the Soviet Union.

In Germany, the French proposed setting up a joint commission for naval information. The proposal prompted a debate between the British, who were sitting on most of the German naval assets, and the French who had lived under German rule for four years and knew something of the personalities involved. It was rejected as the body suggested would duplicate too much work elsewhere to be useful. Having discarded that component, the remaining task was to identify potentially dangerous elements among ex-naval personnel. A report observed,

> 'The German Navy was the least tainted service politically. It was almost wholly free from party influence up to 1943. After that a political officer (N.S.P.O.) was attached to the staff of each Flag Officer. In 1944 a small political section was attached to the O.K.M. The staff of this small political section (16 in number) and the N.S.P.O.'s can all be regarded as "ardent Nazis" and included in the automatic arrest category. We have the names of the O.K.M. staff and are endeavouring to obtain names of any N.S.P.O.'s.'[11]

With no easy category, such as the SS, to select for blanket arrest the naval de-Nazification programme had to rely on a painstaking process of record search and personal interview. By 30th October 1945 some 400,000 out of 680,000 naval personnel records had been found and were being reviewed at the British naval headquarters in the former Melitta paper factory at Minden, not far from Hannover.

In addition, the Royal Navy retained a force of up to 45,000 sailors under German naval organisation and discipline for minesweeping and clearance. There was, at least initially, no shortage of volunteers for this difficult, uncomfortable, and dangerous work under the German Minesweeping Administration (GM/SA). It was at least paid, familiar and social.[12] After the end of hostilities they, with many others, were classed as Surrendered Enemy Personnel (Disarmed Enemy Forces in US parlance), avoiding the repatriation clauses of the 1929 Geneva Convention.

For most German citizens, the de-Nazification process was inevitably done in haste. Some, however, were clearly going to need a closer look – the kind of inspection that only the skills of a detailed interrogation centre could provide. Planning for this had started at least as early as June 1944, and quickly decided that the best leader was Lieutenant-Colonel 'Tin-Eye' Stephens of MI5's Camp 020 near Richmond, Surrey. Initially, MI5 was expected to provide only a token contribution to the new camp's staff. It soon became clear that its clients were as likely to be civilian spies and subversives as the military prisoners that MI19 were used to dealing with. Stephens, never happy with the idea, could see his highly efficient Richmond creation being eviscerated to no good purpose.

In January 1945, an MI5 representative requisitioned Château Val-Duchesse near Brussels for use as a temporary interrogation centre (which later moved to Diest) and arranged for screening facilities to be provided at a nearby prisoner of war camp in Vilvoorde. The first officers detached from Camp 020 and CSDIC UK arrived in April. CSDIC Western European Area (WEA) was born.

Stephens had not given up the fight. A meeting of the Joint Intelligence Committee (JIC) on 1ˢᵗ May was asked to consider whether *'the Sub-Committee renewed their approval to the establishment of an Interrogation Centre in the light of the altered circumstances set out in the minute [creation of an independent US centre]; to what extent 21 Army Group should accept Inter-Service responsibility for the Centre; and whether or not there should be a small C.S.D.I.C. in the U.K. after the formation of a Centre by 21 Army Group.'*

The committee confirmed the principle of a European CSDIC while rejecting the overtly political elements of the proposal. Its reply,

(i) *'Agreed to the formation of a Combined Services Detailed Interrogation Centre under 21 Army Group.*

(ii) *Agreed that the Centre should undertake "responsibilities towards all three Services" and <u>not</u> "some responsibilities towards other Services" as proposed.*

(iii) *Invited the Deputy Directors of Intelligence to consider at their next Meeting whether or not C.S.D.I.C. in the U.K. should continue after the formation of an Interrogation Centre under 21 Army Group, bearing in mind that it would be more economical to abolish the U.K. Centre.'* [13]

In June 1945, the centre moved to Bad Nenndorf, conveniently close to Minden. Here it was officially designated No 74 CSDIC. Stephens moved across from Camp 020, which closed in November.

The focus of its work progressively migrated from operational intelligence (OI) to counterintelligence (CI) as its targets evolved from unrepentant Nazis to Soviet spies, defectors, and infiltrators. By 1947 the centre was suffering from budget and staffing cuts, while too many of the replacement staff were unskilled or, worse, criminal.

In early 1947 several prisoners from Bad Nenndorf needed hospitalisation, and two of them died. Their condition on admission to hospital led to enquiries about the treatment of inmates, allegations of abuse (certainly justified), unwanted attention in Parliament and the press, and eventually the closure of the camp. Stephens and three others were court-martialled. The likely reputational impact, both on British methods in the recent war and on the willingness of future defectors, prompted MI5 to watch developments anxiously from the side-lines. Guy Liddell, Director of Counterespionage, noted in his diary,

> *'Our only fear is that people will say that this is how Camp 020 got their information during the war, and it would therefore be convenient if there were someone there who could unofficially look after our interests.'*[14]

None of the guards and only two of the interrogators were charged, along with a medical officer. The trial was hampered by the lack of personnel trained to use the listening equipment, which might have provided evidence of innocence or guilt. In the event Stephens and one of his co-defendants were cleared of all charges, one case was abandoned before trial and the medical officer was dismissed from the service. Stephens was re-employed by MI5 as a security liaison officer in Accra on the Gold Coast (Ghana).

Liddell's diaries also mention proposals to set up post-war CSDICs in Cyprus, Palestine, Hong Kong, and Singapore. It is not clear how far these ideas progressed.

Post War

CSDIC and NID: Endings and Beginnings

CSDIC operations at Latimer house formally closed in November 1945, Trent Park continued operating until the following month. Latimer is now a hotel, and Trent Park is being developed for residential use at the time of writing, with the intention to include a museum commemorating the work of CSDIC. Wilton Park became No 300 Prisoner of War camp and was used for the re-education of German ex-prisoners of war before their repatriation. In 1954 a bunker was built there as the war headquarters for Eastern Command (including London). The site has since been redeveloped for housing and no trace of its wartime use remains.

As the Second World War segued into the Cold War the need to '*Look into the seeds of time / And say which grain will grow and which will not*' became more vital than ever. As each side acquired ever more powerful weapons the consequences of a single misreading of the other's intention became more horrific. At the same time Britain's retreat from empire helped create the conditions for the range of 'asymmetric conflict', from insurgency to terrorism. An early example was the formation of an *ad hoc* CSDIC in 1950 to help combat insurgents in the Malayan Emergency.[15]

The need for a permanent resource led to the formation of the Joint Services Interrogation Wing (JSIW), based at Templer Barracks in Ashford, Kent. It worked wherever British forces were engaged and helped train many non-military security organisations. The barracks closed in 1997 when the Channel Tunnel Rail Link came through the site, and the Wing's activities have relocated.

The last Director of Naval Intelligence in an unbroken line stretching from William Henry Hall in 1887 was Admiral Sir Norman Denning who, as a Paymaster Lieutenant-Commander in 1937 formed the Operational Intelligence Centre which

289

would give Britain a critical edge in the Battle of the Atlantic. He served in that role from 1959-64 and then, after the amalgamation of the service intelligence branches, as the first Deputy Chief of Defence Staff (Intelligence) from 1964-65.

The need for service-specific intelligence functions never entirely went away and was strengthened after the Falklands War in 1982. Today the Royal Navy recruits and employs intelligence specialists within the Warfare Branch. The availability of a specific career path avoids the need to push resentful seaman square pegs into staff round holes, which so damaged NID during the inter-war years.

---

[1] *Building and Launching of HMS Royal Rupert – the history of the founding of Naval Party 1735*, Royal Rupert Times, 1947, Archive of the Wilhelmshaven Association (TWA), Ref 7669SB. Burton Cope may have written the article.

[2] Ibid. According to Jens Graul the relieving troops were 27th Battalion Royal Marines.

[3] TNA ADM 223/214.

[4] Original in the author's possession.

[5] TNA ADM 283/72, 290/285.

[6] TNA ADM 199/2434

[7] Ibid.

[8] TNA FO 1031/63.

[9] TNA ADM 213/823. P.3.

[10] Sullivan.

[11] TNA FO 1038/145.

[12] Madsen.

[13] The main source for this passage is TNA KV 4/327.

[14] TNA KV4/469. 28th June 1947.

[15] Thomas J Maguire, *Interrogation and 'psychological intelligence'* in Andrew & Tobia, *Interrogation*.

Conclusion

How Come?

There is an enduring fascination with the secret history of the two world wars. While others have looked at prisoner of war interrogation in World War 2 the genesis of the practice in the Great War has so far been neglected. This volume sets out to repair that neglect.

- It argues that British Naval Intelligence pioneered structured prisoner interrogation as an information source and looks at the development of the technique in WW1.

- It focusses on naval issues. In WW1, the technological race was most acute at sea. In WW2, a combined services approach gave British intelligence an immense advantage over the despotic regimes' vicious internecine rivalry, but it is important to recognise that the three services' different perspectives influenced their approaches.

- The naval focus provides an opportunity to consider technology issues in more depth.

- It reviews the work of interrogation centres in the Middle East, Africa, India, Australia, New Zealand, and the USA as well as the UK.

- Two questions run through the book: '*Did it work?*' and '*Did we use torture?*' The answer to the first is an emphatic yes, to the second a qualified no. We will review these in the following pages.

Castaways in Question

The Ethical Dimension

Humanity has tried for centuries, with varying success, to limit the inhumanity of conflict. Among the rules set out by the Hague Conventions of 1899 and 1907 was a set of standards for administering and looking after prisoners of war. These rules said nothing about extracting information from them, which created an opportunity first noticed and exploited by British naval intelligence.

We have seen how, from the beginning, instructions for handling prisoners emphasised fair and civilised behaviour. This is not to be confused with the naivety that sometimes allowed captured officers to give security briefings to their crew or dispose of sensitive documents.

Eyewitness accounts inevitably vary. It is however noteworthy that where we have British and German accounts of the same event, whether capture or interrogation, they can be so different as to strain belief that both are sincere.

There were undoubtedly lapses but interrogators in both wars tried to avoid physical mistreatment. This is not so much due to sensitivity on their part as to the understanding that violence was likely to be counter-productive and fear that word would get out and affect the treatment of British and allied prisoners in enemy hands.

The Geneva Convention (1929) repaired the omission in the Hague Conventions by specifying what information a prisoner could be required to give, and the limits on the incentives which could be used to extract more.[1] The key passage reads,

> *'No pressure shall be exercised on prisoners to obtain information regarding the situation in their armed forces or their country. Prisoners who refuse to reply may not be threatened, insulted, or exposed to unpleasantness or disadvantages of any kind whatsoever.'*

Interrogators in the Second World War certainly bent, if not broke, the spirit of this clause. Suggestions that the Russians were interested in a prisoner, that he would be sent to Canada across supposedly lethal waters, that he would be handed to the British 'Secret Service' or tried for piracy or spying elegantly turned the Nazi Party's own propaganda against its more impressionable victims. Any thawing in the interviewee's demeanour, on the other hand, might be rewarded by a seat or a cigarette. The most intransigent might find themselves in solitary confinement for a spell, though this negated any benefit from the secret microphones. Guy Liddell of MI5 described the fine line between adequate and abusive pressure to a post-war meeting of the Joint Intelligence Committee.

> *'I then read out to the meeting an extract of our minute to the Prime Minister on the whole question which he had approved. We stated "in this country physical violence was not a weapon that an interrogator would ever wish or be permitted to use. Not only is the idea abhorrent to the national conscience but it is a well known fact that such methods as often as not defeat their own ends by providing information which is wholly unreliable. But it would be idle to pretend that an interrogating officer does not, in a large percentage of cases which he handles, put pressure – and often severe and continuous pressure – upon his subject before he can achieve or hope to achieve any result. The form of pressure will vary enormously with different cases, but basically it will, more often than not, be founded on fear – fear for himself, fear for someone else." I made it quite clear to the meeting that if mental pressure was to be prohibited there would be no point in running CSDICs at all.'[2]*

CSDIC UK kept both feet and most of its toes on the right side of the line, but it is difficult to be as confident about some other centres.

The London District Cage at 6-8 Kensington Palace Gardens was an anomalous establishment. It was neither part of CSDIC nor strictly one of the cages used for sorting and classifying prisoners before forwarding them either to CSDIC or an internment camp. There were repeated allegations of harsh interrogation methods, both during the Second World War and afterwards when it was used for war crimes investigations.[3]

Some of the prisoners who had come to the UK after experiencing CSDIC Middle East described extended questioning under bright lights by relays of interrogators, being made to dig what they were told was their own grave, and threats of transport to Russia (again). These allegations were strenuously denied in a history of the service written by Colonel D McMillan (quoted in Global cataclysm was no reason to interrupt the daily internecine conflict at Admiralty. Neither Trench nor the DNI, Admiral Godfrey, were the sunniest personalities in the world and their abrasive relationship came to a head in 1942. Trench's diary records,

(2nd January)

'Campbell has played the dirty on me by making me responsible for the loss of some of our C.B.'s [Confidential Books] at the beginning of the war, which were then on his charge. A very sharp memo will reach the D.N.I. tomorrow on the subject.'

(4th January)

'Forwarded memo to D.N.I. & had an interview with him, during which he got very angry, said I was obstinate & mulish, which is quite correct, but he did not allow me to make any explanation. He said that he himself had received an expression of their Lordships' displeasure. This I could well believe. The impression left on both our minds after the interview was that we both thoroughly disapproved of one another. In addition my feelings are that I have no pleasure in serving in the N.I.D. in this war, after having seen what a well organised & well run N.I.D. was like in the last war. I have now no interest in it & no enthusiasm for it. The D.N.I. has no

*capacity for instilling enthusiasm in his subordinates. A misfit, so
very different from Sir William Hall.'*

Only one winner could emerge from such a clash of horns.
There is no evidence of a direct link, but the diary entry four
months later that the DNI *'wants me to go out to the Middle & Far
East to advise on P/W matters'* may be related.

The six-month trip would take him around the world. By the
time he returned Colin McFadyean was firmly installed in his
job and mainstream interrogation work had moved from Trent
Park to the new centres at Latimer House and Wilton Park.

Ironically, by then Godfrey himself had fallen victim to inter-
service politics and been succeeded by (then) Captain Edmund
Rushbrooke.

Trench held a short and demure farewell gathering at his flat
on 11ᵗʰ June. It was attended by nine favoured colleagues
including interrogators Cope, Mitchell, Rosevere, McFadyean,
Dick Weatherby and Williamson; Mrs Brown (his assistant at
Admiralty), and Esmé Mackenzie, a Wren officer at Trent Park.

On 16ᵗʰ he travelled overnight to Glasgow where he met his
companions for the trip and boarded the commandeered liner
Queen Elizabeth. Observing the first boat drill he commented
that, with ten thousand men and over eight hundred officers
filling every space, a genuine abandon ship order would lead to
disaster. The Cunard catering staff were however still there
however, so the excellent food was some consolation.

The ship got under way around midnight on the 17ᵗʰ/18ᵗʰ
June, initially steaming west with a strong escort at about twenty-
five knots. Frequent drills made the evacuation process slicker,
but Trench observed, *'I have not been allocated to a boat, so I am with
the sinking party.'* The following day she discarded her escort and
headed south, zig-zagging at high speed. She gained Freetown,
Sierra Leone, in the early evening of 25ᵗʰ, carefully timing her

arrival for high tide which was the only moment such a massive ship could enter the port.

They left the following day after taking on oil and water, giving Trench just enough time for a meeting on board with a local intelligence officer about prisoner interrogation. Arriving at Simonstown on 2nd July he discovered that any prisoners landed there were to be sent on to Durban for interrogation, so there was little point in loitering in the Cape area longer than necessary. With the outcome of the North Africa campaign still in the balance air transport was almost unobtainable, so he left by train on 6th, stopping at Johannesburg and Pretoria and arriving on 12th. Meetings at Pretoria and Durban produced material for his first reports.

Trench then arranged onward passage to Kilindini (Mombasa, Kenya) by flying boat. The luggage weight limit for the flight made him abandon his heavy uniform, and an overnight stop in Mozambique, a neutral Portuguese colony, forced him to travel in civilian clothes for fear of internment. He arrived at Kilindini on 16th July and spent ten days in meetings at Mombasa and Nairobi, including a lecture at the local Bletchley Park outpost which was mostly concerned with Japanese traffic.

In August 1941, the General Officer Commanding-in-Chief (GOC-in-C) West Africa had proposed setting up small interrogation centres with listening facilities at Accra and Freetown. Godfrey was initially sceptical, replying,

'With reference to your M.I.9(c)/FOL/42/3 of 25th August, I see no objection to the establishment of a unit in West Africa similar to the C.S.D.I.C. in the United Kingdom and Middle East, but I do not think it desirable from the naval point of view that German naval Prisoners of War should be retained in Freetown or Accra for interrogation.

2. Since German naval prisoners who would be landed in West Africa would either come from U-boats, raiders, or supply ships, the

*information obtained from them is of greater importance to the
Admiralty than to local authorities in West Africa. Therefore we
would prefer that they should be sent to the United Kingdom for
examination here, since all the information which serves as a
background for interrogation is only available in the Admiralty.*

*3.   Should the situation demand we would be glad to send out
naval personnel for one or other of these centres, but meanwhile it is
considered that our interests can be served by means of a watching
brief held by S.O.(I) Freetown.'*

Nonetheless preparations continued, on the assumption that
most prisoners would be Vichy French. The Post Office
Research Station agreed to supply three of the latest listening sets
within existing financial cover.

On 27th October 1941, with everything in train, MI9(c) sent
a cypher telegram to the GOC-in-C West Africa confirming the
arrangements. Crucially, this included a minimum staffing
requirement of twelve intelligence officers, six technicians, five
clerks and nine general duties infantry personnel. All but two or
three key officers were to be found locally. This quickly
produced a reply to the effect that it was impossible to find the
staff from his authorised strength. The equipment supply was
cancelled, and the project stood down. A letter from Major-
General Davidson to Godfrey and Air Vice Marshal Medhurst in
February drove the point home.

*'This is to the effect that, whilst the experts advised that small static
units could be set up at Freetown and Lagos Accra involving an
increase of but two technical other ranks over existing establishments,
the scheme must remain in abeyance for the present, since even the
small increase in European personnel entailed cannot be accepted, in
view of the limitations imposed by the ceiling figures and of the
priority needs of other requirements.*

*If you agree, therefore, I propose to drop the matter for the time
being.'*

The case for a permanent centre in West Africa was difficult to argue, though in practice interrogators were flown from Cairo for preliminary interviews of survivors landed in Freetown.

From December, however, war with Japan and the quick succession of defeats in South-East Asia made a compelling case for better intelligence in the Indian Ocean. Although the Deputy C-in-C Eastern Fleet, Vice-Admiral Peter Danckwerts, was sceptical about the chance of having any prisoners to deal with, Trench's reports added new impetus to work in progress on a CSDIC near Mombasa. A house and grounds were requisitioned at Nyali about six miles away. The plan was that the building would house staff and the M Rooms while tents provided prisoner accommodation and interrogation rooms. Experience in Egypt had shown that their low reverberation gave a much cleaner acoustic environment than permanent buildings, and they had the added advantage of making it easier to move the equipment if necessary.

Colonel Charles Lamplough RM (Deputy DNI) summed up the situation in a memo from Admiralty to MI19 dated 21st October 1942:

> *'According to a report from Colonel Trench, it appears that the construction of a camp at Mombasa may have been commenced, and he suggests that two rooms in this camp should be equipped with special listening apparatus and accommodation provided for the following Naval prisoners of war:- 5 Officers, 10 Chief or Petty Officers, 40 men. He recommends the Naval Interrogation Staff should consist of 2 Japanese-speaking Naval Officers, 1 German-speaking Naval Officer, 1 lady clerk, if possible with a knowledge of Japanese.*
>
> *3. Interrogation of prisoners is robbed of a great deal of its value without the use of listening apparatus, but Trench in his report states that 1 Japanese-speaking Military Officer is expected shortly (report dated July 1942) and 3 or 4 more are to come later. I presume,*

therefore, that these Officers will be available to man the special apparatus.'

German-speaking interrogators would be flown from Cairo if required, while Mombasa's Japanese speakers could reinforce the Indian centre. The twenty-five ratings then undergoing intensive Japanese language instruction in London were not expected to be of much value.

A MI19 minute of 26th October also refers to *'the centre now being formed at MOMBASA.'*

On 26th July Trench set out by flying boat on the two-day journey to Cairo, with overnight and refuelling stops on Lake Victoria and along the Nile. While there he visited the prison camp cum interrogation centre at Al Maadi, where he met Lieutenant-Commander Gustav Rodd to discuss the upgrades needed at Mombasa and received enthusiastic co-operation. While memos of escalating bewilderment flew between Admiralty and MI19 in London Rodd quietly got on with the job, visiting the site in September to plan the installation. At the beginning of November, acting on the principle that it is better to ask for forgiveness than permission, he sent a cypher telegram stating simply, *'Captain Hayward and two signalmen leave today for Mombasa to install centre. Request approval.'*

In the event it seems likely that the Kilindini centre was completed but not routinely used. Commander (Retired) Stephen Lushington, a fluent Japanese speaker, was posted from Trade Division to NID Kilindini on 1st September 1943 as 'Officer i/c Language Personnel' with no-one visibly reporting to him. By October 1944 he led a substantial CSDIC and SEATIC section at Kandy in Ceylon (now Sri Lanka), which was the location first intended for a South-East Asian naval intelligence centre. Survivors of *U-852* (sunk 3rd May 1944) were however brought to East Africa (presumably Kilindini) for preliminary interrogation. Eight, including the captain, were flown directly from there to the UK. Prisoners in both centres admitted the boat's part in the massacre of *Peleus* survivors (see Human Wrongs below), which sealed the fate of three of their officers.

Trench left on 4th August, again by flying boat, on the four-day trip to Delhi. The eventful journey involved an overnight stop at Kalia on the Dead Sea, where the resort manageress spoke only German and was suspiciously curious about Trench's movements. The aircraft was repeatedly plagued by engine trouble which culminated in an extra stopover at Karachi while the offending motor was changed.

On arrival in Delhi Trench made his way to the imposing Red Fort, which housed India's CSDIC. This section had been created recently, when proposals to set up a facility in Singapore and then Burma had been overtaken by the incredibly swift Japanese advance. The equipment destined for Singapore had therefore been diverted to India. Japanese language skills were a major constraint, and it was thought that it might be possible to identify suitable Japanese-speaking Chinese refugees.

There he met an interrogator and the senior available officers, most of whom did not impress him. Meetings the next day with the Directors of Personnel Services and Military Intelligence were enough for him to conclude his business and write up his report.

There were six Japanese army prisoners in residence at the time and Brigadier Cawthorn, the Director of Military Intelligence, was anxious to add naval expertise to his interrogation team. Trench identified three officers in the Royal Indian Navy who were fluent Japanese speakers and suggested they could be trained as interrogators.

The CSDIC India War Diary for June 1945 records that '*Early in the month the special segregation rooms and the D.I. rooms were completed.*' This implies that the Red Fort did not have a functioning M Room at the time of Trench's visit. There is an intriguing suggestion that some of the senior German officers captured in North Africa may have been sent to India, but I have found no corroboration.

Trench's state of mind was bleak. He confided to his diary, *'The Russians seem to be retreating still and everything seems to be going in favour of the Axis. We are doing nothing, waiting for the Russians to be defeated, so that Germany can concentrate on us. I have no confidence at all in our Government – ostrich like they bury their heads in the sand. There seems no prospect of the Allies winning the war; the only hope is that we may avoid losing it, but in any case we shall lose most of our empire.'*

On 13th August Trench set off by an extraordinarily convoluted route for his eventual arrival in Australia. It first involved a return to Cairo by air, then by stages to Durban where he boarded the independently sailing merchantman *Desirade*, about 12,000 tons. Her maximum speed of about 11½ knots ensured a leisurely passage, arriving at Sydney on 27th September.

On arrival he went to the Naval Headquarters on Garden Island and met Admiral Muirhead-Gould, who had formerly been naval attaché in Berlin and was later Flag Officer Western Germany until his untimely death in June 1945.

Trench then travelled overnight to Melbourne, discussing prisoner interrogation with intelligence officers there from 2nd to 5th October. Returning to Sydney, he flew to New Zealand on 8th. While there he observed the interrogation of an army prisoner at Featherston camp, about 41 miles from Wellington.

He then received instructions from the Admiralty to co-ordinate his onward travel with Lieutenant-Commander Ralph Albrecht, USN, who was not due to arrive at Brisbane until about 7th November. This gave him time for a little sightseeing before his return to Australia. Trench had met Albrecht earlier, facilitating his visit to Britain in April 1942 when he had been shown around Trent Park, inspected HMS *Graph* (formerly *U-570*) and the preparation of the Latimer and Wilton Park sites.

Trench flew back to Sydney on 30th October, spent a couple of days there writing up his report, then travelled by train to Brisbane (site of Australia's central interrogation facility at Indooroopilly) on 5th/6th November. Albrecht arrived on 8th. The next few days were spent in further report writing, planning their programme, and in discussions with senior naval, intelligence and political figures.

Trench and Albrecht finally left on Monday 23rd November. They island-hopped across the Pacific, flying via New Caledonia, Fiji, Palmyra Atoll and Honolulu (Pearl Harbour), where they spent five days in further talks and arranging onward transport. They arrived at San Francisco on Wednesday 2nd December, just having time to visit the West Coast interrogation centre at Camp Tracy, Byron Hot Springs before catching an evening train to Washington via Los Angeles and Chicago.

They reached Washington on Monday 7th December and were met by Albrecht's wife and son. Trench dined with the family that evening and spent the next few days meeting British and American naval officers including Albrecht's superior, Commander John Riheldaffer. He also visited Fort Hunt, the recently opened US interrogation centre near Washington.

On 11th December Trench said his farewells and boarded a train to New York where he boarded the SS *Westerland* the next day. Never the most 'clubbable' of people he expressed little gratitude for the open-hearted hospitality he had received in Washington.

Westerland sailed with a slow convoy of about a hundred ships on 13th. The next day, in an unnerving few hours, she was forced to stop and repair a steering gear failure, then put on her unimpressive best speed to catch up with the convoy. A straggler was every U-boat skipper's dream.

The rest of the voyage was uneventful, and Trench arrived at Greenock on 28th, caught the overnight train to London where he found tenants still occupying his flat. He therefore reported directly to the Admiralty where he was informed of a proposal that he should become Deputy Director of Naval Intelligence – Prisoners of War (DDNI(P/W)).

Subsequent events suggest this 'promotion' was more like a palace coup. Colin McFadyean had been promoted (over Cope's head) to Trench's former Admiralty desk NID1 (P/W), and Trench's diary suggests that his official duties took up much less of his time from this point onward. In deteriorating health, he was allowed to retire in December 1944.

At about the same time as Trench's homecoming Major D McMillan, normally based in Cairo, returned from a technical tour of C.S.D.I.C. installations in India, Australia, and America. His experience informed the design of mobile eavesdropping units for use in North Africa, Burma, and Australia. He noted that US-designed equipment was 'very inferior to that developed for use in this country'. Later practical experience found that an American portable tape recorder worked better in tropical conditions than British disc recorders.

McMillan is not mentioned in the Trench diaries so, despite treading the same ground at roughly the same time, it is unlikely their paths crossed.

The Mediterranean Club above).[4]

We should read these contradictory statements in the context of the North African campaign: fast-moving, fluid, dominated by the army. Many prisoners passed through the system when things were going well, and army commanders' chief concern was for operational intelligence which had to be obtained quickly if it was to be of any value. With no time for the methodical approach used by CSDIC UK the Middle East team emphasised direct interrogation over microphones and stool pigeons. The temptation to keep pushing just a little bit harder must have been strong.

Post war intelligence services face a radically different environment, in which opponents may be difficult or impossible to distinguish from a sympathetic civilian society through which they move and do not observe the same operational constraints as British and allied personnel. The conditions for a spiral of violence are self-evident.[5]

Was it Worth it?

What did the interrogators achieve? Intelligence breakthroughs seldom come from a single coup or flash of inspiration, but rather from the careful joining of dots which may be accidental, smudged, or belong to different pictures. We can still point to valuable insights which could only have come from the conversation of people intimately familiar with their subject.

In the First World War the prime concerns of static (as opposed to operational) naval intelligence were to keep pace with U-boat technology and tactics, and to prepare the fleet for the constantly anticipated clash of dreadnoughts.

A steady procession of U-boat survivors passed through the door of Wandsworth and later Cromwell Gardens, along with their captured equipment and documents. Results were patchy at first, as the interrogators learnt their craft and developed standard rules for handling prisoners. As the threat developed so did their skills, allowing them to provide regular updates on the enemy's strength and organisation, technology, tactics, use of wireless, morale, and the effectiveness of Allied counter-measures. Some of the hints dropped toward the end of the conflict about advanced research on torpedo and submarine propulsion were to see fruition in the next war.

Conclusion

The pivotal event as far as surface action was concerned was the Battle of Jutland, or *Skagerrakschlacht* on 31st May to 1st June 1916. With a second encounter always on the cards the Admiralty needed urgently to know why British ships, and especially the cherished battlecruisers, had fared so much worse than their German equivalents. Intelligence Division was able to help. From the year's end onwards a constant stream of deserters and former High Seas Fleet men who had transferred to U-boats or destroyers passed through their hands. They gave up detailed information about the effect of British shells and the actual damage to German ships, the (poor) quality of some British firing, the working of German fire control, night fighting techniques and damage resistance. One deserter even turned up with a sample of a new type of armour-piercing fuse. They also kept up a running commentary on the next generation of German capital ships, which were commissioned after the battle.

The interrogators were less successful in countering armed merchant raiders, because they were few in number and invariably somewhere else by the time their activities were known. If prisoners were taken, they were either from a prize crew, in which case the raider was long gone, or from a chance encounter between raider and warship which was of little value in finding other raiders.

In the Second World War the interrogators' efforts were strengthened by the integration of covert listening and stool pigeons, along with a much better organised intelligence processing and sharing organisation. Their contribution included:

- Keeping naval, air and military intelligence abreast of German 'influence' (magnetic, acoustic and pressure) mine developments. These 'unsweepable' mines could have closed British and Allied ports, starving the country into submission in short order.

- Survivors from supply ships gave the first warning of armed merchant raiders on the loose.
- Providing enough technical detail on the T5 homing torpedo for the Allies to develop an effective counter-measure before it even entered service. This advanced weapon underwent a long and thorough development programme and was expected to be a game changer. Although worrying enough, its overall effect was limited.
- Warning of the existence of the SBT (*Pillenwerfer*) acoustic countermeasure, anechoic coating of U-boats, and floating radar decoys. Advance knowledge of these techniques allowed anti-submarine forces to anticipate and bypass them.
- Keeping the Allies up to date on German radar warning receiver development. This helped the Royal Navy and RAF Coastal Command argue for priority in receiving the new, higher frequency radar sets or, when they were not available, informed the tactics of crews using older equipment.
- Warning of new developments such as supply submarines ('*milch cows*'), four-barrel 20mm anti-aircraft cannon, and the *schnorkel* before their deployment.[6]
- A major contribution to the closure of the blockade-breaker pipeline of essential raw material supplies to Germany.
- Early warning of revolutionary new U-boat designs, without which the reduced pace of conventional submarine construction might have led to unwarranted complacency. If these boats, to which there was no countermeasure, had been available and reliable earlier they would have imperilled the build-up of forces for D-Day and potentially lengthened the war in Western Europe.
- Revealing the vulnerability of the *Elbing* class torpedo-boats, whose radar could only look forward and to the side but was blind aft.

- A clear view of the orders given to the Biscay flotillas in the event of invasion gave the Allies confidence to throw up the 'wall of steel' that prevented them interfering with the D-Day landings.

- A running commentary on the evolution of 'small battle units': human torpedoes, minisubs, explosive speedboats and assault swimmers. Thanks to rushed development and targets alert to the threat, the designers' ingenuity and operators' insane bravery was almost entirely wasted.

- Prisoners who had previously worked on or been posted to coastal artillery installations on the Atlantic Wall filled out useful details on the defences the D-Day landings had to overcome.

- Others who described anti-invasion preparations in areas where *no* landings were proposed (such as the fortification and garrisoning of the Norwegian coastline) helped focus and direct Allied disinformation measures.

- Apparently trivial gossip about bases, home, morale, and radio listening habits informed Allied propaganda.

Winston Churchill famously recalled that the U-boat menace was the only thing that truly frightened him during the Second World War. That menace was countered by the physical courage and endurance of the merchant and naval seamen and the airmen on the front line, directed by the 'brain' of the Operational Intelligence Centre (OIC) and Submarine Tracking Room at Admiralty. The OIC synthesised information from every source it could tap: 'Special' (cryptographic) intelligence, reconnaissance, refugees, diplomats, spies, captured documents – and prisoners. These last were by no means the least. They arrived with fresh information in their heads, doubly valuable because it came backed by experience. It was the interrogators' job to extract that information without damaging the heads.

In general, they did it rather well.

1   Appendices D and E contain the relevant text.

2   TNA KV 4/470. 16th April 1948.

3   See Fry, *The London Cage*, for a full discussion.

4   TNA WO 208/3248. P.11.

5   See Cobain, *Cruel Britannia*.

6   David Syrett (Ed), *The Battle of the Atlantic and Signals Intelligence*.

AFTERWORD

Even today we too often see the facile equation of the words 'German' and 'Nazi' in writings about World War 2. It is not difficult, listening to prisoner transcripts, to find young men who were indoctrinated from an early age into the certainties of that vicious cult. To them any divergence of thought was not simply wrong, but evil.

Yet there were others. Their conversation struggled to find a way through the tensions between their loyalties to country, crew, military duty, coerced political oath, and their own ethics. They remind us that populating our mental landscape with lazy, unidimensional caricatures sets us on the same blank-faced road to perdition as their robotic colleagues.

The moment we look at history through an ideological filter or pour it into a narrative mould, we distort the story and begin to corrupt the lessons we take from it.

> *'When it starts .... There aren't just good men on one side and, and bad men on the other – there are good men on both edges of the middle. And some of them are stupid, but some of them are quite clever .... But just not quite clever enough. And of course, a lot of them are quite ordinary, also. And, then, as one side or the other starts to win, and to show its true colours, they don't know what to do. But by then it's too late, and they haven't anywhere else to go, because they're inside the thing by then – they can't run, then: it's Bergen-Belsen or Siberia, or a firing squad for them – and their families. So what do they do then, eh?'*

Anthony Price: *A New Kind of War.*

Appendix A – NID Interrogation Staff in WW1

Cdr V Brandon RN

Dec 1914-Apr 1919

Brandon was recalled from command of the gunboat *Bramble* on China station in 1914 to form ID German section. He developed, with Trench, the interrogation service from scratch and progressed to Assistant DNI. He served with distinction in a variety of roles until his retirement with the rank of Captain in 1929. Despite fragile health which exempted him from mobilisation his service record notes that he was on loan from the Ministry of Shipping to the DNI for duty at GCCS in May 1940. He died on 3rd January 1944.

Lt Cdr W T Bagot

1914-1918

Walter Theodore Bagot was born in 1885 in Bremen and was apparently brought up by his mother alone. As well as fluent German he had 'slight' knowledge of French and Dutch. He was already on ID staff when Brandon arrived and was retained throughout the war. He was the interpreter at the official 'negotiation' (in fact a dictation of terms) for the internment of the German surface fleet aboard HMS *Queen Elizabeth* on 15th November 1918. In 1926 he translated the official German account of the Battle of Jutland.[1] His career prospects were held back by poor eyesight, lack of interest in sport, and a reputation for a methodical rather than proactive approach to his work. He retired in 1928.

Sub Lt B S R Cope RNVR

Sep 1917-Nov 1919
Born and brought up in Munich, Cope returned to Britain with
most of his family on the outbreak of WW1. He joined the
RNVR in 1916 and was initially posted to HMS *Pekin*, a
minesweeper base in Grimsby. He transferred to ID in 1917
moving to Blackheath and working at Admiralty Annex 2
(Cromwell Gardens Barracks).

Lt Harold George Sydney Dillon RNVR

Nov 1917-Jan 1919
Dillon was a German and Russian speaker born in St Petersburg
who had transferred from the RFC. After being hospitalised with
influenza in January 1919 he undertook a mission to the South
Baltic for the DNI. He was demobilised in July 1920 and died in
1922.

Lt Henry Mowbray Howard RNVR

Oct 1915-Feb 1919
Howard was a qualified interpreter in German and Dutch and
appears to have come to NID's attention through a report on a
submarine survivor.

Capt. B F Trench RMLI

Aug 1915-Apr 1918
Trench was recalled from active service with the armoured
cruiser *Highflyer* to join ID German section. He ran the
interrogation team jointly with Brandon. He was posted to Port
Intelligence Officer Queenstown (Cobh) April 1918.

These are the only staff who I have been able to confirm as
members of the German interrogation team but there were

undoubtedly others. As well as the section's full-time staff there are documented instances of senior officers such as Commander Lord Herschell and Admiral Hall himself taking an interest in specific interviews.

---

[1]   Jellicoe, *The Last Days of the High Seas Fleet*. P.69 (footnote).

Appendix B – NID
Interrogation Staff in WW2

This list is based on the Naval Intelligence Directories (in TNA ADM 223/257 and ADM 223/472), Navy Lists and the diaries of Bernard Trench. Dates may be approximate as official publications took time to catch up with staff movements (if they did at all). Ranks given are those on appointment to the prisoner of war service.

Admiralty

Lt-Col B F Trench RMLI

14/9/39-5/12/44
Recalled from retirement to form naval section. His active interrogation role dwindled as the team grew. Following a global inspection tour of interrogation facilities from June-December 1942 he was 'promoted' to an apparent make-work job, Assistant DNI (Prisoners of War). Retired with severe arthritis pain.

Sub Lt J W McDonnell RNVR

26/4/43-1945
John William McDonnell worked on prisoners' mail censorship at Admiralty.

Charles Mitchell

4/9/39-1945
Charles Mitchell was born in 1912. He was a civilian employee, formerly an expert on pictures and naval history at RN College,

Greenwich.[1] He nonetheless took part in some interrogation work, went to Iceland to retrieve materials from the captured *U-570* and later worked with Forward Interrogation Unit. He lost his first wife in a 1940 air raid and later married Jean Flower, a Wren officer at CSDIC.

German Section

Lt L F Atkinson RNVR

Apr 43-1944?

Little is known about Leslie Fred Atkinson. His tenure with CSDIC seems to have been short, suggesting he was unsuited to the work.

Lt J W de Mussenden Carey

25/8/41-Feb '44

John Wilfred Paul de Mussenden Carey was appointed to progress PoW reports. Trench's diary for 8th February 1944 records, '*Met Carey who has been returned from Italy as not required there.*' He transferred to the Royal Canadian Navy Reserve on 7th November 1954.

Sub Lt B R Connell RNVR

Dec 43-1944

Brian Reginald Connell was a journalist before the war. Following his experience with CSDIC he worked with the Forward Interrogation Unit. In November 1944 he married Wren officer Esmé Mackenzie, a union that lasted until her death in 1996. After the war he became a well-known writer and television journalist.

Lt (Lt-Cdr) B S R Cope RNVR

12/3/40-7/12/44

Burton Cope was born in Munich, where his father was working as a stained-glass painter, in 1885. Most of the family returned to Britain on the outbreak of WW1. He joined the RNVR in 1916 and was quickly assigned to intelligence work. He worked for Cunard White-Star lines in Paris between the wars, returned to Britain in 1940 and re-joined NID. In late 1944 he was posted to Naval Party 1735 (Port Party designated to occupy Wilhelmshaven). On his discharge from the Navy in 1946 he continued working for the Allied Control Commission in Germany until 1948. He died in 1952.

Lt-Cdr E Croghan RNVR

1/9/39-16/12/41

Edward Croghan was born in Johannesburg in 1896. He was a RNAS officer in WW1 and transferred to the RAF on the creation of that service. He resigned his commission in 1919 to resume his medical studies. He died on 16/12/41 when his aircraft was shot down on his way to interview U-95 survivors at Gibraltar.

Lt C W Everett RNVR

8/12/42-1945

Charles Everett was brought up in Germany by his American father and Polish mother. Before the war he worked as a teacher, then as a local representative for a student travel company. After the outbreak of war, he joined the Admiralty, working in the Naval Attaché's office in Bucharest. When Romania joined the Axis in November 1940 he disappeared, resurfacing in Portugal on 18th June 1941 where he worked as Naval Control Service Officer in Oporto, with a covert activity scouting suitable beaches for SOE landings and evacuations. In October 1942 he was declared *persona non grata* and forced to return to the UK.[2] In 1945 he took up a post as Staff Officer (Security) in Emden.

Lt Cdr J E S Fawcett DSC RNR

31/5/44-1944-45
Detached for duty with ACOS(I) (Assistant Chief of Staff (Intelligence)) ANCXF (Allied Naval Commander in Chief Expeditionary Force (Normandy)).

Lt G H Halstead RCNVR

23/10/44-1944-45
John Gelder Horler Halstead (1922-1998) joined the RCNVR on graduating from the University of British Columbia in 1943. He served with Intelligence in Canada, Britain, and Germany until 1946.

2nd Lt F G Havard RM

14/9/39-5/10/39
Brief tenure owing to unsuitability for the work.

Lt R W B Izzard RNVR

27/3/41-1944
Ralph Izzard secured a job through his father's influence with the Berlin bureau of the *Daily Mail*, where through his own talent he quickly rose to lead the bureau. While investigating the 'Venlo incident' (in which two MI6 agents were kidnapped and spirited across the German border) he came within a whisker of being captured himself. He then joined the RNVR as an Ordinary Seaman Gunner but, possibly through his acquaintance with Sefton Delmer in the propaganda section, came to the attention of NID's Ian Fleming. Fleming introduced him to Trench who described him as 'rather a tough person' in

his diary and promptly took him on at CSDIC. From 1944 until shortly after the end of the war in Europe he led the Forward Interrogation Unit, after which he returned to civilian life and a career in journalism – with, it is widely speculated, an intelligence sideline.

Lt P L de Laszlo RNVR

29/3/40-Nov '40

Paul Leonardo de Laszlo (seniority 29th March 1940) was a signals specialist temporarily seconded to NID, rather than a professional interrogator. The latest reports certainly by him were in November 1940. A barrister in civilian life, he was born in Vienna in 1906. After the war he was awarded an OBE in January 1946. He died in 1983.

Lt J P Lunzer RCNVR

25/9/44-1944

Julius Lunzer was a Jewish Canadian citizen of Dutch extraction and worked between the wars as a steward for Cunard. He joined the Royal Canadian Navy in 1941, serving initially in the armed yacht HMCS *Wolf*. By mid-1942 he was working with NID in Ottawa. He joined CSDIC in 1944 and almost immediately transferred to Forward Interrogation Unit. During his work with FIU, he was able to contact surviving relatives in liberated territories.

Lt J S Marriner RNVR

21/1/42-1945

John Stuart Marriner was born in Perth, Western Australia. He was a pre-war journalist and took up a post-war career as a writer on travel and yachting. Part of his wartime service was spent in the United States.

Lt (Lt Cdr) J C McFadyean RNVR

Apr 43-Jan 46

John Colin McFadyean joined the RNVR as a Sub Lieutenant in August 1939 and was posted to HMS *Dunnottar Castle*, an armed merchantman operating out of Freetown, in May 1940. In October 1940 he was a Lieutenant in *Seaborn*, a Naval Air Service station at Dartmouth Nova Scotia. He probably crossed the Atlantic on the 'Destroyers for Bases' ship *Cameron* (formerly USS *Welles*) which was admitted straight to Portsmouth Dockyard for a major refit, and so badly damaged in an air raid on 5th December that she never saw active service. In February 1941 he was on Atlantic convoy duty in *Lancaster*, another D-for-B ship, and by June doing the same job off the UK east coast in *Leeds* - yet another. He joined Naval Intelligence Division in March 1942 and around October / November spent some time in the US. In June 1943 he was promoted Acting Lieutenant-Commander, and about the end of the year moved from Latimer to London as NID 1/PW, responsible for naval interrogation of prisoners from Germany and German-occupied territories. He remained with NID until January 1946 when the Navy List describes him as Rld (Released?).

Cdr C O'Callaghan DSC (Retd)

Feb '40-Feb '43

Charles O'Callaghan was a WW1 veteran. He was a wireless intelligence officer with the Italian section of GC&CS Bletchley Park at the outbreak of the war, but intermittently pops up on German interrogation reports until November 1940. He was a qualified Italian interpreter and appears in Italian interrogation reports as late as February 1943.

Lt R G L Pennell

28/9/39-28/11/40

Richard George Lovell Pennell was assigned to Naval Intelligence from Anti-Submarine Warfare Division while convalescing from a broken leg. He returned to active duty, following which he was awarded a DSC and a Mention in Despatches (MiD) for his service with a Steam Gun Boat on the ill-fated Dieppe raid in August 1942, and another MiD for 'actions with the enemy' with the destroyer HMS *Tartar* in 1943.

Lt M G Reade RNVR

19/3/44-1945

Australian-born Michael Gibbon Reade (1916-2006) had previously served in the destroyer *Georgetown*, earning a DSC *'For skill and enterprise in action against Enemy Submarines'*. After V-E Day he helped interrogate the crews of surrendered U-boats at Loch Ryan.

Lt Cdr P W Rhodes

1/3/40-Jan '42

Philip Rhodes was a WW1 veteran. He survived the sinking by mine of *Audacious* in 1914 and was taken prisoner when commanding a boat's crew from *Crusader* going to the assistance of *Maori*, mined off the Belgian coast on 7/5/1915. His role in WW2 was principally MI9 liaison. Accompanied Operation *Claymore* (Lofoten raid) 3/41. Fragile health from 8/1940. Ran No 9 Intelligence School from January 1942.

Cdr (E) L C Rideal*

28/4/41-31/7/45

---

*   (E) - Engineering

Leonard Chichester Rideal was born in 1891, entered the RN in 1904. He gained qualifications in engineering and German but was turned down for airship service. He retired in 1920, was granted a Board of Trade Master's certificate in 1921 and was re-instated with the rank of Commander in 1931. In a January 1942 reorganisation he was transferred from active interrogation work to Admiralty for 'dockets, routine work, liaison with D.P.W. and M.I.9.'[3] From 1942-5 he compiled the final interrogation reports (CB 04051 series). Frequent periods of sick leave from 1942 suggest deteriorating health. He reverted to the retired list in September 1945 and died in 1966.

Lt W Samuel RNVR

14/1/40-7/2/41

Wilfred Samuel came to the Navy's attention when, as an army intelligence officer, he helped interrogate the survivors of naval Zeppelin *L50* in France. He later transferred to the RAF on its formation in 1918 and was demobilised from there, thus having the unusual distinction of serving in all three services. He was posted to Canada for Canadian intelligence liaison and prisoner of war mail censorship.

Lt (E) H I Scholar RNVR

13/9/43-1945

Harry Scholar was a second electrical engineer, a Czech, recruited to strengthen the team's technical background. He was injured in a car accident on New Year's Eve 1944. A spinal injury not detected until much later led to behavioural issues which forced his transfer to other duties.

Sub Lt (E) P Sieber RNVR

9/6/45-1945

Little is known about Peter Sieber.

Appendix B

Capt J M Weatherby RM

1/11/42-1945

John Mansfield Weatherby (1910-2003) was the third of six brothers (Richard was the youngest). He joined the Royal Marines in November 1942 and NID in early 1943. He was an artist, alumnus of Winchester College and Magdalen College Oxford. In 1954 he moved to Uganda where he remained until his death.

Lt (Lt-Cdr) R M Weatherby RNVR

11/6/40-Nov '45

Richard Mansfield ('Dick') Weatherby (1917-59) was, after Cope, the longest-serving member of the NID CSDIC team and took over from him as its leader. He and his brother were both Wykehamists (alumni of Winchester College). He died in 1959 aged 42, at which time he was a Member of H.M. Foreign Service.

Lt (E) D Welbourn RNVR

8/3/43-1945

After graduation from Emmanuel College, Cambridge in 1937 Donald Welbourn went into the English Electric Co. Ltd. in Stafford, where he became Assistant to the Works Superintendent. He travelled in Germany and Austria before the war, observing the rise of Nazism at first hand and learning German in the process. He joined the RNVR as an electrical branch officer in 1942. Early in 1943 he was pulled from his perilous experimental minesweeping duties and transferred to CSDIC. At first his role was confined to advising interrogators and helping them frame their questions, but as he gained familiarity with the work, he took on interrogation duties himself. After the war he was sent to Germany to assist with the intelligence take there and was able to reacquaint himself with some of his pre-war friends. They commented on his vastly improved command of the language, his new Hamburg accent and much fruitier vocabulary!

Lt S C Cornelius-Wheeler RM

5/2/44-1944
Selwyn Charles Wheeler (1923-2008) was born in Bremen and brought up in Hamburg. After CSDIC he served with Forward Interrogation Unit where he was the last NID commander, handing over to George Blake (MI6) in April 1946. He had a prominent post-war career as a television journalist.

Sub Lt D P W Williamson RNVR

9/6/41-May '43
David Peter Waldron Williamson served in HMS *Antrim* and then *Tweed*, surviving the sinking of *Tweed* on 7/1/44 after his first posting to CSDIC, where he made an immediate positive impression on Bernard Trench. In July 1945 he was working on document translation, certifying at least one later used in the Nuremberg trials. By October 1945 he was still with NID, working on technical liaison (with Gwendoline Neel-Wall). In early 1946 he interrogated *Fregattenkapitän* Wiebe (*U-516*) at CSDIC WEA (Bad Nenndorf) about alleged war crimes in connection with sinking of SS *Antonico*.

Italian Section

The Italian section in the UK and Middle East.

Appendix B

Lt R Burnett RNVR (Sp)

Robert Burnett was promoted to Temporary Lieutenant on 1st April 1942 and assigned to HMS *Nile* (a shore establishment at Alexandria) on 15th June and shown as 'Attached to C.S.D.I.C.' later that month.

Lt E C Davies RNVR (Sp)

28/10/40-NK
Edward Cecil Davies joined the RNVR in October 1940 and was promoted to Acting Lieutenant-Commander in 1944.

Lt H Emmet RNVR (Sp)

20/7/42-NK
Heneage Emmet (1912-1989) was a scriptwriter in civilian life. He joined NID directly as a RNVR Lieutenant in July 1942 and remained with NID throughout the war, transferring to a permanent commission. He eventually progressed to Acting Commander.

When Rosevere and Davies were transferred to Italy in November 1943 Emmet was left in charge of the UK Italian section until Rosevere's return in June 1944. He resumed the role after Rosevere's death in March 1945 and wrote the post-war history of the Italian section.

Lt (acting Lt Cdr) J E S Fawcett DSC RNVR

James Edward Sandford Fawcett DSC (1913-91) was a barrister before joining up. He earned a DSC for his part in a 1942 action against an Italian destroyer. In his post-war career he was a member (1962–1984) then President of the European Commission for Human Rights (1972–1981), and grandfather of later prime minister Boris Johnson. He was director of studies at the Royal Institute of International Affairs (known as

Chatham House) from 1969 to 1973, and professor of international law at King's College London from 1976 to 1980. He also served with German section.

Sub-Lt R O B Long RNVR (Sp)

29/7/40-NK
Little is known about Richard Oliver Bruce Long (1914-82). He was later co-author of *The Sea Wolves. The story of the German U-boats at war, etc* with Wolfgang Heinrich Frank and Carl Dönitz, and *Under Ten Flags* with Bernhard Rogge and Wolfgang Heinrich Frank.

Lt W B Nussbaum RNVR (Sp)

29/7/40-1944?
William Bernard Nussbaum was born in 1894 and served with the Royal Engineers from 1918-19. On his discharge he gave a permanent address in Naples. In 1939 he was living in Islington and working as an exporter of garage equipment. He was engaged as a Temporary Lieutenant (Special Branch) RNVR on 29th July 1940.

Cdr C O'Callaghan DSC (Retd)

Feb '40-Feb '43
See 'German Section' above.

Lt Cdr the Hon G G R Rodd Retd

July '40-1944?
The Hon Gustaf Guthrie Rennell ('Taffy') Rodd was born 13/7/1905 (son of Sir Rennell Rodd, MP for St Marylebone) and died 1974 in Florence, Italy. A former Assistant Naval Attaché in Rome he was responsible for setting up the first Middle East CSDIC at Al Maadi.

Appendix B

Lt Cdr (E) W H Rosevere

25/10/40-28/3/45

William Henry Rosevere, born in 1877, was a First World War veteran recruited to head the Italian section of CSDIC UK. Being also fluent in German, French and Spanish he was earmarked for a post with the occupation forces when he was killed in a road accident on 28th March 1945.

Lt Cdr E S Spence RNVR (Sp)

Little is known about Eric Walter Spence.

Far East

The following list contains a sample of the large and constantly evolving group of junior officers posted to South-East Asia Command. Given the preponderance of sub lieutenants (a naval interrogator would normally be a lieutenant at least) it seems likely their main role was translating captured documents and intercepted signals.

A curious feature of the half dozen representatives selected here is that they formed a cohesive group, apparently being posted to Australia together and then to their post-hostilities assignments in pairs.

Cdr S W Lushington (Retd)

Stephen Wellesley Lushington (1895-1978) was a WW1 veteran recalled to service in 1939. He had the unusual combination of Japanese interpreter qualification and some cryptographic experience. In May 1943 he was poached from Admiralty Trade Division to take charge of language personnel at Kilindini. By 1944 he led the prisoner and captured document section at Kandy in Ceylon (Sri Lanka), which looked after the needs of

Delhi and possibly Kilindini. He had a substantial staff of (mainly) RNVR special service sub-lieutenants who were probably graduates of a crash Japanese language programme taught in London.

Capt K McAlpine Fox RM

Temporary Captain Kenneth McAlpine Fox was second in command.

Lt M Ellerton RANVR

Montague Ellerton was born in 1876 in Kobe, died 11/9/54 in Yokohama. He formerly served with the Australian legation in Tokyo. Wartime service at Kandy and Allied Translation and Interpretation Service (ATIS) Brisbane was followed by post-war work in Manilla. An exception to the general run of junior officers at Kandy, he was not a graduate of the School of Oriental and African Studies (SOAS) crash course in Japanese.

Sub Lt R R Cunningham (Sp)

Rex Rainsford Cunningham was born in September 1918, died 3/8/2004 in New Zealand. He moved on from Kandy to ATIS Brisbane then CSDIC Tokyo after the end of hostilities.

Sub Lt J P Hobson (Sp)

James Peter Hobson (1924-1995) was a SOAS graduate who served at Kandy, ATIS Brisbane and Hong Kong.

Sub Lt J P Judd (Sp)

Jean-Pierre Judd (1924-24-9-2012) served at Kandy, ATIS Brisbane, and Manilla. A SOAS graduate, he returned to the school as a teacher after the war.

Appendix B

Midshipman J P O'Neill (Sp)

Patrick Geoffrey O'Neill served at Kandy, ATIS Brisbane and Hong Kong. He was one of the first SOAS intake – bright sixth formers known as 'Dulwich boys' because they were given lodgings at Dulwich College during their course. He became Professor of Japanese at SOAS from 1968-86.

Sub Lt D T Richnell (Sp)

Donovan Thomas Richnell (3/8/1911-18/2/1994) served at Kandy, ATIS Brisbane and CSDIC Tokyo. He was also awarded a US Bronze Star for liaison service with the US Army Tenth Corps in New Guinea and the Philippines. After the war he built a career in records management, becoming the first Director-General of the British Library Reference Division.

Wrens

3/O E M E Barron

17/12/42-1944-45
Evelyn Mary Eleanor Barron was born in 1915 in Godstone, Surrey. She was promoted from Petty Officer to Third Officer on 24th May 1942, and to Second Officer on 17th May 1943. Late in life she gave an interview to Dr Fry in which she asserted that the Wren officers took part in interrogations.[4]

3/O B M Colls

4/9/44-1944-45
Betty Marion Colls (sometimes given as Collis) was born in 1911 in Norwich and died in 2001 in North Walsham, Norfolk. She obtained a degree in French from the Royal Holloway and Bedford College in 1932. She was promoted from Petty Officer

to Third Officer on 15th November 1942 and to Second Officer on 1st July 1945. After the war she was heavily involved with the WRNS Benevolent Trust. By 1950 she was First Officer, and Director of the Education Department WRNS at Admiralty.

3/O J Flower

29/9/42-4/11/44
Jean Flower was born 1916. In Welbourn's words, '…member of a well-known academic family.' She married Charles Mitchell on 4/11/44 at St Martin-in-the-Fields. She was promoted to 2nd Officer on 29th April 1943.

3/O C M Furneaux

21/6/43-1944-45
Claudia Furneaux was studying modern languages at Somerville College Oxford when war broke out. She interrupted her studies to help with the war effort. After a period listening to German radio transmissions from various stations on the South Coast she was commissioned and posted to Latimer. She met her American husband Harry Lennon, an American interrogator, while in the WRNS. After Harry's death she returned to run the family farm at Fingringhoe in north Essex until her death in 2011. In an interview for her former college magazine, she stated that Wren officers did *not* interrogate prisoners directly, though they could on occasion join them in social pub visits to help loosen their tongues.

PO E J Mackenzie

Jul 41-1944
Esmé Jean Mackenzie (1920-96) was promoted to 3rd Officer 7/12/41 and 2nd Officer on 29/4/43. She left CSDIC by October 1944. Welbourn described her as '…*a vivacious and exceptionally bright girl.*' Her first engagement was brutally cut short in 1941

when her fiancé (Captain Peter Wilkinson, Royal Regiment) accidentally shot himself half an hour before the wedding.[5] She married Brian Reginald Connell on 27/11/1944.

3/0 G M Neel-Wall

17/12/42-1944

Gwendoline Marguerite was born 15/2/1897 to Caroline (nee Kumm born in Berlin, 1858) and Charles Edward Neel in West Ham, Essex. She had a brother, Lionel, and a sister Gladys. Her father was a master mariner born in Jersey. She married 2nd Lieutenant Liam Francis Joseph Wall RFC/RAF (b. 1/9/1895) in Q2 1918 at Brentford. There is no record of him after 1921. She ran a wholesale women's gown supplier, which folded in the crash of the early 1930s. By 1939 she was living in Canterbury, presumably widowed, working as a 'Hairdresser Director Manager' and a Red Cross probationer. From June 1940 to 1941 she oversaw the improvised Y (wireless intercept) station on Portland Bill. She was promoted 3rd Officer 22/10/40 and Acting 2nd Officer 18/12/42. She joined CSDIC by March 1943 and left by October 1944 but remained with NID 24 (German Documents Transit Section and Library) at least to March 1945. For part of this time, she was seconded to NID 30 (30 Assault Unit) to help with 'drawing up supplementary target lists and making preparations for the disposal of captured material'.[6]

Her son Michael was lost with the submarine *Tempest* in February 1942 and her nephew Dennis Kumm with the anti-submarine trawler *Ullswater* later that year. After the war she lived in Sussex. She died in Q1/1968 in Brighton.

2/0 C Thomas

26/6/43-1944-45

Celia Thomas was promoted to Third Officer on 19th July 1941 and to Second Officer on 31st July 1944.

Petty Officers

Name	Served from	Until
CPO Hales	23/6/43	1945
PO V P Lennard	17/4/44	1944-45
PO Writer M Barton	7/6/44	1944-45
PO (S/T) E Duckers	7/6/44	1944-45
PO (S/T) K Pearce	13/6/44	1944-45
PO J E Day	Sep 44	1945

PO – Petty Officer   CPO – Chief Petty Officer   3/O – 3rd Officer

2/O – 2nd Officer   S/T – Shorthand Typist

US Navy

The following US naval officers play a part in our story.

Lt Cdr R G Albrecht

Ralph Gerhart Albrecht was born in 1896 of German heritage. He studied law, qualifying in 1919 and 1923.

He joined the Office of Naval Intelligence (ONI) in WW2 and visited CSDIC UK from March to June 1942 to observe and learn from British techniques. While there he took part in work at Trent Park, visited the new sites under construction at Latimer and Wilton Park, and inspected the captured U-boat HMS *Graph* (formerly *U-570*).[7] At the same time Ralph Izzard was in Washington, advising the ONI (Op-16-Z) on the creation of its equivalent facility at Fort Hunt. He then met his UK host Bernard Trench in Australia and accompanied him on the last leg of his world tour across the Pacific and United States.

Later he drew on prisoner intelligence to broadcast on Voice of America as 'Commander Robert Norden', where he was an effective propagandist.[8]

Appendix B

He was an associate United States counsel at the Nuremberg war crime trials from 1945 to 1947.

He died in September 1985.

Lt. jg. T W Broecker USNR

Lt. Junior Grade Theodore W. Broecker (2/6/1905-7/3/1972) served with the Forward Interrogation Unit in 1944.

Lt H T Gherardi USNR

Harry Taylor Gherardi was born on 3/4/1906, son of (later) Admiral Walter Rockwell Gherardi. He was promoted to Commander in 1944 and retired in 1953, retraining as an architect. He died on 14/1/1974.

Lt John E Lambie, Jr USNR

Lieutenant Lambie served with 30 Assault Unit during the 1944 North-West Europe campaign, liaising with US forces and presumably also as a member of the Forward Interrogation Unit.

Lt Cdr J L Riheldaffer

John Laurence Riheldaffer was born 24/9/1889 of Italian extraction.

He was assigned to the Division of Naval Intelligence in January 1941 and was instrumental in setting up and managing the US prisoner interrogation service. He served until June 1945 during which time he was promoted to captain. His contribution was subsequently recognised by the award of a Legion of Merit.

Bernard Trench met him in Washington on the final leg of his 1942 world tour, and subsequently hosted him during a visit to Britain in March 1943.

---

[1]   TNA ADM 223/464, P.22.

2   TNA HS 9/491-1.
3   Memo S/NID 79 dated 6/1/42 in TNA ADM 223/471.
4   Fry, *The Walls Have Ears*. P.50.
5   *Gloucester Citizen*, 5/3/41. P.2.
6   TNA ADM 223/214, Chapter XIII, P.1.
7   Albrecht letter to Riheldaffer Op-16-Z A6-2(8) dated 22/4/42 (http://uboatarchive.net/POW/POWInterrogationAlbrechtVisit.htm)
8   Riheldaffer interview with *Kapitänleutnant* Müller (U-662), Op-16-Z A6-2(8) dated 24/9/1943 (http://www.uboatarchive.net/U-662A/U-662NordenInterview.htm)

APPENDIX C – U-BOAT SURVIVORS INTERROGATED IN WW2

This is a partial transcript (with some columns omitted) of a paper prepared by the DNI after the Second World War.

7th September 1945

GERMAN U-BOATS
FROM WHICH PRISONERS WERE TAKEN DURING
HOSTILITIES
BY BRITISH AND AMERICAN FORCES

The attached list gives all the German U-Boats sunk, scuttled, or surrendered from which prisoners were taken by British and American forces prior to the surrender of Germany.

2.   It is not always possible to divide prisoners exactly as between British and U.S. forces, but the total number of prisoners taken from these U-Boats can roughly be divided as follows:-

British	3,815
U.S.	1,188
	5,003

(Note: Prisoners taken by Allied forces under British operational control have been counted as British.)
(Sgd.) E. G. N. RUSHBROOKE
DIRECTOR OF NAVAL
INTELLIGENCE

Castaways in Question

U-Boat	Type	C.O.	Date	Ship or Aircraft concerned	Ps/W Officers	Men
39	IX	GLATTES, Gerhard	14.9.39	H.M.S. FAULKNER, FOXHOUND and FIREDRAKE	4	39
27	VIIA	FRANZ, Johannes	20.9.39	H.M.S. FORESTER and FORTUNE	4	34
42	IX	DAU, Rolf	13.10.39	H.M.S. IMOGEN and ILEX	3	14
40	IX	BARTER, Wolfgang (+)	13.10.39	Mined	3	
35	VIIA	LOTT, Werner	29.11.39	H.M.S. KINGSTON, ICARUS and KASHMIR	4	39
55	VIIB	HEIDEL, Werner (+)	30.1.40	H.M.S. FOWEY and. WHITSHED and aircraft of 228 Squadron	3	38
33	VIIA	VON DRESKY, Hans (+)	12.2.40	H.M.S. GLEANER	3	14
63	IIC	LORENTZ, Guenther	25.2.40	H.M.S. INGLEFIELD, NARWHAL ESCORT, and IMOGEN	3	21
49	VIIB	VON GOSSLER, Curt	15.4.40	H.M.S. FEARLESS	4	37
13	IIB	SCHULTE, Max	30.5.40	H.M.S. WESTON	3	23
26	I	SCHERINGER, Heinz	1.7.40	H.M.S. GLADIOLUS and Sunderland F/B No. 510 R.A.A.F.	4	44
32	VIIA	JENISCH, Hans	30.10.40	H.M.S. HARVESTER and HIGHLANDER	4	29
31	VIIA	PRELLBERG, Wilfried	2.11.40	H.M.S. ANTELOPE	5	38
70	VIIC	MATZ, Joachim	7.3.41	H.M.S. ARBUTUS and CAMELLIA	4	21
100	VIIC	SCHEPKE, Joachim (+)	17.3.41	H.M.S. VANOC	1	5
99	VIIC	KRETSCHMER, Otto	17.3.41	H.M.S. WALKER	5	35
76	VIIC	VON HIPPEL, Friedrich	5.4.41	H.M.S. WOLVERINE and SCARBOROUGH	4	38
110	IXA	LEMP, Fritz-Julius (+)	9.5.41	H.M.S. AUBRIETIA, BROADWAY and BULLDOG	4	28
138	IID	GRAMITZKY, Franz	18.6.41	H.M.S. FAULKNOR, FEARLESS, FORESIGHT, FOXHOUND and FORESTER	4	24
556	VIIC	WOHLFARTH, Herbert	27.6.41	H.M.S. GLADIOLUS, NASTURTIUM, and CELANDINE	5	35
651	VIIC	LOHMEYER, Peter	29.6.41	H.M.S. MALCOLM, VIOLET, SCIMITAR, ARABIS and SPEEDWELL	6	39
570	VIIC	RAHMLOW, Hans	27.8.41 (captured)	Hudson a/c S/269	4	39

Appendix C

U-Boat	Type	C.O.	Date	Ship or Aircraft concerned	Ps/W Officers	Men
501	IXC	FOERSTER, Hugo	10.9.41	H.M.C.S. CHAMBLY and MOOSEJAW	6	31
111	IXA	KLEINSCHMIDT, Wilhelm (+)	4.10.41	H.M. Trawler LADY SHIRLEY	2	42
433	VIIC	EY, Hans	16.11.41	H.M.S. MARIGOLD	6	32
95	VIIC	SCHREIBER, Gerd	23.11.41	Netherlands S/M O.21	4	8
131	IXC	BAUMANN, Arend	17.12.41	H.M.S. BLANKNEY, EXMOOR, STORK, AUDACITY, PENTSTEMON and STANLEY	5	43
434	VIIC	HEYDA, Wolfgang	18.12.41	H.M.S. STANLEY and BLANKNEY	3	39
574	VIIC	GENGELBACH (+)	19.12.41	H.M.S. STORK	4	12
451	VIIC	HOFFMANN (+)	21.12.41 (?sunk)	Swordfish a/c --/8l2	1	-
79	VIIC	KAUFMANN, Wolfgang	25.12.41	H.M.S. HOTSPUR and HASTY	4	40
75	VIIC	RINGELMANN (+)	28.12.41	H.M.S. KIPLING	2	28
374	VIIC	VON FISCHEL, Unno (+)	12.1.42	H.M.S/M UNBEATEN	-	1
93	VIIC	ELFE, Horst	15.1.42	H.M.S. HESPERUS	5	35
581	VIIC	PFEIFER, Werner	2.2.42	H.M.S. WESTCOTT	5	36
352	VIIC	RATHKE, Hellmut	9.5.42	U.S.C.G. ICARUS	2	31
568	VIIC	PREUSS, Joachim	28.5.42	H.M.S. ERIDGE, HURWORTH and HERO	5	42
701	VIIC	DEGEN, Horst	7.7.42	U.S. Army Attack Bomber No. 9-29-322, Unit 296 B.S.	1	6
335	VIIC	PELKNER, Hans	3.8.42	H.M. S/M P.247 (SARACEN)		1
372	VIIC	NEUMANN, Heinz-Joachim	4.8.42	H.M.S. SIKH, ZULU, CROOME and TETCOTT, and a/c of 203 Echelon	4	42
210	VIIC	LEMCKE, Rudolf (+)	6.8.42	H.M.C.S. ASSINIBOINE	2	35
379	VIIC	KETTNER, Paul-Hugo (+)	8.8.42	H.M.S. DIANTHUS	-	5
464	XIV	HARMS, Otto	20.8.42	U.S. Catalina a/c PBY-5A-1 of 73 Squadron	5	46
94	VIIC	ITES, Otto	28.8.42	U.S.N. PBY a/c and H.M.C.S. OAKVILLE	2	24
162	IXC	WATTENBERG, Juergen	3.9.42	H.M.S. PATHFINDER, VIMY and QUENTIN	3	46
512	IXC	SCHULTZE, Wolfgang (+)	2.10.42	U.S. Army Bomber B-18A	-	1
353	VIIC	ROEMER, Wolfgang	16.10.42	H.M.S. FAME	5	34
559	VIIC	HEIDTMANN, Hans-Otto	30.10.42	H.M.S. HERO, DULVERTON,	6	35

337

U-Boat	Type	C.O.	Date	Ship or Aircraft concerned	Ps/W Officers	Men
				PETARD, PAKENHAM and HURWORTH, and an a/c of 47 Echelon		
660	VIIC	BAUR, Goetz	12.11.42	H.M.S. STARWORT and LOTUS	3	43
595	VIIC	QUAET-FASLEM, Juergen	14.11.42 (beached and scuttled	Damaged by a/c (5) of 500 Squadron	4	41
331	VIIC	VON TIESENHAUSEN, Freiherr Hans-Diedrich	17.11.42	3 Hudson a/c of 500 Squadron and a/c from H.M.S. FORMIDABLE	4	13
517	IXC	HARTWIG, Paul	21.11.42	a/c from H.M.S. VICTORIOUS	5	45
357	VIIC	KELLNER, Adolf (+)	26.12.42	H.M.S. HESPERUS and VANESSA	-	6
164	IXC	FECHNER, Otto (+)	6.1.43	U.S. PBY a/c	-	2
224	VIIC	KOSBADT (+)	13.1.43	H.M.C.S. VILLE DE QUEBEC	1	-
301	VIIC	KOERNER, Willy-Roderick	21.1.43	H.M.S/M P.212 (SAHIB)	1	-
187	IXC	MUENNICH, Ralph (+)	4.2.43	H.M.S. VIMY and BEVERLEY	3	42
205	VIIC	BUERGEL, Friedrich	17.2.43	H.M.S. PALADIN and BISLEY a/c S.A.A.F.	6	36
606	VIIC	DOEHLER, Hans (+)	22.2.43	Polish Destroyer BURZA and U.S.C.G. CAMPBELL	3	9
444	VIIC	LANGFELD, Josef	11.3.43	H.M.S. HARVESTER and F.F.S. ACONIT		4
432	VIIC	ECKHARDT, Hermann (+)	11.3.43	F.F.S. ACONIT	1	19
175	IXC	BRUNS, Heinrich (+)	17.4.43	U.S.C.G. SPENCER	5	36
203	VIIC	KOTTMANN, Herman	25.4.43	H.M.S. PATHFINDER and a/c from H.M.S. BITER	6	33
439	VIIC	VON TIPELLSKIRCH (+)	4.5.43	Sunk by collision with U.659	2	7
659	VIIC	STOCK, Hans (+)	4.5.43	Sunk by collision with U.439	1	2
528	IXC	VON RABENAU, Georg	11.5.43	H.M.S. FLEETWOOD and Halifax a/c D/58	7	38
128	IXC	STEINERT, Hermann	17.5.43	Brazilian PBM a/c 74-P-4 and 5 and U.S.S. MOFFETT and JOUETT	4	43
569	VIIC	JOHANNSEN, Hans Friedrich	22.5.43	2 a/c from U.S.S. BOGUE	3	22
752	VIIC	SCHROETER, Karl Ernst	23.5.43	A/c from U.S.S. ARCHER	1	12

338

Appendix C

U-Boat	Type	C.O.	Date	Ship or Aircraft concerned	Ps/W Officers	Men
202	VIIC	POSER, Guenter	2.6.43	H.M.S. KITE, WOODPECKER, STARLING and WILD GOOSE	4	26
521	IXC	BARGSTEN, Klaus	2.6.43	U.S.P.C. 565	1	-
118	XB	CZYGAN, Werner (+)	12.6.43	A/c from U.S.S. BOGUE	-	16
97	VIIC	TROX, Hans Georg (+)	16.6.43	Hudson a/c T.459	2	19
409	VIIC	MASSMANN, Hans Ferdinand	12.7.43	H.M.S. INCONSTANT	4	35
506	IXC	WUERDEMANN, Erich (+)	12.7.43	U.S. Liberator A/c of 1st A/S Squadron	1	5
487	XIV	METZ, Helmut (+)	13.7.43	A/c from U.S.S. CORE	4	27
607	VIIC	JESCHONNEK, Wolf	13.7.43	Sunderland N/228 supported by Halifax O/58	4	3
135	VIIC	LUTHER, Otto	15.7.43	H.M.S. MIGNONETTE, BALSAM and ROCHESTER	4	37
67	IXC	MUELLER, Guenther (+)	16.7.43	A/c from U.S.S. CORE	1	2
513	IXC	GUGGENBERGER, Friedrich	19.7.43	U.S., a/c PBM 5 of VP 74 Squadron	1	6
558	VIIC	KRECH, Guenther	20.7.43	U.S. Liberator a/c F/19	2	3
662	VIIC	MUELLER Heinz-Eberhard	21.7.43	U.S. Catalina a/c of VP 94. Squadron	1	2
527	IXC	UHLIG, Herbert	23.7.43	A/c from U.S.S. BOGUE	3	10
598	VIIC	HOLTORF, Gottfried (+)	23.7.43	2 a/c from U.S. Bombing Squadron 107	1	1
459	XIV	VON WILAMOWITZ-MOELLENDORF, Georg	24.7.43	Wellington a/c O/l72	5	36
461	XIV	STIEBLER, Wolf	30.7.43	Australian Sunderland a/c U/461	3	12
462	XIV	VOWE, Bruno	30.7.43	Halifax S/502	8	56
591	VIIC	ZIESMER, Reimar	30.7.43	U.S. Ventura Bomber VB-127-B-10	4	24
199	IXD 2	KRAUS, Hans Werner	31.7.43	Brazilian Catalina a/c	4	8
454	VIIC	HACKLAENDER, Burkhard	1.8.43	Australian Sunderland a/c B/l0	2	12
706	VIIC	VON ZITZEWITZ, Alexander (+)	2.8.43	U.S. Liberator T of 4 A/S Squadron	1	3
489	XIV	SCHMANDT, Adalbert	4.8.43	Sunderland G/423 R.C.A.F.	3	48
615	VIIC	KAPITZKY, Rolf (+)	6.8.43	U.S. A/C (5) from Squadron 204 and U.S. Ship	3	40

U-Boat	Type	C.O.	Date	Ship or Aircraft concerned	Ps/W Officers	Men
664	VIIC	GRAEF, Adolf	9.8.43	A/c (4) from U.S.S. CARD	3	41
604	VIIC	HOELTRING, Horst	11.8.43	Damaged by a/c and scuttled. Ship's company picked up by U.185, q.v.	1	8
468	VIIC	SCHAMONG, Clemens	11.8.43	Liberator a/c D/200	3	4
458	VIIC	DIGGINS, Kurt	22.8.43	H.M.S. EASTON and H.H.M.S. PINDOS	5	38
185	IXC	MAUS, August	24.8.43	A/c from U.S.S. CORE	2	23
523	IXC	PIETZSCH, Werner	25.8.43	H.M.S. WANDERER	4	33
643	VIIC	SPEIDEL, Hans	8.10.43	Liberator a/c T/120 and Z/86	3	15
419	VIIC	GIERSBERG, Dietrich	8.10.43	Liberator a/c R/86	1	-
533	IXC	HENNIG (+)	16.10.43	Bisley a/c E and H/244	-	1
470	VIIC	GRAVE, Guenther (+)	16.10.43	Liberator a/c E/120 and Z/120		2
841	IXC	BENDER, Werner (+)	17.10.43	H.M.S. BYARD	1	26
732	VIIC	CARLSEN, Peter	31.10.43	H.M.S. DOUGLAS and IMPERIALIST	2	17
340	VIIC	KLAUS, Hans Joachim	1.11.43	H.M.S. FLEETWOOD, ACTIVE and WITHERINGTON, and Wellington a/c R and W/179	4	44
848	IXD	ROLLMANN, Wilhelm	5.11.43	a/c of 107 Squadron U.S.N. and U.S.A.A.F.	-	1
536	IXC	SCHAUENBURG, Rolf	20.11.43	H.M.C.S. NENE assisted by H.M.S. SNOWBERRY and H.M.C.S CALGARY	3	14
172	IXC	HOFFMANN, Hermann	13.12.43	A/c (6) from U.S.S. BOGUE and U.S.S. GEORGE E. BADGER, DUPONT, CLEMSON and INGRAM	4	42
593	VIIC	KELBLING, Gerd	13.12.43	H.M.S. CALPE and U.S.S. WAINWRIGHT	5	46
73	VIIC	DECKERT, Horst	16.12.43	U.S.S. TRIPPE and WOOLSEY	4	30
231	VIIC	WENZEL, Wolfgang	13.1.44	Wellington a/c L/172	5	38
177	IXD	BUCHHOLZ, Heinz (+)	6.2.44	Liberator A/c PB4Y of VB-107 based on Ascension Is.	2	11
406	VIIC	DIETERICHS, Horst (+)	18.2.44	H.M.S. SPEY	4	37
386	VIIC	ALBRECHT, Fritz	19.2.44	H.M.S. SPEY	2	16
264	VIIC	LOOKS, Hartwig	19.2.44	H.M.S. STARLING and WOODPECKER	6	45
761	VIIC	GEIDER, Horst	24.2.44	2 U.S.N. Catalinas of 63 Squadron; 1 U.S.N.	3	42

U-Boat	Type	C.O.	Date	Ship or Aircraft concerned	Ps/W Officers	Men
				Ventura of 127 Squadron; 1 R.A.F. Catalina of 202 Squadron; and H.M. Ships ANTHONY and WISHART		
257	VIIC	RAHE, Heinz (+)	24.2.44	H.M.C.S. WASKESIU	1	17
91	VIIC	HUNGERSHAUSEN, Heinz	26.2.44	H.M.S. AFFLECK, GORE and GOULD	3	13
358	VIIC	MANKE, Rolf (+)	1.3.44	H.M.S. AFFLECK, GARLIES, GORE and GOULD	-	1
472	VIIC	VON FORSTNER, Freiherr Wolfgang Friedrich	4.3.44	Swordfish a/c B/816 from H.M.S. CHASER, and H.M.S. ONSLAUGHT	2	27
744	VIIC	BLISCHKL, Heinz (+)	6.3.44	H.M.C. Ships ST. CATHERINES, CHILLIWACK, GATINEAU, FENNEL, CHAUDIERE and H.M. Ships ICARUS and KENILWORTH CASTLE	3	37
973	VIIC	PAEPENMOELLER, Klaus (+)	6.3.44	Swordfish a/c X/816 from H.M.S. CHASER	1	1
845	IXC	WEBER, Werner (+)	10.3.44	H.M.S. FORESTER and H.M.C.S. ST. LAURENT, OWENSOUND and SWANSEA	3	42
450	VIIC	BOEHME, Kurt	10.3.44	U.S.S. MADISON and H.M. Ships EXMOOR, BLANKNEY, BLENCATHRA and BRECON	4	47
575	VIIC	BOEHMER Wolfgang	13.3.44	U.S.S. HOBSON and HAVERFIELD H.M.C.S. PRINCE RUPERT, a/c from U.S.S. BOGUE, Wellington a/c B/172 and Fortress R/206 and J/220	4	33
801	IXC	BRANS, Joachim (+)	16.3.44	U.S.S. CORRY and BRONSTEIN and a/c (3) from U.S.S. BLOCK ISLAND	1	46
1059	VIIF	LEUPOLD. Guenther	19.3.44	U.S. a/c TBF and FM from U.S.S. BLOCK ISLAND	2	6
223	VIIC	GERLACH. Peter (+)	30.3.44	H.M.S. TUMULT, BLENCATHRA,	3	24

U-Boat	Type	C.O.	Date	Ship or Aircraft concerned	Ps/W Officers	Men
				HAMBLEDON and LAFOREY		
856	IXC	WITTENBERG, Friedrich	7.4.44	U.S. Task Group 21.15 and Task Force 27.6.2	3	25
515	IXC	HENKE, Werner	9.4.44	A/c from U.S.S. GUADALCANAL and U.S.S. PILLSBURY, POPE, FLAHERTY and CHATELAIN	4	39
68	IXC	LAUZEMIS, Albert (+)	10.4.44	A/c from U.S.S. GUADALCANAL	-	1
448	VIIC	DAUTER, Helmut	14.4.44	H.M.S. PELICAN and H.M.C.S. SWANSEA	5	37
550	IXC	HAENERT, Klaus	16.4.44	U.S.S. JOYCE, PETERSON and GANDY	3	9
852	IXD	ECK, Heinz	3.5.44 (scuttled)	Damaged by Wellington a/c T and B/621 of the Aden Command	5	54
371	VIIC	FENSKI, Horst	4.5.44	U.S.S. JOSEPH E. CAMPBELL, PRIDE, F.F.S. SENEGALAIS and H.M.S. BLANKNEY	5	45
473	VIIC	STERNBERG, Heinz (+)	6.5.44	H.M.S. STARLING, WREN and WILD GOOSE	1	29
765	VIIC	WENDT, Werner	6.5.44	a/c from H.M.S. VINDEX and H.M.S. BICKERTON, BLIGH and AYLMER	2	9
66	IXC	SEEHAUSEN, Gerhard (+)	6.5.44	U.S.S. BUCKLEY and a/c from U.S.S. BLOCK ISLAND	4	32
616	VIIC	KOITSCHKA, Siegfried	17.5.44	U.S.S. ELLYSON, BIBB, GLEAVES, MACOMB, HAMBLETON and H.P. JONES and Wellington X, A and H/36	6	47
960	VIIC	HEINRICH. Guenther	19.5.44	U.S.S. NIBLACK and LUDLOW, and Wellington a/c H and U/36 and Ventura a/c V/500	4	16
453	VIIC	LUEHRS, Dierk	21.5.44	H.M.S. TERMAGANT, TENACIOUS and LIDDESDALE	4	45
505		LANGE	4.6.44 (captured)	U.S.S. GUADALCANAL Group	5	53

Appendix C

U-Boat	Type	C.O.	Date	Ship or Aircraft concerned	Ps/W Officers	Men
490	XIV	GERLACH, Wilhelm	12.6.44	A/c from U.S.S. CROATAN and U.S.S. FROST, HUSE and INCH	7	53
715	VIIC	ROETTGER, Helmut (+)	13.6.44	A/c Canso T/162, R.C.A.F.	-	16
860	IXD 2	BUECHEL, Paul	15.6.44	A/c (7) from U.S.S. SOLOMONS	2	18
767	VIIC	DANKLEFF, Walter (+)	18.6.44	H.M.S. FAME, HAVELOCK, INCON¬STANT and HOTSPUR	-	1
971	VIIC	ZEPLIEN, Walter	24.6.44	H.M.C.S. HAIDA and H.M.S. ESKIMO, and Liberator a/c O/311 (Czech)	4	44
269	VIIC	UHL, Georg (+)	25.6.44	H.M.S. BICKERTON	4	35
390	VIIC	GEISSLER, Berthold (+)	5.7.44	H.M.S. TAVY and WANDERER	-	1
233	XB	STEEN, Hans (+)	5.7.44	U.S.S. BAKER and THOMAS	3	26
243	VIIC	MARTENS, Hans (+)	8.7.44	Australian Sunderland a/c H/10	2	36
672	VIIC	LAWAETZ, Ulf	18.7.44 (scuttled)	Damaged by H.M.S. BALFOUR	4	42
671	VIIC	HEGEWALD, Wolfgang (+)	4.8.44	H.M.S. STAYMER and WENSLEYDALE	2	3
736	VIIC	REFF, Reinhard	6.8.44	H.M.S. LOCH KILLIN	3	16
608	VIIC	REISENER, Wolfgang	9.8.44	Liberator C/53 and H.M.S. WREN	4	47
385	VIIC	VALENTINER, Hans Guido	11.8.44	Sunderland P/461 R.A.A.F. and H.M.S. STARLING	4	37
270	VIIC	SCHREIBER, Heinrich	13.8.44	Sunderland A/461, R.A.A.F.	5	66
741	VIIC	PALMGREN, Gerhard (+)	15.8.44	H.M.S. ORCHIS	-	1
230	VIIC	EBERBACH, Heinz-Eugen	20.8.44	-	4	47
413	VIIC	SACHSE (+)	20.8.44	H.M.S. FORESTER, VIDETTE, and WENSLEYDALE	1	-
1229	VIIC	ZINKE, Armin (+)	20.8.44	A/c (7) from U.S.S. BOGUE	1	17
407	VIIC	KOLBUS, Hans	19.9.44	O.R.P. GARLAND assisted by H.M.S. TROWBRIDGE and TERPSICHORE	3	44
859	IXD 2	JEBSEN, Johann (+)	23.9.44	H.M.S/M TRENCHANT	1	10

U-Boat	Type	C.O.	Date	Ship or Aircraft concerned	Ps/W Officers	Men
168	IXC	PICH, Helmuth	6.10.44	H.Neth.M.S/M ZWARDVISCH	4	1
1006	VIIC	VOIGT, Horst	16.10.44	H.M.C.S. ANNAN	3	41
1209	VIIC	HUELSENBECK, Ewald (+)	18.12.44	Struck rocks and sank	1	41
877	IXC	FINDEISEN. Eberhard.	27.12.44	H.M.C.S. ST. THOMAS	5	50
1199	VIIC	NOLLMANN, Rolf (+)	21.1.45	H.M.S. MIGNONETTE and ICARUS	–	1
425	VIIC	BENTZIEN, Heinz (+)	17.2.45	H.M.S. LARK and ALNWICK CASTLE	–	1
300	VIIC	HEIN, Fritz (+)	22.2.45	H.M.S. RECRUIT and PINCHER	3	38
1018	VIIC	BURMEISTER, Walter (+)	27.2.45	H.M.S. LOCH FADA	1	1
681	VIIC	GEBAUER, Werner	11.3.45	U.S.N. Liberator N/103	3	35
1003	VIIC	STRESSING (+)	(20.3.45 (23.3.45	Rammed by H.M.C.S. NEW GLASGOW) Scuttled.)	3	28
399	VIIC	BUHSE, Heinz (+)	26.3.45	H.M.S. DUCKWORTH	–	1
1195	VIIC	CORDES, Ernst (+)	6.4.45	H.M.S. WATCHMAN	2	16
1024	VIIC	GUTTECK, Joachim (+)	12.4.45	H.M.S. LOCK GLENDHU	1	36
1206	VIIC	SCHLITT, Karl Adolf	14.4.45	Damaged and sank owing to faults in boat.	4	42
1063		STEPHAN, Karl Heinz (+)	16.4.45	H.M.S. LOCH KILLIN	1	16
546	IXC	JUST	24.4.45	U.S. Ships of T.G. 22.1	3	30
307	VIIC	KRUGER	29.4.45	H.M.S. LOCH INSH	2	12
				Total:	**526**	**4,477**
				Grand Total:		**5,003**

Transcriber's notes:

- The source is a document in the National Museum of the Royal Navy archive. For reasons of space a column giving the co-ordinates of each sinking has been omitted.

- Some commanding officers' names may be incorrect or incomplete. No effort has been made to check or rectify the data in the original document. (+) by a C.O.'s name indicates that he perished in the conflict. No effort has been made to correct known errors in this tagging (for example see U-444).

- The original phonetic rendition of umlaut vowels (e.g. 'oe' for 'ö') has been retained.
- Extra spaces embedded within dates have been removed for ease of reading.
- The source is a photocopied document, extremely faint in places, with the top of the first page masked out. Despite every effort to avoid transcription errors, a few may persist.
- A/c – Aircraft.

Appendix D – Hague Convention (1907) Extract

REGULATIONS RESPECTING THE LAWS AND CUSTOMS OF WAR ON LAND

SECTION I: ON BELLIGERENTS

CHAPTER II: Prisoners of war

Art. 4. Prisoners of war are in the power of the hostile Government, but not of the individuals or corps who capture them.

They must be humanely treated.

All their personal belongings, except arms, horses, and military papers, remain their property.

Art. 5. Prisoners of war may be interned in a town, fortress, camp, or other place, and bound not to go beyond certain fixed limits; but they cannot be confined except as in indispensable measure of safety and only while the circumstances which necessitate the measure continue to exist.

Art. 6. The State may utilize the labour of prisoners of war according to their rank and aptitude, officers excepted. The tasks shall not be excessive and shall have no connection with the operations of the war.

Prisoners may be authorized to work for the public service, for private persons, or on their own account.

Work done for the State is paid for at the rates in force for work of a similar kind done by soldiers of the national army, or, if there are none in force, at a rate according to the work executed.

When the work is for other branches of the public service or for private persons the conditions are settled in agreement with the military authorities.

The wages of the prisoners shall go towards improving their position, and the balance shall be paid them on their release, after deducting the cost of their maintenance.

Art. 7. The Government into whose hands prisoners of war have fallen is charged with their maintenance.

In the absence of a special agreement between the belligerents, prisoners of war shall be treated as regards board, lodging, and clothing on the same footing as the troops of the Government who captured them.

Art. 8. Prisoners of war shall be subject to the laws, regulations, and orders in force in the army of the State in whose power they are. Any act of insubordination justifies the adoption towards them of such measures of severity as may be considered necessary.

Escaped prisoners who are retaken before being able to rejoin their own army or before leaving the territory occupied by the army which captured them are liable to disciplinary punishment. Prisoners who, after succeeding in escaping, are again taken prisoners, are not liable to any punishment on account of the previous flight.

Art. 9. Every prisoner of war is bound to give, if he is questioned on the subject, his true name and rank, and if he infringes this rule, he is liable to have the advantages given to prisoners of his class curtailed.

Art. 10. Prisoners of war may be set at liberty on parole if the laws of their country allow, and, in such cases, they are bound, on their personal honour, scrupulously to fulfil, both towards their own Government and the Government by whom they were made prisoners, the engagements they have contracted.

In such cases their own Government is bound neither to require of nor accept from them any service incompatible with the parole given.

Art. 11. A prisoner of war cannot be compelled to accept his liberty on parole; similarly the hostile Government is not obliged to accede to the request of the prisoner to be set at liberty on parole.

Art. 12. Prisoners of war liberated on parole and recaptured bearing arms against the Government to whom they had pledged their honour, or against the allies of that Government, forfeit their right to be treated as prisoners of war, and can be brought before the courts.

Art. 13. Individuals who follow an army without directly belonging to it, such as newspaper correspondents and reporters, sutlers and contractors, who fall into the enemy's hands and whom the latter thinks expedient to detain, are entitled to be treated as prisoners of war, provided they are in possession of a certificate from the military authorities of the army which they were accompanying.

Art. 14. An inquiry office for prisoners of war is instituted on the commencement of hostilities in each of the belligerent States, and, when necessary, in neutral countries which have received belligerents in their territory. It is the function of this office to reply to all inquiries about the prisoners. It receives from the various services concerned full information respecting internments arid transfers, releases on parole, exchanges, escapes, admissions into hospital, deaths, as well as other information necessary to enable it to make out and keep up to date an individual return for each prisoner of war. The office must state in this return the regimental number, name and surname, age, place of origin, rank, unit, wounds, date and place of capture, internment, wounding, and death, as well as any observations of a special character. The individual return shall be sent to the Government of the other belligerent after the conclusion of peace.

It is likewise the function of the inquiry office to receive and collect all objects of personal use, valuables, letters, etc., found on the field of battle or left by prisoners who have been released on parole, or exchanged, or who have escaped, or died in hospitals or ambulances, and to forward them to those concerned.

Art. 15. Relief societies for prisoners of war, which are properly constituted in accordance with the laws of their country and with the object of serving as the channel for charitable effort shall receive from the belligerents, for themselves and their duly accredited agents every facility for the efficient performance of their humane task within the bounds imposed by military necessities and administrative regulations. Agents of these societies may be admitted to the places of internment for the purpose of distributing relief, as also to the halting places of repatriated prisoners, if furnished with a personal permit by the military authorities, and on giving an undertaking in writing to comply with all measures of order and police which the latter may issue.

Art. 16. Inquiry offices enjoy the privilege of free postage. Letters, money orders, and valuables, as well as parcels by post, intended for prisoners of war, or dispatched by them, shall be exempt from all postal duties in the countries of origin and destination, as well as in the countries they pass through.

Presents and relief in kind for prisoners of war shall be admitted free of all import or other duties, as well as of payments for carriage by the State railways.

Art. 17. Officers taken prisoners shall receive the same rate of pay as officers of corresponding rank in the country where they are detained, the amount to be ultimately refunded by their own Government.

Art. 18. Prisoners of war shall enjoy complete liberty in the exercise of their religion, including attendance at the services of whatever church they may belong to, on the sole condition that they comply with the measures of order and police issued by the military authorities.

Art. 19. The wills of prisoners of war are received or drawn up in the same way as for soldiers of the national army.

The same rules shall be observed regarding death certificates as well as for the burial of prisoners of war, due regard being paid to their grade and rank.

Art. 20. After the conclusion of peace, the repatriation of prisoners of war shall be carried out as quickly as possible.

APPENDIX E – GENEVA CONVENTION (1929) EXTRACT[1]

Convention relative to the Treatment of Prisoners of War, 118 L.N.T.S. 343, entered into force June 19, 1931.

(List of Contracting Parties)

Recognizing that, in the extreme event of a war, it will be the duty of every Power, to mitigate as far as possible, the inevitable rigours thereof and to alleviate the condition of prisoners of war; Being desirous of developing the principles which have inspired the international conventions of The Hague, in particular the Convention concerning the Laws and Customs of War and the Regulations thereunto annexed,

Have resolved to conclude a Convention for that purpose and have appointed as their Plenipotentiaries:

(Here follow the names of Plenipotentiaries)

Who, having communicated their full powers, found in good and due form, have agreed is follows.

PART I: GENERAL PROVISIONS

Article 1. The present Convention shall apply without prejudice to the stipulations of Part VII:

(1) To all persons referred to in Articles 1, 2 and 3 of the Regulations annexed to the Hague Convention (IV) of 18 October 1907, concerning the Laws and Customs of War on Land, who are captured by the enemy. (2) To all persons belonging to the armed forces of belligerents who are captured

by the enemy in the course of operations of maritime or aerial war, subject to such exceptions (derogations) as the conditions of such capture render inevitable. Nevertheless these exceptions shall not infringe the fundamental principles of the present Convention; they shall cease from the moment when the captured persons shall have reached a prisoners of war camp.

Art. 2. Prisoners of war are in the power of the hostile Government, but not of the individuals or formation which captured them.

They shall at all times be humanely treated and protected, particularly against acts of violence, from insults and from public curiosity.

Measures of reprisal against them are forbidden.

Art. 3. Prisoners of war are entitled to respect for their persons and honour. Women shall be treated with all consideration due to their sex.

Prisoners retain their full civil capacity.

Art. 4. The detaining Power is required to provide for the maintenance of prisoners of war in its charge. Differences of treatment between prisoners are permissible only if such differences are based on the military rank, the state of physical or mental health, the professional abilities, or the sex of those who benefit from them.

PART II: CAPTURE

Art. 5. Every prisoner of war is required to declare, if he is interrogated on the subject, his true names and rank, or his regimental number.

If he infringes this rule, he exposes himself to a restriction of the privileges accorded to prisoners of his category.

No pressure shall be exercised on prisoners to obtain information regarding the situation in their armed forces or their country. Prisoners who refuse to reply may not be threatened, insulted, or exposed to unpleasantness or disadvantages of any kind whatsoever.

If, by reason of his physical or mental condition, a prisoner is incapable of stating his identity, he shall be handed over to the Medical Service.

Art. 6. All personal effects and articles in personal use -- except arms, horses, military equipment and military papers -- shall remain in the possession of prisoners of war, as well as their metal helmets and gas-masks.

Sums of money carried by prisoners may only be taken from them on the order of an officer and after the amount has been recorded. A receipt shall be given for them. Sums thus impounded shall be placed to the account of each prisoner.

Their identity tokens, badges of rank, decorations and articles of value may not be taken from prisoners.

PART III: CAPTIVITY

SECTION I: EVACUATION OF PRISONERS OF WAR

[Article 7 omitted]

Art. 8. Belligerents are required to notify each other of all captures of prisoners as soon as possible, through the intermediary of the Information Bureaux organised in accordance with Article 77. They are likewise required to inform each other of the official addresses to which letter from the prisoners' families may be addressed to the prisoners of war.

As soon as possible, every prisoner shall be enabled to correspond personally with his family, in accordance with the conditions prescribed in Article 36 and the following Articles.

As regards prisoners captured at sea, the provisions of the present article shall be observed as soon as possible after arrival in port. *[Articles 9-76 omitted]*

PART VI: BUREAUX OF RELIEF AND INFORMATION CONCERNING PRISONERS OF WAR

Art. 77. At the commencement of hostilities, each of the belligerent Powers and the neutral Powers who have belligerents in their care, shall institute an official bureau to give information about the prisoners of war in their territory.

Each of the belligerent Powers shall inform its Information Bureau as soon as possible of all captures of prisoners effected by its armed forces, furnishing them with all particulars of identity at its disposal to enable the families concerned to be quickly notified, and stating the official addresses to which families may write to the prisoners.

The Information Bureau shall transmit all such information immediately to the Powers concerned, on the one hand through the intermediary of the protecting Powers, and on the other through the Central Agency contemplated in Article 79.

The Information Bureau, being charged with replying to all enquiries relative to prisoners of war, shall receive from the various services concerned all particulars respecting internments and transfers, releases on parole, repatriations, escapes, stays in hospitals, and deaths, together with all other particulars necessary for establishing and keeping up to date an individual record for each prisoner of war.

The Bureau shall note in this record, as far as possible, and subject to the provisions of Article 5, the regimental number, names and surnames, date and place of birth, rank and unit of

356

the prisoner, the surname of the father and name of the mother, the address of the person to be notified in case of accident, wounds, dates and places of capture, of internment, of wounds, of death, together with all other important particulars. Weekly lists containing all additional particulars capable of facilitating the identification of each prisoner shall be transmitted to the interested Powers. The individual record of a prisoner of war shall be sent after the conclusion of peace to the Power in whose service he was.

The Information Bureau shall also be required to collect all personal effects, valuables, correspondence, pay-books, identity tokens, etc., which have been left by prisoners of war who have been repatriated or released on parole, or who have escaped or died, and to transmit them to the countries concerned.

Art. 78. Societies for the relief of prisoners of war, regularly constituted in accordance with the laws of their country, and having for their object to serve as intermediaries for charitable purposes, shall receive from the belligerents, for themselves and their duly accredited agents, all facilities for the efficacious performance of their humane task within the limits imposed by military exigencies. Representatives of these societies shall be permitted to distribute relief in the camps and at the halting places of repatriated prisoners under a personal permit issued by the military authority, and on giving an undertaking in writing to comply with all routine and police orders which the said authority shall prescribe.

Art. 79. A Central Agency of information regarding prisoners of war shall be established in a neutral country. The International Red Cross Committee shall, if they consider it necessary, propose to the Powers concerned the organization of such an agency.

This agency shall be charged with the duty of collecting all information regarding prisoners which they may be able to obtain through official or private channels, and the agency shall transmit the information as rapidly as possible to the prisoners' own country or the Power in whose service they have been.

These provisions shall not be interpreted as restricting the humanitarian work of the International Red Cross Committee.

Art. 80. Information Bureaux shall enjoy exemption from fees on postal matter as well as all the exemptions prescribed in Article 38.

PART VII: APPLICATION OF THE CONVENTION TO CERTAIN CATEGORIES OF CIVILIANS

Art. 81. Persons who follow the armed forces without directly belonging thereto, such as correspondents, newspaper reporters, sutlers, or contractors, who fall into the hands of the enemy, and whom the latter think fit to detain, shall be entitled to be treated as prisoners of war, provided they are in possession of an authorization from the military authorities of the armed forces which they were following.

[Articles 82-97 omitted]

---

[1]   University of Minnesota Human Rights Library web site

BIBLIOGRAPHY

Admiralty Hydrographic Department reports in the ADM 344 series are drawn from sources including direct observation, charts and sailing directions from France and the Baltic littoral.

Abrutat, David. 2019. *Vanguard: The true stories of the reconnaissance and intelligence missions behind D-Day.* 1st. London, Annapolis: Unicorn Publishing Group, Naval Institute Press.

Admiralty. 1919. "ADM 137/3917: Original history sheets of UB type German submarines: UB74-UB155." London: The National Archives.

—. 1909. "ADM 344/436: MS memorandum by Lieutenant Vivian Brandon, 23 March 1910, describing contents of 'Kattegat, Sound, Belts and Baltic Sea' compiled from photographs taken during HMS Cornwall cruise, 1909; sketch made during same cruise." London: The National Archives, 31 12.

—. 1909. "ADM 344/437: Europe, N Coast and Scandinavia: Denmark and Sweden; Kattegat, vicinity; thirteen items on one sheet. By HMS Cornwall, 1909." London: The National Archives, 31 12.

—. 1910. "ADM 344/442: Europe, N Coast and Scandinavia: Denmark, E Coast; Jylland (Jutland); Kattegat to Lille Baelt (Little Belt); three items on one sheet: (HMS Cornwall, 1909?)." London: The National Archives, 31 12.

—. 1910. "ADM 344/443: Europe, N Coast and Scandinavia: Denmark, E Coast and Sweden, W Coast; Kattegat to Samso Baelt, Store Baelt (Great Belt) and Oresund (The Sound); sixteen items on one sheet: (HMS Cornwall, 1909?)." London: The National Archives, 31 12.

—. 1910. "ADM 344/444: Europe, N Coast and Scandinavia: Denmark, E Coast and Sweden, W Coast; Oresund (The Sound) and Store Baelt (Great Belt); ten items on one sheet: (HMS Cornwall, 1909?)." London: The National Archives, 31 12.

—. 1910. "ADM 344/445: Europe, N Coast and Scandinavia: Denmark, E Coast and Sweden, W Coast; Kattegat to Oresund (The Sound) and Sjaelland (Zealand); six items on one sheet: (HMS Cornwall, 1909?)." London: The National Archives, 31 12.

—. 1909. "ADM 344/450: Europe, N Coast and Scandinavia: Denmark, E Coast and Sweden, W Coast; Oresund (The Sound) and Store Baelt (Great Belt); thirteen items on one sheet: (Lt V Brandon, HMS Cornwall, c1909)." London: The National Archives, 31 12.

—. 1910. "ADM 344/451: Europe, N Coast: Denmark, E Coast; Store Baelt (Great Belt) and Lille Baelt (Little Belt), vicinity; fifteen items on one sheet: (HMS Cornwall, 1909?)." London: The National Archives, 31 12.

—. 1910. "ADM 344/452: Europe, N Coast: Denmark, E Coast; Lille Baelt (Little Belt) and Kieler Bucht, approaches; seventeen items on one sheet: HMS Cornwall, 1909." London: The National Archives, 31 12.

—. 1910. "ADM 344/453: Europe, N Coast: Denmark, E Coast: Lille Baelt (Little Belt) and Kieler Bucht, approaches; eighteen items on one sheet: HMS Cornwall, 1909." London: The National Archives, 31 12.

—. 1910. "ADM 344/454: Europe, N Coast: Denmark, E Coast; Lille Baelt (Little Belt), vicinity; eleven items on one sheet: HMS Cornwall, 1909." London: The National Archives, 31 12.

—. 1910. "ADM 344/455: Europe, N Coast: Denmark, E Coast and Germany; Lille Baelt (Little Belt) and Kieler Bucht, vicinity; eleven items on one sheet: (HMS Cornwall?), 1909." London: The National Archives, 31 12.

—. 1910. "ADM 344/463: Europe, N Coast: Germany; Schleswig-Holstein, E Coast; Kieler Bucht to Fehmarnsund; 'Coast of Prussia'; eleven items on one sheet: (HMS Cornwall, 1909?)." London: The National Archives, 31 12.

—. 1910. "ADM 344/478: Baltic Sea: Germany and Poland; Rugen to Gulf of Gdansk (Danzig); fourteen items on one sheet: HMS Cornwall, 1909." London: The National Archives, 31 12.

—. 1910. "ADM 344/480: Baltic Sea: Germany and Latvia; Stein Ort, vicinity and Liepaja (Libau); 'The Kourland Coast'; four items on one sheet: HMS Cornwall, 1909." London: The National Archives, 31 12.

—. 1909. "ADM 344/498: Scandinavia: Norway, SW Coast; Utsira to Larvik; three items on one sheet: HMS Cornwall, 1909." London: The National Archives, 31 12.

—. 1909. "ADM 53/18956: Admiralty, and Ministry of Defence, Navy Department: Ships' Logs, HMS Cornwall." London: The National Archives, 18 12.

Air Ministry Directorate of Intelligence. 1939. "AIR 40/2394: Interrogation of German and Italian Prisoners of War: Reports Vol 1, 1939 Sept-Dec." London: The National Archives, 31 12.

—. 1945. "AIR 40/2636: Intelligence from interrogation: the work of ADI(K), 1939-1945." London: The National Archives.

—. 1942. "AIR 40/3102: CSDIC (UK): special extracts from SR drafts; information obtained from Axis POWs." London: The National Archives, 31 12.

—. 1945. "AIR 40/3104: CSDIC (UK): special extracts from SR drafts; information obtained from Axis POWs." London: The National Archives, 31 12.

—. 1944. "AIR 40/3106: Special SR Reports Nos 1-134: information obtained from Axis POWs." London: The National Archives, 31 12.

Bibliography

—. 1940. "CSDIC (UK) reports SRA 1-499 (incomplete): information obtained from German Air Force POWs." London: The National Archives, 11 09.

Amersfoort, Herman, and Wim Klinkert, . 2011. *Small Powers in the Age of Total War, 1900-1940.* Leiden, Boston: Brill.

Andrew, Christopher, and Simona Tobia, . 2020. *Interrogation in War and Conflict: A comparative and interdisciplinary analysis.* Abingdon: Routledge.

Anon. 1947. "Building and Launching of HMS Royal Rupert." *The Royal Rupert Times*, 12, 34th ed.

ARW. 1973-04. "Hall and Godfrey-Doyens of Naval Intelligence." *The Naval Review* 125-138.

Beesly, Patrick. 1982. *Room 40: British Naval Intelligence 1914-18.* London: Hamish Hamilton.

—. 1980. *Very Special Admiral: The life of Admiral J H Godfrey CB.* 1st. London: Hamish Hamilton.

—. 2006. *Very Special Intelligence: The Story of the Admiralty's Operational Intelligence Centre 1939-1945.* London: Chatham Publishing.

Bell, Falko. 2015 31:4. "One of our Most Valuable Sources of Intelligence: British Intelligence and the Prisoner of War System in 1944." *Intelligence and National Security* 556-578. http://www.tandfonline.com/doi/abs/10.1080/02684527.2015.106231 9.

Birch, Frank, and William F Clarke. 2009. *Room 40: German Naval Warfare 1914-1918.* Edited by Hans Joachim Koerver. Vol. I: The Fleet in Action. 3 vols. Berlin: Schaltungsdienst Lange o.H.G.

Bittner, Dr Donald F, and John Coleby. 1993. *Royal Marines Spies of World War One Era.* Portsmouth: Royal Marines Historical Society.

Black, Nicholas. 2009. *The British Naval Staff in the First World War.* Woodbridge: Boydell.

Boyd, Andrew. 2020. *British Naval Intelligence Through the Twentieth Century.* 1st. Barnsley: Seaforth Publishing. https://www.pen-and-sword.co.uk/British-Naval-Intelligence-through-the-Twentieth-Century-Hardback/p/17926.

Brooks, Tom. n.d. "Naval Intelligence at Fort Hunt Park: One of ONI's most successful HUMINT operations of World War II." 3. Accessed 12 21, 2021. https://ncisahistory.org/wp-content/uploads/2021/11/Naval-Intelligence-at-Fort-Hunt-Park.pdf.

Buchheim, Lothar-Günther. 1973. *The Boat (Das Boot).* 2nd. Translated by J Maxwell Brownjohn. Glasgow: Wm Collins Sons & co.

Burt, Kendal, and James Leasor. 2006. *The One That Got Away.* Barnsley: Pen & Sword.

Bywater, Hector Charles, and H C Ferraby. 2015. *Strange Intelligence: Memoirs of Naval Secret Service.* London: Biteback Publishing Ltd.

Clayton, J W, and Rodger Winn. 1998. "The Battle of the Atlantic and Signals Intelligence: U-boat situations and trends, 1941-1945." *Navy Records*

Society. Vol. 139. Edited by David Syrett. Aldershot: Ashgate Publishing Ltd.

Cobain, Ian. 2012. *Cruel Britannia: A secret history of torture.* London: Portobello Books.

Colvin, Tony. 2010. "Wilhelmshaven." *After the Battle,* 148 ed.: 2-41.

Corbin, Alexander D. 2009. *The History of Camp Tracy: Japanese WWII PoWs and the Future of Strategic Interrogation.* Fort Belvoir: Ziedon Press.

Cradock, Percy. 2002. *Know Your Enemy: How the Joint Intelligence Committee Saw the World.* London: John Murray.

Díaz-Benítez, Juan-José. 2018. "German Supply Ships and Blockade Runners in the Canary Islands in the Second World War." *The Mariner's Mirror* 318-329.

Director of Torpedo, Anti-Submarine and Mine Warfare Division. 1945. "ADM 199/1789: U-boats sunk or damaged and US Fleet Anti-Submarine Bulletins." London: The National Archives.

Dönitz, Karl. 2000. *Memoirs: Ten years and twenty days.* Translated by R H Stevens and David Woodward. London: Cassell Military Paperbacks.

Dunn, Steve R. 2018. *Bayly's War; The Battle for the Western Approaches in the First World War.* 1st. Barnsley: Seaforth Publishing.

—. 2017. *Securing the Narrow Sea.* 1st. Barnsley: Seaforth Publishing.

Foley, Michael. 2015. *Prisoners of the British.* Stroud: Fonthill.

Foreign Office. 1988. "FCO 15/5366: Alleged British war atrocity in Indonesia: sinking of a Japanese coaster by HM Submarine Sturdy, 25 November 1944." London: The National Archives, 31 12.

—. 1946. "FO 1031/63: Enemy Personnel Exploitation Section (EPES) Interrogation reports: vol I." London: The National Archives, 12.

—. 1945. "FO 1038/145: Commission for Naval Information." London: The National Archives.

—. 1918. "FO 383/442: Germany: Prisoners, including: ... Treatment of Lieutenant S Spindler of the ship Libau, while interned at Cromwell Gardens Barracks, London." London: The National Archives.

Forstner, Georg-Günther von, Paul König, and Edgar von Freiherr Spiegel von und zu Peckelsheim. 2010. *U-Boat War 1914-1918 Volume 2: three accounts of German submarines during the Great War.* Leonaur.

Fry, Helen. 2014. *Spymaster: The Secret Life of Kendrick.* London: Marranos Press.

—. 2017. *The London Cage: The Secret History of Britain's WWII Interrogation Centre.* London: Yale University Press.

—. 2019. *The Walls Have Ears.* 1st. New Haven and London: Yale University Press.

—. 2023. *Women in Intelligence: The hidden history of two world wars.* 1st. London: Yale University Press.

Bibliography

Fürbringer, Werner. 1999. *FIPS: Legendary U-Boat Commander.* 1st UK. Translated by Geoffrey Brooks. Barnsley, South Yorkshire: Pen & Sword.

Gibson, R H, and Maurice Prendergast. 2015. *The German Submarine War 1914-1918.* Uckfield: Naval & Military Press.

Graul, Jens. 2014, 2018. *Wilhelmshaven: Captain Edward Conder and the new beginning 1945.* Translated by Elizabeth Tarrant. Wilhelmshaven, London: Brune-Mettckner.

Hastings, Max. 2015. *The Secret War: Spies, Codes and Guerrillas 1939-1945.* London: William Collins.

Henry, Alexander. 2021. *War Through Italian Eyes: Fighting for Mussolini, 1940-1943.* Routledge: Abingdon.

Hewitt, Nick. 2013. *The Kaiser's Pirates: Hunting Germany's Raiding Cruisers 1914-1915.* Barnsley: Pen and Sword.

Hinsley, Harry. 1993. *British Intelligence in the Second World War (Abridged Edition).* London: HMSO.

Hinsley, Harry, and C A G Simkins. 1990. *British Intelligence in the Second World War.* Vol. 4. London: HMSO.

Hinsley, Harry, Edward Eastway Thomas, C F G Ransom, and R C Knight. 1984. *British Intelligence in the Second World War.* Vol. 3 Part 1. London: HMSO.

Home Office. 1946. "HO 334/164/19474: Naturalisation Certificate: Stefan Georg Klein. From Austria." London: The National Archives, 10 09.

—. 1957. "HO 405/3688: Barazetti A & W F." London: The National Archives, 31 12.

Hore, Peter. 2021. *Bletchley Park's Secret Source: Churchill's Wrens and the Y Service in World War II.* Barnsley: Greenhill Books.

—. 2009. *Sydney Cipher and Search: Solving the last great naval mystery of the Second World War.* Rendlesham: Seafarer Books.

Institute Henry Dunant. 1931. *Convention relative to the Treatment of Prisoners of War, 118 L.N.T.S. 343, entered into force June 19, 1931.* . 19 06. Accessed 05 09, 2019. http://hrlibrary.umn.edu/instree/1929c.htm.

Jackson, Robert. 1964. *A Taste of Freedom.* London: Arthur Barker Ltd.

Jackson, Sophie. 2012. *British Interrogation Techniques in the Second World War.* Stroud, Gloucestershire: The History Press.

Jago, Michael. 2013. *The Man Who Was George Smiley: The Life of John Bingham.* London: Biteback.

James, Admiral Sir William. 1955. *The Eyes of the Navy: A Biographical Study of Admiral Sir Reginald Hall.* London: Methuen & Co.

Jellicoe, Nick. 2021. *George Jellicoe: SAS and SBS Commander.* Barnsley: Pen & Sword.

—. 2016. *Jutland - The Unfinished Battle.* Barnsley: Seaforth.

—. 2019. *The Last Days of the High Seas Fleet.* 1st. Barnsley: Seaforth Publishing.

King-Hall, Stephen. 1952. *My Naval Life, 1906-1929.* London: Faber & Faber.

Kirby, Geoff. 1972. "A History of the Torpedo Parts 3-4." *Journal of the Royal Naval Scientific Service* 27 (2): 78-105.

Kleinman, Steven M. 2002. "The History of MIS-Y: US strategic interrogation during World War II." Washington: Joint Military Intelligence College, 08. 162.

Kluiters, F A C. n.d. "Bill Hooper and secret service." Accessed 09 20, 2022. https://www.nisa-intelligence.nl/PDF-bestanden/Kluiters_Hooper2XV_voorwebsite.pdf.

Koerver, Hans Joachim. 2020. *The Kaiser's U-Boat Assault on America: Germany's Great War Gamble in the First World War.* 1st. Barnsley: Pen & Sword.

Konstam, Angus. 2016. *Jutland 1916: Twelve hours to win the war.* London: Aurum Press Limited.

Krammer, Arnold. 1983. "Japanese Prisoners of War in America." *Pacific Historical Review* (University of California Press) (Vol. 52, No. 1): 67-91. Accessed 12 26, 2021. https://www.jstor.org/stable/3639455?origin=JSTOR-pdf.

Laird, Matthew R. 2000. ""By the River Potomac": An Historic Resource Study of Fort Hunt Park, George Washingtom Memorial Parkway, Mount Vernon, Virginia." Washington: National Park Service. vi,146. Accessed 12 20, 2021. https://archive.org/details/byriverpotomachi00lair.

Lampersberger, Josef. 1962. "Eyewitness account by Josef Lampersberger of his anti-Nazi activism, kidnapping by Gestapo and mistreatment in custody." *Testifying to the Truth: Eyewitnesses to the Holocaust.* Wiener Holocaust Library for the Study of the Holocaust & Genocide. Accessed 05 28, 2023. https://www.testifyingtothetruth.co.uk/viewer/metadata/104840/1/.

Landau, Henry. 2015. *The Spy Net: The Greatest Intelligence Operations of the First World War.* London: Biteback Publishing Ltd.

Liddell, Guy. 1940. *KV 4/186: Liddell Diaries. Volume 2 of the diary kept by Guy Liddell, the head of the Security Service's B Division, during the Second World War, including index.* London: The National Archives.

Lincoln, Ashe. 2017. *Secret Naval Investigator: The Battle Against Hitler's Secret Underwater Weapons.* Barnsley: Frontline Books.

Lomas, Dan. 2018. "The drugs don't work: intelligence, torture and the London Cage, 1940–8." *Intelligence and National Security* (Routledge) 33 (6): 918-929. Accessed 12 30, 2023. doi:https://www.tandfonline.com/action/showCitFormats?doi=10.1080/02684527.2018.1478629.

Madsen, Chris. 1998. *The Royal Navy and German Naval Disarmament 1942-1947.* London: Frank Cass.

Mallett, Derek Ray. 2012. "Prisoners of War-Cold War Allies: The Anglo-American Relationship with Wehrmacht Generals." College Station, Tx: Texas A&M University, 14 02. 415. Accessed 12 13, 2021. https://oaktrust.library.tamu.edu/handle/1969.1/ETD-TAMU-2009-08-869.

Bibliography

Mallman Showell, Jak P. 2013. *Dönitz, U-boats, Convoys.* Barnsley: Frontline Books.

—. 1973. *U-Boats Under the Swastika: An introduction to German submarines 1935-1945.* Shepperton: Ian Allan Ltd.

Massie, Robert K. 2003. *Castles of Steel: Britain, Germany and the winning of the Great War at sea.* London: Jonathan Cape.

McKee, Fraser M. 1993. "An Explosive Story: The Rise and Fall of the Common Depth Charge." *The Northern Mariner* III (1): 45-58. Accessed 01 11, 2019. https://www.scribd.com/document/240217873/An-Explosive-Story-The-Rise-and-Fall-of-the-Common-Depth-Charge.

McLachlan, Donald. 1968. *Room 39: Naval Intelligence in Action 1939-45.* London: Weidenfeld and Nicholson.

Messimer, Dwight R. 1997. "Heinz-Wilhelm Eck - Siegerjustiz and the Peleus Affair." In *Silent Hunters: German U-boat Commanders of World War II*, by Theodore P. Savas, 137ff. Da Capo Press.

Moore, John Hammond. 1978. "Getting Fritz to Talk." *The Virginia Quarterly Review*, Spring. Accessed 12 27, 2021. https://www.vqronline.org/essay/getting-fritz-talk.

Naval Intelligence Division. 1939. "ADM 1/10069: PRISONERS OF WAR AND INTERNEES (79): Conduct of Prisoner of War Camps and morale of German prisoners." The National Archives.

—. 1941. "ADM 1/10176: Investigation into possibilities of midget submarines." London: The National Archives, 22 02.

—. 1939. "ADM 1/26868; Interrogation of PoWs." London: The National Archives, 12.

—. 1916. "ADM 1/8446/15: Procedure to be adopted regarding Prisoners of War captured from Enemy Submarines." London: The National Archives.

—. 1939. "ADM 1/9777: ADMIRALTY (5): Submarine Intelligence Summaries No's 3-6 ." London: The National Archives.

—. 1917. "ADM 137/1629: Intelligence." London: The National Archives.

—. 1918. "ADM 137/1906: Secret Packs of the Commander-in-Chief Grand Fleet 1914-1918, Vol XXVI." London: The National Archives.

—. 1918. "ADM 137/1907: Secret packs of the Commander in Chief Grand Fleet, Volume XXVII, pack 0017, sections 4-5." London: The National Archives.

—. 1918. "ADM 137/1908: Secret Packs of the Commander-in-Chief Grand Fleet 1914-1918, Vol XXVIII." London: The National Archives.

—. 1918. "ADM 137/1933: Secret packs of the Commander in Chief Grand Fleet, Volume LIII, pack 0022, section I." London: The National Archives, 11.

—. 1918. "ADM 137/3060: Interrogations of survivors of captured and sunk German submarines, etc." London: The National Archives.

—. 1918. "ADM 137/3875: Reports concerning cruises, interrogation of survivors, machinery and fittings of German submarines." London: The National Archives.

—. 1918. "ADM 137/3876: Interrogation of survivors of German submarines." London: The National Archives, 11.

—. 1918. "ADM 137/3881: German surface craft: specifications, movements, details of damage and losses sustained at Jutland." London: The National Archives.

—. 1918. "ADM 137/3896: German vessels: interrogation of prisoners of war from German ship BRESLAU: activities of and attacks on German vessels GOEBEN and BRESLAU and effect on relations with Turkey." London: The National Archives.

—. 1918. "ADM 137/3897: German submarines UC 16–UC 44: interrogation of survivors, translations of German officer's diary, and letters of prisoners of war." London: The National Archives.

—. 1917. "ADM 137/3899: History sheets of German submarines UB1–UB47: Miscellaneous notes and letters of crews." London: The National Archives.

—. 1918. "ADM 137/3900: History sheets of German submarines UB48–UB140: drawings of vessels, details of activities, diaries and letters." London: The National Archives.

—. 1917. "ADM 137/3903: Papers concerning German submarines U60–U90: details of U boats, descriptions of sinking of merchant vessels and U boat activities, and interrogation statements of prisoners." London: The National Archives.

—. 1917. "ADM 137/3909: Papers and reports concerned with activities of German surface raiders SEEADLER and LUTECE." London: The National Archives.

—. 1919. "ADM 137/3964: German airships: brief history, compiled mainly from interrogation of survivors of crashes 1915-1919." London: The National Archives.

—. 1918. "ADM 137/4688: Naval intelligence: note on duties of I.D. section 16a." London: The National Archives.

—. 1950. "ADM 186/805: British & Foreign Merchant Vessels Lost/Damaged by Enemy Action during WW2 amended up to 2nd September 1945. Also includes records for German Naval survivors, Oct 1939-Dec 1940." *BR 1337*. London: The National Archives, 1940 Dec.

—. 1941. "ADM 186/806: Interrogation of German naval survivors." London: The National Archives.

—. 1942. "ADM 186/807: Interrogation of German naval survivors." London: The National Archives.

—. 1943. "ADM 186/808: Interrogation of German naval survivors." London: The National Archives.

—. 1944. "ADM 186/809: Interrogation of German naval survivors." London: The National Archives.

Bibliography

—. 1945. "ADM 199/2434: History of occupation by Allies of Walterwerke Kiel and account of general activities May-November 1945." London: The National Archives, 11.

—. 1944. "ADM 199/2478: Director of Naval Intelligence: movements of small craft and personnel to Mediterranean, questionnaires and Prisoners of War statements: includes CX material." London: The National Archives, 31 12.

—. 1945. "ADM 199/443; Pre and post-surrender intelligence and policy in relation to Germany." London: The National Archives.

—. 1947. "ADM 213/823: Interrogation of Brückner-Kanis team in Germany by E Norton and DB Welbourn Feb 1947." London: The National Archives, 02.

—. 1944. "ADM 223/144: Summary of statements by German prisoners of war." London: The National Archives, 01 04.

—. 1970. "ADM 223/214: Appendix 1 (Part 5): History of 30 Commando (later called 30 Assault Unit and 30 Advanced Unit also known as Special Engineering Unit)." *NID Vol 46*. London: The National Archives, 05 09.

—. 1945. "ADM 223/257: Naval Intelligence Division: staff and duties." London: The National Archives.

—. 1944. "ADM 223/286: Operational Intelligence Centres: formation and history." London: The National Archive, 04.

—. 1947. "ADM 223/297: Notes and extracts from volumes of paper collected by Admiral Godfrey." London: The National Archives.

—. 1947. "ADM 223/297: Notes and extracts from volumes of paper collected by Admiral Godfrey." London: The National Archives.

—. 1942. "ADM 223/352: DNI Notes." London: The National Archives.

—. 1944. "ADM 223/355: DNI Notes (Apr-June 1944)." London: The National Archives, 06.

Naval Intelligence Division. 1944. "ADM 223/357: DNI Notes (Oct-Dec 1944)." London: The National Archives.

—. 1950. "ADM 223/464: History of Naval Intelligence and the Naval Intelligence Department 1939-1945." London: The National Archives.

—. 1943. "ADM 223/467: NID monograph: NID (I)." London: The National Archives.

—. 1945. "ADM 223/472: NID memoranda: NID organisation and establishment." London: The National Archives.

—. 1948. "ADM 223/473: NID memoranda: training and administration." London: The National Archives.

—. 1947. "ADM 223/475: Intelligence Collection Methods." London: The National Archives.

—. 1944. "ADM 223/487: NID & OIC Intelligence Reports & Papers: France." London: The National Archives.

—. 1944. "ADM 223/501: 30 Assault Unit: targets." London: The National Archives.

—. 1950. "ADM 223/619: The Navy and Naval Intelligence 1939-1942: afterthoughts by Admiral J H Godfrey (former DNI)." London: The National Archives.

—. 1919. "ADM 223/637: Agents' Reports: Naval." London: The National Archives, 02.

—. 1945. "ADM 223/851: NID volume: Secret Intelligence Service (SIS)." London: The National Archives.

—. 1945. "ADM 234/578: Naval staff history: defeat of the enemy attack on shipping." London: The National Archives.

—. 1939. "ADM 234/994: German submarines in question and answer." London: The National Archives, 09.

—. 1941. "ADM 239/603: Treatment and handling of prisoners of war in ships affecting capture." *CB 3074.* London: The National Archives.

—. 1945. "ADM 283/72: Enemy scientist interrogation report: Professor Walter." London: The National Archives, 30 05.

—. 1945. "ADM 290/285: Interrogation by joint team of Dr Walter, head of Walter-Werke, Kiel, on hydrogen peroxide propulsion of torpedoes and submarines." London: The National Archives, 26 05.

—. 1914. "Naval Intelligence on Germany obtained in 1914, including reports from British warships attending the formal re-opening ceremony of the Kiel Canal in June 1914." London: The National Archives.

Neitzel, Sönke. 2013. *Tapping Hitler's Generals: Transcripts of Secret Conversations 1942-45.* Translated by Geoffrey Brooks. London: Frontline Books.

Neitzel, Sönke, and Harald Welzer. 2013. *Soldaten: On Fighting, Killing and Dying.* Translated by Jefferson Chase. London: Simon & Schuster UK Ltd.

Neuner, Matthias. 2014. "When Justice Is Left to the Losers: The Leipzig War Crimes Trials." *Historical Origins of International Criminal Law.* Vol. 1. Edited by Morten Bergsmo, Wui Ling and Ping Yi. Brussels: Torkel Opsahl Academic EPublisher, 12 12. https://www.legal-tools.org/doc/8a075f/pdf/.

Nudd, Derek. 2017. *Castaways of the Kriegsmarine.* Portsmouth.

Nudd, Derek. 2019. "The Battle of Jutland, Through a Looking-glass." *The Mariner's Mirror* (Routledge) (105:4): 425-441.

Offley, Ed. 2011. *Turning the Tide.* New York: Basic Books.

Packard, Wyman H. 1996. *A Century of US Naval Intelligence.* Washington: Office of Naval Intelligence and the Naval Historical Center. Accessed 12 23, 2021. https://archive.org/details/centuryofusnaval00wash.

Paterson, Lawrence. 2006. *Weapons of Desperation: German frogmen and midget submarines of World War II.* 1st. London: Chatham Publishing.

PWE. 1944. "WO 208/5617: Interrogation of POWs in World War II: Operation OVERLORD; use of POWs in propaganda to the enemy." London: The National Archives, 30 04.

Bibliography

PWIS. 1944. "WO 165/39; MI9 War Diary, includes Camp 020 (Interrogation of Prisoners of War), Wilton Park, Beaconfield, Bucks and IS9." London: The National Archives, Dec.

—. 1945. "WO 166/17838: War Diary, `Z' Sec. C.S.D.I.C. (India)." London: The National Archives, 30 06.

—. n.d. "WO 208/3248: Notes on Combined Services Detailed Interrogation Centre (CSDIC)." London: The National Archives.

—. 1945. "WO 208/3256: Mediterranean and Middle East theatres: use of 'X' source (concealed microphones) in interrogation centres run by CSDIC 1940-1945." London: The National Archives.

—. 1945. "WO 208/3258: Notes on CSDIC: Mediterranean reports." London: The National Archives.

—. 1944. "WO 208/3439: Operation Overlord: information required." London: The National Archives, 25 07.

—. 1941. "WO 208/3442: Prisoners of war holding strong anti-Nazi views." London: The National Archives, 09.

—. 1942. "WO 208/3443: War Office camps for X and Y prisoners of war." London: The National Archives, 02.

—. 1942. "WO 208/3452: CSDIC: East Africa." London: The National Archives.

—. 1942. "WO 208/3453: CSDIC's abroad: policy." London: The National Archives.

—. 1943. "WO 208/3454: CSDIC: North Africa." London: The National Archives, 12.

—. 1941. "WO 208/3455: Survey of CSDIC work in UK 1.1.1941 - 30.6.1941." London: The National Archives, 31 12.

—. 1943. "WO 208/3460: CSDIC(UK) and MI 19 (RPS): comments on value of work." London: The National Archives.

—. 1943. "WO 208/3461: CSDIC's: inclusion of Allied personnel." London: The National Archives.

—. 1941. "WO 208/3518: Supply and operation of CSDIC mobile unit." London: The National Archives, 09.

—. 1944. "WO 208/3527: Special camp for anti-nazi POws: suggested transfer from No 1 Camp to No 7 Camp." London: The National Atchives, 07.

—. 1940. "WO 208/4119: Interrogation Reports on German Prisoners of War: SRA 441-651." London: The National Archives, 09.

—. 1940. "WO 208/4121: Interrogation Reports on German Prisoners of War Nos 862-1007." London: The National Archives, 11.

—. 1941. "WO 208/4122: Interrogation Reports on German Prisoners of War Nos SRA 1008-1195." London: The National Archives, 01.

—. 1941. "WO 208/4123: Interrogation Reports on German Prisoners of War Nos 1196-1629." London: The National Archives, Feb-Apr.

—. 1941. "WO 208/4141: Interrogation Reports on German Prisoners of War Nos SRN 1-240." London: The National Archives, 04.

—. 1941. "WO 208/4142: Interrogation Reports on German Prisoners of War Nos SRN 241-560." London: The National Archives, 07.
—. 1942. "WO 208/4143: Interrogation Reports on German Prisoners of War Nos SRN 561-1040." London: The National Archives, 09.
—. 1943. "WO 208/4147: Interrogation Reports on German Prisoners of War 2200-2450." London: The National Archives, 11.
—. 1944. "WO 208/4148: Interrogation Reports on German Prisoners of War Nos 2451-2699." London: The National Archives, 31 01.
—. 1944. "WO 208/4149: Interrogation Reports on German Prisoners of War Nos 2700-3500." London: The National Archives, 31 03.
—. 1944. "WO 208/4150: Interrogation Reports on German Prisoners of War Nos 3501-3359." London: The National Archives, 30 04.
—. 1944. "WO 208/4151: Interrogation Reports on German Prisoners of War Nos 3360-3650." London: The National Archives, 31 05.
—. 1944. "WO 208/4152: Interrogation Reports on German Prisoners of War Nos 3651-3790." London: The National Archives, 30 06.
—. 1945. "WO 208/4156: Interrogation Reports on German Prisoners of War: SRN 4251-4560." London: The National Archives, 31 01.
—. 1945. "WO 208/4157: Interrogation Reports on German Prisoners of War: SRN 4561-4857." London: The National Archives, 30 09.
—. 1944. "WO 208/4163: Interrogation Reports on German Prisoners of War Nos 1731-1949." London: The National Archives, 28 02.
—. 1945. "WO 208/4164: Interrogation Reports on German Prisoners of War Nos 1950-2141." London: The National Archives, 31 08.
—. 1944. "WO 208/4196: Interrogation reports on German and Italian prisoners of war (CSDIC)." London: The National Archives, 31 08.
—. 1945. "WO 208/4198: Special extracts from interrogation reports on German and Italian prisoners of war (CSDIC)." London: The National Archives, 31 08.
—. 1945. "WO 208/4200: Special extracts from interrogation reports on German and Italian prisoners of war (CSDIC)." London: The National Archives, 31 03.
—. 1945. "WO 208/4970: The Story of MI19." London: The National Archives.
—. 1946. "WO 208/5158: Enemy PoW interrogation reports: wireless and signals intelligence." London: The National Archives, 03.
—. 1942. "WO 208/5521: Interrogation Reports on German Prisoners of War Nos GRN 6-12." London: The National Archives, 19 05.
—. 1945. "WO 208/5540: Interrogation Reports on German Prisoners of War: SIR 1300-1399." London: The National Archives, 13 01.
—. 1945. "WO 208/5541: Interrogation Reports on German Prisoners of War: SIR 1400-1499." London: The National Archives, 26 02.
—. 1941. "WO 208/5621: Expansion of CSDIC UK; justification for Wilton Park Centre." London: The National Archives, 31 01.

—. 1944. "WO 208/5629: Operations of Combined Services Detailed Interrogation Centre (CSDIC) in Mediterranean Theatre, January-March 1944." London: The National Archives, 30 06.

—. 1946. *WO208/1485: Japanese prisoners of war; statistical returns, interrogation reports and information summaries.* London: The National Archives.

Ramsay, David. 2008, 2009. *'Blinker' Hall: Spymaster.* Stroud: The History Press.

Ranft, Bryan, Alan Cowpe, Hugh Lyon, Philip Towle, David Henry, Geoffrey Till, and Anthony Wells. 1977. *Technical Change and British Naval Policy 1860-1939.* 1st. Edited by Bryan Ranft. Sevenoaks: Hodder & Stoughton.

Rankin, Nicholas. 2011. *Ian Fleming's Commandos: The Story of 30 Assault Unit in WWII.* London: Faber & Faber.

Robinson, Derek. 2006. *Invasion, 1940.* London: Constable & Robinson Ltd.

Roskill, Stephen. 2013. *Churchill and the Admirals.* Barnsley: Pen & Sword Books Ltd.

—. 2016. *Naval Policy Between the Wars: Vol 1, The period of Anglo-American antagonism 1919-1929.* Vol. 1. 2 vols. Barnsley: Seaforth Publishing.

—. 2016. *Naval Policy Between the Wars: Vol 2, The period of reluctant rearmament 1930-1939.* Vol. 2. 2 vols. Barnsley: Seaforth.

—. 2004. *The War at Sea 1939-1945: Volume 1, The Defensive.* Edited by Sir James R M Butler. Vol. 1. 3 vols. Uckfield: Naval & Military Press Ltd.

—. 2004. *The War at Sea 1939-1945: Volume 2, The Period of Balance.* Edited by Sir James R M Butler. Vol. 2. 3 vols. Uckfield: Naval & Military Press Ltd.

—. 2004. *The War at Sea 1939-1945: Volume 3 Part 1: The Offensive 1st June 1943-31st May 1944.* Edited by Sir James R M Butler. Vol. 3 Part 1. 3 vols. Uckfield: Naval & Military Press Ltd.

—. 2004. *The War at Sea 1939-1945: Volume 3 Part 2: The Offensive 1st june 1944-14th August 1945.* Edited by Sir James R M Butler. Vol. 3 Part 2. 3 vols. Uckfield: Naval & Military Press Ltd.

Royal Marines. 1944. "ADM 202/599: War Diary, 30 Assault Unit Vol 2." London: The National Archives, 08.

Saunders, Andy. 1990. "'Luftwaffe' Hospital, Woolwich." *After the Battle,* 38-43.

Scheer, Reinhard. 2014. *Germany's High Sea Fleet in the First World War.* Barnsley, S Yorkshire: Frontline Books.

Security Service. 1956. "KV 2/2690: Josef Lampersberger." London: The National Archives, 31 01.

—. 1948. "KV 2/3767: Georg Schwarzloh." London: The National Archives, 12 02.

—. 1946. "KV 4/327: Establishment and formation of Combined Services Detailed Interrogation Centre (CSDIC) Western European Area." London: The National Archives, 31 12.

—. 1945. "KV 4/466: Diary of Guy Liddell, Deputy Director General of the Security Service, June to November 1945." London: The National Archives, 18 11.

—. 1946. "KV 4/467: Diary of Guy Liddell, Deputy Director General of the Security Service, November 1945 to September 1946." London: The National Archives, 25 09.

—. 1947. "KV 4/468: Diary of Guy Liddell, Deputy Director General of the Security Service, September 1946 to March 1947." London: The National Archives, 03 03.

—. 1947. "KV 4/469: Diary of Guy Liddell, Deputy Director General of the Security Service, May to December 1947." London: The National Archives, 31 12.

—. 1948. "KV 4/470: Diary of Guy Liddell, Deputy Director General of the Security Service, 1948." London: The National Archives, 31 12.

Special Operations Executive Personnel Files HS9/491/1. 1946. "Charles William EVERETT - born [1908]." London: The National Archives, 31 12.

Straus, Ulrich. 2003. *The Anguish of Surrender: Japanese POWs of World War II*. Seattle: University of Washington Press.

Sullivan, Matthew Barry. 1979. *Thresholds of Peace: German Prisoners and the People of Britain 1944-1948*. London: Hamish Hamilton.

Toliver, Raymond F. 1997. *The Interrogator: The Story of Hans Joachim Scharff, Master Interrogator of the Luftwaffe*. Atglen, PA: Schiffer Publishing Ltd.

Trench, Bernard Frederick. 1939. "Diary 11 Feb 1938 - 29 Nov 1939." *Personal Papers*. Vol. 2017/24/27. Portsmouth: NMRN.

—. 1943. *Diary 15 Sep 1941-3 Dec 1943*. Vol. NMRN 2017/24/29. Portsmouth: NMRN.

—. 1941. *Diary 30 Nov 1939-14 Sep 1941*. Vol. NMRN 2017/24/28. Portsmouth: NMRN.

—. 1945. *Diary 4 Dec 1943-30 Jan 1945*. Vol. NMRN 2017/24/30. Portsmouth: NMRN.

U Boat Archive. n.d. *British Interrogation Reports*. Accessed 11 09, 2019. http://uboatarchive.net/BritishInterrogationReports.htm.

Vincent, Jeff. 1990. "The Combined Services Interrogation Centre." *After the Battle*, 44-52.

Waller, Derek. 2017. "The Surrender, Capture and Recovery of U-570." *For Posterity's Sake*. Accessed 07 06, 2020. http://www.forposterityssake.ca/RCN-DOCS/HMCS-NIAGARA-U-570-by-Derek-Waller.pdf.

Walter, Brian E. 2020. *The Longest Campaign: Britain's maritime struggle in the Atlantic and northwest Europe, 1939-1945*. Oxford: Casemate Publishers.

Welbourn, Donald Burkewood. 2008. *An Engineer in Peace and War: A Technical and Social History*. Edited by Margaret Hardy. Vols. 1 - 1916-1952. 3 vols. Lulu.com.

Bibliography

Wells, Anthony Roland. 1972. "Studies in British naval intelligence 1880-1945." London: King's College.

Wentzel, Fritz. 1975. *Single or Return? The story of the only German POW to escape from the West and get home.* 1st NEL Paperback. Translated by Edward Fitzgerald. London: New English Library.

Wheeler, Shirin. 2023. *Charles Wheeler: Witness to the twentieth century.* London: Manilla Press.

INDEX

Index

About the Author

Derek Nudd's rare blend of arts and science degrees and a career in the defence engineering industry are a valuable grounding for insights into technical intelligence in the Second World War. He has published two other books, and several articles on the theme of naval intelligence. He has written, edited and spoken in the field of naval and maritime history, appeared on television and acted as historical consultant to TV productions.

Armageddon Fed Up with This is the true story of one articulate artillery conscript's journey from raw gunner to professional sergeant, preserving a humorously caustic take on army life along the way.

The tale is told through his letters home, and woven into the social, political and military mayhem going on around him.

"Everyone should own a copy of this book" –
That's Books and Entertainment

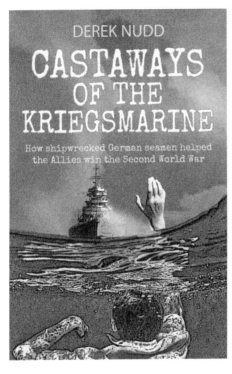

December 1943 brought little cheer to Hitler's Kriegsmarine.

Two hundred and fifty exhausted, disoriented survivors converged on two remote English country houses. They had lived through Nazi shipwrecks from North Africa to North Cape, from blockade runner to battleship.

They met a highly tuned intelligence production line created to draw valuable information from their heads as quickly and painlessly as possible.

Read how it was done, how it tilted the balance of the sea war, and the human stories behind the machine.

"It should be on the shelves of anyone interested in the Kriegsmarine or WW2 at sea."
Navy News

Derek's web site is at https://www.dnudd.co.uk.